FrontPage 2000:
Get Professional Results

About the Author

Sherry London is an artist, a writer, and a teacher—which is exactly what a going-into-college aptitude test predicted. She was a Contributing Editor for *Computer Artist* magazine (before that publication's untimely death) and has written for *Pre, MacWeek, MacUser, Digital Vision,* and the combined *MacWorld/MacUser* magazine. She currently writes for *Electronic Publishing* magazine. She has taught Photoshop and pre-press in the Continuing Education Department at Moore College of Art and Design in Philadelphia, and currently teaches QuarkXPress, Adobe GoLive, and Flash at Gloucester County College. She has spoken at a number of conferences, including the Thunder Lizard Photoshop Conference and the Professional Photographers of America convention. She has written a number of books on Photoshop, Painter, Illustrator, and After Effects.

FrontPage 2000:
Get Professional Results

Sherry London

Osborne/McGraw-Hill

Berkeley New York St. Louis San Francisco Auckland Bogotá
Hamburg London Madrid Mexico City Milan Montreal New Delhi
Panama City Paris São Paulo Singapore Sydney Tokyo Toronto

Osborne/**McGraw-Hill**
2600 Tenth Street
Berkeley, California 94710
U.S.A.

For information on translations or book distributors outside the U.S.A., or to arrange bulk purchase discounts for sales promotions, premiums, or fund-raisers, please contact Osborne/**McGraw-Hill** at the above address.

FrontPage 2000: Get Professional Results

1234567890 DOC DOC 019876543210

ISBN 0-07-212269-2

Publisher
Brandon Nordin

Associate Publisher and Editor-in-Chief
Scott Rogers

Acquisitions Editor
Megg Bonar

Project Editor
Mark Karmendy

Acquisitions Coordinator
Stephane Thomas

Technical Editor
Jody Cline

Copy Editor
Dennis Weaver

Proofreader
Carol Burbo

Indexer
Carol Burbo

Graphic Artists
Beth Young, Brian Wells, Bob Hansen

Computer Designers
Liz Pauw, Roberta Steele, Gary Corrigan

Series Designer
Peter F. Hancik

This book was composed with Corel VENTURA™ Publisher.

To the "real" Village Flowers: Mary Alice McGrath, and in memory of Patrick McGrath. Your flowers filled my house with fragrance and the pixie dust that you threw on the flowers brought a spark of magic—until Pat's untimely death caused your doors to close forever. To friendship that will never die and to memories of a place of great beauty.

Contents at a Glance

Contents

Part II
Implementing Your Web Site

Part IV

The Fun Stuff: Adding Interactivity to Your Site

Acknowledgments

The creation of any book is a group enterprise, and this book is no exception. You would not be reading this without the contributions of many people. Some of the important contributions, such as the design, layout, production, and printing of the book, were made by people whose names I don't know, but I thank them anyway.

I have written many books, but I have never enjoyed working with a group of people as much as I have enjoyed this experience. I'd like to thank my agent, Margot Maley Hutchinson of Waterside Productions for many things—including introducing me to the folks at Osborne. I'd like to thank Megg Bonar, Acquisitions Editor, for asking me to write this book, and for being such a warm and caring human being. Stephane Thomas, Acquisitions Coordinator, was always accessible and went way beyond her "job definition" to provide assistance and support. Mark Karmendy coordinated the editing and production of this book with efficiency and panache. Jody Cline did an incredible job on the tech edit for the book. I was always able to count on her to catch any blunders or to suggest a better way of presenting the material. Dennis Weaver did an excellent job of copy editing the material so that all the words were consistently capitalized or not capitalized—a task for which I sincerely thank him because it is one of my least favorite things to do. He also made sure that what I wrote made sense, which was an occasional challenge when my mind said one thing and my fingers typed another.

I'd like to thank the folks who helped me gather the material for the book. My husband Norm, a technical genius, wrote the first draft of the "Publishing, Maintaining, and Troubleshooting Your Web" chapter. My son, Dan, a trained musician/songwriter whose "day job" is working as Web developer, helped me with the chapters on HTML and audio/video. Jim Mundy, a California-based Web developer and JavaScript expert, contributed his expertise to the DHTML and FrontPage components chapters.

I'd also like to thank the artists who allowed me to display their creativity. First among them, I'd like to thank Kelly Loomis. Her work leaves me awestruck. I have never seen such beautiful Web interface designs. I'd like to thank Paul

Vineburg for permission to use his MEGA template in this book. His techniques for creating navigation bars helped me a lot. I'd also like to thank Bradley Schenck for the use of his Celtic graphic.

Introduction

Microsoft FrontPage is a WYSIWYG (what-you-see-is-what-you-get) layout program for Web site design. It lets you develop Web pages without having to write the HTML code yourself. With the advent of Office 2000, FrontPage is now an integral part of the Office suite of products. This means that you can use many of the new features in FrontPage in a very integrated environment. FrontPage 2000 has many new features:

- New Web templates to create a variety of site structures
- Web Wizards to design complex sites
- New themes
- The ability to create your own themes and package them without the need for an add-on product
- Integrated development and management environment
- Project management capabilities
- Group authoring capabilities
- Support for dynamic HTML and cascading style sheets
- Ability to integrate with Word, PowerPoint, Access, and Excel content
- Powerful clip art library included
- Ability to work in HTML view with the security that FrontPage will not change your code

What's Special About this Book

FrontPage 2000: Get Professional Results covers all of the features you need to make using FrontPage easy and productive and then goes further to explain how to make your Web sites truly professional. It includes tips, pointers, and short essays to help you use your Web site to *communicate* with the audience.

I have written this book to include not only the specific features of FrontPage 2000 but to also cover a great deal of information about designing a Web site that delivers your message effectively. (There is a difference between effectiveness and efficiency. An old programmer's tale defines efficiency as "building the bridge right" while effectiveness is "building the right bridge." It does you no good to erect the world's best-built bridge over the wrong river!) I'll help you to avoid the pitfalls of incorrect bridge-building through the use of several special features in this book:

- **Numbered steps** explain clearly how to accomplish complex tasks.
- **Annotated figures** lay out the steps needed to accomplish various tasks in FrontPage.
- **"Tips"** offer you useful shortcuts or techniques. You'll find some of my best advice here in the margins!
- **"Professional Pointers"** guide you to the wisdom of professionals.
- **"New in 2000" notes** let you know which features are new in this version of FrontPage.
- **"Cross-Reference" notes** help you to quickly find related material elsewhere in the book.

Perhaps the most exciting feature of this book is the Web Gallery. Found in the center of the book and in full-color, the Web Gallery helps you clearly visualize the effects used in the book's examples. Not only do you learn how to create the effects in the examples, but you can mine them for ideas and inspiration as well.

Who Needs this Book

I have designed this book for beginning and intermediate users who are familiar with Microsoft Windows (95, 98, or NT) and with a word-processing program such as Microsoft Word. I don't assume that you have any knowledge of graphics or of Web page design or HTML. For those of you who are creating your first Web site, you'll be up and running by Chapter 4. If you've done this a number of times already, then you'll learn about ways to make your sites look good and to communicate clearly using the features contained in FrontPage 2000.

FrontPage 2000: Get Professional Results starts out with the basics and then presents the rest of FrontPage's features systematically and comprehensively. If you read it from cover to cover, it will bring you to an intermediate-to-advanced level of knowledge and skill.

There are some things that this book won't do. It won't teach you to become an HTML or JavaScript expert. It won't enable you to go into the graphic arts business. It won't cover the supporting technologies for the Web (database integration, ASP, XML). These topics are beyond the scope of the possible for one book. It will, however, help you to learn what makes a Web site look professional and to use the features of FrontPage to achieve these professional results.

How this Book Is Organized

The organization of this book is carefully thought out to present material from the simple to the complex and from the general to the specific.

Part I, "Getting Ready to Design a Web Site," introduces you to the planning stage of a Web site design project. If you don't know what to build, it's unlikely that it will ever be what you need. Chapter 1 takes you through the questions that you need to ask to decide what kind of a site to build. It also introduces you to twelve example sites that you'll meet throughout this book. Chapter 2 introduces you to the FrontPage interface and application. Chapter 3 helps you to find the resources and documents that you need and shows you how to create the structure of your site. Chapter 4 takes you through the process of creating a Web site and lays a foundation for the rest of the book.

Part II, "Implementing Your Web Site," tackles the specific topics that you need as you actually build your pages. Chapter 5 teaches you about the text features of FrontPage, and Chapter 6 shows you how (and when) to create hyperlinks. It also introduces you to the shared borders and navigation bar features that differentiate FrontPage from the other visual Web site design programs. To my mind, these features are worth the entire price of admission. No other program has this kind of power. Chapter 7 teaches you how to use graphics wisely on your pages, and Chapter 8 tells you how to use themes and how to create your own.

Part III, "Advanced Options," covers a number of more advanced but important issues. Chapter 9 shows you how to publish your Web site and how to install and use the FrontPage extensions. Chapter 10 shows you how to use tables to present tabular data and to control the layout of your pages. Chapter 11 introduces you to frames and framesets and helps to tame that very troublesome topic.

Part IV covers the "Fun Stuff: Adding Interactivity to Your Site." In Chapter 12, you'll learn the basics of HTML and why learning a bit of HTML will take you a long way. Chapter 13 covers Dynamic HTML and shows you how to create page transitions, fly images through your site, and create rollovers. Chapter 14 shows you how to integrate audio and video into your site and how to create animated GIF images. Finally, Chapter 15 shows you how to use the various FrontPage components to perform tasks like creating hit counters, mouseovers, collapsible lists, forms, and discussion groups that would otherwise require advanced programming skills.

How to Use this Book

Tip: You'll find tutorial images to help you work through the exercises in this book on the Web at www.osborne.com. The images on the Web are organized by chapter so you can easily find the image you need to work with.

If you're a beginner, you should start from the beginning and read until you have enough information to create a Web site. Try out the features as you read. If you need to build a specific site, start planning it in the first chapter and expand on it as you work through the book. As you continue reading, you can improve and refine your site based on the material presented in each new chapter. You can work through the chapters with the examples that I include or you can use the steps on your own material.

If you have used FrontPage before but you want to improve your skills and increase your knowledge, you can skim over the material in Part I (read Chapter 3 carefully, however) and then go directly to the chapters that contain the topics you need.

Have Fun!

However you use this book, enjoy the process and the satisfaction you will get from creating effective, professional Web sites.

Sherry London
January, 2000

Part I

Getting Ready to Design a Web Site

chapter 1

So What Do I Need to Do?

In this chapter, you:

- Learn about the need to plan your Web site

- Find out about the elements that make up a Web site

- Discover what makes a good Web site

- Identify factors that lead to a good surfing experience for site visitors

- Storyboard your site

- Choose a theme for your site

- Plan ways to build expandability into your site

You've decided to create a Web site. You either feel that a Web site is needed, or someone in your department has "volunteered" you for this task. Web site design can be fun or it can be very frustrating. *FrontPage 2000 Professional Results* is designed to help make the Web site design experience as pleasant and trouble-free as possible for you.

You want your Web site to look good. You may be an artist or a programmer, or you might have no design or programming experience whatsoever. Whatever your background, however, you know that it's important for your Web site to achieve professional results. This book makes the assumption that you have no previous Web site design or programming experience and that you have an immediate need to build a site. A number of example sites are provided for you to work on, but you'll get the best results if, after you finish working through each chapter, you then apply what you've learned to your own project. That way, when you finish the book, your Web site will be operational, as well.

Getting Started for Professional Results

Microsoft FrontPage 2000 is a Web site creation and maintenance program. It helps you create your site and place it on the Internet, where it can be seen by anyone with a modem and a browser.

The native language of the Web is HTML (Hypertext Markup Language), a type of coding scheme that is placed around regular text so that a Web browser (the software that allows you to surf the Web) knows how the text should be displayed. HTML isn't hard to learn, but FrontPage allows you to create your pages without having to learn to code in HTML. This makes it much easier to get up and running. FrontPage also provides some wonderful bells and whistles that add features and fun to your Web sites after they are built.

You won't learn very much about using FrontPage in this chapter. This book is going to take you through all the steps of building a Web site, and the first step is designing your site. You'll be "formally introduced" to FrontPage in Chapter 2. For now, you need to decide what your Web site is all about.

Planning vs. Serendipity

A very old piece of advice states that if you don't know where you're going, any road will take you there. If you get into your automobile and randomly drive until you get tired, you've reached your destination when you stop, because you planned to go somewhere, and you've arrived at "somewhere." However, if you end up two blocks away from your house after 10 hours of driving, have you really taken the most efficient route to get there?

Serendipity can be fun. You get to places that you didn't know existed and you can meet interesting people and have many adventures along the way. However, by its nature, Web site design isn't random. You are creating a site that communicates your purpose in building it, and if you don't have a purpose, your site won't either. Your site will fail before it starts.

Aiming for the Goal Line

The Internet—and the World Wide Web—have become the new communication medium for the new millennium. The Web promises instant access to information about businesses and people worldwide. Each site on the Web has a purpose for being there, though the purpose might differ. Your site needs a purpose, as well.

Why create a Web site?

Why are Web sites created? A business might create a site to sell its products. A software company might want a site to provide technical support. An individual might want to create a site to help family keep in touch or to impress friends. An artist might create a site to give prospective clients the ability to preview a portfolio of work.

Each site might have a different rationale for existing, but certain basic types of sites emerge. FrontPage (as you can see in Figure 1-1) divides them into eight categories, and when you create a new Web site, you can select from any of the eight types.

Each choice contains the options that are most appropriate for that type of site:

- **One Page Web**   The One Page Web site allows you to create single pages. Most Web sites will be larger than one page, but if you don't like to plan in advance, or you really only need one page, this is a convenient way to start.

- **Corporate Presence Wizard**   The Corporate Presence Wizard walks you through the process of creating a Web site for a large corporation. It allows you to create pages for contacts, products, news, and feedback. It also allows you to create a table of contents for easier navigation, and a search process for your site so that site visitors can easily find what they need.

- **Customer Support Web**   The Customer Support Web option creates the pages necessary to provide 24-hour customer support. Although it's aimed at software companies, it can be tailored to meet your individual needs.

- **Discussion Web Wizard**   The Discussion Web Wizard helps you to build a site that is *threaded* (messages are kept in order for others to read). You can set up a chat area where visitors can talk about the topic of your site—a site to discuss science fiction, politics, diabetes, or any other topic that you want. FrontPage 2000 allows you to build this site with very little programming intervention, and to maintain it online.

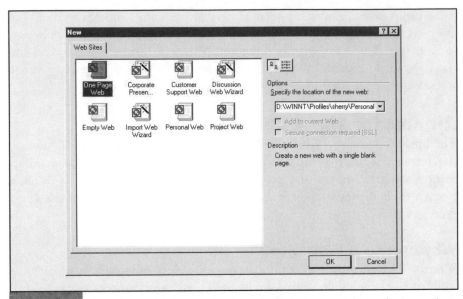

FIGURE 1-1 The New Web Sites selection window shows eight Web site options

- **Personal Web**   The Personal Web site is for the individual who wants to put up a family or vanity site. When you select this option, FrontPage 2000 automatically creates pages for family photos and for links to your favorite other Web sites.

- **Import Web Wizard**   You can import a Web site that you had previously created in HTML or in another Web creation program and use it as the basis of the new Web site. The Import Web Wizard performs this magic for you. Even if your site was not created in FrontPage originally, by using the Import Web Wizard, you can get the benefit of all of the FrontPage-specific features to enhance your site.

- **Project Web**   The Project Web option allows you to create a site to make the management of a project easier. This type of site is designed for intranets. An *intranet* is a network within a corporation that is only accessible to members of that corporation or department, but which uses Internet features to communicate.

- **Empty Web**   The final type of Web site that you can create is the Empty Web site. This site type is for the person or business that wants a unique site and prefers to begin with a blank canvas. When you create an empty Web site, FrontPage offers no suggestions about what it should contain.

The case studies

The type of Web site that you design will depend on the purpose of the site. A large, entertainment corporation, such as Disney, requires a massive Web site that uses cutting-edge technology. A staid insurance company might want a much smaller, more traditional site to just let people know where they can find an agent and how they can contact the company in case of claims.

Because Web site needs vary significantly, you will find a variety of case studies as you work through this book—an even dozen of them. Although you won't create each one from start to finish, you'll have a chance to work with the specific (fictional) sites listed in Table 1-1.

Site Name	Description
www.homenclosure.com	HomeNclosures manufactures and sells room additions.
www.villagefrs.com	Village Flower Shoppe is a full-service flower shop.
www.candymancorp.com	The Candyman, Inc. is a distributor of bulk candies.
www.accessability.com	Access-Ability is a nonprofit organization that promotes awareness about handicapped access.
www.sweaterlink.com	Sweater Link is a magazine that publishes a variety of knitting patterns and instructions.
www.vidaliaheaven.com	Vidalia Heaven is a farmer's cooperative that grows the sweet Vidalia onions that have recently become so popular. Its purpose is to attract attention to the onions and their side products. The site will point to the e-commerce sites of its members.
www.inscopa.com	The Insurance Company of Southern Pennsylvania needs an intranet site where they can post personnel news and deliver online training to their employees.
www.stockchatter.com	Stock Chatter is a members-only discussion group that compares investments and exchanges stock news.
www.thesmythes.com	The Smythe family has decided to create a Web site of their own for their extended family and their friends. They also want to exchange email and postcards with other families around the globe.
www.myskateweb.com	Sue Ellen is a deeply involved fan of figure skating and has decided to create a Web site that links to all types of figure-skating information and news.
www.settlementserv.com	Settlement Services, Inc. is the division of a national real-estate chain that deals with home settlements and mortgage commitments. The Web site that they want to construct will help their clients track the progress of their mortgage applications and of all of the steps that lead to settlement on a home.
www.prancingpixel.com	The Prancing Pixel is a graphic arts company run by a starving artist. This will be a portfolio site.

TABLE 1-1   Fictional Web Sites that Will Be Discussed in This Book

What Is a Web Site?

Of course, you all know what a Web site is, or you wouldn't have purchased this book! However, let's take a closer look at some of the elements that can be included on a Web site. These elements—text, graphics, links, forms, and effects—are like an artist's set of paints. They are the basic building blocks of a Web site.

Text

Perhaps the most basic element in all Web sites is text. Although the Web was created, in part, to allow for nontextual information to be transferred over the Internet, most Web sites still contain more text than any other element. The text communicates the majority of the information on most sites.

Originally, on the Web, you had little control over the way text was displayed. As site designer, you could specify the relative size of the font, but the browser determined which font was used. You could choose a larger size for headlines and a smaller size for the body text of the site. The user could (and still can) specify within the browser that headline type is to be 24 points or 12 points.

New techniques are available now that give site designers more control. Cascading style sheets give you the option of specifying fonts and setting precise styles for headlines and body copy. You'll learn much more about creating text in Chapter 5.

Graphics

Some of the pleasure of surfing the Web comes from the graphics that are so liberally sprinkled across Web sites. Pictures do convey information—not the same type of information as text, but they add a dimension that text cannot achieve.

A Web site could present paragraph after paragraph about the beauty of its floral offering for Valentine's Day, and try to describe the carnations, daisies, and red glitter hearts that decorate its baskets. Figure 1-2 shows it much faster and better than any number of words possibly could.

A Web site can contain many other graphic elements, in addition to images. The buttons that you click to move from one location to another are usually graphics. The background for a Web site might be a repeating pattern or a soft image that sets off the text. The entire navigational system for the Web site might be a large, segmented graphic, like the one created for Prancing Pixel, shown in Figure 1-3.

Graphics add interest and "eye candy" to a Web site, but they need to be carefully prepared. Graphics-heavy sites often cause visitors to quickly exit because the pages take too long to load. Chapters 3 and 7 will tell you much more about preparing graphics for the Web.

FIGURE 1-2 A Valentine's Day basket from Village Flower Shoppe

Links

Hyperlinks (known more often as "links") allow you to move from place to place on the Web as you follow a specific line of thought. Let's say that you wanted to find information about taking a trip to London. You might first check a search engine, such as AltaVista (www.altavista.com). One link in that list takes you to London Events (www.london.eventguide.com). This page consists of a lot of links to various attractions, hotels, and shops. You can find out about ordering products from Marks and Spencer (a popular London department store) or learn how to order theatre tickets online. The links allow you to hop and skip about as your fancy dictates.

You could be reading about art and follow a link to the National Gallery of Art. You could be looking at a page about a specific artist and learn about his or her works, and then click on a link to information about the art movement or the

FIGURE 1-3 Prancing Pixel's interface design is a multipart, segmented graphic

specific time period in which a piece was painted. You might end up far away from your original Web site.

One of the most useful things that you can do for your site visitors is to provide them with a good set of links to topics of interest. Depending upon the specific purpose of your Web site, you might even be able to join a Web "ring"—a group of Web sites about related topics that point to each other. Chapter 6 will tell you much more about creating links.

Forms

Many Web sites also contain forms. Forms allow visitors to enter online orders, send email to the site administrator, fill out surveys, or chat with one another. The data entered into a form can be sent to the site administrator as an email, or can be added to an Access database (or another linked database).

Forms can be quite complex, but FrontPage 2000 makes them much easier to create. If your Internet service provider (ISP) has FrontPage Extensions on the server, the process of creating forms becomes quite easy and automatic. FrontPage Extensions are services that are installed on a server to implement special FrontPage-only features. They are an added benefit of using Microsoft FrontPage for site development and maintenance. You'll learn how to create forms in Chapter 12, and Chapter 16 will tell you much more about FrontPage Server extensions and components.

Effects

You might want to include special effects in your site. These effects can be *roll-overs*—where a button or object on screen changes as the mouse moves over it, or a variety of colored balls follow your cursor as you move it. They could be static animations or special sounds. They can be dynamic—transition effects like dissolve that appear when the screen loads. (A *dissolve* is method of moving from one screen to another so that the change is decorative as well as functional. An example of a dissolve is the Venetian Blind effect where screen 1 changes into screen 2 in sections that look like multiple window shades. Figure 1-4 shows one screen changing into another using this effect in the Skate Web site.

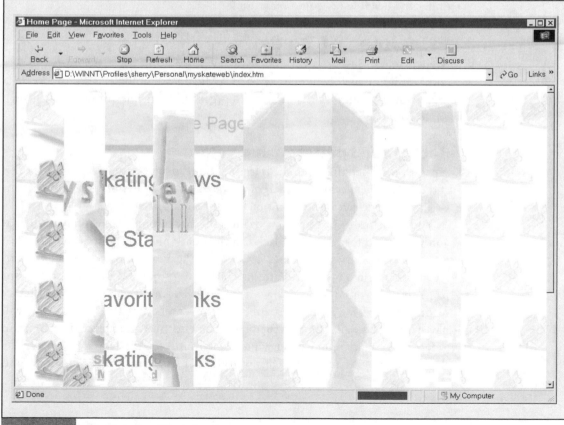

FIGURE 1-4   The Venetian Blind dissolve

Special effects can be added to Web sites through the use of JavaScript (a scripting language) or Dynamic HTML (an extension to standard HTML). The standards for these techniques are not quite set in stone, and the two major browsers—Netscape Navigator and Microsoft Internet Explorer—use different versions of the commands and behave differently. However, if you're brave (and/or your ISP also uses FrontPage Extensions), you can add a lot of excitement and fun to your Web site by adding special effects. You'll learn how to add effects to your site in Chapters 13, 14, and 15.

What Makes a Good Web Site?

If you've surfed the Web at all, you've noticed that some sites seem better than others. "Better" is, of course, a subjective term, and what seems "better" to you might not meet someone else's idea of "better." However, this book is designed to help you create professional-looking Web sites, and there are certain features that a "professional-looking" site calls to mind. Many of these features also come under the heading of "common sense."

Principles of Design

Even if you're not an artist and have no interest in art, a passing familiarity with design issues will help you to avoid classic pitfalls and to create a professional-looking site. The following general principles of design will help guide your way.

Background patterns and colors

A professional-looking Web site is legible and readable. It uses plain fonts for text and displays them at a size that is comfortable for a majority of readers. Fine print is okay on contracts but it won't make your site popular.

Your text needs to stand out against the background color or pattern that you've selected for your site. Black text on a dark blue background is so hard to read that most site visitors would say "Why bother?" and move on. Wild patterns are another prime offender. Patterns are fun to create and easy to add to your pages, but they need to be used with extreme caution. If you have any difficulty reading your screen as you create the site, you can be sure that your visitors will have trouble, as well. One way to use patterns effectively is to place the pattern in a decorative margin and use a white background for the text area. Figure 1-5 shows a glaring example of what not to do. The pattern is much too busy and

FIGURE 1-5 Patterns should be subtle—this one is not

obscures the text. Figure 1-6 is better; it shows the pattern removed from the button area and toned down so that it no longer conflicts with the text.

You can use black text on a white background for maximum visibility, or white text on a black background for drama (even though it is a little bit harder to read). Colorful sites are cheerful to visit, but the colors do need to relate to one another and provide some contrast. For example, green text on a yellow background would be difficult to read. A combination of purple, orange, and green lettering could create an interesting effect, but one that many of your site visitors might find extremely unappealing.

If you're not artistically trained, it's easier to think about colors for a Web site as you would articles of clothing. If you wouldn't wear the colors together, you probably shouldn't dress your screen in them either.

FIGURE 1-6 This pattern is much better

Creating an identity

A professional-looking Web site has a unique identity that carries throughout the pages in the site. Each page should repeat a common element to make all of the pages look as if they belong together.

The common element can be a small logo repeated on each page, a unique navigational device, a border color, or all of these together. In addition, the "look" of the site should be appropriate for your business. To use a very morbid example, most folks would be less than thrilled with a Web site for a funeral home that was dressed up in screaming bright primary colors (red, yellow, blue) and looks like a it was designed by kindergartners. That look might do quite well for a nursery school site, however.

A sedate corporate site might use shades of gray and maroon, while a site for an artist's portfolio might use any color or weird combination that the artist prefers. You need to evaluate the message that you want to send about your site before you start to design it. Do you want your site to be "staid," "safe," or "conservative"? Do you want to look "progressive" or "daring" or "cutting edge"?

In general, you want to choose one theme for your site, and make most of the pages conform to that theme. Microsoft FrontPage helps you control the look and image for your site by allowing you to choose from their list of themes. A FrontPage *theme* is a set of colors for background, foreground, text, visited and unvisited links, and the background pattern, border patterns, and images. You don't need to choose a preset theme from the Themes list, but you should create your own identity for your pages.

Graphically speaking

Another concept from the graphic arts is that of "whitespace." Whitespace refers to the amount of blank background area on a page. In print advertisement and marketing, the concept of whitespace is also used to target specific audiences. It is believed that large amounts of whitespace appeal to an older and more upscale audience, while pages with little whitespace appeal to a younger or less upscale group of people.

Whitespace also can be represented as the amount of clutter on your page. Although a very cluttered page can be well-designed, it takes more skill to create an appealing busy page than it does to create an appealing quiet page. The music-video look is quite cluttered, but can be dynamic and modern. It is appropriate for some types of enterprises.

The idea of identity, which was introduced previously, also relates to the graphics used for the site. If you're creating a site for an architectural firm, you might want to use Art Nouveau images throughout the site. The Vidalia Onion site that you'll create in a later chapter will undoubtedly use onions as a motif.

As you place items on your pages, you need to look at them for *balance*, another graphic arts term. A balanced page feels as if both sides of the page weigh the same amount. A page can be balanced if it is symmetrical—it has the same elements on both sides of the page, or if it has similarly sized elements on both sides of the page. A page can be asymmetrical and still balanced if the elements on one side seem to equal the elements on the other side in importance. A large graphic on the right side of the page can be balanced with two small text boxes on the other side.

A bit of spell-checking

Few things look less professional than misspelled pages. FrontPage has a built-in spelling checker, so it will automatically catch most of your typing mistakes.

However, it won't mark as a mistake a word that you've spelled correctly but isn't grammatically correct. For instance, if you accidentally write, "You online orders are welcome at this site," the FrontPage spelling checker will not know that the correct grammatical usage is "Your" and not "You." If the spelling checker finds the word in its dictionary, it's sure that the word is correct.

Know your audience

It might seem to be a trite saying, but knowing your audience is one of the most important ingredients for success. You need to know the taste and expectations of your audience and what you—and they—hope to achieve on your Web site.

You also need to know about the equipment that your visitors will use to access your Web site, because that should influence the decisions you make about the technical design of your site. Part of designing a "professional-looking" site is making it efficient and fast-loading for the computers and modems that you expect your audience to be using.

BANDWIDTH CONSIDERATIONS   Bandwidth is the first hurdle for your site. People access the Web from computers (usually, though other devices are also possible) that are attached to modems. A modem allows the computer to send digital data through telephone or cable lines, and these lines transfer data at specific speeds.

Modem speeds have increased dramatically over the past several years. A 14.4Kbps (kilobytes per second) connection is now considered very slow, and only older modems are still limited to this speed. More common are the 28.8 and 33.6Kbps modems, although those, too, are slow. A 56.6Kbps (v90) is a more reasonable modem speed. Even faster access is provided by dedicated ISDN lines, T1 lines, and the new cable-modem services available from local cable companies.

Figure 1-7 shows the Smythe family's dog. In Photoshop, the original image was 2.21MB. If that image were to be placed on a Web site exactly as it was prepared for printing in this book, using high-quality JPEG compression, it would theoretically take 29 seconds under ideal conditions to download on a 56.6Kbps modem. (If this sounds like Greek to you right now, just take note of the relative times to download. The specifics of JPEG and baud rate will be made clear to you as you work through this book.) If you were to use a 14.4 modem, the image would take at least 111 seconds to download.

Two issues are at play here. One is the difference in speed between the 14.4 and 56.6Kbps modems. Twenty-nine seconds versus 111 seconds is an enormous difference. The other issue is that the image prepared for printing is much too large, anyway. The dog's image, which prints at approximately three inches

FIGURE 1-7   The Smythe's dog

wide, would occupy almost nine inches on the screen. Graphics that are prepared for printing, therefore, are not suitable for publication on the Web. They need to be altered. If you scan images or acquire them from a digital camera, you will probably see the recommendation to use 300 dots-per-inch as the image resolution. This image resolution is suitable for print production but results in an image that is much too large to fit on a Web page (and that takes far too much time to download).

You should alter the image so that it is appropriate for the size of monitor you expect most of your visitors to have, and for the speed of the modems that you expect will be used by the visiting population. The correct size (in number of pixels) for the Smythe's dog is about one-third of the size needed for printing. At that reduced size, the image would, in theory at least, download to a 56.6Kbps modem in four seconds, but would take a minimum of 12 seconds on a 14.4 modem. While it's reasonable to wait for 4 seconds to view an image, 12 seconds is a bit too long for an individual image. Site visitors have short attention spans, and in 12 seconds they could be at someone else's site!

If you expect that the people who would be interested in your site have modern equipment and large monitors, you can prepare your Web pages for a larger screen and use a more graphics-intensive

Tip: When considering the actual file size of individual images, it's best not to have files that exceed 40K. These seem to load at reasonable speeds. Also be aware that the more graphics you place on your page, the longer it takes the entire page to appear.

layout. You can also consider using special effects, such as movies and audio. If, however, you expect that many of your users will have old equipment, slower modems, and 640×480 monitors, you will need to carefully prepare your site to make it load as quickly as possible.

BROWSERS AND OTHER VISUAL DELIGHTS   If you want to include special effects (or even display large graphics or use creative layout methods, such as tables or frames), there's another catch or "gotcha" to be aware of when preparing pages for the Web. All browsers are not alike. Some of the browsers being used are old and obsolete. You have no control over either the choice of the browser your visitors will use or the settings that are applied to that browser.

All browsers are not created equal. The two most common browsers are Netscape Navigator and Microsoft Internet Explorer, and there are multiple versions of these two in use. The version 2 and 3 browsers from both companies are still widely used, particularly on older computers, and they can do much less than the version 4 (or 5) browsers that were released later. Other, less popular, browsers have (or lack) features that are part of the "big two."

Significant differences exist in the ways that Netscape and Microsoft have implemented the handling of moving video images, animated GIF files, dynamic HTML (DHTML), and JavaScript. Techniques that work on one browser might not be visible on the other browser, or might even crash it. You need to decide whether you will develop your Web site so that everyone is welcome (which means testing and optimizing for the lowest common denominator), or whether you will standardize on one version of one browser and tell your visitors that either they need to use what you suggest or they might not be able to see all of your content.

You also need to know whether your users are generally using the same type of computer or whether you expect to attract a mixed group of Windows, Mac OS, and Unix users. Microsoft Internet Explorer 4.5 for Mac OS does not have the same DHTML abilities as does Internet Explorer 4.0 for Windows. Many JavaScript commands that work under Windows do nothing at all on the Mac.

Storyboards and Flow Charts

Once you've decided the purpose of your Web site and determined the technological level of your audience, you are ready to begin planning the site. Planning does help. It keeps your site from becoming a haphazard jumble of pages that look like they were thrown together by whim or fancy.

One of the best techniques for planning a site is to prepare a set of storyboards. Storyboarding is a technique borrowed from the entertainment and animation industries to show the progression of a story over time. When you create a Web site, you, too, are telling a sort of story. You need to make sure that the story line is clear and that the reader (or visitor) is never lost. The other helpful planning technique is the flowchart—loved by managers the world over for making structures clear.

If you go into a full-service bookstore, you'll find several rows of books devoted to the Web and to Web site design. One of the best books is David Siegel's *Creating Killer Web Sites,* second edition (Hayden Books, 1997). David Siegel is a noted artist and typographer. His ideas on Web site design have changed the way in which many designers work.

David Siegel recommends that you pick a metaphor to use as the main navigational device for your site (a site devoted to NASCAR, for example, might use controls that look as if they were designed to drive a car). You need to pick an appropriate metaphor that is familiar to your visitors. For example, an e-commerce site usually uses the metaphor of a shopping basket. If the site specializes in woman's clothing, it would seem odd for the "buying" part of the site to use a metaphor of putting fish into a bucket.

You need to select a metaphor (if you are planning to use one) before you begin to storyboard. You also need to decide whether your site will have an entranceway. This is another of David Siegel's terms. He recommends an entranceway that intrigues visitors and entices them further into the site. The traditional method of site design placed all of the options on the first page, but David Siegel feels that this encourages the visitor to look and run. Many sites today, therefore, just have page openers, such as the one shown in Figure 1-8, that show an opening image and a message that essentially says "Click Here to Enter."

Some sites also benefit from a long entranceway that allows for wandering before the visitor reaches the "meat" of the site. You will also generally attract more visitors if you can provide something for them to play with or take away. This should be an element that is updated or changed frequently so that you can get people to come back to your site multiple times. Sometimes, allowing your site visitors to send a "postcard" from your site to a friend both captures the interest of your visitors and brings in their friends. You should plan this type of giveaway before you begin to design the site.

A Little Organization Goes a Long Way

Flowcharts can help you create a well-organized site. If you take the time to sit and plan the sequence in which pages appear and are linked to one another, then you are really thinking through the entire structure of your site.

You can elect to flowchart or storyboard or both. I tend to make a flowchart first, so that I am sure of what I want to do, and then I begin to scribble tiny thumbnail sketches. If I storyboard first, I usually discover that I've forgotten something critical in the site navigation. Once the site navigation is set, I can

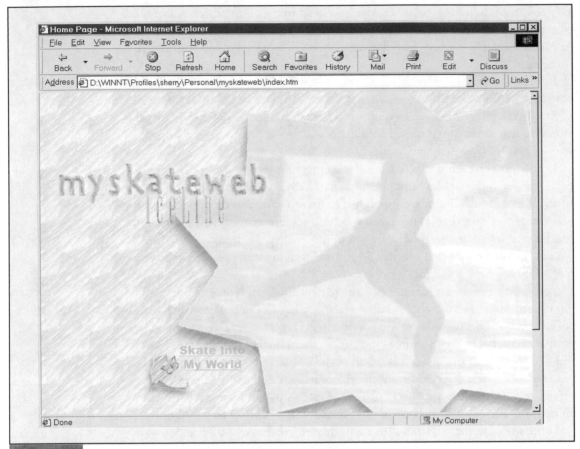

FIGURE 1-8 The opening page for www.myskateweb.com

then create the storyboards and begin to fill in my content. Depending upon the client, I may need to make multiple passes through these steps before everyone is happy with the design.

Two Example Web Sites

Let's look at two different example Web sites from the list in Table 1-1. The Smythe family is creating a personal Web site, a family photo-adventure. The Vidalia Onion cooperative wants a site that gives the history of Vidalia onions and which will funnel viewers to linked sites to purchase the onions.

A closer look at the Smythe family

The Smythe family has selected the URL of www.thesmythes.com and has purchased the rights to use that domain name. They plan to keep their site updated every month. They have even purchased a digital camera to make it easier to put photos up on their site and to change them fairly often.

The Smythe family consists of six people and a dog. Susan, the mother, is forty years old. She works part-time as an accountant and is very interested in clogging, a form of folk dancing brought to the United States by Dutch settlers. Her husband, John, is forty-five years old and is a construction worker. They have four children. Jeff, the oldest, is seventeen; Jayne is fifteen; Dick is eleven; and Sally is three. Jeff is interested in music and plays the guitar. Jayne is primarily interested in boys, but she also volunteers at the local hospital. Dick likes to collect rocks and wants to be a geologist. Sally just wants to play with her friends, although she loves her Barbie dolls. Recently, Jayne and Sally (with Susan's approval) have started a collection of Beanie Babies®.

Tip: Your Internet service provider (ISP) can arrange to secure a domain name for you. You ought to first surf the Web to make sure that the name is not currently in use. When you ask for the rights to that domain name, another search is made to make sure no one else has registered it. Your ISP will bill you for the fee to register your domain name.

The Web site is Susan's idea. Although she objected to the amount of time that John spent on the computer when he first brought it home, she has decided that a family project to create and maintain a Web site could help everyone in the family work together and share ideas. She feels that it will create a common interest among the children and that it will also allow John to share his love of the computer with them all. In addition, she's hoping that they will be able to find pen pals from around the country and, perhaps, from all over the world.

Susan has seen some sites where visitors are encouraged to send a postcard from the site to their friends. She'd like to add a slightly different twist. She would like site visitors to actually send a postcard from their hometown to the Post Office box that she has rented for this purpose. For each postcard that she receives, the entire family will write a short thank-you note and send a postcard of their hometown to the sender. Susan thinks that it would be a wonderful experience for the children to learn about other people and other places.

By thinking this through, Susan has realized that there are a number of pages that need to be created. She wants an entrance page, a main page, a page for each family member (even for Doggie, the cocker spaniel), a page where visitors can sign in and send email, a page for family outings and Christmas letters, a Beanie Babies® page, and a page for scanned thumbnails of all the postcards the family receives.

Based on the knowledge of what she wants to accomplish, Susan designed the flowchart in Figure 1-9. It looks like she will have a minimum of 27 pages in the

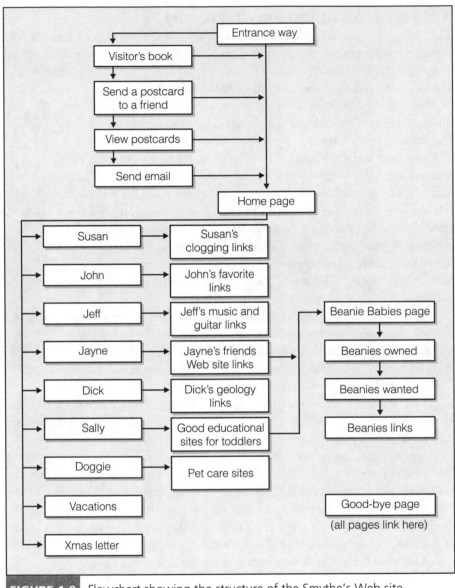

FIGURE 1-9   Flowchart showing the structure of the Smythe's Web site

Web site. All pages will point to the Home page and the Good-bye page. Each
child and the dog will also have a page of private photos and a page of links.

All about onions

The Vidalia Heaven cooperative is proud of the giant onions grown by its members. Vidalia onions are unusually sweet onions that can only be grown in several counties of Georgia. Only those counties are entitled to use the Vidalia label. The onions take about eight months to grow, harvest, and prepare for market, which makes them a much more time-consuming product than ordinary onions. The soil in the several counties in Georgia is thought to be what makes these onions so sweet.

Vidalia onions are available for only a few months each year. The first crop typically reaches market in May or June and the onions are no longer available by Thanksgiving. If you travel through Georgia in the summer months, you can buy these onions at almost any roadside stand. You can also get Vidalia onions at many supermarkets in the United States. Most supermarkets run out of Vidalias by mid-October, although specialty markets might carry them through the autumn.

The Vidalia Heaven cooperative consists of nine member farms. These farms sell their onions, relishes, and onion-related products via the Internet, as well as through their traditional retail outlets. The purpose of the site is to interest the site visitor in onion lore, facts, and recipes so that the visitor is lured into going to a member site to place an order. A secondary purpose is to entice the site visitors to consider Vidalia, Georgia, as a stop on a trip south. The tourist money is highly appreciated in this locale.

The "giveaway" for this site is a 10 percent discount coupon good on an order of onions at any of the member sites. It is awarded if the visitor can score 80 percent or higher on the 10-question quiz about onion lore. The quiz has many questions, but 10 are randomly selected at any given time. There are no limits on how often a visitor can play, but they can only use one certificate per 10-pound order.

The entrance way for the site is a series of images, sounds, and "word pictures" in praise of Vidalia onions. For example, you can listen to the sizzle of onions sautéing in a pan, or hear the crunch of cold, juicy onions in a sandwich.

The main pages of the site feature the history of the Vidalia onion, scientific facts about onions as a health food, care and storage of Vidalia onions, the growth cycle of the onions, and recipes featuring Vidalia onions. The quiz is on the exit page.

Figure 1-10 shows a quickly drawn storyboard of the three top-level pages in the prospective Vidalia Heaven site. The storyboards give a vague idea of the design approach with some private notes as to how items might be implemented. They also show the navigational items on the pages.

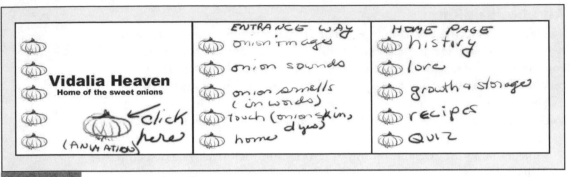

FIGURE 1-10   Storyboards for www.vidaliaheaven.com

Choosing a Theme

Each site needs a distinct identity. This identity is based on a combination of factors: the colors in your site, the graphic elements, the site layout, and the text styles. It can also include the metaphor that you've decided to use. In short, your site's theme encompasses all of those decisions that affect the personality and interior design of your pages.

What Your Site Says About You

If clothing and deportment are a person's first clue to the personality of someone they have just met, the design of your site is the visitor's first clue to the content that they expect to find in the site. I once received a catalog for knitting yarns, and the catalog was hand-typed (and misspelled) with numerous items crossed out. It was 28 pages long, and each page contained 50 items listed by name, single-spaced with a price next to it. The catalog was unreadable and visually unbearable. I never ordered from that store, even though they probably had one of the best selections of yarn in the country.

Your site can be inviting or it can be as painful an experience as the yarn catalog. The Candyman Corporation's Web site has the potential of being as awful as the yarn catalog. Like the yarn catalog, it contains hundreds of products that need to be listed. The challenge for that site will be to keep the number of items displayed on each page at a manageable number and to allow viewers to display pictures of the candy that they want.

You also need to make sure that your interior design is appropriate. You might be able to use a Wild West theme for the candy distributor if you pretend that the candy is all stored in a stagecoach and needs to be protected from outlaws who3 want to hijack it. The theme is a bit of a stretch, but it could work. If you took, instead, the theme of pickles, onions, and relishes (appropriate to the Vidalia Heaven site) and used it for the Candyman site, your audience would probably think that you'd gone insane.

Introducing FrontPage Themes

You might be a bit worried by now that you need to be an artist or designer in order to create a Web site. One of the benefits of using FrontPage as your design program is that you don't need to be an artist if you prefer not to decorate your site by yourself. FrontPage 2000 contains numerous themes, which are predesigned looks for your Web site.

Each theme sets the background color, link color, visited link color, selected link color, text color, and graphic elements for your entire site. You can modify the themes in many different ways. Many vendors also sell or allow you to download additional themes.

You've read almost an entire chapter without doing any work yet. The time has arrived for you to launch FrontPage and create a theme for the Smythe's Web site. You'll build more of this site in Chapter 4, and you'll learn more about creating and modifying Themes in Chapter 7.

1. Launch FrontPage by double-clicking its icon or by selecting it from the Windows Start menu.

2. Choose File | New | Web, as shown next. (FrontPage calls a "Web site" a "Web.")

3. Name your Web site. Allow FrontPage to place it into the default location for now (the default is a folder called My Webs). Press ENTER to create the Web site.

4. You'll then see the same screen that was shown in Figure 1-1. Select the Personal Web option from the collection of icons. Press ENTER.

5. After a few moments (or more—this can be slow), you'll see your new Web site. Figure 1-11 shows the result on my computer. Your starting screen will vary based on the last Theme that you chose.

Tip: You need not stick to the common "8.3" DOS format for a Web site name, but don't use any special characters or spaces in the name of the site that you create.

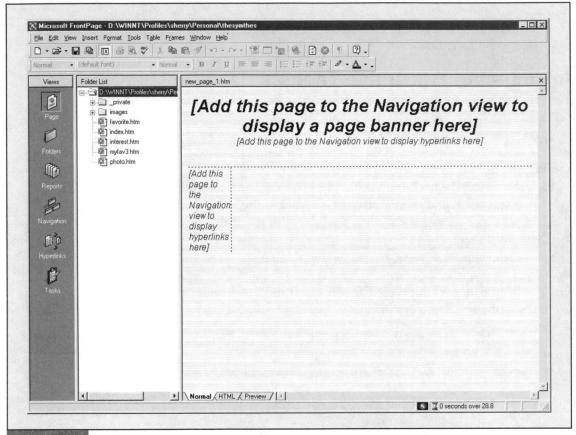

[Add this page to the Navigation view to display a page banner here]
[Add this page to the Navigation view to display hyperlinks here]

[Add this page to the Navigation view to display hyperlinks here]

FIGURE 1-11 The new Web appears

6. Now that you have a Web site, choose Format | Theme from the top menu bar as shown here:

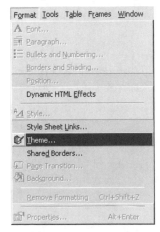

7. The screen shown in Figure 1-12 appears. Scroll to the Poetic theme in the list at the left side of the dialog box. Poetic is a casual theme with a light style that is suitable for a personal Web site.

8. Click the checkboxes to select the Vivid Colors, Active Graphics, and Background Picture options. Click OK to finish making choices.

9. Choose File | Save and then File | Exit to save your Web site and close FrontPage.

That's all there is to it. Of course, if you want to modify your theme, it takes a bit more work, but creating a new Web site and adding a theme is as easy as clicking a few buttons.

The theme consists of the graphic elements, the background picture, and the link colors. By selecting the Vivid Colors option, you altered the link colors and some of the graphics to make them brighter. The Active Graphics option instructs FrontPage to write the code to allow the buttons to change when you move the mouse pointer over them (these are called *rollovers*). The Background Picture option tells FrontPage to use the pattern or picture stored in the theme. If

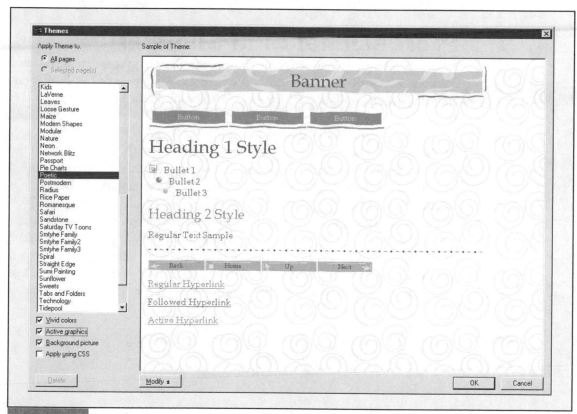

FIGURE 1-12 Choose Poetic as the theme

this checkbox is not selected, you'll get a plain background (which can often be more desirable). Try opening the Themes dialog box again and turning the various checkboxes on and off. See what changes occur in the preview window to the right. Explore some of the other built-in themes.

Building Expandability into Your Site

One of the very useful features of FrontPage is that it allows you to expand your site when you need to. You might not know in advance just how many pages you'll need, and sometimes the content of a site grows quickly. You can add pages at any time.

You haven't read about this yet, but FrontPage also gives you the ability to change the navigational structure of your site. This is important because you don't want to lock yourself into a structure that can't easily be changed. With FrontPage 2000, you can easily change your site.

Professional Skill Summary

In this chapter, you've learned about some of the thought processes that you need to apply before you begin to create a Web site. Learning to use FrontPage is not enough. Unless you know *what* you want to build, knowing *how* to build it is irrelevant.

You've learned some of the basic principles of building a good Web site, and you should be better able to objectively analyze Web sites as your browse the Web. When you visit a new site, you should be able to see if the designer has used easy-to-follow navigational elements and has created an appropriate design for the site.

You've learned how to determine the purpose of your site and how to pick its personality. You've also learned how to outline your site using either a flowchart or a storyboard. Finally, you learned how to create a new FrontPage Web site and attach a theme to it. In Chapter 2, you will be formally introduced to FrontPage and learn about its interface and the variety of ways that you can view your site.

Creating a Framework

In Chapter 1, you learned about some of the things that you need to think about if you're going to create a Web site. In this chapter, you'll get a chance to meet FrontPage and learn how its menus and commands are structured to make it easier for you to create Web sites. FrontPage 2000 has taken a leap forward in integrated functionality. You need to learn how to harness its power.

Finding a Home for Your Web

You have two decisions to make as you start to create your Web site. You need to determine who will host your Web site and you need to decide where you will develop your Web site.

Locating an ISP

If your site is to be available on the Internet, you need to have a server to make the site available to the world. You can create your own server if you wish. This is a path taken by many large corporations. However, you need to have the technical competence to run your own Web server. Giving you that competence is beyond the scope of this book.

If you are developing a site meant to be used within a corporation (an intranet), you will also need to have your own server in place. You need to have the technical people who can build and maintain this server for your company. Again, this type of technical knowledge is beyond the scope of this book.

For most readers, your most likely choice will be to find an ISP (an Internet service provider) or a Web hosting service to host your site. The service provider should be able to provide the technical support to fix any server-related issues on your site. If a link is broken because you forgot to update it, that is not the service provider's problem. However, if a page is missing due to a hard disk error, then the service provider should be able to fix that 24 hours a day. The service provider should also be able to provide you with the information that you need to upload your site to their server and to achieve compatibility with their server.

Servers typically use either UNIX, Mac Server, or Windows NT. The capabilities and requirements for these different operating environments differ somewhat, and your service provider needs to tell you what features of FrontPage will (or won't) run on their particular configuration.

You need to decide if you will need FrontPage Extensions before you choose a service provider. FrontPage Extensions are necessary if you want to use the many Dynamic HTML effects, the forms, and the scrolling banners that are built into FrontPage. Many ISPs do not have FrontPage Extensions, or charge you extra to use them. Therefore, you need to check on this before you begin your site development.

You also need to decide if you want to register a domain name. A domain name is the URL name or address that you choose for your site (for example, my Web site is www.londoncomputing.com). This name needs to be unique, and only one such site can exist within the country of origin. There is a one-time fee to register a domain name, and you must make smaller additional payments biannually as well.

If you are planning to create a personal Web site, your current ISP (the one who provides your Internet connection) might be able to offer you a small site at no extra charge. Personal Web sites usually allow only small amounts of data to be stored on the server, permit a low number of hits per month, and don't permit products to be sold on them.

You don't need to have a domain name in order to create a Web site. Your ISP will allow you to share their domain name (example: www.ispname.com/~yoursite). This is a somewhat less expensive alternative, but it has several pitfalls. It lacks the name recognition that you might want if you are developing a commercial site, and if you change ISPs, it will be difficult for your customers to find you again. If you actually register a domain name, you can change ISPs as needed without affecting your "address" on the Web.

Of course, there are other questions that you need to ask of your ISP as well. These include:

- Do I get email accounts with this service? Can I send as well as receive email?
- How much disk space comes with the account?
- What happens if I use up all of my disk space?
- Is there a limit to the number of "hits" that my site can get without incurring an extra fee?
- Can I use this site for commercial purposes?
- Does the ISP provide e-commerce services (such as accepting credit cards)? How much do they cost?
- Is there an FTP server that I can use to enable my site visitors to download material from my site? Is there an extra fee for this service?
- Does the site allow me to use CGI scripts if I need them? (CGI scripting is an alternate means of providing many of the services of FrontPage Extensions. Many CGI scripts are available on the Net and can save development time.)

Developing Your Site

FrontPage is quite particular as to where you can create your Web. It needs to have all of the resources for your pages in one location. Actually, a little organization is a good thing. By insisting that everything for your Web be in a central location and that all of its parts be known to the Folders view (which you'll meet in a few minutes), FrontPage is ensuring that *you* stay organized as well.

New in 2000: FrontPage 2000 is much friendlier to hard-disk based development than FrontPage 98 was. It has new features that make it easier for you to upload ("publish") your Web to your ISP or WWP, even if the service that you're using doesn't have FrontPage extensions.

▶ Tip: This book will usually assume that you are developing the site on your own hard drive. If you need to be anywhere else, you'll be told so explicitly. So, unless you're specifically requested to use your online connections or load Personal Web Server, you can create your practice Webs on your hard drive.

However, you do have a few choices to make before you start to develop your Web. Although FrontPage insists that your entire Web be kept in one folder, it isn't as fussy as to where that folder is kept. You have three basic options as to where to build your Web pages. You can develop your pages on your local machine, on the Microsoft Personal Web Server or online—in the "published" location for your Web. Let's look a bit more closely at each of these options.

Starting live

Your Web will ultimately live on the Internet (or company intranet), so why not develop it where it will be used? This approach has many advantages. You can immediately test your pages and your links. When the site is finished, it is immediately available. You'll learn as you develop what works and what doesn't work on your ISP's server. You'll also be able to ask friends or associates to check out your site using various browsers with different operating systems to make sure that your site is accessible by many different platforms.

Building on a local machine

When you build your Web site, you might not be completely sure of what you want to do. You might want to experiment and to try a variety of techniques. You might also be unable to develop your site quickly in the press of other business that you need to conduct.

If you put your fledgling efforts in full view, you could attract potential customers but lose them with an incomplete site. If your domain name is registered, you have little means of keeping folks from landing on your half-built site. If you want to register a domain name (as in www.*myname*.com), you need to have at least a placeholder Web page or you lose the right to use that domain name. However, a holding page indicates an obviously unstarted site, while a site in progress might have just enough content in it to frustrate visitors.

If you feel that Web development is an activity that should be done in private, you might feel more comfortable developing your Web on your own hard drive. That way, you can get yourself organized and make as many attempts as you want without feeling that you've exposed yourself to the world "half-dressed." When your site is ready, you can publish it on your Web server.

If you choose to develop on your own hard drive, you won't be able to test your pages completely. Most of the scripting capabilities cannot be previewed. While you can load individual pages into your browser, many of them are not fully operational unless a server environment surrounds them.

Using Personal Web Server

Microsoft Personal Web Server provides what might be a reasonable "third" approach. If you want to develop your site in private but also want to be able to test (most of) your site as you develop it, you can use the Microsoft Personal Web Server. This software creates a Web server on your own hard drive. All of your pages use their Universal Resource Locators (URLs) rather than the hard drive addresses. All of the links and effects become operational. You cannot test database queries or anything that requires Server Extensions using this approach and it is difficult to test the performance of your Web on different platforms. (If you develop under Windows, you can't determine if someone with a Mac can see all of your effects). However, if you also host a local area network at your site and it has Macintosh computers attached to it, you could even test your site's performance on the Mac.

New in 2000: Personal Web Server no longer ships in the same package as FrontPage.

If you have Windows 98, however, you can download a copy of Personal Web Server or see if it is on your version of Word's installation CDs. It is also on the Windows 2000 installation disks if you've purchased Windows 2000.

Let's Meet FrontPage 2000

Microsoft FrontPage 2000 is the fourth release of the Web design, creation, and maintenance package that Microsoft originally purchased from Vermeer Technologies in 1995. Each release has brought changes and improvements to the package. This release is the first one in which all of the elements of FrontPage— creation, site maintenance, and page layout—are included in the same program. The components of FrontPage98, FrontPage Explorer, FrontPage Editor, and Personal Web Server have been replaced by a single package (that no longer includes the Personal Web Server).

FrontPage has become so important a part of Microsoft's vision of the future that it is now tightly tied-in to Microsoft Office, and even comes included in a special Office 2000 bundle. The interface of Microsoft FrontPage 2000 has been revamped to move it closer to Office 2000. If you are already a user of Office applications, you'll find that FrontPage looks very familiar.

A Quick Interface Tour

You can begin your exploration of FrontPage by looking at Figure 2-1. It shows the FrontPage screen before anything "real" has been opened. Let's take a closer look at it.

The application window name at the very top of the screen shows you that you are working in Microsoft FrontPage 2000. The row underneath the window title is the menu bar. The navigation bars are below the menu bar. Shown in Figure 2-1 are the standard navigation and the formatting bars. The navigation bars will automatically change depending upon your view and the commands that you are using. For example, when you work with Dynamic HTML, the Dynamic HTML navigation bar will be visible.

Figure 2-1 shows the lower portion of the screen divided into two major parts. The left side says Views, and the right side shows

Tip: You can right-click anywhere in the navigation bar area to show a menu of all available navigation bars, and add that bar to your screen.

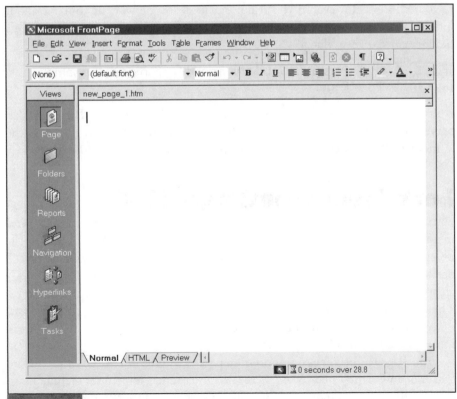

FIGURE 2-1   FrontPage starts up with an empty, blank document

new_page_1.htm. The Views section allows you to quickly change the way that you can work with FrontPage (more about that in a short while). The new_page_1.htm is living inside of your workspace. The workspace shows you the object or item that is currently being changed, viewed, or created. In the example in Figure 2-1, you are simply editing (or viewing) a single page that is not linked to a Web.

The tabbed area across the bottom of the workspace allows you to quickly change your viewing and/or editing mode in FrontPage. You can work in Normal mode (which is the *almost*-WYSIWYG—what-you-see-is-what-you-get—editor), HTML mode (which allows you to enter or change HTML code directly on the screen), or Preview mode (so that you can see how the page will look when displayed on the Internet).

A Look at the Menus

FrontPage 2000 contains all of the usual menus (File, Edit, Window) plus additional choices for using FrontPage. All of the commands are accessible via these menus at the top of the application window (see Figure 2-1). The menu bar is *dockable*. This means that you can drag it away from the top of the window and place it somewhere else in the window; the navigation bars under it are dockable as well.

New in 2000: FrontPage 2000 uses adaptive menus that display your most recently used menu choices and hide some of the others choices on the menu bar.

As a convenience to the user—though you might disagree—Microsoft has decided to use adaptive menus in FrontPage 2000. Each menu displays two upside-down caret symbols at the bottom to indicate that some of its choices are not being shown. If you hold your mouse cursor over the symbol (or linger on the menu) for a few seconds, the missing choices appear.

Tip: Microsoft FrontPage calls Web sites that it is creating or managing "Webs," so this book will also start to use that terminology.

Tip: Preview mode is not precise. Different browsers will show the page differently. The Preview tab at the bottom of the workspace only shows you how the page will look using Microsoft Internet Explorer 3, 4, or 5 (depending on which one is the latest version installed in your computer). If your most recent copy of the Internet Explorer is earlier than version 3, you won't be able to preview using the Preview tab. To see how other browsers display your page, choose File | Preview in Browser from the FrontPage menu bar.

You don't need to use the adaptive menus if you don't like them. Choose Tools | Customize and click on the Options tab. In the Options section, click on the "Menus show recently used commands first" checkbox to remove the checkmark. Your menus will now behave the way they did in Office 98.

If you do like the adaptive menus, you have a different option. By default, the option below the "Menus show most recently used commands first" checkbox is selected. This option automatically shows all of the options on the menu after a short delay. If you don't want to see the other menu options unless you specifically request them, you can uncheck this checkbox.

Toolbars

As you saw in Figure 2-1, the standard and formatting toolbars appear when you launch FrontPage. Figure 2-2 shows the additional toolbars that appear. You can also select which ones you wish to see at any time.

The standard toolbar contains functions that are common to most Office applications as well as some functions, such as Preview in Browser, Folder List,

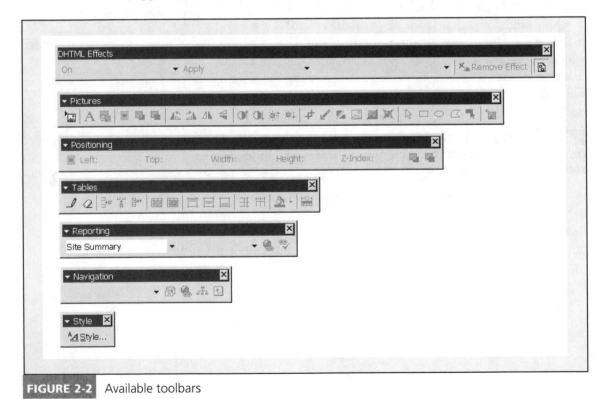

FIGURE 2-2 Available toolbars

and Insert Component, which are unique to FrontPage. The items on this toolbar are those that you use most often. The formatting toolbar is also standard to most Office applications. It allows you to format text and, select the font, style, and text size. You can also set your text alignment and change the text to bold, italic, or underlined.

The other toolbars contain more specialized functions, and many of their options shown in Figure 2-2 are grayed out. The toolbars are only active when you are completing a specific task. The DHTML effects toolbar enables you to add dynamic effects to your pages. The pictures toolbar is operational when you are working with images, as it enables you to perform straightforward tasks such as importing an image, cropping it, rotating it, positioning it, and changing the contrast and brightness.

Cross-Reference: Chapter 13 tells you about Dynamic HTML and using the DHTML toolbar, and Chapter 7 tells you all about graphics.

The positioning toolbar also requires an object—i.e., something that can be positioned. It helps you to specify the exact spot in which to place text or images. It also allows you to change the stacking order of images and layers.

Cross-Reference: You'll also find out about the positioning toolbar in Chapter 13.

The tables toolbar enables you to create tables, add and delete rows and columns, merge cells, and perform other table-design-related tasks. The reporting toolbar is only active when you are in Reports view. It allows you to select the specific reports to view.

Cross-Reference: Tables are discussed in Chapter 10, and the reports are discussed in detail in Chapter 9.

The navigation toolbar works in Navigation view, and you'll try it out later in this chapter. The style toolbar allows you to create and manage cascading style sheets.

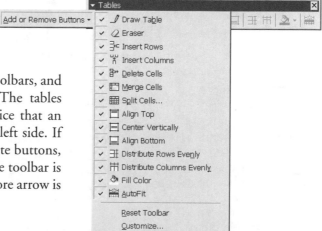

You can add or delete the items on the toolbars, and create your own toolbars if you prefer. The tables toolbar is shown here in the margin. Notice that an undocked toolbar has a small arrow on its left side. If you click on the arrow, you can add or delete buttons, and a list of available buttons appears. If the toolbar is docked at the top of the application, the More arrow is on its right.

Getting Started

Now that you've seen the "outside" of FrontPage and had a chance to think about how you want to approach developing your own Web, it's time to look inside FrontPage more carefully. You'll be taking a more creative tour in Chapter 4, when you get to create a preliminary site for the Smythe family, but for now you'll just use a simple one-page site. In this section, you'll learn some of the most basic commands needed to open, close, save, and delete FrontPage Webs.

Creating a New Web

You actually created your first Web in Chapter 1, but you did it without much explanation. The File | New | Web command is used to create totally new Webs. FrontPage defaults to the MyWebs folder within FrontPage. That's as good a location as any other to store all of your Webs. One of the key concepts in FrontPage, however, is that you need to manage the items in the Web through the program itself. Once you place something inside a folder in your Web, you cannot move or delete it using the normal operating system methods. FrontPage will do all of the management for you. Try this short demo to create a new Web.

1. Launch FrontPage. You'll see the same window shown in Figure 2-1.

2. Choose File | New | Web.

3. In the "Specify the location of the new web" field, you can see that FrontPage chooses a default location and name for your Web:

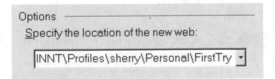

Leave the directory path alone (it points to your Personal folder as designated for your installation). The very last portion of the path is the Web name. Change the suggested name to **FirstTry**.

4. Choose a one-page Web from the opening dialog box.

5. Click on OK to close the dialog box.

6. The new_page1.htm file that appeared when you launched FrontPage is still in your workspace. This page doesn't belong to your Web. Click on the tiny x in the upper-right corner of the page to close the document. Since you've made no changes to it, you won't be asked to save it.

Tip: You can easily overlook the field that contains the suggested name for your Web. If you select a template for the Web and double-click on it, the Web is named and saved, and you've had very little say in what it was called.

7. Creating a Web, however, has made a change in your screen from the image in Figure 2-1. Figure 2-1 shows a View menu and the workspace. In Figure 2-3, you can see a third screen area has been added to the window. It is the Folder menu. Double-click on the file index.htm to open it. This is the main page of your one-page Web. Since you didn't attach a theme to the Web, you only see a blank document.

Tip: You can rename a Web by selecting Tools | Web Settings. In the General tab, select Web Name and type in a new name for the Web. FrontPage automatically updates all of the links.

Arranging Your Screen Space

FrontPage works best on a large, high-resolution monitor. On a 14" monitor, you'll feel quite cramped and crowded. You may hide the Views bar if you want (Select Views | Views Bar to toggle the bar on or off). You could also right-click on the Views bar and select Hide Views from the context-sensitive menu that pops up.

If you want to work with the Views bar and the Folder list as well as the workspace on the screen, you can change the relative amounts of space occupied by each one. If you place your cursor over the line that divides the Views bar from the File list (or the line that divides the File list from the workspace), your cursor

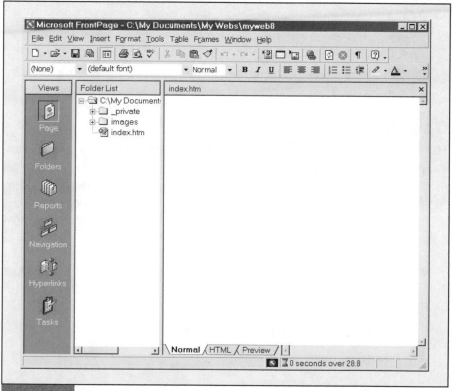

FIGURE 2-3 FrontPage adds a new page area for folders when you create a new Web

changes into a double line with an arrowhead pointing out from each line like the one shown here in the margin. When you see the column size cursor, you can drag the cursor in either direction to change the size of the column. You can make the Views bar and the Folder list columns more narrow so that you can see more of your Web page on your monitor.

Closing a Web

Closing a Web is a surprisingly nonobvious step in FrontPage. The File | Close command closes only the open page within the Web but doesn't close the Web itself. Try it.

1. Choose File | Close. The document index.htm closes. The Folder list remains visible so that you can open any page that you want. The Web is still the open and active object in FrontPage.

2. Double-click on the index.htm page to open it again.

The command that you need to use to completely close a Web is the File | Close Web command—and for some odd reason, the command is hidden by the adaptive menus when you first begin to work with FrontPage.

1. Click on the File menu to open it. Either leave the menu open for a few moments or click on the double down arrows at the bottom of the menu. You'll see the Close Web option.

2. Click on the Close Web command to close the entire Web. The Folder list disappears as well.

Opening a Web

You open a Web using the File | Open Web command. Try it.

1. Choose File | Open Web. In the dialog box, select the FirstTry Web that you just created. Click on Open. Figure 2-4 shows the Open Web dialog box. Notice that you have a panel of choices to the left of the standard Windows File | Open dialog box. This panel enables you to click to choose a Web from History, My Documents, Desktop, Favorites, or Web Folders. This panel lets you quickly choose where FrontPage looks first to find a Web to open.

2. The Web opens, but there is no document in the workspace. Double-click on the index.htm entry in the Folder list to open the actual page into the workspace.

You can also open a page explicitly. Here's how:

1. Choose File | Open.

FIGURE 2-4 The File | Open Web dialog box

2. Navigate to the location of the page that you want to open. As you can see in the bottom of the screen:

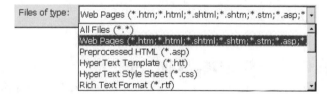

   you have a list of available file types. If you select the All Files option and open a file type that FrontPage cannot open (such as a Photoshop .psd file), FrontPage switches to that application to open the file.

3. Select index.htm and click on Open. FrontPage opens the entire Web as well as the page that you want to edit.

You can use either the Open or Open Web command as you prefer. Open is probably faster when you already know which page you want to edit, but Open Web works just as well.

Deleting a Web

If you need to delete an entire Web, you must do it through the facilities in FrontPage. Do not use the normal Windows Delete on the Web folder because it will confuse FrontPage. If you've looked carefully at the File menu, you might have noticed that there is no Delete option on it—even when you view the full menu. This means that you need to learn a different way to delete Webs.

Since the FirstTry Web was just that—practice, with no included content—you can safely delete it. Here's how:

1. In the Folder list to the right of the Views menu, right-click on the top-level folder in the list. You'll see the menu shown here:

2. Click on the Delete option. Another dialog box appears. Select the "Delete this Web entirely" radio button and click on OK. Every trace of the Web is removed.

The Workspace Tabs

Now that you know how to create, save, open, and delete a Web, it's time to learn about the three ways you can work with a Web page. Of course, you're going to have to create a new Web before you can continue . . .

1. Choose File | New Web and create a one-page Web called SecondTry.
2. Double-click on the index.htm document to open it.

Notice the three tabs sitting in the workspace window. They are the tabs that enable you to work in Normal, native HTML, or Preview mode.

Normal

By default, when you edit a page, you are in Normal mode. Normal mode gives you full access to all of FrontPage's editing capabilities and features. In the index.htm document, type "**Welcome to my SecondTry Web site.**" Press the ENTER key and type a new line: "**I am doing this just for practice.**" You can see the screen in Figure 2-5.

Notice the underline underneath the word "SecondTry." FrontPage is automatically spell checking your document and lets you know (by underlining the offending word) that it cannot locate that spelling in its dictionary. Since this really *is* just for practice, don't worry about the unknown spelling for now.

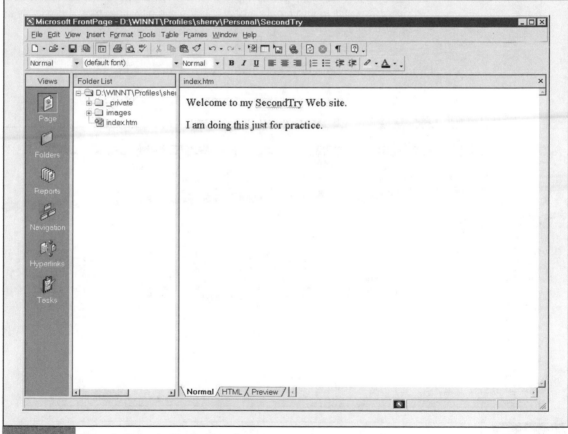

FIGURE 2-5   Entering text in Normal mode

HTML

Click on the HTML tab. You'll see the screen shown in Figure 2-6. Notice that FrontPage has already generated the starting code for you. The title of the page is "Home Page." You can see your two lines of text enclosed in paragraph markers (the <p> symbols). The HTML term for an item in <> is *tag*. Basically HTML is a tagging (or *markup*) language. The tags tell the browser how to display the various items in your page.

You can change the page directly in the HTML view by following these steps:

1. In the title tag, change the text so that the line reads as follows:

   ```
   <title> My New Home page </title>
   ```

2. Place your cursor just to the right of the last </p> tag in the document and press the ENTER key to create a new line. On the new line, type this exactly as shown here:

   ```
   <p>This site will be updated very soon. Watch for it!</p>
   ```

Figure 2-7 shows the HTML window when you are finished typing.

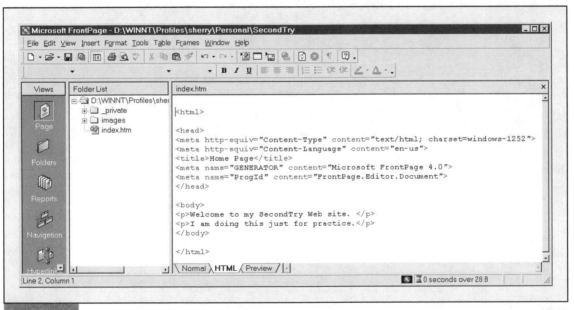

FIGURE 2-6   The HTML mode window

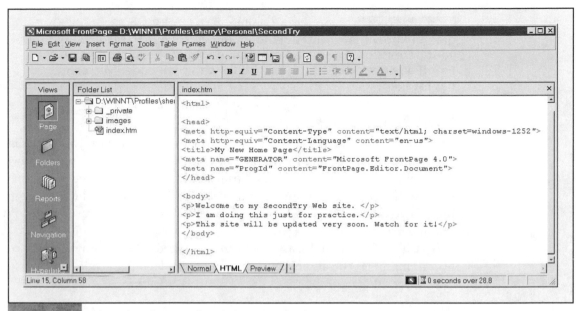

FIGURE 2-7 Changing the text directly in HTML mode

3. Switch to Normal mode by clicking on the tab. Figure 2-8 shows the changes you have made. You cannot see the change of title in Normal mode at all.

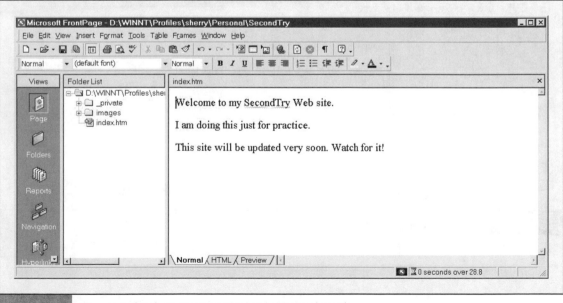

FIGURE 2-8 You can clearly see your new text in Normal mode

New in 2000: If you were familiar with FrontPage 98, you'll be glad to know that FrontPage no longer edits your HTML code without your permission. Frustrated programmers have been requesting that FrontPage get rid of its urge to fiddle with their code. Microsoft has listened!

Preview Mode

Click on the Preview tab. There is a subtle change in your screen as you can see in Figure 2-9. Notice that none of the editing tools are active. Preview mode shows you approximately how your finished page will look when displayed in Internet Explorer. If you want a more accurate idea, you'll need to use the Preview in Browser command on the File menu. Figure 2-10 shows the screen opened in Internet Explorer 5.0.

To use the Preview in Browser command, you need to have a browser installed in your machine. You also need to save your open document (File | Save) first.

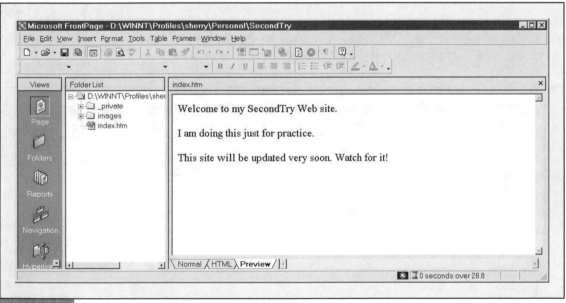

FIGURE 2-9 The open document in Preview mode

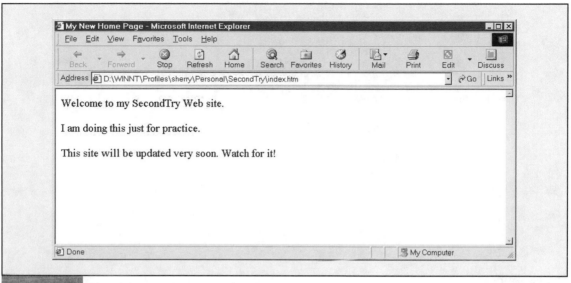

FIGURE 2-10 The document in Microsoft Internet Explorer

(If you forget, you'll get a reminder dialog box asking if you want to save changes before previewing.)

1. Choose File | Preview in Browser. A list of available browsers appears. This list contains the browsers that FrontPage knows are installed in your system. Choose whichever browser you prefer from your list.

2. Click on OK. The browser opens and displays the page. Figure 2-11 shows the same page displayed in Netscape Communicator 4.5.

Notice the difference in text size between Figure 2-10 and 2-11. The fonts are the same, but the preferences for fonts are set differently on my machine. The font is set to Medium in Internet Explorer and Large in Netscape Communicator. Although I did not change the default preferences in either program (and most users won't change them either), the page still looks different. This is just one of the difficulties that you will find in designing for the Web. Your pages look different in different browsers.

Since the browsers in Windows look different, I thought you might also like to see this very simple page as it looks on the Macintosh. The HTML code saved under FrontPage actually crashed Internet Explorer 4 on the Macintosh and wouldn't load from the disk without crashing until I manually removed all of the hard carriage return characters in the file. Netscape Navigator 3.0 had no

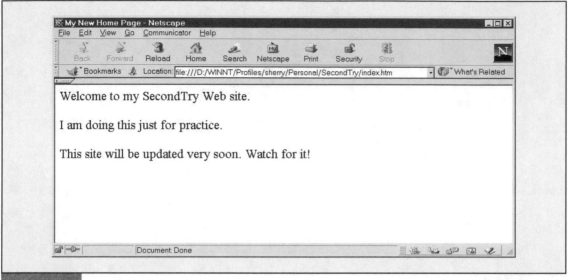

FIGURE 2-11 The **index.htm** page displayed in Netscape Communicator 4.5

problems with the page at all. Figure 2-12 shows the page window (sized exactly the same as it was under Windows) in Netscape Navigator 3.0 and Figure 2-13 shows the page in Internet Explorer 4.0. One thing that you should immediately notice is the difference in font sizes between the two platforms.

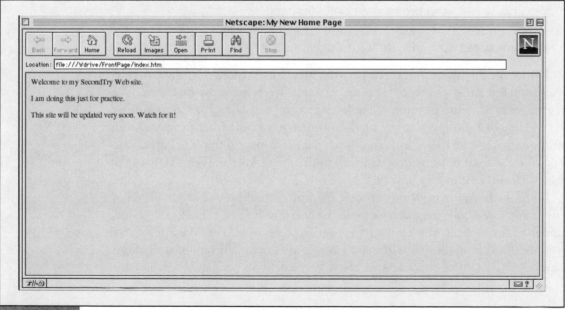

FIGURE 2-12 The **index.htm** page in Netscape Navigator 3.0 on the Macintosh

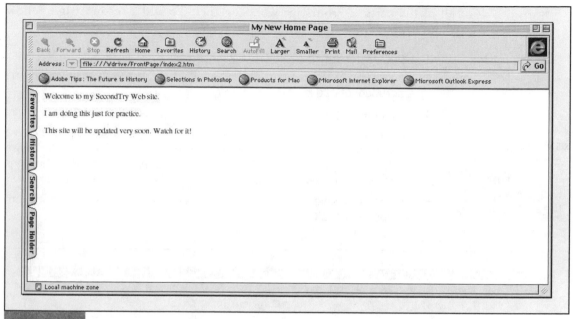

FIGURE 2-13   The index.htm page in Microsoft Internet Explorer 4.0 on the Macintosh

A View from the Bridge

FrontPage also gives you a large number of other features in addition to the ability to create and edit Web pages. The icons in the Views section of the screen allow quick access to these features. You've already met the Page view—that's the view that allows you to create and edit Web pages.

In addition to Page view, you can access:

- **Folders view**   To organize and manage files and folders
- **Reports view**   To analyze your Web and manage its content
- **Navigation view**   To plan the navigational structure of your Web
- **Hyperlinks view**   To view the connections that exist between pages
- **Tasks view**   To create and manage the tasks needed to make the site operational

Page View

You already know about Page view since you've been working in it, but a one-page Web doesn't give you much scope for seeing what the other views can do. You need to add another page and create at least one link in order to see how all of the parts of FrontPage work together. To add a second page, follow these steps:

1. Open the SecondTry Web if it isn't already open.

2. Choose File | New | Page to see the New Page dialog box. It gives you a wide assortment of pages from which to choose.

3. Select the Frequently Asked Questions page. Click on OK.

4. When the page appears, it already contains the logic for the page. It also contains the start of commonly asked questions. Type in some nonsense questions using the starting part of the questions. Type in the same questions in the related answers on the page. Figure 2-14 shows my nonsense questions.

5. Choose File | Save. The name probably defaults to table_of_contents.htm. Accept the default.

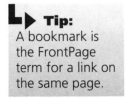

Tip:
A bookmark is the FrontPage term for a link on the same page.

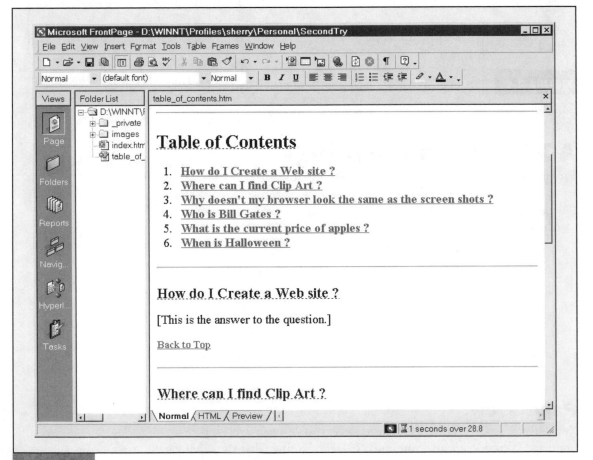

FIGURE 2-14 Nonsense questions added to the FAQ page

Now, you need to create a link from this page to return to the home page, and from the home page to link to the FAQ page. These basic links are easy to create. Follow these steps:

1. Near the top of the FAQ page, type the words **Go Back Home**. Highlight the text that you've just typed.

2. Choose Insert | Hyperlink. A dialog box opens. It defaults to the structure of the open Web. In this case, because you want to choose a page that's internal to your Web, you can easily select the index.htm page by clicking on its name in the dialog box. You'll see that as soon as you select the document, FrontPage enters its name into the URL field in the dialog box.

3. Click on OK to save the link.

4. Save the page (File | Save). Open the index.htm page in Page view by double-clicking on it in the Folder list.

5. Add a hyperlink to the FAQ page by typing "**Go To Table of Contents**" under the text that is already on the home page. Then create the hyperlink as you did in Steps 2 and 3 (choose table_of_contents.htm as your link page, however). Click on OK and then save the changes to the home page.

6. If you want, try out your links in Preview mode.

Now you have enough data in your Web that you can take a look at the other available views.

Folders View

Click on the Folders View icon in the Views bar. As you can see in the following illustration, the workspace disappears and in its place you can see a detailed listing of all of the files and folders in your Web. Clicking once on a folder in the Folder list opens the folder. Clicking on the minus sign in front of the top-level folder collapses it. The folder then shows a plus sign next to it. Clicking on the plus sign expands the folder again.

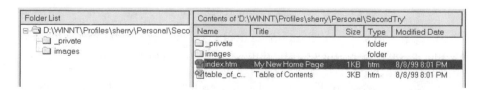

You can change the location of files in Folder view. If you had pages that you wanted to hide from the site visitor, you could drag these pages while in Folder view into the _Private folder that was automatically created when you created

Tip: You can test the bookmarks in Normal mode by pressing the *CTRL key and clicking on the link.*

Tip: FrontPage generally uses the name of the first link on the page as the default name for the page when you've added a page after the Web has been created. If there are no links on a page, the name generally defaults to new_page_x.htm.

your Web. You might want to hide style sheets, for example, from your visitors by dragging them into the _Private folder.

If you move a page containing links into a different folder within your Web while in Folder view, FrontPage automatically updates the links to that page.

Cross-Reference: You'll see how you can update links in Folders view in Chapter 6.

Reports View

Click on the Reports View icon in the Views bar. You'll see a summary report about your Web site similar to the one shown in Figure 2-15. This report lists a total of all of the files in your Web, shows if you have any broken links or slow pages, and lets you view the tasks that you've assigned to get the Web site created.

The Summary report is also a Reporting menu. You can double-click on any item to easily specify the report that you want to see. You can see the list of available reports here:

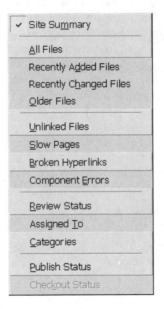

These reports appear on the Reporting floating menu and on the View | Reports menu. As you can see, they mostly duplicate the items on the summary-level report in Figure 2-15.

The Summary report shows that there are 14 links in the Web so far. None of them are broken. You can request a detail report on pages in your Web. As you can see in the following illustration, you see some extra information such as the name of the person who created the page and when it was last modified.

Name	Title	In Folder	Size	Type	Modified Date	Modified By	Comme
index.htm	My New Home Page		1KB	htm	8/8/99 8:01 PM	Sherry	
table_of_c...	Table of Contents		3KB	htm	8/8/99 8:01 PM	Sherry	

Navigation View

Navigation view allows you to create navigation bars for your Webs. You can specify which pages are included or not included in the navigation scheme and you can use this information to build a table of contents.

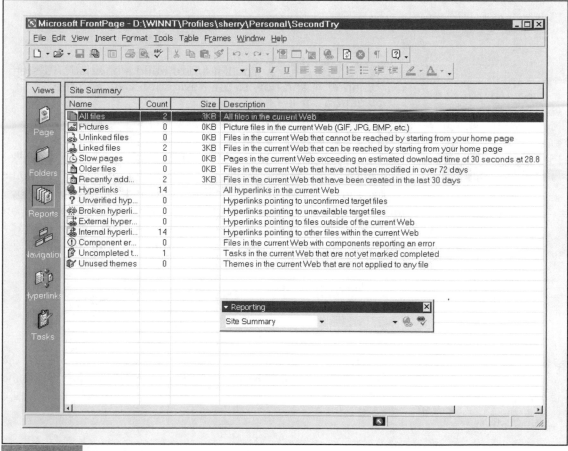

FIGURE 2-15   Reports view

Tip: The "Table of Contents" feature and the page that you saved as Table of Contents aren't the same thing at all. Inserting an "official" table of contents is a feature that uses components and requires FrontPage Extensions. It's confusing that FrontPage automatically saves a FAQ page that has no other links on it yet as "Table of Contents."

Click on the Navigation view icon in the Views bar. The navigational structure for this Web is shown in the following illustration. Of course, the Web structure is very simple right now, but when you get multiple branching pages, this view is extremely useful.

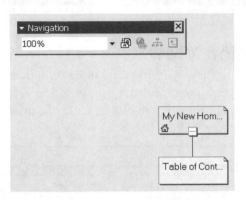

Tip: If you switch to Navigation view on your own system, you won't see the structure just shown unless you build it yourself. It doesn't appear automatically.

Cross-Reference: You'll learn to build a navigation system in Chapter 4, and how to use Navigation view and the navigation bar in Chapter 6.

Hyperlinks View

Hyperlinks view enables you to see which pages in your site are linked to other pages. In your Web, you have an infinite loop. The home page allows you to jump to the FAQ page, and the FAQ page allows you to jump back to the home page. It's perfectly legal to have this type of loop in a Web site (although the thought of an infinite loop is enough to give any programmers among you nightmares). The Hyperlinks view for this simple site is shown here.

index.htm   index.htm
table_of_contents.htm

Tip: The links on your pages don't show up in Hyperlinks view unless you've first saved the page.

You need to select a page to be able to see the links coming into the page and leaving it. The previous illustration shows just the home page pointing into the FAQ page and out of it. The next illustration shows what happens when you click on the tiny plus sign on the page symbol.

As you can see, the process of pointing back and forth could go on forever (but it serves no useful purpose to keep expanding the linked images here because they only point back to one another).

Tasks View

Tasks view is the final view on the Views bar. You might be developing the Web site by yourself, or, you might share responsibility for this Web with many other people. In either case, many tasks are involved in building a Web site, and it is all too easy for you to forget some of them.

FrontPage contains a built-in project management system to help you to manage all of the tasks that must be accomplished. You can link tasks to specific pages, or you can add tasks as simple reminders. As you begin tasks and finish them, you can keep the project management system updated about the status of the task.

You can add and edit tasks in a multitude of ways. You can add a new task from the File menu (File | New | Task), or you can add a new task from the Edit menu (Edit | Tasks | Add Task). You can also add a task from within the Folder list by right-clicking on the associated file name and choosing Add Task from the context-sensitive menu or any place where you can right-click on the name of an HTML file.

To add a linked task while in Folders view, you need to right-click on the name of the file in the contents window. Shown here are several fictional tasks that I added to this Web.

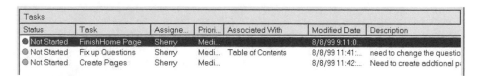

Cross-Reference: You'll learn how to use the project management system in Chapter 8.

Professional Skill Summary

This concludes the quick tour of FrontPage. You've learned how to create, open, save, and delete Webs and individual pages. You've created your first hyperlink and had a chance to tryout all of the views and workspace modes.

You've also examined the menus and toolbars that help you to create your Web sites. You've learned how to turn off the adaptive menus if they annoy you. You've also learned how to modify toolbars and view multiple toolbars at one time.

Although you didn't develop any more of the case study Web sites in this chapter, you should be starting to feel more at ease with the program. You've seen how all of the pieces fit together to enable you to create a Web site. You've seen some of the reports that FrontPage can produce, and you've learned how to create tasks as reminders of work yet to be done.

You've also learned about the development process of a Web site—where to store your files, the advantages and disadvantages of developing your site online or on your own hard drive, and questions to ask of an ISP before signing up for a site.

In the next chapter, you'll learn about the content that you"ll need in order to develop your site. You'll learn about the supporting program needed, and a bit about the technologies involved.

chapter 3

Gathering Documents and Graphics

In this chapter, you:

- Gather the materials that you will need for your site

- Learn how other Office applications can interact with FrontPage to give added functionality to the program

- Discover some of the advantages of using Adobe Acrobat on your site

- Learn about the variety of graphics applications and graphics utilities available if you want to produce your own graphics

- Learn where to look for graphics if you absolutely cannot and will not create your own images

- Learn about the basics of planning for multimedia

Using FrontPage to design a Web site is much like using a page layout program to produce a brochure. In its most basic form, a page layout program is a repository for materials that were created elsewhere. In typical page layout projects, articles are written in Microsoft Word or another word processor, graphics are created in Photoshop or Illustrator, and everything is put together and composed in QuarkXPress or Adobe InDesign.

When you create a Web site in FrontPage, you follow a similar process. You can create your text in either Word or in FrontPage itself, but the other elements—graphics, moving images, and sound—must be developed elsewhere and placed into FrontPage in a coherent fashion.

This chapter talks about gathering your materials—a very important step in creating a Web site. If you have nothing to put on your pages, you have no reason to create a site to display it. I hate to belabor the point, but you really do need to plan what you're going to do before you do it. If you let your site grow haphazardly, it will quickly become a management nightmare.

Planning for Change

One of the major decisions that needs to be made, even before you begin to gather materials for your site, is how often you want to add new material to your site. This seems as if it is a minor point, but it is really one of your most critical decisions. Many of your other decisions flow from this one.

Some commercial sites exist on the Web only as global yellow pages entries. The site announces the existence of a business, its location, and telephone number. In some cases, the site even gives a bit of primary information about the company. This type of site does not need to be updated. It's only purpose is to be there as a placeholder to allow prospective customers to find its name and address. Once the single page is done, it won't need to be touched unless the shop hours change. Of course, no one is going to come back to the site, either—unless they forgot the phone number!

Of the example sites in this book, www.stockchatter.com has the most frequent need for updates. The site would like to have a live feed to the latest stock prices. It needs to update news at least once per day, and preferably by the hour. The company that produces StockChatter needs to either find a totally automated way of keeping its site updated, or it needs to devote staff to keep the site up-to-date. As you can see, the update needs of this site become a major consideration in the design process.

Some of the example sites need less frequent updates. Settlement Services, for example, needs to keep its listing of available houses updated, but the settlement interface portion of the site doesn't need to change very often (the data for the individual settlements needs to be frequently updated, of course, but only the individual home buyer sees this data). Since this is a utility site, you don't need to keep trying to bring people in for repeat visits. They will use the site until they settle on their home and then probably not visit it again until they are ready to buy another home. Settlement Services certainly might want to send them periodic reminders of their existence—perhaps even offering a gift certificate to a local store or some other type of cash reward for referrals. However, once the site is operational, it should (mostly) take care of itself—except for the clerical updates to the settlement files.

The Candyman, Inc., site needs to be updated with a special promotion for each holiday. Candyman, therefore, needs to know that it will have to commit time and resources for new site developments at least every other month. Valentine's Day, Secretary's Day, Mother's Day, Independence Day, Halloween, Thanksgiving, and Christmas are all good holidays for candy.

Your business might have a "natural" update rhythm to it, or you might want to change your content more frequently so that you make it enjoyable for repeat visitors. Bringing folks back to your site more frequently can encourage them to purchase more of your products. The more often they visit; the more often they buy. Running specials or giveaways can entice visitors to your site.

You might also want to encourage repeat visits in order to boost your site "hits." If you wish to display advertising on your site, the income that you generate from the ad might be linked to the number of visitors to your site. There are many different types of programs that enable you to earn commissions for referrals to other sites. I will absolutely not recommend any of them. That decision is entirely yours. However, if you want to explore the world of paid links and advertising, you might want to investigate the Associates program at Amazon.com. This gives you a decent place to begin learning about various ways to earn advertising income on the Web and gives you a reputable starting point. You need to be very careful about choosing a cross-marketing program, because many of those that are available are multilevel marketing programs (MLMs), which were more commonly known as "pyramid" marketing structures in the past. There are a lot of get-rich-quick schemes floating around, and they will rarely enable *you* to "get rich quick."

The topic of ads and linking to earn extra money exposes the seamy underbelly of the Web very quickly. I have written this book assuming that you wanted to created a Web site to promote an existing business or that you wanted to create a Web-based business that sold a *real* product or service. However, you can also create a Web site that does little more than send people to other sites that sell something. If you want to explore this facet of the Web, type "**Making Money Web**" into one of the Web search engines. In this case, I recommend that you use AltaVista as your search engine with the Family option turned on if you find "adult content" offensive (as I do). Just be a very careful consumer of the marketing expertise that some of these—cleaner—sites wish to sell.

What Kind of Documents Will I Need?

Your Web site consists of text, graphics, sound, and moving graphics. The mix of these elements and the decision to include all or some of them is completely yours. FrontPage is not the creation point for most of these needed resources. They must be built in other programs and imported into FrontPage (except for text, of course).

Even though graphics are important on the Web, much of your site will probably contain text. Graphics are time-consuming to download, so they need to be used with a bit of restraint. Words, however, can be displayed in whatever quantities you wish. One of your first tasks, then, after you've designed the structure of your site, is to gather or create the text that you will need on the pages.

This can be as simple as writing some descriptive captions for the candies in the Candyman Web site, or as complex as gathering all of the documents needed to populate the Web sites of Access-Ability, the SweaterLink site, or the INSCOPA personnel site.

If you are going to use text from documents that are already in existence, you need to determine how to get them online. You also need to be certain that you have the rights to post them online. Once you've gathered the text documents, you also need to organize them in a coherent way. That organization will be the backbone of the your Web structure.

Let's look for a moment at the organizational challenges facing Access-Ability. This site wants to provide help to people who have mobility problems. It needs to give them both information and links to information about ways to make life easier. It has a huge file of articles regarding products for easier living, making travel arrangements, and legal rights for the mobility-challenged. How could you organize this wealth or material if you were designing the Access-Ability site?

One easy way to create the site would be to give each document a title and assign keywords to it (a *keyword* is a word that identifies the topic of the article). Just as you use a search site such as Yahoo or Lycos and locate content by typing in keywords, so you could find articles by typing keywords into a site-based search engine. FrontPage contains a Search Form component so that you can implement a site-wide search relatively easily.

If your entire site interface consists only of a search form, however, you risk boring or frustrating your users. Therefore, in addition to the search component, you need to find a way to slice up the content of the site into sections to give the site visitor an idea of what the site contains. You could divide the site by area of use: such as Home, Work or School, and Travel. Another possible set of categories would be Products, Facilities, and Legalities.

Either set of categories would work; you need to decide the method that you want to use. The key ingredient is to determine the broad categories that cover all of the material that you want to display. You can always add categories later, but try to think your way through all of the possibilities before you start.

In the example categories above, another question to ask is which method results in the least duplication of material. If the site were organized by "Home, Work or School, and Travel," you could list "Products" as a subcategory within each major topic. If there is a large overlap in the products used in each of the categories, "Products" should be a major category of its own. If you can keep the overlap low (for example, the wheelchairs that are meant for home use are different than the ones designed for outdoor use), you can safely use "Home, Work or School, and Travel" as your main categories. Of course, one benefit to placing information on the Web is that you can use hyperlinks to branch to topics of interest, and you don't need to send your readers in only one direction. If a lot of the same products are used in the Home, Work, and Travel locations, you could link to the product pages and you don't need to place them on the Web multiple times.

FrontPage and Office 2000—
A Close Partnership

Microsoft has designed Office 2000 as an integrated Internet-aware application. All of its pieces work together and all of them share a common interface. They can use the same themes as FrontPage. They can all save data in HTML format for immediate placement on the Web.

The Office 2000 Server Extensions (an advance from the earlier FrontPage Extensions) enable you to place live Excel or Access data on your Web site. You can convert PowerPoint presentations into Web presentations simply by saving your work for the Web.

Every Office 2000 application has a Web toolbar and a Save to Web option. This enables members of your work group to prepare content in the program with which they are most familiar.

> **Tip:** Although you can create Web pages from within any of the Office 2000 applications, you should use each application for the task it does best.

Word

Word 2000 has been tuned to work with FrontPage. You can open and save documents directly into HTML format—that is now one of the "native" formats of Word. This means that you can create all of your text inside of Word and easily bring it into FrontPage, or create text-based pages completely within Word.

Word 2000 has added a new Web view to the views available in Word 97. If you size your windows for the size of the Web page, you can get a fairly good preview of your page as you create it. You can use the Web toolbar to create forms or pages with checkboxes, drop-down menus, radio buttons, and other navigational aids (although this is probably best done within FrontPage). You can also create links from within Word by choosing the Insert | Hyperlink command.

When you save files as HTML, you can use the tools on the File | Save as Web Page dialog box to customize the options for the Web. When you select the Web Options submenu on the Tools menu, you'll find four tabs full of settings:

- **General tab**   This option lets you decide what version of HTML code to write. It also enables you to automatically use cascading style sheets (CCS) if you want.

- **Files tab**   This tab contains a variety of options dealing with file locations, long file names, and the editor to assign to documents placed on the Web.

- **Pictures tab**   This tab lets you format your Web screen for a specific size and enables you to choose the method needed to display your graphics in a page.

- **Encoding tab**   This tab allows you to specify the language symbols to use.

You can drag and drop text directly from Word into FrontPage. Figure 3-1 shows the preceding sentence being dragged into a FrontPage document. You simply need to arrange your desktop so that you can see both programs at the same time, as shown in the following steps:

1. If Word occupies the entire window, the center icon at the top right of the screen shows overlapping documents like this:

Click on the icon (the ToolTip cursor says "Restore"). Your application window gets smaller and the icon in the center of the top bar becomes:

Now you can move the Word window anywhere on your monitor.

2. Launch FrontPage. Restore the application so that you can move it as well.

3. Place the two windows next to one another.

4. Make Word active by clicking in that window. Select your text inside of Word by dragging and highlighting with the mouse.

5. Drag the selected text into the FrontPage document.

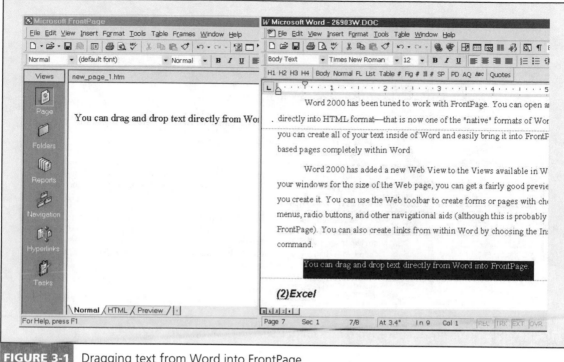

FIGURE 3-1   Dragging text from Word into FrontPage

You can also drag an entire Word document from the desktop into FrontPage. Figure 3-2 shows this operation in progress. The procedure is similar to dragging and dropping text, as shown in the following steps:

1. Locate the Word document on the desktop (you can look in My Computer to find it).
2. Size FrontPage so that you can see it and the desktop at the same time.
3. Select the icon for the document on your desktop.
4. Drag the icon into FrontPage.

Excel

Excel has also been tuned to work with the Web. You can save a spreadsheet for the Web either as a static image or as an active spreadsheet. The "Add interactivity" checkbox on the File | Save as Web Page dialog box, shown in Figure 3-3, controls whether the pages is linked to a "live" spreadsheet or simply placed on the Web for information. When Selection: Sheet is chosen and the "Add interactivity" box is checked, the spreadsheet can be edited online.

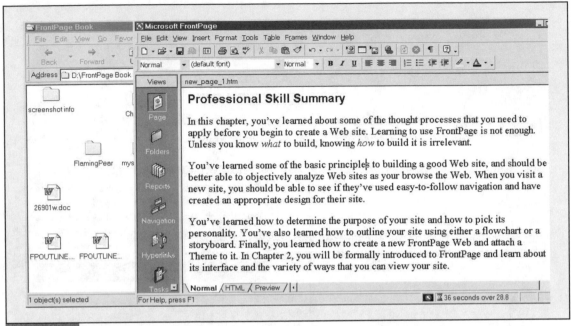

FIGURE 3-2 Dragging an entire Word document from the desktop into FrontPage

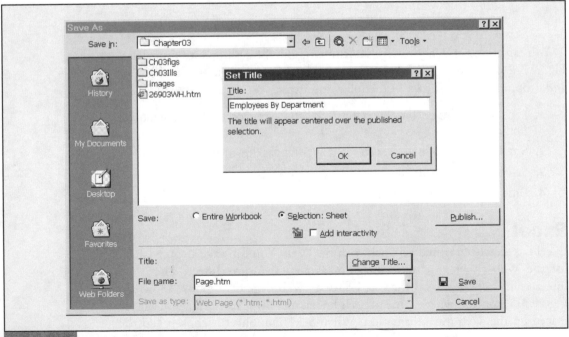

FIGURE 3-3 Saving an Excel spreadsheet for the Web

However, there's a catch (of course) to this very powerful feature. Lest you think that you can simply place a live spreadsheet on your Web site and anyone can use it, you need to remember that Microsoft earns money from the sale of Excel. Therefore, the only folks who would be able to manipulate the spreadsheet are the ones who have a valid license for Excel 2000 on the computer from which they are surfing the Web.

What is the consequence of this requirement? You cannot use Excel to create a mortgage payment calculator and expect to have all of your site visitors able to use it. This would be a wonderful feature for the Settlement Services example Web site, but too few of their customers are likely to own Excel. However, the Insurance Company of Southern Pennsylvania (INSCOPA) can place active Excel spreadsheets into their intranet if they wish, because they already know that all of their employees have valid licenses to use Excel.

Excel has some additional features that are visible in Figure 3-3. You can save a single sheet of the workbook for the Web, and you can change the title of the sheet when you save it. The title and the file name are not the same thing.

You can place the saved spreadsheet into FrontPage by selecting Insert | File from within FrontPage. If you only select File | Open and choose the saved HTML page, you will launch Excel instead (unless you changed your preferences in Excel). Figure 3-4a shows the Normal mode version of the saved spreadsheet, Figure 3-4b shows the spreadsheet in HTML mode, and Figure 3-4c shows the Preview mode of the page.

You can also embed Excel charts and pivot tables into your Web pages. Excel charts create excellent information graphics when you need to visually communicate numeric data. Pivot tables are reports that show summaries of spreadsheet information in a manner that can be controlled by the user. The charts and pivot tables can be live if Excel is installed on your site visitor's machine.

Access

Microsoft Access is the database component of the Office applications. A database is useful in organizing data. The spreadsheet example shown in Excel could have been generated from the data in an Access database. If INSCOPA keeps an Access database of employees and departments, the interconnectivity of Office would allow the company to quickly produce the spreadsheet.

You could also directly embed a database into a Web page. You embed a database into a Web page by creating a data access page from within Access. This page enables you to choose fields and add tools, sorting and grouping controls. It is similar to designing a form.

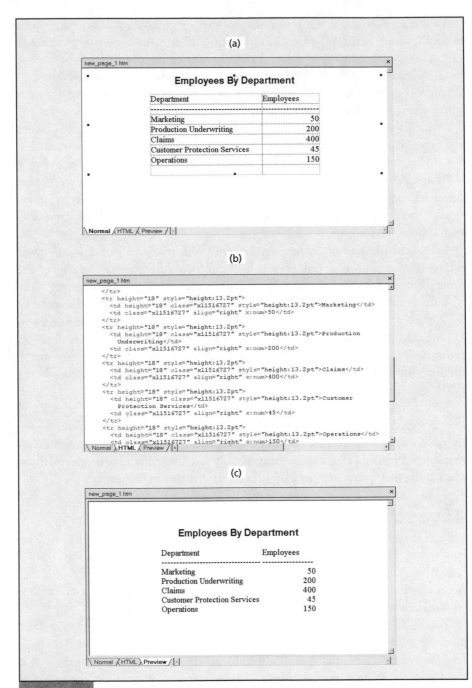

FIGURE 3-4   Saved Excel spreadsheet in Normal (a), HTML (b), and Preview (c) modes in FrontPage

You can create three types of data access pages—pages for interactive reporting, data entry, or data analysis. Your site visitor needs a valid Access 2000 license and a Microsoft Internet Explorer 5 browser to work with the data access page over the Web. The page is downloaded to the individual computer. The site visitor can change the sorting or reporting any way he or she likes. The data itself resides in the original database on the server or other accessible location. So long as the site visitor only changes the way the data is displayed, the underlying data is not changed. However, if any changes are made to the data itself, the original database is updated.

Access provides one easy way to maintain the settlement history of each of the Settlement Services customers.

The company could create an Access database and a secretary could update each task as it is completed. They could then prepare static reports for each customer and allow only the customer to access his or her own data. (An alternate method for Settlement Services to consider is to use the task management features built into FrontPage.) Figure 3-5 shows a sample of an Access interactive reporting data access page as it would appear in Internet Explorer. The image is taken from Microsoft Access Help.

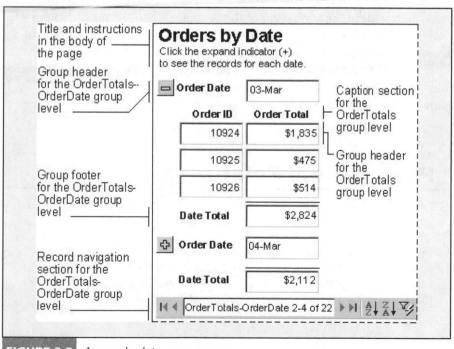

FIGURE 3-5   A sample data access page

PowerPoint

Microsoft PowerPoint is a presentation program. Originally, the program created slides that could be assembled digitally and then imaged to a slide recorder to produce physical media (i.e., slides) that were projected onto a screen with a slide projector. Of course, PowerPoint can still do that, and many organizations still deliver slide presentations for sales, marketing, and financial services (and whatever other departments use them).

A growing trend, however, has been to keep the digitally created presentation on a digital medium. You can show a PowerPoint presentation on a computer screen with the added benefit of being able to animate it. You can link audio to the slides much more precisely on the computer than you can by cueing the slide projectionist to change to the next slide.

You can place your entire slide show on the Web. This enables an organization to make an archive of their slide presentations and make them available to people not able to attend the original presentations. You can design your presentation directly for the Web in PowerPoint if you want and save it as HTML. You can still edit it in PowerPoint. However, you can use this presentation as part of your FrontPage content.

When you create a presentation for the Web, you can embed links and allow your site visitor to skip over areas of the content. When the presentation is displayed on the Web, the outline of the slide show appears on the left side of the browser and enables the visitor to jump from slide to slide.

If you want, you can even set up a specific time to *broadcast* your presentation and "go live" over the Web. This broadcast feature is new to PowerPoint 2000. It allows you to schedule a presentation and then show it at the specified time.

Professional Pointer

Be careful of animations that require a mouse click in your presentation if you are showing it on the Web. Unless you also include a "click here" or some other visual clue, your site visitors won't know that the animation is there. You might want to make the animation time sensitive or otherwise automatic. You also need to choose the colors in your slide show with care. The deep colors that project so well for slides can be too intense or too dark on a monitor.

FrontPage and Adobe Acrobat

Adobe Acrobat is one of the most useful "helper" applications if you need to send fully formatted pages across your Web site. Acrobat was designed to enable cross-platform viewing of formatted documents that contain graphics without the viewer needing to own copies of the programs that created the documents. This means that a QuarkXPress document can be saved as a Portable Document File (.pdf) with all of the text and graphics included. The viewer can download the document from your Web site and read it with the original formatting intact. All of the fonts, all of the graphics—everything shows up exactly as it was designed. It doesn't matter if the original document was created on a Mac or on the PC. It will look the same regardless of where it was created.

In order to view .pdf files, your site visitors need to have Adobe Acrobat Reader on their system. Acrobat Reader acts as a plug-in or help application to both Netscape Navigator and Internet Explorer. It is a commonly available freeware program. Although Adobe sells the complete version of Acrobat, the Acrobat Reader is free, so that your site visitors can easily obtain a copy.

If you are creating a Web site that contains a lot of information (such as the Access-Ability site) and that information already exists as formatted text, you might consider turning the documents into Acrobat files and placing them on your Web site. You can then allow your site visitors to search for the documents that they want to read and download them.

You will need a full copy of Adobe Acrobat in order to be able to create (*distill*) Acrobat files. (The full version is not free.) The full version of Acrobat installs a menu option into both Microsoft Word and Microsoft PowerPoint that enables you to save your documents directly to Acrobat (.pdf) format. You can visit the Adobe Web site (www.adobe.com) for more details.

Paint and Drawing Programs

Once you've assembled the text for your Web site, you need to think about the graphics. You can either create your own graphics or use packaged graphics on your site. Although FrontPage gives you some graphics manipulation commands, you cannot create original graphics within FrontPage.

What kinds of graphics exist? The basic division is between raster and vector graphics. Raster graphics consist of pixels (a pixel is the smallest unit that your monitor can display). Raster graphics are also called *bitmapped* graphics. Painting programs create raster graphics. The key ingredient of a raster graphics program is that the program only understands pixels. Although you can tell the computer to keep groups of pixels together, the program itself does not differentiate between one part of the image or another. It can't tell the difference between a hat and a light bulb.

Vector graphics keep shapes in the program. A vector graphics program defines shapes using formulas or positional code. For example, a square is internally defined to a vector program as having a starting point, a length, and a width. From these numbers, plus the stroke and fill attributes, the program can redraw the square any time it needs to display it. It takes up much less space to write a vector file. Vector files let you easily layer objects, move them, and resize them.

However, everything that is displayed on the computer monitor is in pixels, and even vector graphics need to be changed to pixels to be displayed (a process called *rasterizing*). Vector graphics programs don't handle photographic images. Although some programs can display them, a vector (drawing) program cannot edit the underlying pixels.

Both raster and vector graphics programs have their uses for the Web. Most Web graphics are created in raster programs, but vector images actually compress better into the .gif format. They use fewer colors and convert to become much "cleaner" and sharper images. Of course, the style of graphics created by each program type does differ. The vector graphics tend to be more "hard edge" and crisp than raster graphics. They are very useful for logos and some types of animation.

Most artists use both raster and vector graphics programs. Let's take a look at some of the programs available in each category.

Painting Programs

The most commonly used painting program for graphic artists is Adobe Photoshop (www.adobe.com). This program is the "gold standard" to which all others are compared. Photoshop 5.5 (the current version) allows you to scan images, color correct them, and prepare them for the Web. You can save images as .gif, .jpg, or .png files (the most common formats for the Web) and compare three versions of the file to the original for quality, size, and download speed, as shown in Figure 3-6.

Photoshop 5.5 includes ImageReady 2.0, a program that allows you to create .gif animations, slice images, and create image rollovers. You can easily move files from one program to the other.

Tip: With the introduction of Photoshop 5.5, ImageReady will no longer be sold as a stand-alone program.

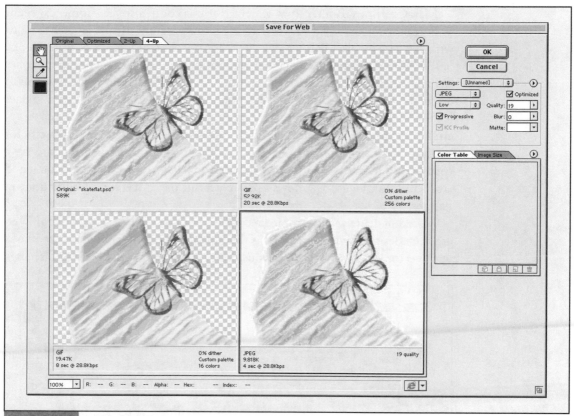

FIGURE 3-6 The **Save for Web** command in Photoshop allows you to compare options

Cross-Reference: If you don't know what .gif animations, rollovers, and image slices are, see Chapter 7, 10, 13, and 14.

Although Photoshop is a spectacular program, it isn't for everyone. The program is expensive, so if you only want to create simple images, you might not want to splurge on a $600+ piece of software. Less expensive alternatives do exist.

Corel PhotoPaint (www.corel.com) is a perfectly serviceable program that does many of the same things as Photoshop. Many folks in the PC world actually prefer it to Photoshop because they feel it doesn't have as large a learning curve and it has more bells and whistles. You can create animations and image maps, and save images as .gif, .jpg, or .png. However, Corel PhotoPaint doesn't give you the same preview controls as Photoshop. Corel PhotoPaint is available as a stand-alone program or as part of the CorelDRAW Graphics Suite.

MetaCreations Painter (www.metacreations.com) also has some excellent Web features. Painter is a very interesting raster program. It enables you to paint with "natural media." You can use chalk, crayons, impasto, mosaics, watercolors, oils, or almost any other media that you can image. You can change the brushes to make almost any texture or effect that you want. Painter 6 even allows you to create multibristle brushes that pick up multiple colors. You can save your images for the Web, create animations, and set up image maps. Painter also has a wrap-around file format that enables you to create seamless tiles that are very useful for background images on your Web pages. Although other graphics programs have tried to mimic Painter's use of traditional media, Painter was the first to do it and is still the best. Figure 3-7 shows a possible home page for Access-Ability done in Painter.

Macromedia (www.macromedia.com) has some excellent programs for Web graphics design as well. Fireworks is their paint program, although it also works with vector graphics. It enables you to create images for the Web and change

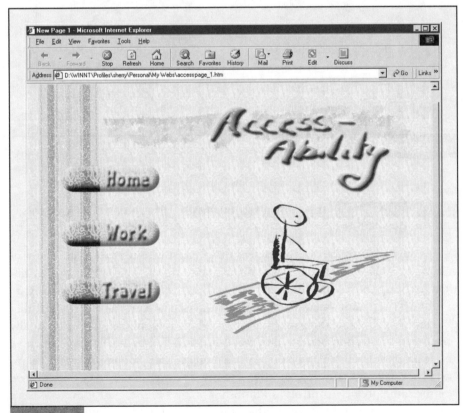

FIGURE 3-7   Web site interface created in MetaCreations Painter

them into Web-compatible formats. You can create animations, image maps, and rollovers. You can slice images as needed to make tables. You can also see a preview for quality and download time when you save your images. If you only create graphics for the Web, Fireworks might be all you will ever need.

Photoshop, Painter, Corel PhotoPaint, and Fireworks are all professional-level commercial painting programs. JACS PaintShop Pro (www.jasc.com) is a relatively inexpensive (about $99) program that is used by many of the Web graphics designers. It contains many of the same features as Photoshop, at a fraction of the cost. You cannot work with channels as easily and it is not the easiest program to use for traditional CMYK printing, but for Web work or presentation graphics, it is an excellent choice at a low price. It also includes vector layers, so you can get the best of both worlds. Figure 3-8 shows the PaintShop Pro 6 interface with a button filled by a variety of special effects.

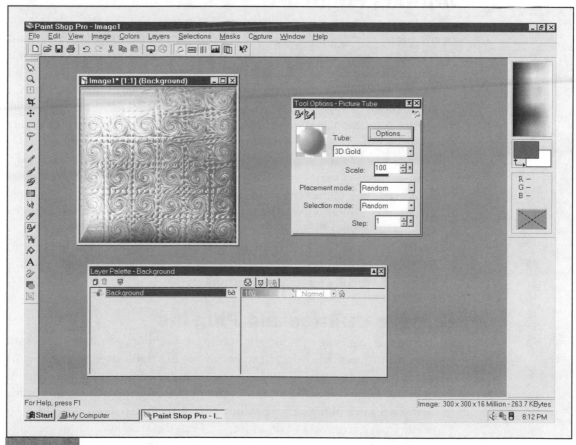

FIGURE 3-8   PaintShop Pro 6 interface

You might also have the graphics tools that you need included in the version of Microsoft Office that you purchased. Microsoft sells Image Composer and PhotoDraw. Image Composer is only available with the stand-alone version of FrontPage 2000. If you want more information about it, you can read the Microsoft Image Composer FAQ at: http://www.microsoft.com/FRONTPAGE/imagecomposer/faqs.htm.

PhotoDraw (www.microsoft.com) is the newer graphics program from Microsoft. It combines both raster and vector features and includes a large number of graphics to get you started. You can scan images and apply special effects. You can color correct images and you can save them for the Web. PhotoDraw is included with the Premium version of Office 2000 and can be purchased as a stand-alone product for an estimated price of $149.

Drawing Programs

The most popular vector drawing programs are Adobe Illustrator (www.adobe.com), Macromedia Freehand (www.macromedia.com), and CorelDRAW (www.corel.com). These "big three" have a constant feature war and try to contain fairly similar features.

Vector programs are good choices to build the basic shapes that you need for Web graphics. You can create the shapes for your buttons (and the shapes can be much more creative than simple circles, squares, or lozenges). You can then bring these shapes into your drawing program and turn them into Web art.

Vector programs can also create very small graphics that download quickly. You can create a "cartoon look" for your Web site, or create sites that are quite sophisticated but still manageable in size.

Micrografx Draw (www.micrografx.com) is a lower-cost alternative to CorelDRAW, Adobe Illustrator, or Macromedia Freehand. Micrografx Draw was actually one of the first Windows graphics programs, but it lost out to CorelDRAW over the years. Micrografx then lowered the price of the package and has made a choice for lower-end graphics.

Graphic Utilities and Plug-ins

In addition to acquiring a painting or drawing application, you'll probably want special-effects filters that help you to create buttons, banners, and other visual treats for your Web pages. There are a huge number of these plug-in programs around, and many of them work with a variety of raster graphics programs. Some of them even work inside of Adobe Illustrator or the other vector programs.

While I can't give you an exhaustive list, I can describe some of my personal favorites. If you want to create buttons for the Web, you can use the native facilities in Photoshop, Painter, or CorelDRAW. However, if you want additional possibilities, Extensis PhotoTools (www.extensis.com) is an excellent choice. It allows you to create your own bevels, and does a variety of both beveling and embossing tasks. It also creates original textures that you can use as the basis for other effects. Its shadow filters are quite good, and you can create both drop and cast shadows. PhotoTools is a "workhorse" filter. It is a good, solid worker and does its job. It isn't flashy or exciting, but it works hard and its interface is one of the most usable around. Figure 3-9 shows the Extensis TextureMaker, a filter that is part of Extensis PhotoTools.

Alien Skin Eye Candy (www.alienskin.com) is another program that specializes in beveling and embossing. One of the wonderful things that this filter can do is create geometric shapes such as stars. You can specify the number of points on the star or sides to a polygon, and you can control the angle of the shape and the depth of the points.

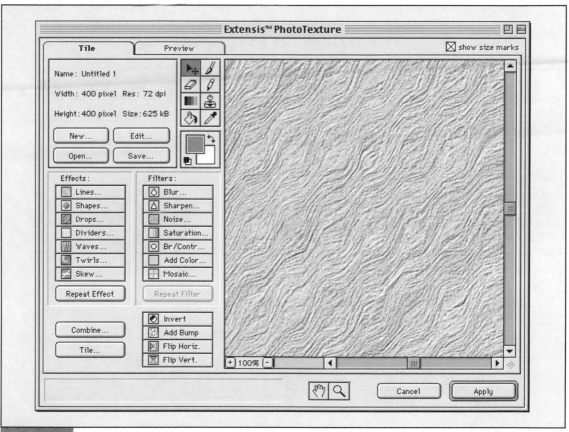

FIGURE 3-9 Extensis PhotoTools TextureMaker

MetaCreations is the home of Kai's Power Tools (though no longer of Kai Krause, the genius behind these filters). Kai's Power Tools were one of the very first third-party plug-ins around, and they caused quite a commotion when they were first released. KPT is now at version 5.0, and the filters have gotten even better. The ShapeShifter filter is awesome in the buttons and effects that it can create. Here is a button created in KPT 5 on top of a texture that was generated with Extensis PhotoTools:

I have recently become obsessed with a plug-in that is available only on the Web. It's called BladePro, and you can find it at www.flamingpear.com. This plug-in creates the most amazing jewels and metallic effects I've ever seen. There is an entire ring of Web sites devoted to BladePro, and you can download hundreds of presets (filter settings) for it. If you start at the BladePro site, you are automatically connected to the ring of related sites. You can download this filter and try it free for 15 days. Figure 3-10 shows the BladePro filter in action.

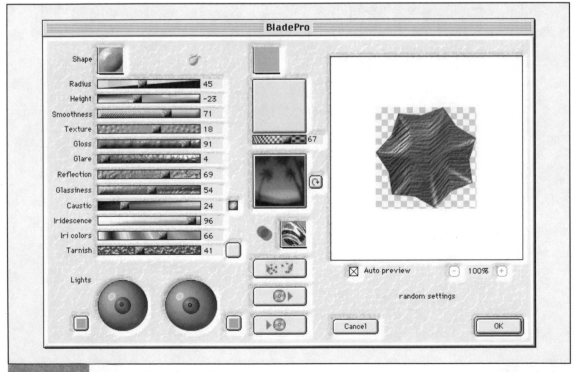

FIGURE 3-10   BladePro filter from Flaming Pear

FIGURE 3-11 Xaos Tools Terrazzo pattern-making filter

If you like to create patterns and play with painted textures, look at the Web site of Xaos Tools (www.xaostools.com). They have two excellent filters. Terrazzo is a pattern creator. It takes your basic image and changes it into a repeating tile based on one of the 17 possible ways to mathematically create a repeating tile. Figure 3-11 shows some of the buttons developed in BladePro being turned into repeating patterns.

Xaos Tools also sells Paint Alchemy, a brushing engine that creates wonderful textures and painted effects.

But I Can't Draw!

I can almost hear some of you muttering "Of what use are paint programs to me when I can't even draw a straight line?" Believe me, the computer can draw a straight line for you. All you need is the interest and a spark of creativity and you can train yourself to create eye-catching graphics.

However, even if you decide that you hate to create graphics, you can still decorate your Web site. The easiest way, of course, is to use a theme that is built into FrontPage. That's the route my husband took when he put up a Web site for London Computing (www.londoncomputing.com) and I was too busy to help out. My husband is a total techie, and has no interest in creating graphics. Yet the site is quite presentable. FrontPage took care of all of the details.

If you want to expand your options beyond the themes, you can use clip art or even buy a predecorated site for sale.

Clip Art

Clip art is the name given to images that are already created and "ready to wear." You can find almost any element as clip art. You can get dingbats for buttons; you can find buttons by the dozens already made. You can locate photographic clip art and vector art of objects and symbols. You can pay a lot for clip art or you can pay nothing.

Eyewire (www.eyewire.com) is an online retailer of fonts and clip art. They were once a part of Adobe Systems, where they were known as Image Club Graphics. When they separated from Adobe, they chose the name Eyewire. They stock a wonderful assortment of objects and images. Their catalog is available online, as are all of their products. They also have a large number of tutorials on the site.

Most software catalogs contains large numbers of clip art products as well. One of my favorite clip art collections is not available from stores. It is the Ultimate Symbol Design Elements collection (www.ultimatesymbol.com). This collection contains symbols for all occasions. They also have a Nature Icons collection that is equally useful. You can get a set of free samples at their Web site.

WebSpice (www.webspice.com) takes another approach to clip art. They have an enormous collection of buttons and clip art for Web sites. They also sell additional themes for FrontPage. You can take a tour of their products and learn about their online subscription service that lets you download graphic elements as you need them. The tour gives you access to about 10,000 pieces of free clip art. The next series of figures shows you the steps needed to choose a button for your site.

1. You first select the shape of the button, as shown here:

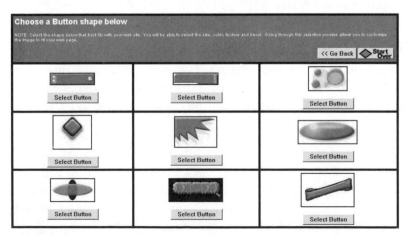

2. Select the size of the button, as shown here:

3. Select the pattern on the button, as shown here:

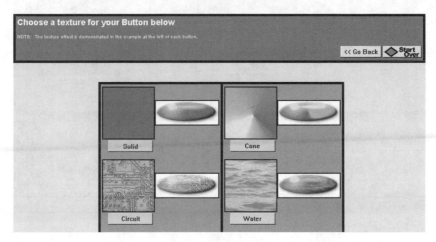

4. Select the type of embossing for the button, as shown here:

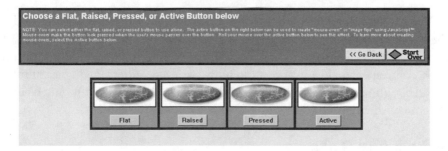

5. Select the color(s) for the button shown in Figure 3-12. The figure also tells you how to create the rollover since the button that is shown is a rollover button. What you cannot see in the grayscale image is the variety of colors in which this button is offered.

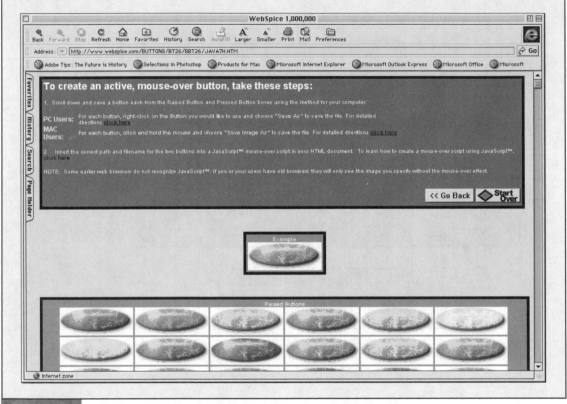

FIGURE 3-12 WebSpice site—selecting a button color for a rollover button

You can find thousands of sites for free clip art on the Internet. Just try typing the words "**Free clip art**" into a search engine. Obviously, some of the free clip art is worth what you pay for it, but some is quite wonderful. You need to read the license agreement on free stuff very carefully, however, as there might be a number of restrictions on the use of the images. Frequently, free clip art can only be used on noncommercial sites.

Sites for Sale

If you have a personal site that does not sell anything, you can use any of the linkware Web sets to create the interface to your Web site. If a Web set is linkware, that means that the artist allows you to use the set free of charge, but you must display the artist's logo on your site. That logo is an active link back to the site where you obtained the images.

Some of these artists allow commercial sites to use their images for a fee. For an additional fee, you can obtain the exclusive rights to a set. The artists will even create custom buttons for you. One site charges $60 for exclusive use; another might charge $150. Some of the linkware is the most exquisite graphics I've ever seen. There is a ring of Digital Divas sites that are spectacular. Kelly's 7Rings site (www.7rings.com) is a good place to start. Her interface is extraordinary. Her linkware sets have the look of art nouveau jewelry. She also has links to other artists' works. Another good link page can be found at: http://www.fortunecity.com/victorian/byzantium/260/vs-links.html on the Visual Sonnets site.

Media Marvels

You might want to use video or animations or audio as another component of your Web site. Again, you have the choice to build or buy. You need to carefully think about using either video or audio on a site, however, because they can be quite slow to load. Macromedia Flash is the choice of many graphics professionals for small, fast-loading animations based on vector graphics.

You also need to determine if the audio or video is going to annoy your site visitors. I find spinning buttons to be particularly annoying and generally click off of any site whose animations move so fast that they make me dizzy. I also make a fast exit from any site that spontaneously plays music for me. If I need to surf in a room with other people, I'd prefer to do it in silence. If you are going to play music on your site, you might want to prominently display a control to turn it off.

The Sights: Planning for Video

Adobe Premiere is one of the most capable of the video capture programs if you want to import your own video into the computer. You can add amazing special effects or animations of still images with Adobe After Effects.

Macromedia Flash is the new darling of the Web for creating fast-loading vector-based animations. The program is excellent, and Macromedia provides top-notch technical support. Most of the new Web browsers support the Flash format without the need to download a plug-in.

Once you've created your video, you need to compress it and make it as small as possible for download. Media Cleaner Pro by Terran (www.terran.com) is the choice of professionals. If you search for "**video compression software**" you will find other choices as well.

Cross-Reference: There are a lot of other ghoulies and gotcha's when you use video on the Web. Chapter 14 discusses the main points that you need to know.

The Sounds: Planning for Audio

You can get yourself into trouble using audio without careful planning. You need to understand the various audio formats and how users will interact with them. Do your site visitors need to download a special helper application in order to listen to the audio? How quickly can the audio be transferred to your visitors' sites?

Audio takes time to download as well as to play. You need to decide if you will download the audio or stream it. Streaming audio means that the sounds will play even as they are downloaded.

You also need to decide what format to use for the audio material. You can use MP3 as the format, but this format requires an MP3 player and takes a long time to download. It is, however, the best-quality sound available on the Internet—but it is used to record entire songs, not usually just for sound effects.

Real Audio (RA file format) needs the Real Audio plug-in. This is the Web's most popular format for streaming audio. This format also gives you the option of trading sound quality for faster download speed.

The Windows native sound file format is the .wav file. This is great for sound effects like quacking and mooing, and it plays directly on the user's sound card. However, the quality of sounds saved in this format is directly linked to the quality of the sound card in the user's computer.

AIFF files are the Mac's way of recording sounds. They, too, depend upon the quality of your site visitor's sound card.

The other popular sound format is MIDI. This file format is fairly small, but it only contains information to re-create the sound, and the creator of the sound file has no way of controlling how well or poorly the sound is reproduced on the user's computer.

Cross-Reference: You'll learn more about using audio in Chapter 14.

Professional Skill Summary

Although this chapter might have been a bit dry, it covered a lot of the background that you need to know as you begin to gather documents for your Web site. Because of the nature of the material, there were not many chances for you to try other features of FrontPage. We'll fix that in the next chapter, where you'll get a chance to create an entire Web site.

In this chapter, you learned about the other products on the Microsoft Office suite and how to use them with FrontPage. You also learned how to drag and drop text from Word into FrontPage.

You learned how Adobe Acrobat can transfer formatted documents over the Web with all formatting intact—even if the person reading the file has none of the same programs or fonts. You also learned about a large number of painting and drawing programs that can be used to help you create graphics for your site.

You discovered some options if you won't draw or can't draw but want to decorate your Web sites with graphics. You were also introduced to the concept of linkware, which can help you to create wonderful personal sites. In addition, you learned the very basic facts about using audio and video.

I hope you'll follow some of the links and URLs that you were given in this chapter. Although it is quite time-consuming, you'll expand your own options by learning what others are doing on the 'Net' and seeing the results you can get with various software products.

Site Building

You've spent three chapters learning about some principles of design for Web pages, exploring FrontPage, and gathering materials. Now it's time to finally start creating Webs. You've already created a very simple Web with a theme, and a One Page Web with no theme. In this chapter, you'll create all of the pages shown in the flowchart for the Smythe's Web site (you saw this flowchart in Chapter 1). You will learn how to create a navigational system for your own site as well.

Creating a Web with only one page, or creating a site using one of the "patterns" that FrontPage has already set up, is easy. Creating a Web where the pages differ from the standard pattern is a bit trickier. You'll get the hang of it here, and then you'll be able to apply the knowledge to your own sites. If you only build a standard site, then you're restricting your creativity and setting unnecessary limitations on the design and expansion of your site.

I want you to build the structure for a complete site in this chapter, even if you don't fill in all of the details. Because we'll discuss many of these topics again, however, I will concentrate more on the step-by-step instructions (the "how") than the explanations (the "why"). When I don't fully explain why I'm asking you to do something, rest assured the explanation will appear later in the book.

The Smythes Get a Web Site

In Chapter 1, you saw the flowchart that Susan developed for the Web site she wants to create with her family. You're going to actually create that structure now. Although it is a bit complex, it provides excellent practice for you. Once you understand what you're doing, it will no longer seem as complicated.

If you don't want to work through the exercise that I've created, then make a flowchart for your site. Use the same type of format that I used, and figure out what pages you will need to create and how you want your site visitor to get to them from the other pages in your site.

Here's the plan for creating the site:

1. You need to create your flowchart to determine as best you can the main pages that you will need.

2. You need to decide which template (if you want to use one) will be closest to the needs of your site.

3. You need to create the Web.

4. You need to choose a theme and add it to your site.

5. You need to see if any pages in your site can be used as templates for the new pages that you will need to create. Most sites cannot use every page created by the Web template or wizard and need pages that weren't created.

6. You need to delete the pages on the site that were automatically created by the Web template and that you know you won't need to use.

7. You need to create and save the extra pages that you want on your site (using the templates for the pages that you set up in Step 5).

8. You need to change the titles of all of the pages that you created so that they use the names that you want to show up on your Web.

9. You need to create shared borders to display the same elements on every page.

10. You need to specify the type of buttons that you want to appear in the navigation bars on the shared borders.

11. You need to build the navigation system by linking documents into the Navigation View flowchart.

12. Finally, you need to add all of the text and graphics that make the site "live" and change it from FrontPage's idea for a Web to your own.

Creating the Web

Launch FrontPage. Although you chose a Poetic theme for this site in Chapter 1, you're going to apply a different theme this time around. (If you are "doing your own thing," feel free to use any theme that you want. You do need to use a theme to try out this feature, however, because the theme helps to create the navigation system for you. In Chapter 6, you'll see how you can create a navigation system without using a theme.)

1. Choose File | New | Web. Choose the Personal Web. Name this Web **SMYTHE**, and allow FrontPage to place it in the default folder for Webs.

2. Choose Format | Theme and select the Bubbles theme as shown in Figure 4-1. Use the default theme but make sure that the Vivid Colors and Apply using CCS boxes are not checked.

3. If there is an unsaved page named new_page_1.htm that's open in the workspace window, close it before you go on. Double-click the index.htm page to open it. Figure 4-2 shows the page as it should look on your computer.

Select Bubbles theme

Uncheck "Vivid colors" box

Uncheck this box as well

FIGURE 4-1   Selecting the Bubbles theme

Look carefully at the Folder list (you can see it in Figure 4-2). It shows the various pages that were created by the Personal Page template. In addition to index.htm, the template created favorite.htm, interests.htm, photo.htm, and myfav3.htm.

Open each page and look at it. The photo page has a few sample photos (which you'll replace a bit later). The interests page has a bulleted list of interests. Both the favorites page and myfav3.htm are link pages—they contain a number of "dummy" hyperlinks to other Web sites.

So, where do you go from here? You've created the site and it has a few pages, but nothing here agrees with the flowchart in Chapter 1 that shows how the site should look. Figure 4-3 shows the flowchart that Susan created. As you can see, you've got a lot of work to do!

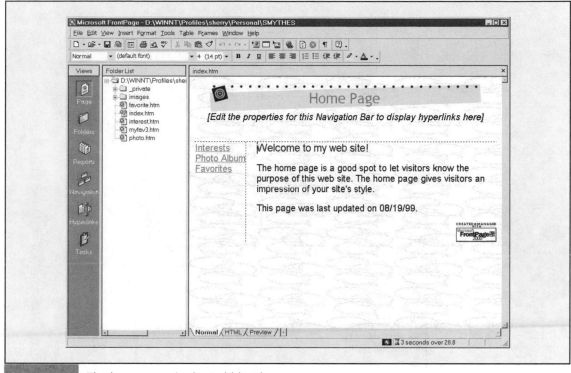

FIGURE 4-2 The home page in the Bubbles theme

When you create a site using the Personal Page template (or any other template), the site only contains the pages that Microsoft thought you would want. This rarely agrees with reality. Whenever you create a new site using a template, you will need to determine which pages you want and which pages you don't want.

Choosing the Site Templates

After you've created a Web, you still need to build it. You can approach this task in many ways. The more inexperienced designers tend to start by creating the home page before they begin to worry about what to do with the other pages. This is usually a mistake. If you focus too closely and too quickly on the design of the home page, you might be painting yourself into a corner. You need to know the requirements of most of your pages before you begin to flesh out *any* of the pages.

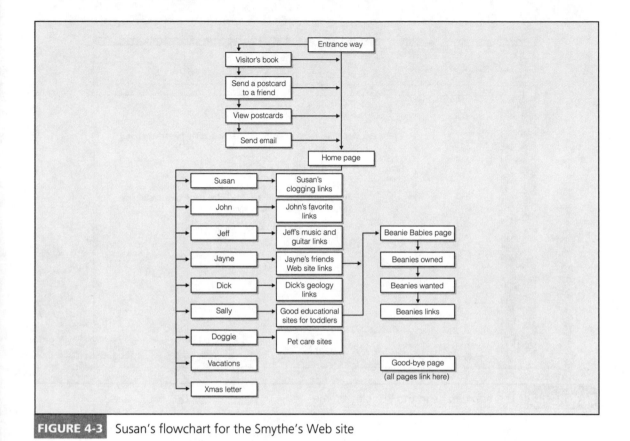

FIGURE 4-3 Susan's flowchart for the Smythe's Web site

Note: This is a problem that many designers have when they want to use FrontPage to create a site that has both a "traditional" home page and entranceway with a splash screen. Although we won't actually create the entranceway here, you need to think about what it will need when you're ready to create it.

Since you've already created (or been given) a flowchart, you can start there to see what types of pages you are going to need. The flowchart for the Smythes shows the site to be divided into two major flows: the Entrance Way and its pages, and the home page and the main pages on the site.

The Entrance Way needs a splash screen (a page that just serves as the introduction), a page for postcards, a guest book, and a comments page. While the splash screen needs to be custom designed, the other three screens can use standard templates that come with FrontPage 2000.

In the main section of the Smythe's site, you have a home page, an interest or photo page for each of the family members, and a link page for each of the family members. In addition, you have a page for vacations and for the annual Christmas letter. The Personal Page template has already created skeleton pages that you can use for these. index.htm is a perfectly serviceable home page outline, and the vacation page and family interest pages can use the photo.htm page as their structure. The link pages can easily use the favorite.htm page as their template.

When you create a site on your own and use a template, you should try to find pages in the template that are close to what you actually want on your site. You can use those pages to create new templates for the pages that you want to add.

Your first task, therefore, is to save the example pages that are already created templates of your sample pages so that you can use them to build the additional pages that you need. After that, you need to create the pages and create the navigational system.

Saving Your Own Templates

Before you create new pages, you need to save the pages that you want to copy as template files. A template file is a pattern file with its own extension (.tem) that can be reused many times but not easily written over. Template files can be stored in your Web or stored with the templates that are installed with FrontPage. If you might want to use the templates with a different Web, then you should store them in the Template directory so that they automatically appear when you select File | New | Page.

The following set of instructions shows you how to save a page in your site as a template file:

1. Open the page in your site that you want to save as a template file (in the Smythe example, open photo.htm in the workspace by double-clicking the file name in the Folders list).

2. Choose File | Save As and select FrontPage Template from the "Save as type" drop-down menu in the dialog box.

> **Tip:** You can also open an .htm file by right-clicking on its name in the Folders list and selecting Open from the pop-up menu.

> **Tip:** When you name your files, use lowercase letters only and try to stick to the 8.3 DOS file-naming format. Although it isn't strictly necessary, some servers (UNIX machines in particular) are case sensitive, and using a consistent lowercase helps cut down on problems.

File name:	photo.tem
Save as type:	Web Pages (*.htm;*.html;*.shtml;*.shtm;*.stm;*.asp;*

All Files (*.*)
Web Pages (*.htm;*.html;*.shtml;*.shtm;*.stm;*.asp;*.
FrontPage Template (*.tem)
Active Server Pages (*.asp)
HyperText Template (*.htt)
HyperText Style Sheet (*.css)

You can change the file name if you want or leave it as photo.tem.

The Save as Template dialog box appears.

You'll usually want to save the template with the other templates, so you don't usually want to check this checkbox

L ▶ Note: Where does FrontPage put the templates that you've just saved? They go into the Templates folder in the Microsoft Office Applications folder. The drive on which this is stored will vary based on where you told Windows to install the applications.

You can type a descriptive name into the Title field. This name is the one that will identify the template in the Templates dialog box when you select a template for a new page. You may also select a different file name for the template by changing the name that appears in the Name field. Finally, you can type in some descriptive text for the template that you'll be able to read in the dialog box that allows you to select a page template. Don't place a check in the Save Template in Current Web checkbox. Click OK to save the page as a template. Repeat Steps 2 and 3 for the favorite.htm page.

Adding and Deleting Pages

Your next task is to make the pages in the Web conform to the list of pages in your flowchart. If you look at Figure 4-3 again, you'll notice that the flowchart for the Smythe Web site shows nine pages coming from the home page. Nine selections are really too many choices from a single screen. Research has shown that most people have a "comfort level" of three to seven choices. When you design a navigational structure, the research also shows that most pages (or at least the most commonly used pages) in your Web site should be accessible in no more than three clicks. Therefore, you need to consider the hierarchy of your pages very carefully. If your own site hierarchy has more than seven choices coming from the home page, take some time to think if there is a different way that you can break up the structure.

Because the Smythe flowchart indicates nine selections from the home page, you might consider placing a level "above" these pages. If you look at the topics of the nine pages, you'll notice that they aren't all of the same subject matter. You have the six (or seven, if you include the dog) family members who get individual pages, and then a page for vacations and a page for the Christmas letter. Therefore, you could make the hierarchy deeper by adding a level above the individual pages that only points to the individual pages. Figure 4-4 shows the new hierarchy.

Before you can actually create the navigation system, however, you first need to create the pages. You'll create the new pages by levels so that you can keep track of them, and link them into the navigation system in stages. You need to delete the unnecessary pages that the Web template created first and then create the additional pages that you need.

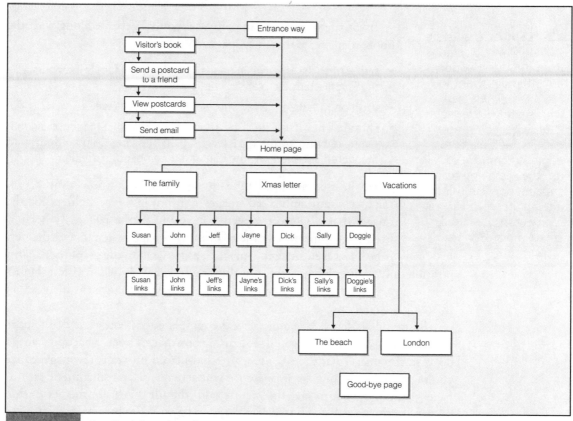

FIGURE 4-4   The final flowchart for the Smythe's Web site

Here's how to delete a page:

1. In Page View mode, right-click the file that you want to delete in the Folders list.

2. Select Delete from the drop-down menu and click the Yes button when asked if you are really sure that you want to delete this page.

3. If you are following the Smythe example, delete the myfav3.htm page and the interest.htm page. If you are using your own example, see if there are any pages on the site that you know you won't use. Delete them now.

Once you have deleted all of the pages that you don't need, you can add pages that you do need. Here's how to add a new page:

1. Make sure that you are in Page view. Choose File | New | Page. From the list of templates, select the template that you want to use.

2. Save the page by choosing File | Save As. Choose an appropriate name.

▶ Tip: You must be in Page view (selected from the Views window on left) if you want to use a template when you create a new page. Otherwise, you simply get a default blank page. You must also use the File menu to create a new file using a template. If you simply type CTRL-N, you'll only create a blank page.

If you are developing the Smythe family Web site along with the book, then create these new pages:

- family.htm (this is the main page that links to the family members. Use the favorite.tem template to create it.)

- vacation.htm (Use the favorite.tem to create it as well.)

- christmas.htm (Use the One Column Body with Staggered Sidebar template but read the next section first. The One Column Body with Staggered Sidebar template contains an embedded image.)

If you use one of the built-in page templates from FrontPage, it might contain embedded images that are just placeholders for the images that Microsoft expects you to put in the pages. By default, FrontPage wants to save these "dummy" images when it saves the new page. However, since the image is, as they say in the graphic arts, "for position only," you might not want to clutter up your Web folder with it. Here's how to save a page created by a template without having to save the images that the template contains.

Choose File | New | Page and select the template that you want. If the page contains embedded images, you'll see a dialog box that asks you what you want to do with the image that the page template has placed on your new page. Since you're going to toss out the image once you actually place real content on this page, you don't want to save the picture with the file. Click on the Set Action button. In the next dialog box, select the Don't Save radio button. Click OK to close that dialog box and click OK again to close the first dialog box and finish saving the page.

If you have any pages in the Web that are not named properly (for example, the two pages that you used as templates if you are creating the Smythe Web site), you need to rename them now. Renaming the pages will allow you to more easily move them into the correct hierarchical position in Navigation view. Here's how to rename a page:

1. In Page view, right-click the page that you want to rename in the Folders list. From the pop-up menu that appears, select Rename. (You can use the favorite.htm page in the Smythe site as an example.)

2. Type the desired new name (**suelinks.htm** if you're following along with us) into the file Name field that opens up.

```
Folder List
└─ D:\WINNT\Profiles\shel
   ├─ _private
   ├─ images
   │  family.htm
   │  suelinks.htm
   │  index.htm
   │  photo.htm
   │  vcation.htm
   │  xmas.htm
```

3. Press the ENTER key when you've finished typing in the new name.

4. If you are following the Smythe exercise, rename the photo.htm document as susan.htm.

Changing the Document Titles

After you have added and deleted pages in your Web to try to make the Web template that you used conform to your idea for the site, the Folder list tends to get a bit messy. If you've renamed documents, then the name that you gave the file when you renamed it doesn't match the name that FrontPage uses to identify it (because the document has another property called its *title*)—that you didn't change. Before you go any farther, you have some housekeeping to do.

You should take some time to make sure that all of your pages are properly named and titled so that the menu system that you want to create will say the "right" thing. Both you and your site visitor would get confused if a page about clogging is called "Downloads" in the button that leads you to it. If you renamed any of your pages, you will definitely need to clean up their titles. If you simply created new pages, then the title of the new page is usually New_Page (and it needs

Tip: You don't need to choose Rename from the context-sensitive menu in order to be able to change a document name, although it's sometimes easier. Click once on the desired document in the Folders list and wait a few seconds. The name is selected. If you click on the document name again, the field should open up for editing (*should* is the operative word here—sometimes the interface gets a bit recalcitrant).

Tip: When you choose the title for a page, consider what you want your site visitors to call it. The title is used for the buttons and navigation, so it needs to be short enough to fit on the button. However, it is also used in the page banner (if you use one) to act as the title of the page. As the title of the page, the name needs to be descriptive enough to be of use. "Home Page" fits on a button, but it doesn't tell the site visitor *whose* home page they are visiting.

to be changed). If you used a template, then the template gave the new page its title—and you still need to change it to conform to what you want to name the document.

When you save a page, that name becomes the name used to access the document from the Web server. However, each document has another property, the *title*, which is used to identify the document in "common English." The title of the document and its file name are not the same thing. The titles in all of the pages that you created above are probably quite inappropriate. There are two methods that you can use to change the title of a page. The method that you select depends upon whether or not you've linked the page into the navigation system yet. If the page shows up in the navigation workspace window (i.e., it is linked into the hierarchy), then you can change the title of the page directly in the navigation workspace window. The labels that show up on the navigation flowchart are the titles of the pages. If the pages don't appear in the navigation workspace (i.e., they aren't linked to anything yet), then you need to change the titles using the Folder list.

Changing document titles in the navigation workspace window

If your pages are already linked to the navigation system, you can change the title of the page directly on the navigation flowchart in the workspace. Here's how:

1. Make sure that you are in Navigation view.

2. Click on the entry that you want to change in the navigation workspace window to select it. Wait a few seconds and click once on it again (or right-click and select Rename from the context-sensitive menu).

3. Type the name of the new page title into the now-open field. You don't need to clear the field; just begin typing once the field is selected and you have an I-beam cursor. Either press the ENTER key or click out of the field to register the changed title.

4. If you are following the Smythe's example, click on the Photo Album entry and change the title to Susan's Page, then click on the Favorites entry and change its title to Susan's Links.

Figure 4-5 shows the changed titles. The entries are still in the wrong place in your structure, however.

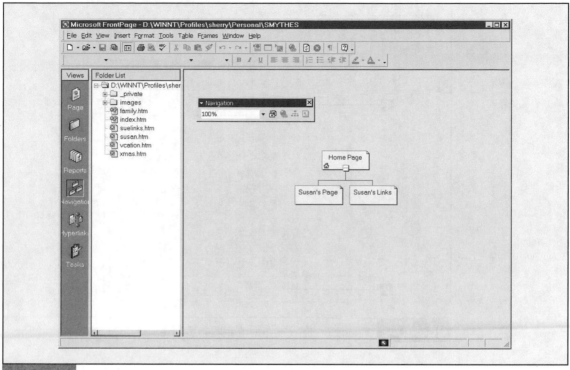

FIGURE 4-5 Renamed titles show up in the Navigation view

Changing document titles in the Folder list

If you've been following the Smythe example, then you still need to change the titles of all of the pages that you created using the templates. These pages all have the same title. If you're using your own material, then your new pages need a change of title as well.

These pages have not yet been linked to the main navigational structure of your Web, so you need to alter their titles in the Folder list by using the Properties command.

To change the title of a document, right-click the page name in the Folder list. From the context-sensitive menu, select Properties. In the Properties dialog box, select the General Properties tab. Figure 4-6 shows you where to enter the new title for your document.

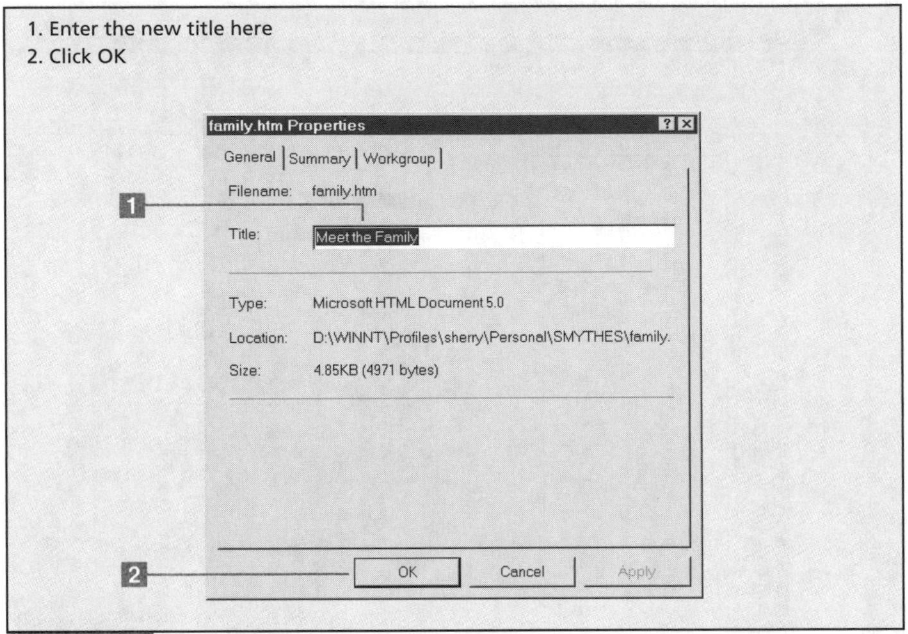

1. Enter the new title here
2. Click OK

family.htm Properties

General | Summary | Workgroup |

Filename: family.htm

Title: Meet the Family

Type: Microsoft HTML Document 5.0

Location: D:\WINNT\Profiles\sherry\Personal\SMYTHES\family.

Size: 4.85KB (4971 bytes)

OK   Cancel   Apply

FIGURE 4-6   Changing the document title in the General Properties dialog box

If you are following the Smythe's example, change the title of the vacation.htm document to Our Vacations, family.htm to Meet the Family, and christmas.htm to Christmas Letter.

You won't see the result of these changes until you move on to the next portion of the chapter and create your navigation system.

Creating a Navigation System

Now that you've added the top level of pages and titled them correctly, you can link them together in the Navigation view. By adding a level of pages and then linking them before you add the next set, you can keep your structure in focus as you work. If you add everything first and then try to name and link everything, you'll probably feel a bit overwhelmed.

Several different ways exist to make the navigational structure match the Smythe's site flowchart in Figure 4-4 (or your own flowchart, for that matter). If the flowchart that you see in the Navigation View workspace doesn't match your planned flowchart, then the easiest way to fix the problem is to remove everything from the Navigation View flowchart but the Home Page icon.

You can remove an icon from the Navigation View flowchart by clicking the icon that you want to remove. Then, choose Edit | Cut (or press CTRL-X). This clears the entry from the Navigation View workspace but leaves it in the Folder list.

If you are using the Smythe example, cut both the Susan's Page icon and the Susan's Links icon from the Navigation View flowchart. This leaves only the Home Page icon. Once you've removed the old structure, you can make a fresh start.

Removing the icons from the Navigation View flowchart causes some major changes to your Web. When you created the Web using the Personal Page template, FrontPage automatically created the Navigation View flowchart structure. This structure caused navigation buttons to appear at the top of your pages so that you could link from page to page (The home page allowed you to move to the photos page, etc.). When you remove page icons from the Navigation View flowchart, you also remove the corresponding buttons and links from the pages themselves. If you look at your site now in Page view, you have no way to move from page to page. The buttons and page banner are gone (but you can get those back in a little while).

Once you have cleared away the original structure, you're ready to create the top level of your flowchart. You can add a new entry to the flowchart by dragging the page name from the Folder view to the correct place in the Navigation View flowchart in the workspace window.

Here are the changes to make for the Smythe's Web:

1. Click to select the family.htm document in the Folder list window.

2. Drag the document into the Navigation View workspace window. As you drag, a line will connect from the new file to the index.htm document. Drag the family.htm document until it is directly underneath the index.htm icon and then release the mouse button.

3. Select the christmas.htm document in the Folders list and drag it to the right of the Meet the Family icon. It, too, connects to the Home Page icon.

4. Now, drag the vacation.htm document into the Navigation window to the right of the Christmas Letter icon. The new structure is shown here:

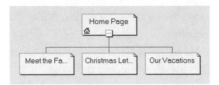

You need to understand a bit about hierarchical flowcharts to fully see what you are building. The FrontPage navigation system is basically like an organization chart for a large corporation. It is a pyramid structure where the very top level consists of only one entry (the CEO or home page). The next level under the CEO contains the "direct reports." In the Smythe example, these direct reports are the Meet the Family, Our Vacations, and Christmas Letter pages. Each of these pages might, in turn, have pages underneath them (except for the Christmas Letter page that is, for the moment, an individual contributor).

The relationships in the flowchart are described in terms of "parent-child." The home page is the "parent" of the Meet the Family, Our Vacations, and Christmas Letter pages. Those pages are considered to be "child" pages of the home page. Taken together, these four pages form the top-level structure of the navigation system.

Unless you intend to have a very tiny site, you have more pages to add to the navigation flowchart than those that form the top level of the chart. Certainly the navigation system for the Smythe's site is still far from complete. However, before you finish adding all of your pages to the Navigation View flowchart, I'd like to introduce you to FrontPage's Shared Borders command. This command allows you to standardize and automate the navigation of you site.

Shared Borders

When you created the Smythe's Web using the Personal Page template, you took the first steps in developing a navigational system for the Web site. The template contains buttons and banners (as well as other graphics) that show you the page titles and allow you to link from page to page. What makes these buttons and banners appear on your pages? How does FrontPage know where to put the buttons, and which pages link to other pages?

The answers to these questions are found in the Shared Border feature of the program. The Shared Border feature allows FrontPage to automatically use and maintain the navigational structure that you create in Navigation view. A shared border is an area at the top, left, right, or bottom of the Web page that is used by every (participating) page on your site. Any text or graphics that you place in the shared border is seen on every Web page that uses the shared border.

You use the Shared Borders command to designate the sides of your Web pages that you want to be shared. Each page then presents a consistent set of information to the site visitor. If you place a navigation bar into the shared border, then the Shared Border command uses the navigation structure (the flowchart that you created in Navigation view) to determine which links need to appear on each page. If you change the navigation system, FrontPage readjusts the links.

Shared borders and navigation bars together create the system that lets you move between pages in your Web. If you don't use these features, then you need to place every button and every link one at a time. The time savings and efficiency of the combination of shared borders and navigation bars is astounding. The process is a troika that you have already begun:

1. Create the Navigation View flowchart so that FrontPage knows which pages are supposed to link to which other pages on the site.

2. Create shared borders so that all pages use the same elements in the same location.

3. Insert a navigation bar to automatically decide which type of links appear on the page.

Shared borders and the navigation bars work together so that you can specify a navigation bar in a shared border and the navigation bar appears on every page. Furthermore, you can tell FrontPage the type of buttons that you want to appear in the navigation bar, and FrontPage uses the information in the Navigation View flowchart to place the specified level of links into the navigation bar. Therefore, the actual buttons that appear on each page are context sensitive and you don't need to hand-place any of the buttons. FrontPage does it all for you automatically.

Tip: You can return to Page view easily from any other view by double-clicking the name of a document in the Folders list.

Tip: You need to check the "Apply to All pages" checkbox if you want to be able to include navigation buttons in the shared border. If you want to include a navigation bar on a single page, you need to do it manually, and you'll learn how in Chapter 6.

Adding a shared border

Now that you've designed the highest level of the navigation system flowchart, let's look at the shared borders. After you create your shared borders, you'll then learn how to specify the details for the navigation bars. Here's how to create a shared border:

Switch back into Page view by clicking on the Page View icon in the Views window and double-clicking on the index.htm page in the Folders list. Choose Format | Shared Borders. You can share any of the four border areas on a page. Figure 4-7 shows the options that you should select for the Smythe example. The "Include navigation" checkboxes allow you to automatically create a navigation bar in the top or left shared borders.

Once you've told FrontPage which borders to share, you need to specify what to put in each border. Figure 4-8 shows the border areas in the Smythe's home page. The dotted lines on the figure indicate the various border areas. Although the home page looks as if it only has room for borders, not to worry! The border areas move to surround the content that you place in the pages.

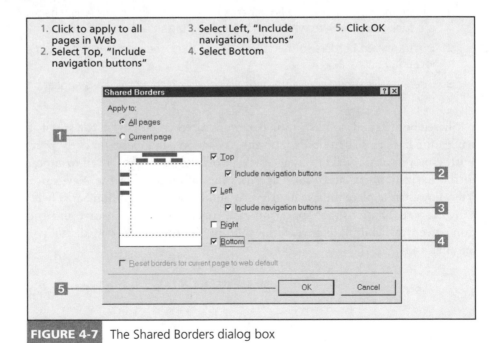

1. Click to apply to all pages in Web
2. Select Top, "Include navigation buttons"
3. Select Left, "Include navigation buttons"
4. Select Bottom
5. Click OK

FIGURE 4-7 The Shared Borders dialog box

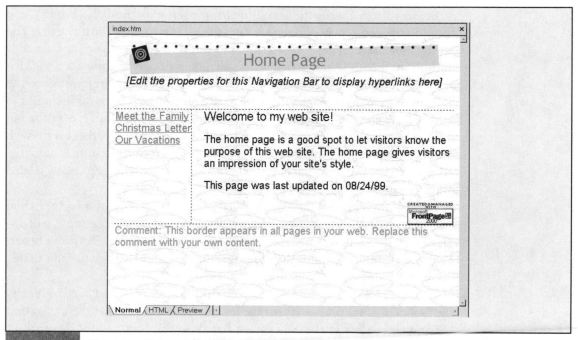

Shared borders on the home page

Specifying the buttons to appear on a navigation bar

Here's how to specify the navigation bar properties for a shared border (if you are using navigation bars in both the top and side borders, then you need to specify the navigation bar properties for each border separately). To specify the navigation bar properties, you need to first select the navigation bar. Here's how (it can be a little bit tricky):

1. Double-click the document in the Folders list window to open the page in the workspace. In the Smythe example, open family.htm.

2. Drag your cursor into the area within the top border of the page until your cursor turns into a hand holding a small document (it will do this over a button or banner or the text telling you to edit the navigation bar properties). Click to select the top border.

3. Right-click the selected area to view the context-sensitive menu. Choose Navigation Bar Properties. (You can also press ALT-ENTER after you have selected something on the navigation bar.)

Before you can specify the navigation bar properties in the dialog box that you have just opened, you need to understand the various levels of the hierarchy. The Navigation Bar Properties dialog box shows you six possible arrangements of buttons on the navigation bar. You can decide to display buttons on a page for any of the six choices listed on Figure 4-9. The black boxes on the figure show the buttons that would appear on the shaded page for each of your possible choices.

The Back and Next buttons are a useful choice if your material is organized in that type of sequence (for example, Adobe has Photoshop tutorials on its Web site that show eight or nine steps; Next and Back make sense in that context). Next and Back are confusing if the child links under a parent aren't really related to one another.

For the top border of the Smythe Web site, it makes sense to select the child level of buttons to display. That means that the home page, for example, will display buttons to link to Meet the Family, Our Vacations, and Christmas Letter. Figure 4-10 shows the completed navigation bar properties for the top shared border on the Smythe's Web site.

If you are following our Smythe Web site example, you also need to specify the navigation bar properties for the left shared border. Select the navigation bar and right-click to the Navigation Bar Properties command. Figure 4-11 shows the settings for this navigation bar (vertical settings will work best along a vertical edge).

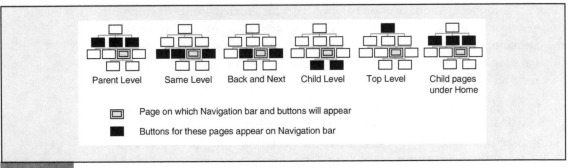

FIGURE 4-9   The navigation bar properties choices for navigation buttons

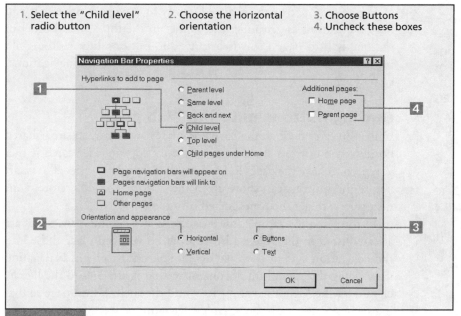

FIGURE 4-10 Setting for the top shared border on the Smythes Web site

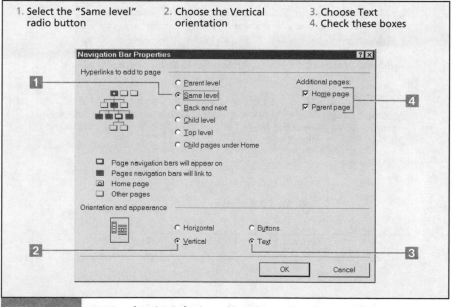

FIGURE 4-11 Setting for the left shared border on the Smythe's Web site

Tip: If you have a page that continues to display the message "Edit the properties of this Navigation Bar to display Hyperlinks here" and there aren't any links to display, you can get rid of the message by selecting the sentence and replacing it with a space. *Do not delete the message completely.* If you remove the entire line and leave no space in its place, your navigation system will disappear from the top shared border for all of your pages.

Figure 4-12 shows the changed family.htm page. Notice that you have no buttons as yet under the banner in the top shared border of the family.htm page. This is because the buttons link to the child pages and you haven't entered any child pages into the navigational system yet.

Getting buttons onto the Web page

Once you have defined the navigation bar for your Web site's shared borders, the buttons should automatically appear. The catch is that you need to have the pages linked into the Navigation View flowchart before the buttons can show up in the Web pages. Therefore, your next step is to get the pages linked into the flowchart.

In the Smythe example, the susan.htm and suelink.htm pages are already listed in the Folder List window, so you can place those into the navigation system now. To do so, you need to be in Navigation view. Drag the susan.htm document so that it attaches to the hierarchy under the Meet the Family icon and the suelink.htm page so that it attaches underneath the Susan's Page icon.

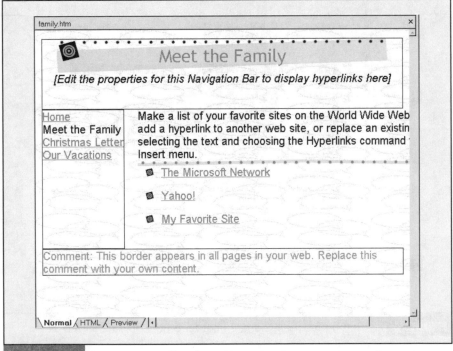

FIGURE 4-12   Meet the Family page with navigation system started

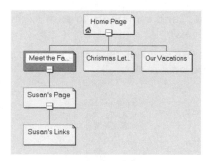

When you develop your own Web site, you can link into the navigation system of any page that you've already created and saved. To place the page in the navigation system, it needs to be in the Folder list. A page doesn't show up in the Folder list until it has been saved.

The top part of the changed Meet the Family page is shown here. Note that you can now see a button link to Susan's Page.

Adding text in a shared border

Shared borders can contain more than a page banner and a navigation bar. In fact, you don't need to have a page banner of buttons in every shared border. Let's put some text into the shared border area at the bottom of the image so that you can see how useful a feature this is. After you enter the text, you'll format it so that it is less distracting on the page.

1. In Page view, open the index.htm page in the workspace. (You actually could open any page that uses the bottom shared border.)

2. Click on the bottom shared border (the text tells you to add/replace the border with your own content). Type **http://www.thesmythes.com** or the Web address that you want to enter.

3. After you've typed the URL, press SHIFT-ENTER to start a new line. Pressing the SHIFT key as you press the ENTER key keeps FrontPage from inserting a paragraph tag (and thus inserting a blank line between sentences).

4. Type the next line: **Page Design by Susan Smythe** and press SHIFT-ENTER. (Again, if you are creating your own page, type in the appropriate text.)

5. Type the final line: **Send comments to susan@thesmythes.com** (or your desired email address).

6. Select all three lines and click on the Font Size menu in the text toolbar (by default, the font size is set to Normal).

Set the font size to 1, which makes the text show up at the smallest size in your browser. This helps to keep the bottom border from overwhelming the page content.

 7. Click on the Center button, shown here in the margin, in the text toolbar.

The three lines of text now appear in all of your Web pages. Figure 4-13 shows the home page with the new bottom shared border.

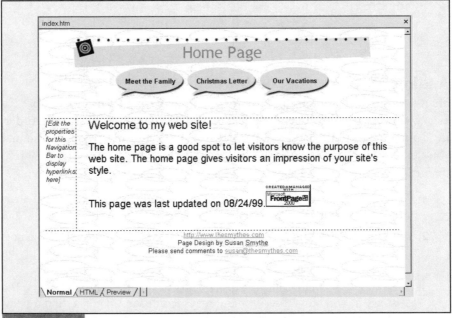

FIGURE 4-13 The bottom shared border contains the URL and an email address

Professional Pointer

The bottom shared border is ideal for listing the Web address and an email address. If a search engine directs site visitors to your site, many of them might end up on a page deep within your site and have no idea where they are. In addition, a number of other sites now want to "para-site" existing sites (i.e., display your site within a frame as if it belonged in their site). Lycos, the search engine, does this, and when it sends you to a site you have no idea where you are if you want to bookmark it in your browser. Therefore, it's a really good idea to make certain that your URL appears on every page of your site. If a user sees your pages within someone else's site, at least they'll be able to get to you directly if your URL is on the page. It need not be large or obvious; it just should be there.

Adding graphics to a shared border

You can also add graphics to the shared border at the bottom of the page. When you create home page using a FrontPage template, the Microsoft FrontPage logo appears on it. This logo is a small graphic that would be appropriate to place in the shared borders area (although it is not a critical component of your Web site). In this section, you'll move it from the page area to the shared border. Follow these steps:

1. Click on the FrontPage logo in the index.htm page. You can see the original placement of the logo in Figure 4-13.

2. The logo becomes selected when you click it, and it acquires a "bounding box"—an outline with small control handles in it. Cut this image (Edit | Cut or CTRL-X).

3. Place your cursor at the start of the first line in the bottom shared border area and Paste (Edit | Paste or CTRL-V).

4. After you paste the graphic, press the SPACEBAR three times to add some room between the graphic and the URL.

Adding Text

This chapter is a smorgasbord of page development techniques. It is a little appetizer for the main course (the rest of the book). I hope that by following the Smythe

Web site example, you'll be able to see how a Web site is constructed—from concept to at least one finished page. Since text is such an important part of developing a Web site, the next item on the list for you to "taste" is text. Let's design the family.htm page for the Smythe site. If you aren't following the example, then you can use whatever elements you have available to you.

This page won't use the shared borders, but it will use a list, graphics, and links. This will give you some practice creating these elements as preparation for Part II of this book.

Cross-Reference: Chapter 5 discusses text, Chapter 6 covers the process of creating hyperlinks, and Chapter 7 talks about graphics.

The Smythe's Meet the Family page introduces the family members to Web visitors and shows a picture of each person. It also deliberately parodies the old "Dick, Jane, and Sally" books from the early 1950s. Since a picture is a perfectly good linking device, and short pages load faster than long ones, it makes sense to use the pictures of each family member as the link to the family member pages instead of having FrontPage place buttons in the top shared border area. By creating this page, you'll learn to custom tailor the pages in your site instead of blindly accepting FrontPage's default behavior. While your pages should be consistent, it's more critical that the navigation be appropriate to the content of the page.

Customizing the page properties

The first thing that you might need to do for a page that you want to customize is to remove the shared borders (for this page *only*). Once you've removed the shared border, you have the freedom to design the page so that it is a "special" page on your site. Here's how to remove the top shared border area for the family.htm page in the Smythe's Web site:

1. In Page view, open the family.htm page in the workspace.
2. Choose Format | Shared Borders. In the dialog box, click the Current Page radio button so that the changes only affect this page. Then, remove the checkmark in the Top Border checkbox. Click OK.

When you remove the shared border on a page, the page banner that shows the title of the page and the buttons that link the page also disappear. You won't need the button links if you want to use a list of pictures as your links on the page, but the page still needs a title. You can manually insert a page banner into a page (even if you are not working in a shared border).

Inserting a page banner

If you need a title for your page and want to maintain a consistent look to your pages, the easiest way to do this if you're using a theme is to insert a page banner. When you use a page banner with a graphic on it on every page, the site visitor soon comes to identify that graphic with your site. In addition, FrontPage automatically generates the title for the page on the page banner.

To insert a page banner (which gives your page a title that site visitors can see), place your cursor at the top of the page. Choose Insert | Page Banner. In the dialog box, select the Picture radio button. The title of the page appears. Click OK. The page banner appears again and presents the title of the page. It's that easy! FrontPage already "knows" the title that you want on the page because you placed it into the General Properties dialog box soon after you created the page.

Cleaning up the page

Your page might also contain elements left over from the original template that created it. The easiest way to clean up the page is to click all of the elements that you don't want and delete them. You can delete any "leftover" elements (like the horizontal line graphic and any default links on the page) by selecting them and pressing the BACKSPACE key.

Adding a list to the page

You can create a list on the page by typing your desired text and then clicking the Bullets icon in the formatting toolbar.

The design plan for the Smythe site calls for a list of family members and a brief description about each of them (in typical Dick/Jayne/Sally English). Here's how to enter it:

1. Type the following text into the first available place on the page: **Susan: "I'm the mommy. I like to quilt and clog."** In this example, it's OK to type the punctuation as shown.

2. Click the Bullets icon in the formatting toolbar.

    Press the ENTER key to end the line. Because you're using a theme, the bullets are all graphics designed to coordinate with that theme.

3. Type the following lines (with punctuation intact), and press the ENTER key after each line:

    John: "I'm the daddy. I like computers."
    Jeff: "I'm the oldest. I'm 17 and I play the guitar."
    Jayne: "I'm 15. I'm a candy-striper at the local hospital."

Tip: Internet Explorer uses smaller text sizes than Netscape Navigator at the same settings. The Normal font size in Internet Explorer results in a page that is too large for easy viewing in Netscape Navigator.

Dick: "I'm 8. I want to be a geologist someday."
Sally: "I'm 3. I like Beanie Babies and Barbie dolls."
Doggie: a brown cocker spaniel who likes to play.

4. Leave all of the family's names in Normal font size. For each line, select the text after the colon and change the font size to 2.

Making formatting changes

You might decide that you don't like the default text styles in your Web. Sometimes, the text size just looks too large for the area. On the Meet the Family page for the Smythe's Web site, the menu text on the side shared border is uncomfortably large. It doesn't need to be that big on any of the pages that use the left-side shared border.

The links shown in the left-side shared border are "convenience links," placed there to make it easier for the site visitors to navigate the site. All of the text on the left-side shared border would benefit from being made smaller. Here's how to do it:

1. Click the links in the left-side shared border area to select them.

2. From the Font Size menu on the text toolbar, select Size 1. Here's how the page with the bulleted list completed should look:

Adding Graphics

You can add graphics to your pages almost as easily as you add text. In this next example, you'll add a small picture of each family member to the list item that introduces them. If you're not working this example, you can use any graphics to which you have access.

Here's how to add graphics to the page:

1. Download the folder of graphics (family.zip) from the Osborne Web site for this book. Unzip the file onto your hard drive.

2. Place your cursor in front of the first list entry (for Susan). Choose Insert | Picture | From File. Near the bottom of the dialog box are two small icons. They are on the same line as the URL. The first one lets you select graphics from a Web site, and the second one allows you to choose graphics from your hard drive. Click on the second icon and navigate to the location where you unzipped the family.zip file that you downloaded.

3. Select the file tsusan.gif. Click OK. The image appears between the bullet and the text. Press the SPACEBAR twice to add some room between the text and the graphic.

4. Place your cursor in front of the each name and insert the corresponding image file.

Figure 4-14 shows the page with all of the graphics added.

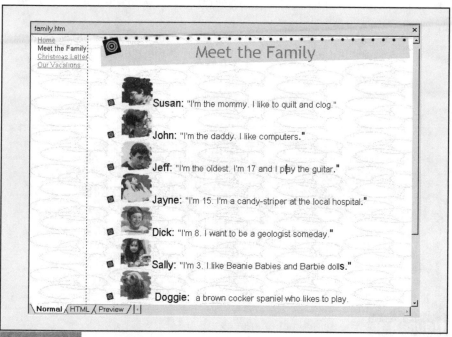

FIGURE 4-14   Graphics added to the family.htm page

Adding an Animation

You can add a gif animation to your Web page as easily as you can insert a picture. A gif animation is simply a .gif file with a number of images stored in it. The images seem to move because they are played one after another. The gif animations are the easiest form of animation on the Web. I used Adobe ImageReady to create the animation that you'll place into the home page; however, you can use a variety of other products (some of them were discussed in Chapter 2 and more will be discussed in Chapter 14).

The gif animation that I created for the Smythe's Web site is a simple merge of photos of the family members that seem to blend into one another as the animation plays. Figure 4-15 shows the frames of the animation.

1. Before you add the animation to the home page, you might want to prepare the page a bit. Switch to Page view and open the index.htm page in the workspace. This is always the default name for a FrontPage home page.

Tip: Check with your Internet service provider to determine what standards they have for naming your home page.

2. In the center of the page, delete the two paragraphs of text that tell you what to place on the page.

3. In the top line, change "Welcome to my web site!" to "Welcome to our web site!"

4. With the top line of text selected, change the font size to 6 and center the text (click the Center button in the text toolbar).

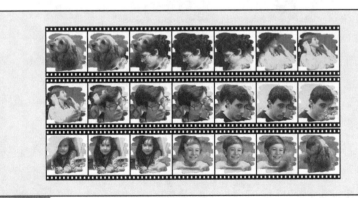

FIGURE 4-15 The .gif animation frames

These changes are purely cosmetic. On your own sites, you need to make whatever changes are needed to the default home page that your template creates.

To actually place the gif animation, you need to first download the image tfamilyan.gif from the Osborne Web site for this book (or find a different gif animation to use). Then:

1. Place your cursor in front of the word "Welcome."

2. Choose Insert | Picture | From File. Navigate to the place where you stored the downloaded gif animation and select it.

3. Switch to Preview mode. The animation should be visible.

4. Save the page. Embed the image and save it with the page by changing folders so that it's placed into the Images folder. Figure 4-16 shows the new home page.

FIGURE 4-16 The redesigned home page

Adding Links

You can add links to any text or graphic. Chapter 6 discusses links in much more detail. In this section, you'll learn a very basic technique to create a hyperlink.

The graphics that you placed on the Meet the Family page can act as links to the pages that contain photos of the individuals in the family. (Or, any graphics on your site can act as links to any other pages.)

In general, in order to create a link between two pages in a Web site, you need to have both pages show up in the Folder list (we'll talk about the exception in a moment). susan.htm is the only page that you've added underneath the Meet the Family page so far. Therefore, it's the only link that you can create right now. Follow these steps:

1. Click on the tsusan.gif image to select it.

Tip: You can also type CTRL-K to create a hyperlink for selected text or graphics.

2. Choose Insert | Hyperlink as shown in Figure 4-17. Click the susan.htm file to make that the URL for the link. Click OK to exit the dialog box.

3. Since some users might want to click on the text instead of the picture, select the text on the Susan line. Again, choose Insert | Hyperlink, and link to the susan.htm page.

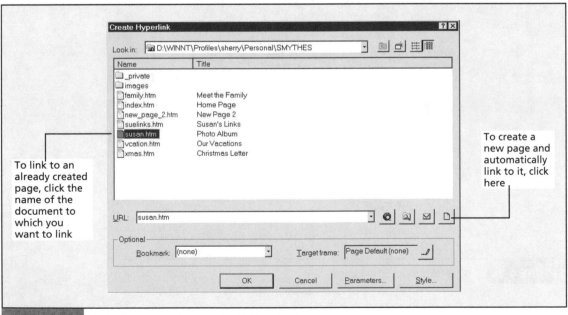

FIGURE 4-17 Selecting susan.htm as the linking URL

If you want to add the rest of the links to the family member pages, you can use the icon shown in Figure 4-17 to create a new page at the same time that you create the link to it.

Saving Your Web

After you create and modify your Web, the changes are not automatically saved. You need to save each page individually. How do you know which pages need to be saved? The easiest way is to just respond when FrontPage prompts you to save before you exit the program. Of course, the safer method is to save each page after you make a change to it. I wish there were a "Save Web" command in FrontPage, but there isn't. Saving a file is still done one at a time (but, at least FrontPage does prompt you for all of the pages that need saving). To save your pages (and not exit), here's what to do:

1. Choose File | Save. Since you added so many images, you'll be prompted for a place to save them. You've already seen this dialog box when you saved the templates earlier in this chapter.

2. This time, you want to save all of the embedded images. Click on the Change Folder button in the Save Embedded Images dialog box and navigate to the Images folder within your Web. Select that folder and save the images.

Previewing Your Site

You should now preview the site so far. First, look at the Web in the Preview window. This shows the way that the pages would look in Internet Explorer 5. Then, choose File | Preview in Browser and select each of the browsers that you have on your system. Evaluate the way the pages look in each browser so that you can make changes if you need to.

> **Note:** Before you can use the Preview in Browser command, you need to save each page that has changed. You'll be prompted to do this when you select the Preview in Browser command.

Finishing the Navigational Structure

Now that you've had a chance to create some text, add some graphics, add a link, and preview the results, you might want to finish creating the navigation system for the Smythe site or finish creating the pages in your flowchart for your own site.

When you create you own site, you'll want to use the pages that you have planned to include in your site. If you are following the Smythe example, here's how to create the remaining pages. As you can see, this is a summary of all that you've learned to do in this chapter.

1. Switch to Page view. For each page, choose File | New | Page and select the photos.tem template. Create a new page and immediately save it. Don't embed the images. These are the page names to save:

   - john.htm
   - jeff.htm
   - jayne.htm
   - dick.htm
   - sally.htm
   - doggie.htm

2. When you've created these pages, right-click on them one at a time in the Folder list and choose Properties. Change the title for each page as needed. For example, john.htm gets the title "John's Page." Do this for all of the family pages.

3. Change to Navigation view. Drag each of the family files into the Navigation window so that they attach under the Meet the Family icon.

4. Go back into Page view. Create and save the following pages as you did in Step 1. This time, use the favorites.tem template:

   - johnlink.htm
   - jefflink.htm
   - jaylink.htm
   - dicklink.htm
   - sallink.htm
   - doglink.htm

5. Click on each link file and change its title to reflect the name of the family member plus the word "Link" (e.g., johnlink.htm gets the title "John's Links").

6. Go back to Navigation view. Drag each link file underneath the correct individual file. Figure 4-18 shows the entire structure.

7. Fix the links on the Meet the Family page so that they all work.

8. Turn off the left shared border on the home page (only).

9. Try out the new site in Preview mode or Preview in Browser. All of the links should work. Notice how the buttons change color when the mouse is on top of them.

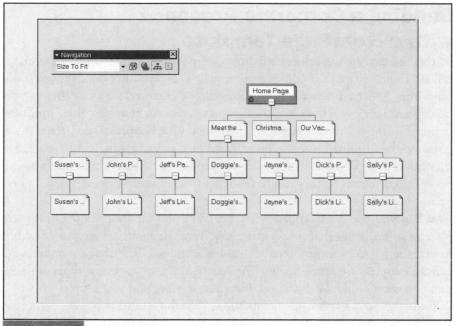

FIGURE 4-18 Link pages added to Navigation view

Using the Wizards

You've just created and modified a "canned" Web site to make it conform to your vision (or my vision) of what it ought to be. FrontPage gives you a number of prepackaged Web site templates. Some of them are complex enough to include wizards—"smart" programs that help you to make the necessary choices as you build the sites.

FrontPage contains wizards for a corporate presence on the Web, a discussion group site, and an import Web (where the documents already exist on your hard drive or on another site). It also automatically creates Webs for customer service and project management that you can customize once the pages are established. Let's take a quick look at the Corporate Presence Wizard (you'll learn about the wizard to create a discussion group in Chapter 15, and you'll use the Import Web wizards to see how to import some resources in Chapter 7).

Building a Corporate Presence with a FrontPage Template

In this section, we'll work on building a corporate presence using a company called HomeNclosures, a home improvement company that builds room additions onto houses. These room additions can be enclosed patios or they can be minigreenhouses. We'll assume the company wants to showcase their products online, but they obviously can't sell anything online because a salesperson must go out to the customer's site and measure the property to give a final estimate. So, they can use this Web site to show off their products and also to collect info about potential customers so they can have their national group of salespeople follow up on the leads.

When you use the Corporate Presence Wizard, you are prompted for each piece of information that the template requires. The items are fairly predictable in that the wizard wants to know the name, address, URL, phone number, and contact people for your company. The wizard also asks about the types of pages that you want on the Web and products and services that you supply.

Based on your answers to the questions that the wizard asks, the Corporate Presence Wizard creates the relevant pages and enters your company's data into title and help fields.

Ten screens are used in the Corporate Presence Wizard to collect all of your choices, and in the figures that follow I'll show you, in sequence, the options available and how to get the most out of this wizard.

To begin, choose File | New | Web and select the Corporate Presence Wizard. I've named the Web HomeNclosures.

Next, you'll select the specific main pages that you'll need for your site. HomeNclosures doesn't need a search screen because they don't have an extensive list of products. They probably don't need a table of contents, either. Figure 4-19 shows the main pages that would be used for the HomeNclosures site.

The next screen, shown in Figure 4-20, allows you to select all of the topics that you want to appear on your home page.

Next, you'll select the topics that you want to appear on the What's New page, and then select the number of products and services to feature. The wizard creates a new page for every item that you specify and for each product and service. Figure 4-21 shows the options found on these two pages and the choices that HomeNclosures would make.

If you were creating this Web for a hardware store, which carries thousands of products, you would not want to use this method of listing the products because it would be extremely cumbersome. For HomeNclosures, with only two main products (patio enclosures and greenhouses) and two services (landscaping and decks), this template works well.

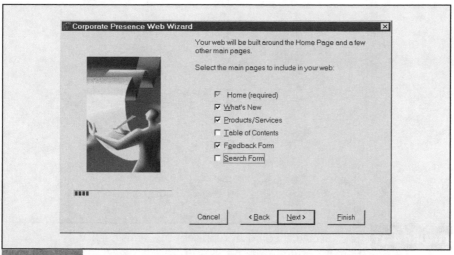

FIGURE 4-19 Select the main pages that you'll need for your site here

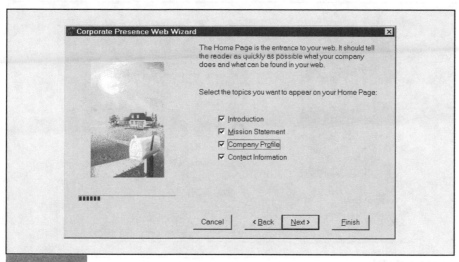

FIGURE 4-20 Select the sections that you want on your home page

The Corporate Presence Wizard automatically creates a feedback form so that site visitors can send their comments to the company. The information that this form requests would be a good source for leads. You can checkmark any of the boxes shown on Figure 4-22 and a request for that information will be added to the feedback form that the wizard creates. To make the feedback form into something that is appropriate for HomeNclosures, you could change the name of the form to "Request for Appointment" or something similar. Because HomeNclosures does residential work, you don't need to collect any company affiliation or job title for the respondents.

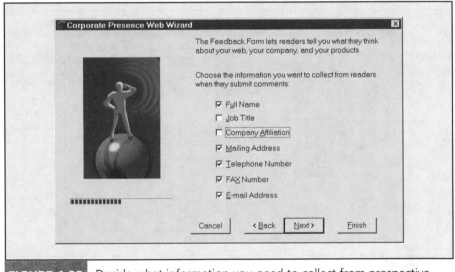

FIGURE 4-21 The selected checkboxes represent the items needed by
HomeNclosures

FIGURE 4-22 Decide what information you need to collect from prospective
customers

The next two pages of the wizard ask you to enter all of the company address
information and company contact information. The contact information is used
on the bottom shared border to allow site visitors to contact the company.

Your next step is to select a theme for your site from the wizard. Choose Romanesque for the HomeNclosures theme. HomeNclosures builds room additions,

and the Roman border on this theme suggests columns and architectural details (the Blueprint theme also works well for this site).

Once you've selected the theme, the only thing left is to decide if you want to view the task list as soon as the site is created. The task list would help you to determine what work still needs to be done to make the site operational.

Building a Customer Service Site with a FrontPage Template

When you decide to create a FrontPage Web and start to consider which template to use as the basis for your site, you need to consider both the purpose of the site and the type of site that each template creates. Sometimes, there is no "perfect" fit between a template and a client. The Customer Service template is designed to allow software companies to provide online support. However, you can "force" it to fit other needs.

SweaterLink, is a subscription service that provides a huge variety of knitting patterns to subscribers for an annual fee. This site will also offer a discussion group and pattern help, and is designed so that the subscriber can search for a specific type of pattern to knit, download the instructions, report pattern errors, and chat with other knitters. In addition, SweaterLink provides online enrollments so that a new site visitor can immediately become a member of the group.

The Customer Service template comes closest to creating the needed site. However, the Customer Service template is really designed for a software firm that needs to allow customers to have access to technical documents and needs to collect bug reports. If you apply a bit of creativity, you can change the language and the intention of some of the "automatic" pages so that you get a workable Web site for non-software-related businesses.

When you choose the Customer Service template, everything is automatically created for you. This template is not a wizard. Therefore, you need to first create the site and then modify it. Figure 4-23 shows the original home page and all of the related files that are automatically added to your Web.

After I created the SweaterLink site, I made three major types of changes. I changed the labels on some of the template documents that FrontPage provided, (Bugs became Pattern Problems, Download became Knit Patterns) and I changed the positioning of items in the menu to place the more common or more important choices higher in the list. I also added an enrollment form that allows visitors to sign up for the service. That was not part of the original Customer Service template. Figure 4-24 shows, in Preview mode, the changes that I made to the original generated site to make it more appropriate for a company that provides knitting patterns.

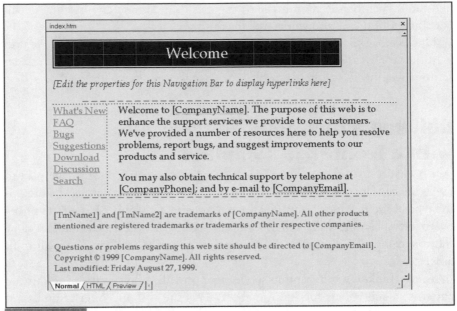

FIGURE 4-23 The original Customer Service template Web

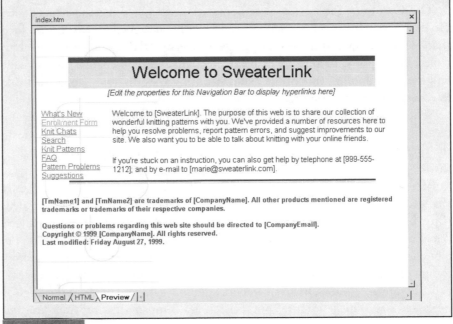

FIGURE 4-24 Web modified to customize the template for SweaterLink

Some Thoughts on Site Design and Template Use

When you need to create a Web site for your company, yourself, or a client, you first need to decide which template to use as a basis. You don't need to use a template at all, of course, but using one gives you an immediate structure that you can modify. If the needs of the Web site are close to any of the templates, then you can use that template as your starting point.

You need to make sure that you don't let the precreated material dictate your final site design, but any template can be wrestled into an alternate pattern so long as you know what you are trying to achieve.

You can select a theme in the same way. Pick something that is close to what you had in mind. It need not be perfect, but it should be "in the ballpark" in terms of style. You can then modify that theme to create something entirely different. However, I've found that starting with a theme makes it easier for me to see how the site works and to decide what I really want it to look like. It's also easier for

a client to approve a site once they see something working. So, getting a prototype of the site up quickly has benefits both to the designer and the client.

Finally, you need to think about the fact that your pages can be much larger than the screen used to display them. Since your monitor acts like a window that only reveals part of the page, you need to design your page so that the most important "stuff" goes near the top. Newspapers use the design concept of "above the fold" to create their front pages. All stories on the front page of a newspaper are important, but the reader is going to notice the ones "above the fold" first. If you purchase your paper from a vending machine, the stories above the fold are the only ones visible when you look at the paper before you buy it. Since some folks will never scroll through your entire page online, you need to place the most critical elements within the top 640 × 480 or 800 × 600 pixels of the screen.

Professional Skills Summary

This chapter covered a lot of material to allow you to create a complete Web. You've learned how to specify the template and the theme and how to modify the documents that are created. You've built a navigation bar and navigation structure almost from scratch. You've learned how to create, save, and use a page template. You've also learned how to add and delete new pages for your Web.

In addition, you've had a chance to add some text to a page, add some graphics, create links, and select an animation. You've also learned how to use the Corporate Presence Wizard and seen how a standard Customer Service template can be changed to become the structure for a slightly different type of site.

This ends the first section of the book. You've met FrontPage and learned the basics. Part II continues the journey by delving more deeply into designing text, graphics, pages, and links, and into publishing and maintaining your Web.

Part II
Implementing Your Web Site

chapter 5

All About Text

In this chapter, you:

- Learn to lay out pages

- Move text by dragging and dropping it

- Spell check your pages

- Use the Thesaurus

- Learn which font formatting features are safe to use in any browser

- Learn about cascading style sheets

- Create paragraph styles

- Format lists with bullets, numbering, or symbols

- Add comments to your pages that are not visible to the site visitor

- Learn ways to break up the space on a page

A picture might be worth a thousand words, but words take up much less room and sometimes even communicate better. Words will probably be the most numerous component of your Web pages.

FrontPage makes it very easy to format the text that you want to display. If you are familiar with Microsoft Word, you'll feel right at home. When you place text on the Web, however, you need to be very careful about knowing your audience. The older browsers don't provide the Web site designer with very much control over the display of information. Developing a text Web page is not as easy as using a page layout program to design a brochure. At least when you create a brochure, you can expect the text to look the same way printed as it did on your monitor. When you place text on the Web, to a certain extent, all bets are off.

Content, Structure, Style

When you lay out text and design a Web page, you are really doing three things at once, as there are three elements that interlock to form a page. These elements are content, structure, and style. Let's look at each in turn.

The *content* of your page is the actual text that it contains. The text has no particular font or typeface or typographic character whatsoever. All that is meant by "content" is the text itself—and the meaning that it conveys.

The *structure* of your page is the method that you use to show hierarchy and order. The title of a page, a list on a page, a form that contains areas for you to enter information—all these are things that give structure to your pages. When you designate an element on your page as a heading, you are structuring the content of your page.

The *style* of the text concerns a number of elements that include the typeface used, the size of the typeface, and the characteristics of the typeface (bold, italic, underlined, etc.). Taken together, these elements form the style component of the page.

Although content, structure, and style overlap (by tradition, for example, footnotes, which are a structuring device, use small print), it is helpful if you can attempt to separate these elements in your mind as you read the material in this chapter. Think about the words that you want to use (content), the way that you need to arrange them on the page (structure), and the physical look of the words that you arrange (style).

HTML and CSS

The section heading above—HTML and CSS—reads like alphabet soup. HTML (*Hypertext Markup Language*) is the "native language" of the Web. FrontPage basically acts as a translator and facilitator. To protect you (or free you) from the need to master HTML coding tags, you tell FrontPage how you want your page to look by selecting word-processing-like commands. FrontPage, in turn, writes the HTML code necessary to display your page on a Web browser just like you want it to look.

That's a nice theory, and it's close to the truth. FrontPage certainly tries its best to do what you want it to do. The problem is, as you've read before in this book, that each browser has its own way of displaying things. In addition to that, HTML is no longer the only standard for creating text on the Web.

You can also add style to your content by using cascading style sheets (CSS). You'll learn more about them later in this chapter. For now, you need to know that when you format something in FrontPage, it is going to either write HTML or CSS commands that you can see in the HTML view for the page. Unless you set a lower standard of browser compatibility (telling FrontPage that you want your Web to be usable by folks with older browsers), FrontPage will allow you to use both HTML and CSS features when you place text on your pages. However, that could be a big mistake.

A browser that doesn't "understand" CSS is supposed to ignore the CSS commands on a page. However, if you haven't given any thought to formatting your page so that it looks good in older browsers, then many of your Web site visitors could be very unhappy with your site.

This chapter, then, discusses both adding text with standard HTML commands and using the newer CSS style sheets. The first part of the chapter, however, deals exclusively with HTML and text. You need to be able to control the final code that FrontPage writes and understand which features require CSS and which do not.

It's Just Like Using Word

In this section, I want to talk about setting type (or just placing words on your page). I am going to assume that you've used a word-processing program at some point, so that the concept of computer typing is not foreign to you.

Creating text in FrontPage is similar to creating text in Microsoft Word, except that you might not have as much control over the formatting. I say "might not" because two different technologies exist for displaying text on the Web. The simplest method is the standard HTML way of formatting a page. This method gives you the minimum of control over how your page is displayed, but every browser can display it properly. Using plain HTML text, you can control the content of your text, but HTML has some very specific formats that structure the page. Except for changes built upon the structure of the page (headings, lists, etc.), you have little ability to style your text. The browser that your site visitor uses makes the decisions about the font, the size, and, in some cases, whether to display boldface or italic (although you do have some control in HTML over the font, font size, bold, and italic).

Later in this chapter, you'll also learn about cascading style sheets, a formatting method that only works in version 4.0 and above browsers (although the level 3.0 browsers understand a few of the formatting commands). This method allows you to suggest a typeface and standardize styles within your document. It enables you to apply specific styles (combinations of typeface, type size, and type attributes) to a particular typographic element, such as headings and lists and URLs, and goes hand in hand with the structure of your document.

Microsoft Word has built-in features that make placing text on a page very simple. FrontPage uses the same commands and methods as Word, and shares the same drag-and-drop, spelling, and grammar checking methods.

Setting Browser Compatibility Levels

You can tell Microsoft FrontPage which browsers your site visitors will most likely be using and it will enable or disable features so that your pages are accessible to those browsers. You should do this before you begin to place text on a page. The setting is for an entire Web, however, so that once you change it, you don't need to alter it for every page in the Web.

In the examples for the first part of this Chapter, you'll need to set your compatibility levels to level 3.0 browsers because you will be learning how to have FrontPage generate standard HTML for the Web page. When you create your own pages, you need to make the decision as to which browsers you will support.

Choose Tools | Page Options. Figure 5-1 shows you the options to select within the dialog box. Notice the technologies that "go away" when you ask FrontPage to maintain compatibility with version 3.0 browsers. Among the technologies that are unchecked is CSS, because this technology isn't supported until you specify that your Web page should be compatible with version 4.0 browsers. Click OK to close the dialog box after you've made your changes.

Let's take a look first at placing "regular" text—called "body copy" by many writers—into a page.

Adding Content

The first step in learning to use text on a Web page is to get the text into the Web page. You can type it directly onto the page, but you can also import it from a file.

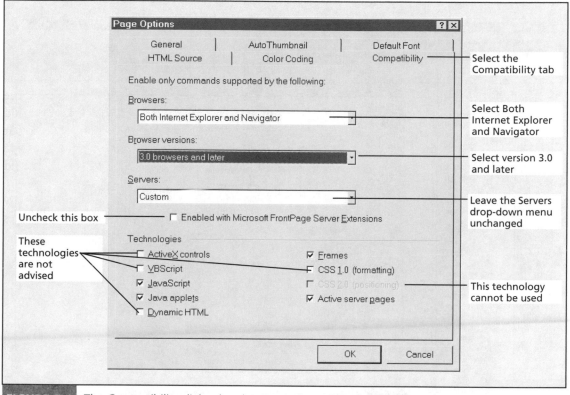

The following callouts appear to the right of the dialog box:

- Select the Compatibility tab
- Select Both Internet Explorer and Navigator
- Select version 3.0 and later
- Leave the Servers drop-down menu unchanged
- This technology cannot be used

The following callouts appear to the left of the dialog box:

- Uncheck this box
- These technologies are not advised

FIGURE 5-1 The Compatibility dialog box lets you select technology options

The next example, which uses the Smythe's Web site that you started to create in Chapter 4, enables you to import text that can be formatted. If you are creating your own page, rather than following this example, you would simply substitute your materials for the ones called for here.

To see how to import text, you are going to add some text to Susan's page. You can find the text file, clog.txt, at the Web site for this book. The file contains a brief history of clogging, Susan's favorite form of exercise. Follow these steps:

1. Open the susan.htm page in the Smythe's Web site (or open your desired page).

2. Delete all of the text and images (but not the navigation buttons) on the page. Your page should look like Figure 5-2 when you've finished deleting the pictures and dummy links that came with the page.

Tip: If you aren't using a theme on your page, you won't need to perform the clean-up operation. However, if there are things on the page that you don't want, just delete them first.

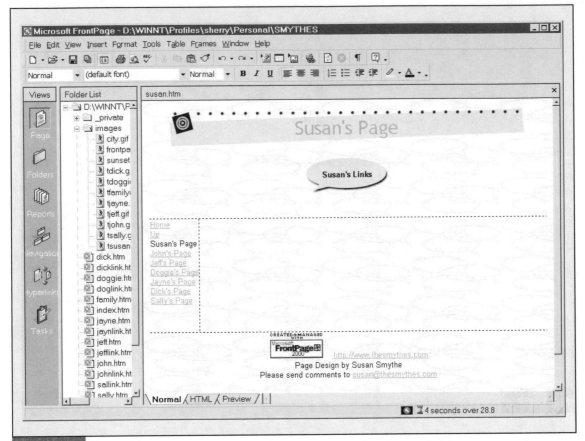

FIGURE 5-2 The susan.htm page cleaned up so that it can accept new material

3. Now you can insert the text. Choose Insert | File. Navigate to the copy of clog.txt that you downloaded (or to your desired text file) and change the Files of Type menu so that it reads Recover Text From Any File (*.*). Select the clog.txt document and click Open.

4. In the Convert Text dialog box, select the "Normal paragraphs" radio button.

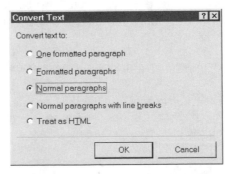

5. Click OK. Figure 5-3 shows the text plunked into the text area on the page.

The page now has content, but it has no structure and no style. The entire text uses a single font. Because it lacks a paragraph structure, it is virtually unreadable. If the text file that you want to use is already formatted in paragraphs, you are that much the better. However, if you are trying to work with a page that is a jumbled mass of text with no order to it, you will need to get some type of structure before you can really begin to see what other formatting changes you might want to make.

If you want to break up the text into paragraphs, you need to press the ENTER key at the end of each chunk of text that needs to be a paragraph. Whenever you press the ENTER key, you create a new paragraph (not the type of paragraph that you learned to write, perhaps, in elementary school, but a paragraph so far as FrontPage is concerned). The critical thing to know about a new paragraph is that every time you create one, HTML leaves a blank line in between the

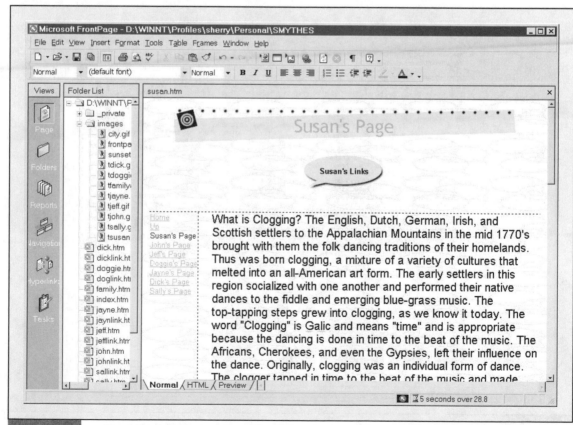

FIGURE 5-3 The susan.htm with text placed on the page

paragraphs. In standard HTML, you have no control over the size of the blank space between paragraphs.

Let's get the paragraphs fixed because until they are in place, you probably won't even be able to force yourself to read the content. Figure 5-4 shows you where to place your cursor in the text. Press the ENTER key at the location of the arrows in the figure to create new paragraphs.

What a relief for sore eyes! Just the breaking up of the text into chunks has made an immediate improvement, because it adds some visual structure for the reader to follow.

Tip: You need to structure your content in order to make it readable. Paragraphs either need to have space left between them, or the first word of the paragraph needs to be indented. Don't use both techniques at one time, however.

Now that you've given some structure to the content, what happens when you change the size of your browser window? Site visitors have many different

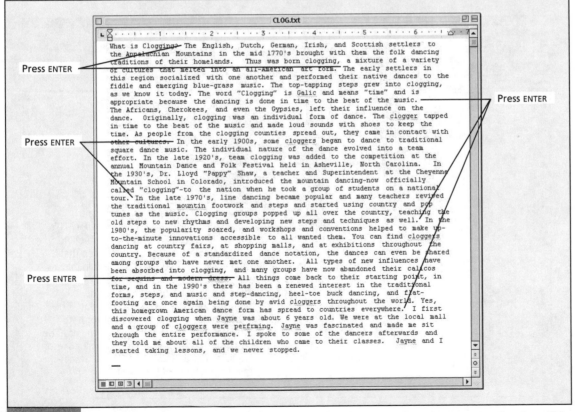

FIGURE 5-4 Press the ENTER key to create new paragraphs to make the text readable

monitor capacities and can make their browser windows any size they wish (so long as it fits on their screen).

Try this to test out the text wrap feature. Click the Restore Window icon at the upper right of the FrontPage window to allow FrontPage to occupy less than the maximum amount of the screen space. Click the Preview tab to view the text as it would look in Internet Explorer. Drag the lower-right corner of the document window around to change the size of the window. Notice that text resizes to fit the window. This is because of a feature known as "automatic text wrap." It's a major benefit because you don't need to worry about whether text will fit on a site visitor's screen. Your visitor's browser takes care of all that for you.

Cross-Reference: You'll learn about using tables in Chapter 10.

Tip: A number of studies have been done to determine the "readability" of a page. The most comfortable line length seems to be about 12 words per line. If there are many more words than this, the reader is likely to lose his or her place when moving to the next line of text. You can control the line length by setting margins using cascading style sheets, using the Indent buttons to bring your text in from the edges in "standard" HTML, or by using tables as a layout device.

Editing Content

FrontPage gives you many facilities for editing the text content that you place in your pages. You have the standard cut and paste commands to allow you to move and remove items from the document. You can also drag and drop text within the document, check your spelling, use the Thesaurus, and find and replace words. Let's try a few of these features.

Drag and Drop

You can select text and move it around once you've selected it. Once the text is selected, you simply place your cursor on top of it, and drag it to the desired location. Look at this selection from the text:

> The Africans, Cherokees, and even the Gypsies, left their influence on the dance. Originally, clogging was an individual form of dance. The clogger tapped in time to the beat of the music and made loud sounds with shoes to keep the time. As people from the clogging counties spread out, they came in contact with other cultures.

The last sentence in this paragraph (which is paragraph 3 in the text) actually sounds as if it makes more sense at the start of the paragraph. Click the first word in the last sentence of the paragraph (As). Press the mouse button and drag the mouse over all of the text in the sentence. Release the mouse button when all of the text in the sentence is selected.

Place your cursor on the word "As" in the selected sentence and drag the word until the I-beam cursor is in front of the sentence that starts the paragraph. Release the mouse button. The text that was selected is dropped into place.

Gallic
Gaelic
Garlic

Ignore All
Add

Spell Checking

You'll notice some red underlines in the text that you placed into Susan's page (or on your own pages if FrontPage doesn't recognize some of your typing). The red underlines indicate misspelled words. Basically, there are two types of misspelled words—words that are spelled incorrectly based on the dictionary that FrontPage uses, and words that the internal dictionary doesn't know about.

When you encounter misspelled words, such as the word "Galic" in the text on Susan's page, you'll see it is underlined. To quickly correct a spelling error, place your cursor over the word and click the right mouse button. Choose the correct spelling—in this case, Gaelic—from the pop-up Spelling menu.

The next underlined word in Susan's page is "clogger." It happens to be spelled correctly, but it is not in the dictionary that comes with FrontPage. Choose Add from the right-mouse Spelling menu. All of the underlines disappear from clogger but not from cloggers. You're dealing with a very literal machine that has no idea that cloggers is the plural of clogger. You'll need to right-click the word "cloggers" and add it to the dictionary as well.

To correct the spelling in your document as a whole, select Tools | Spelling. Figure 5-5 shows you how. The Spelling dialog box appears until you have checked through all of the misspellings in your page.

Tip: If you don't see any underlined spelling mistakes, then you need to enable the Check Spelling as You Type checkbox. Choose Tools | Page Options | General. Click the appropriate checkbox in the Spelling section of the dialog box.

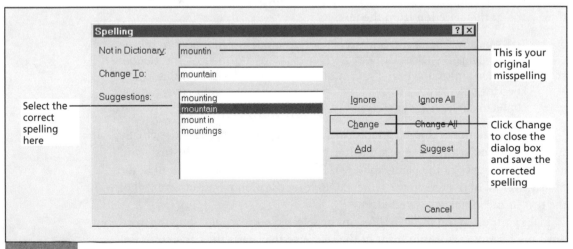

FIGURE 5-5 The Spelling dialog box

Find and Replace

You can also search for words or parts of words in the document and replace text with other text. If you notice a consistent misspelling in your text, or decide that you want to replace every instance of the word blue with the word red, FrontPage has the ability to do this in much the same way that search and replace works in Microsoft Word. (You can also do this by using the Change All button in the spelling dialog box.) In the document we've been building here, the article about clogging, you might notice that there is consistently an apostrophe between the decade number and the plural "s" that follows it. This is grammatically incorrect. To write about the sixties as "The '60s" is fine, but to say "in the 1960's" is not. You can search for every instance of this misuse and correct it very easily.

Because the one consistent thing in all of the dates is the apostrophe, FrontPage can first search for the apostrophe, and then replace it with nothing—which corrects the mistake.

1. Choose Edit | Replace.
2. Type an apostrophe (') into the "Find what" field.
3. Leave the "Replace with" field blank.
4. Click the Find Next button. If the word that is found needs to be corrected, then click Replace. FrontPage will immediately repeat the search until it runs out of examples.

Creating Structure and Style

At the start of this chapter I suggested that you mentally separate the structure of a document from its style or the way that it's displayed. Since we are considering only a plain HTML page right now, the structure of the document generally mandates the style.

You've Got Sizes and You've Got Colors

In the Tools | Page Options | Compatibility dialog box, you told FrontPage that you wanted to use only the features that would be enabled in an early browser (version 3.0 of Netscape Navigator or Internet Explorer). Because of that, you've seriously limited your typographical options. However, you have the confidence that all of your site visitors will be able to properly view your page. Even with fewer options, you can still create attractive pages.

For the text on your page, you can select the relative size of the text, the color of the text, and a few attributes such as bold, italic, or underline. Figure 5-6 shows the formatting toolbar and the names of the formatting items on the toolbar. Here are some of the changes that you can make:

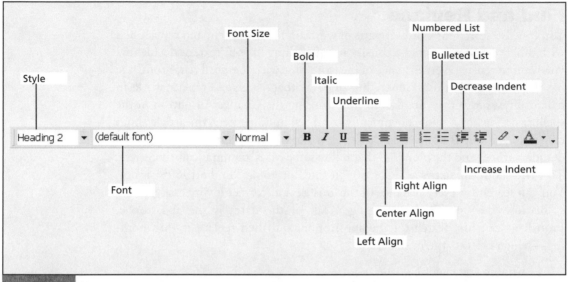

FIGURE 5-6 The Style, Font, and Font Size menus

Let's format Susan's page in the following steps to see what type of style you can add to the HTML:

1. To change the text to a different style, click the Style menu in the text toolbar and select the desired style. (The menu shows six heading styles. Heading 1 is the largest and Heading 6 is the smallest).

2. Align the text (left, right, or center) by clicking on the desired alignment icon.

3. Select the text whose color you want to change. Change the color of the text by clicking on the Color drop-down in the Font menu. Select one of the standard colors (maroon, for example, the fourth one from the left on the top row).

4. You can change the font size by selecting the word or paragraph and choosing the new font size in the formatting toolbar, as shown in Figure 5-6.

5. You can make a word bold, italic, or underlined by clicking on the icons shown in the formatting toolbar in Figure 5-6.

Tip: HTML allows you to select Headings 1–6. Although you may use up to six levels of headings, you might not be able to distinguish headings 4, 5, or 6 from your body copy. Therefore, as a practical matter when using HTML, it's best to use just the top three levels of heading.

Tip: Underline indicates a hyperlink on the Web. Don't underline anything else if you can possibly avoid doing so.

Figure 5-7 shows the clogging article and some formatting changes that you can make to it for practice.

Using standard HTML, you can also create text that is indented on both the right and left sides. FrontPage uses the HTML tag <blockquote> to create these margins. To create the margin, you need to click the Increase Indent icon shown in Figure 5-6. You may select it multiple times to make a larger indent. The text moves over toward the right but keeps its original alignment.

You can "set" poetry or other text without carriage returns (i.e., paragraph breaks) if you don't want to see extra paragraph-type space between the lines. After you type the line, press the SHIFT key and the ENTER key. This forces a line break but not a paragraph break.

Figure 5-8 shows a poem that Jayne wrote when she was six. You can type this in at the bottom of Susan's page if you want to practice indenting and not leaving paragraph breaks.

Tip: The "normal" font size is 3. By changing the font to size 2, you are making it smaller. Don't count on the point sizes listed next to the font size options as truly showing up on your page, since point sizes will vary by browser and by the default font size that the user can set on the browser. However, the relative sizes are accurate. Size 2 is smaller than Size 3 but larger than Size 1. You can select from seven sizes.

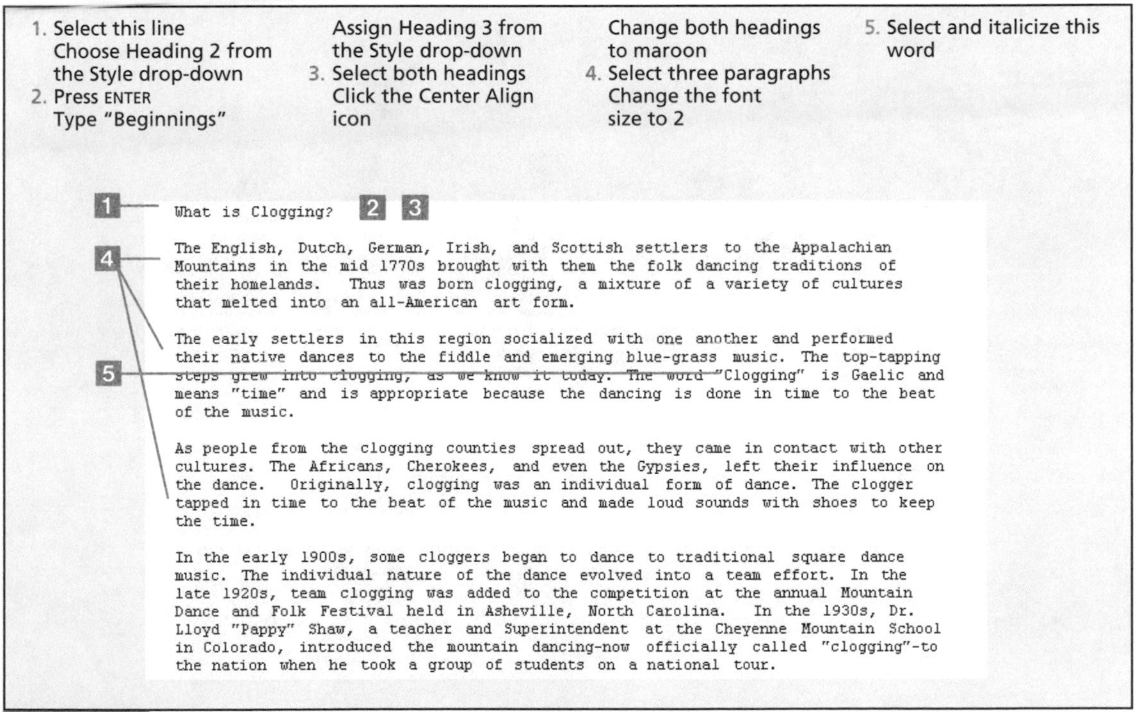

1. Select this line
   Choose Heading 2 from
   the Style drop-down
2. Press ENTER
   Type "Beginnings"

Assign Heading 3 from
the Style drop-down
3. Select both headings
   Click the Center Align
   icon

Change both headings
to maroon
4. Select three paragraphs
   Change the font
   size to 2

5. Select and italicize this
   word

What is Clogging?

The English, Dutch, German, Irish, and Scottish settlers to the Appalachian Mountains in the mid 1770s brought with them the folk dancing traditions of their homelands. Thus was born clogging, a mixture of a variety of cultures that melted into an all-American art form.

The early settlers in this region socialized with one another and performed their native dances to the fiddle and emerging blue-grass music. The top-tapping steps grew into clogging, as we know it today. The word "Clogging" is Gaelic and means "time" and is appropriate because the dancing is done in time to the beat of the music.

As people from the clogging counties spread out, they came in contact with other cultures. The Africans, Cherokees, and even the Gypsies, left their influence on the dance. Originally, clogging was an individual form of dance. The clogger tapped in time to the beat of the music and made loud sounds with shoes to keep the time.

In the early 1900s, some cloggers began to dance to traditional square dance music. The individual nature of the dance evolved into a team effort. In the late 1920s, team clogging was added to the competition at the annual Mountain Dance and Folk Festival held in Asheville, North Carolina. In the 1930s, Dr. Lloyd "Pappy" Shaw, a teacher and Superintendent at the Cheyenne Mountain School in Colorado, introduced the mountain dancing-now officially called "clogging"-to the nation when he took a group of students on a national tour.

FIGURE 5-7 Follow the numbered instructions to format Susan's page

Typography for the Web

Be restrained with your use of styles, font styles, colors, and special effects. You don't really want your page to look like a high-tech ransom note. I was teaching at Drexel University in 1984 when the Macintosh was first introduced. One of my students handed me a term paper written entirely in outline font. I handed it back. It was totally unreadable. If you get too "creative" with your pages, they too will become unreadable. There is a difference between illegible and unreadable. On an illegible page, you would not be able to discern the letterforms at all. On an unreadable page, you can figure out the letters but it's too much work to do so.

Bold should be used sparingly because it makes the eye stop suddenly as it scans the page. Try using italic for emphasis if you want to define something or call the reader's attention to it. Use that sparingly as well. If you change text colors on your page, do so for structural reasons. Don't use the blink effect at all—ever. It's not supported in Internet Explorer 4 and it's universally detested by those folks who have to watch the page go on and off like Rudolph the Reindeer's nose.

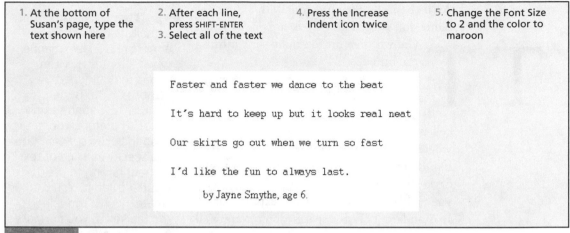

1. At the bottom of Susan's page, type the text shown here
2. After each line, press SHIFT-ENTER
3. Select all of the text
4. Press the Increase Indent icon twice
5. Change the Font Size to 2 and the color to maroon

Faster and faster we dance to the beat

It's hard to keep up but it looks real neat

Our skirts go out when we turn so fast

I'd like the fun to always last.

by Jayne Smythe, age 6.

FIGURE 5-8   Setting a poem

Fonts (and Other Web Layout Annoyances)

So far, you've used most of the native HTML font-styling commands. However, you haven't changed fonts yet. A font is a collection of characters that were designed to be used together and are of a particular weight and size. A typeface or type family is the more general name for the shape of the letters that make up a font. A font is an instance of a typeface.

Semantics aside, you acquire fonts (typefaces, font families) either by installing your operating system (which adds the standard fonts), by installing an application that includes fonts, or by purchasing specific fonts. In order to see a particular font on a Web page, the *site visitor's own system* must contain that font. Although you may specify whichever font you want the Web page to display, if it isn't installed on your user's system, they will see the default font for their browser. You may specify fonts in either HTML or cascading style sheets. In either case, the font needs to be on the visitor's computer in order to be used for display.

How do you know if the font that you want to use is installed on your site visitor's system? You don't and you can't even predict if it will be there. However, just about everyone has some flavor of Times (or Times New Roman) or Helvetica (or Arial). These fonts are safe to use, although they get boring to see after a while. They are the default fonts for most browsers, so even if you don't specify them, they are most likely to be used anyway. Times is a *serif font* (shown below on the left—its letters have little feet on them), and Helvetica or

T T

Arial (basically the same font with a different name for Mac and PC) is a *sans serif font* (shown here on the right—it's missing the little feet):

A third common font is Courier. This is a *monospaced* font (every letter is exactly the same width). This font is excellent for displaying code in a program or wherever you need to keep a consistent spacing. If you select the Formatted style from the Style drop-down on the formatting toolbar, you will normally change your text to Courier. In standard HTML, spaces don't count (all extra spaces are removed). The HTML tosses out multiple spaces in a line. However, using the Formatted style allows you to keep as many spaces as you want.

> **Tip:** FrontPage actually handles spaces in a more reasonable manner when it writes HTML. It enters multiple spaces as " ". This is the symbol for a nonbreaking space. Therefore, you get to keep the extra spaces that you specify in a line of text without having to use Courier to do it. You can create indents by typing the tab key as you normally would. FrontPage writes a tab character as three nonbreaking spaces.

What You'd Like to Be Able to Do vs. HTML Realities

Typography for print design has been standardized and enhanced over the 400+ years since the invention of the first printing press. Graphic artists know how to lay out pages for print and are able to specify many different adjustments to make a page look good. Examine Figure 5-9. It shows a variety of typographic adjustments in this article written for publication in a newspaper.

All of the changes shown to the article can be made in print. Very few of them can be made in standard HTML. The Web was originally designed to make it easier for scientists to exchange data. The scientists weren't interested in graphics—they wanted a faster medium in which to share ideas with each other. To create that faster method of communication, they designed HTML, a text-based standard that was to be machine-independent and machine-readable (so that some searching could be done automatically). My favorite line in a book on Web design was that they then created a standard for typesetting and graphics that only a machine—or a scientist—would want to read.

Actually, it's not that bad. However, to a traditionally trained graphic designer, Web design is a major challenge. When a designer lays out a page, the page is expected to stay put. On the Web, nothing is stationary. You cannot count on your site visitors to have standard software programs, work at a specified resolution or number of colors, or keep their browser set to a consistent size.

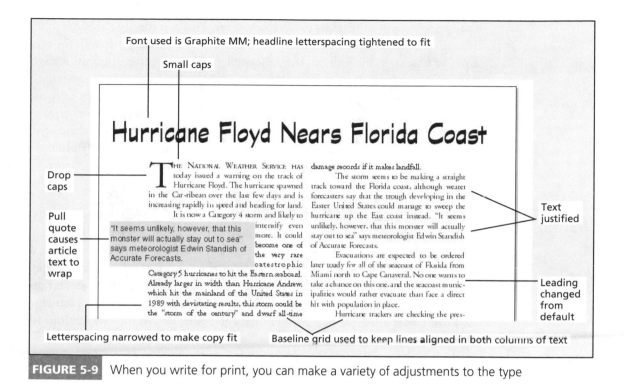

FIGURE 5-9 When you write for print, you can make a variety of adjustments to the type

You can specify fonts, but you can't know which font will eventually be used. Standard HTML doesn't support drop caps (the large initial uppercase letters that begin the first paragraph of some articles). Standard HTML doesn't permit you to letterspace or word space (add or remove spaces between words and letters to make the content fit into a specific space). You can center-, right-, or left-justify text in HTML, but you can't right- and left-justify it at the same time. Inserting pull quotes into an HTML page is possible but very difficult. Baseline grids are unknown. HTML doesn't contain a tag for small caps. You cannot adjust leading (the spacing between lines of text). Most site visitors probably won't feel the lack of these items, but many graphic artists are uncomfortable without these features.

Enter cascading style sheets, or CSS.

Cascading Style Sheets

Cascading style sheets (CSS) is an attempt to bring some of the printed typographical niceties to the Web. Cascading style sheets give back the control over the appearance of the text to the Web designer. You can specify the fonts to use (though you have no more control over what font will actually display), the type size and type style, the indents, the right and left margins, paragraph justification, and many other facets of typography.

You can apply these styles—by creating a style sheet that lists each element you specify—to any piece of text on your page without (so the theory goes) disturbing the underlying HTML structure of the page. You can save these style sheets and apply them to multiple pages at one time. You can also apply multiple style sheets to the same page. If not quite typesetting nirvana, CSS comes close.

A Solution with a Catch

Of course, all of the control that you get with CSS comes at a price. That price is compatibility with all browsers. The version 3.0 browsers from Netscape and Microsoft did understand some of the CSS commands. Unfortunately, they didn't understand them all, and the ones that Netscape did allow weren't always the same ones that Internet Explorer could understand. Also, Netscape and Microsoft browsers differed between their Mac and Windows versions in what they could display.

Both Netscape Navigator and Microsoft Internet Explorer have done a much better job with their version 4 browsers, and still better with version 5.0 (of which Internet Explorer is the only example as we go to print). However, cross-platform and cross-browser differences still exist with command support being missing, buggy, or quirky for some of the CSS features. You can find the complete list of which commands are supported by which browsers at http://webreview.com/wr/pub/guides/style/mastergrid.html. This site also contains a shorter "safe list" that indicates which commands generally work in all of the level 4.0 and above browsers.

Professional Pointer

Before you use any CSS commands, you need to decide if your site visitors are likely to be able to see them. If you think that most of your visitors will be using level 4.0 browsers, then you will produce a much more pleasing and better-structured site if you use the CSS commands. Stick to the "safe" commands and test, test, test, your results in as many browsers and on as many platforms as you can.

CSS Primer

Now you know what HTML can't do and CSS can do, but you still have very little clue as to what CSS is and how you use it. A cascading style sheet is a set of formatting rules that is attached to a Web page or a group of Web pages and tells the browser how to format the various HTML tags in a page.

The logic behind a cascading style sheet is similar to that of creating and using styles in Microsoft Word. When I began to write this book, Osborne sent me a Microsoft Word template to use. That template contained all of the styles that I needed in order to create the chapters. For example, I was sent the "Body" style. This is the style for paragraphs of text. The first line is indented. The lines are spaced approximately 1.5 lines apart. The font used is Times New Roman in Normal weight at 12 points. A .6 inch space separates each paragraph. The style contains no tab settings. It is left-aligned and not justified. Widow and orphan control is on.

All of the typographic controls described above created a Word "style." My Osborne template contains styles for numbered lists, for "special" text like Tips and Sidebars, for figure and table captions, for formatting keyboard commands, and for various levels of headings. As I write this book, all I need to do is compose the text and then apply a style to various sections. For example, if I continue writing a number of paragraphs after this one, I won't need to apply a new style until I write something that isn't a paragraph—a figure caption or a list would need a new style. However, the Body style contains instructions that the next paragraph is supposed to be Body style as well.

Of course, the text that you're reading isn't in Times New Roman at 12 points. I really don't know what it is, because that's a decision that the production folks at Osborne will make after I've sent them all of the chapters for the book. However, because all of my text is tagged with a specific style, the production department can easily redefine the style and the entire chapter instantly is reformatted. That's the power of styles.

Cascading style sheets will do exactly the same thing for your Web pages. Once you define all of the characteristics that you want in your page, you can create the style sheet. After you link your page to the style sheet, a change to the style sheet will make an instant change in the formatting of your pages.

FrontPage supports three of the four possible types of cascading style sheets. You can *link* to your style sheets, *embed* them in a page, or use them *inline*—i.e., apply them to a specific instance in the text. You decide which method to use based on your answers to these questions:

- How often are you going to need to change a style that you have defined?
- How general a formatting option do you want?

Figure 5-10 shows the hierarchy of the three types of style sheets.

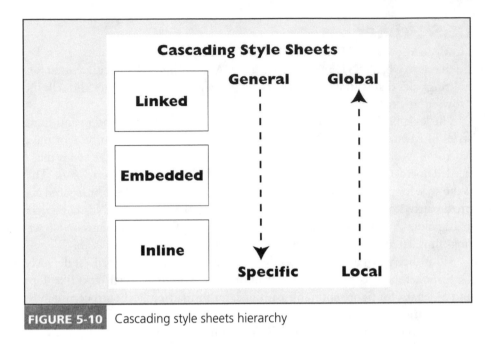

Cascading style sheets hierarchy

Styles *cascade*. That's why they are called "cascading style sheets." This means that once you apply a style to a specific HTML tag, it applies to that tag all of the time unless you change it. If you create a style sheet and link 3,000 (or even 2) pages to it and then decide that you'd rather use New Century Schoolbook for your normal font rather than New Times Roman, then you can replace the font face in the style sheet. Immediately, all of the pages that are linked to that style sheet also change. A linked style sheet is actually a blank document with embedded style sheets that lives outside of your Web. When you link it, you physically create a link statement in each of your pages.

If you embed the styles at the top of each page and then decide to change the font for all of the pages in your Web, you need to open and make the changes to every page that you want to change (possibly 3,000 changes instead of one). However, by embedding a style sheet in a page, you can override any styles that exist in the linked (external) style sheet. Another facet of cascading is that styles placed lower in the hierarchy override styles defined higher up.

For the most control, you can place the style definition inline—wrap it into the tag that's attached to an element. You would do this if you had specified, for example, that all top-level headings (the H1 tag) would be green and on this particular headline, you want the text to be red. You don't want to create all of your styles this way, however, because you then lose the ability to make global changes. An inline style needs to be modified one at a time. However, it also overrides any styles placed higher up in the document, so if you need to alter your original style choices in only one spot, an inline style is the way to do it.

In the sections that follow, you'll learn how to create a style sheet, link to a style sheet, create an embedded style sheet, create inline styles, modify an existing style sheet, and modify and use style sheets with themes. That's a tall order, but it gets easier with every example that you try.

Paragraphs with Individual Style

A bit earlier in this chapter, you learned how to format elements of the text by tagging them as Normal, Heading 1, etc. from the formatting toolbar. You discovered that the main structural elements in a page were the body (i.e., the paragraph text), and the headings (Heading 1–Heading 6). There are other structural elements in addition, but these are the most frequently used ones.

As it happens, these are also the elements that are most commonly redefined by a style sheet. Let's dive in and look at an already created style sheet. Figure 5-11 shows the various parts of the street.css style sheet; street.css is one of the style sheets that is installed when you install the FrontPage themes. You can see many of the familiar elements in this style sheet. It defines the style for the body and for all of the headings (h1-h6), as well as defining styles for links (a:link, a:visited, and a:active) and for tables.

The basic changes that are made in this style sheet are to colors or to fonts. Let's use this style sheet and see what you get when you link a new page to it. You're going to first create a new empty page and add some text to it. You'll format the text the way that you've already learned, and then link this page to a copy of the street.css style sheet. That way, you'll be able to see how your styles immediately change. Follow these steps:

1. Launch FrontPage but don't open any Webs (if you have one open, choose File | Close Web to shut it down).

2. Choose File | New | Page. Select a Normal page from the dialog box and click OK.

3. In the new page, type the text as shown in Figure 5-12 and apply the formatting by selecting the indicated style from the Style drop-down menu in the formatting toolbar. This just gives you some text with which to play.

4. Next, you're going to copy a style sheet into a new document. This is an easy way to get a style sheet to customize. Choose File | New and click the Style Sheet tab. Select the Street document as shown in Figure 5-13.

Tip: When you change the page options compatibility settings for a Web, the settings sometimes persist even when you close that Web and create a new one. Each time you open a new Web, change the compatibility settings for the Web. If your settings permit version 3.0 browsers, then you won't be able to see the style sheets.

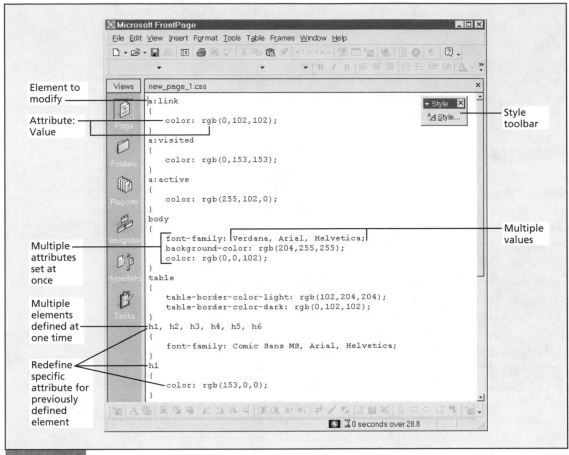

Element to modify

Attribute: Value

Multiple attributes set at once

Multiple elements defined at one time

Redefine specific attribute for previously defined element

Style toolbar

Multiple values

FIGURE 5-11 The anatomy of a style sheet

5. Save the new document as trial.css (File | Save As). Place it anywhere on your hard drive where you can find it again. Close trial.css.

6. The document that you created in Steps 1–3 above should still be open (and visible once you close trial.css). Make the document active.

7. Choose Format | Style Sheet Links. Click the Add button and locate the saved trial.css. Click OK twice to back out of the open dialog boxes. As soon as you click OK, the style sheet takes control. There's quite a difference in the text, as you can see in Figure 5-14.

Tip: It's easier to create a new document and copy the style sheet than it is to find the style sheet and open it. In my system, the Microsoft-installed style sheet documents (.css files) are in the Templates folder of my Microsoft Office installation. This happens to be on my G: drive. However, the location is likely to be different on your system.

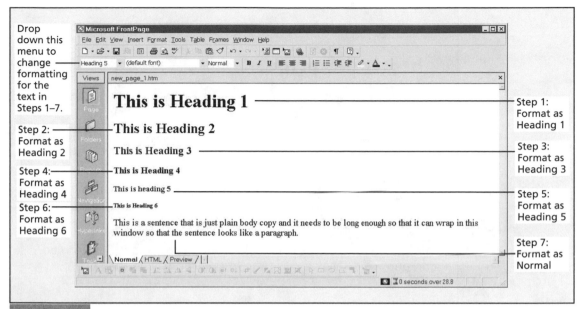

FIGURE 5-12   Type some text and format it

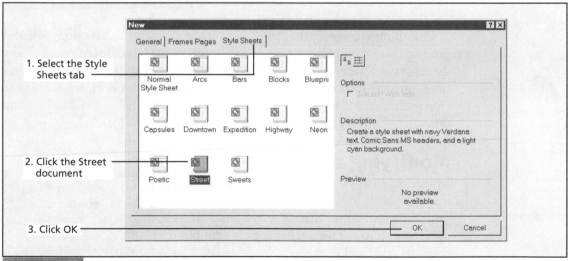

FIGURE 5-13   Selecting a built-in style sheet to modify

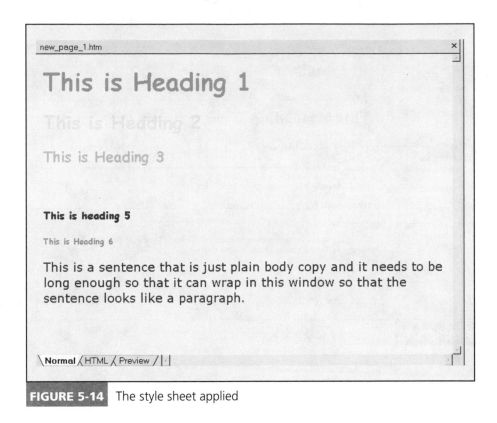

FIGURE 5-14   The style sheet applied

One of the changes in the text is that Heading 4 seems to have disappeared. I promise that I didn't plan it—whoever created the style sheet for Microsoft chose the same color for Heading 4 as he or she used for the page background. The result is invisible text, which is not the world's most useful look. However, you can change that (and if there hadn't been a glitch in the style sheet, I'd have found something different for you to change.

Modifying a Style

In order to modify a style sheet, you need to open it again. Use the File | Open command and navigate to the style sheet that used to control your document. If you've been following my example, open the trial.css document.

The .css document that you open is a "pure" HTML document. There's nothing to view in Page view or Preview mode, because the document only

L▶ Tip: If you receive a message from FrontPage asking if you want to "check out" the file, you need to check in with your system administrator to determine the enabling security technologies at your installation.

contains the style sheet definitions. Therefore, you could modify the HTML directly (and in Chapter 9, you'll learn how to do that). The safest way to change the style sheet, however, is to use the FrontPage commands and let FrontPage make the changes for you—at least until you understand the underlying HTML of the page.

The problem with the trial.css style sheet is located in two definitions. The Body definition contains the statements "background-color: rgb(204,255,255);" and the Heading 4 definition says "color: rgb(204,255,255);"— the statement changes the background color to RGB 204, 255, 255 and the h4 statement sets the foreground to RGB 204, 255, 255. One of these statements needs to change. My suggestion is to change the h4 definition to use a different color. Here's how to make the change, but these steps also apply to any other change that you want to make to an element:

1. Choose Format | Style or click the style toolbar. In the List box, select User-Defined Styles. Click the h4 element in the Styles list and click Modify as shown in Figure 5-15.

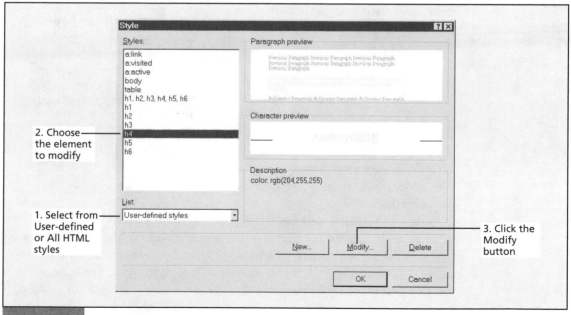

FIGURE 5-15 Selecting an element to modify

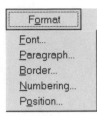

2. The Modify Style dialog box appears, but all that it does is show a preview of the current style. Click the Format button. A variety of choices appear. Select Font from the drop-down menu.

3. You can change the font, the font style, the font size, the font effect, or the font color. Click the Color button and select Teal (the last color on the menu) from the drop-down menu.

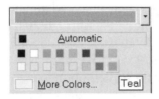

4. Click OK and continue to click the OK button until all dialog boxes are closed. The style sheet definition for h4 is changed to color # 008080 (FrontPage writes the hexadecimal number instead of the RGB value, but it makes no difference; the critical issue is that you've selected a new color for h4 text).

5. Save the style sheet (File | Save). Close the style sheet. Now you can see the Heading 4 line in your document.

Fashion Your Own Style

You don't need to base your style sheet on one that already exists. You can create your own style sheet from scratch in a manner that is similar to the way in which you modified the style sheet above. You can create a blank style sheet and change HTML elements in it exactly the way that you selected the h4 element and changed its color. You click the style toolbar and then select the element to modify from the All HTML styles (rather than the "User-defined styles" list). For each element that you select, you can modify the Font (family, size, style, effect, or color), or change the Paragraph, Border, Numbering, or Position settings.

Tip: You can only style the Position settings if you have chosen CSS 2.0 in the Tools | Page Options | Compatibility Technologies dialog box.

When you create a totally new style sheet, you don't need to define every possible element in your document. In programmer's terms, the elements in your Web all have "inheritance," which means that there is a default style to everything. The native HTML carries its own style with it. If you don't change that default style in your style sheet, it will be used if nothing else is in the way. So, if you don't select a color for your text, for example, the color used will be the browser's default color for that element.

Professional Pointer

Some Thoughts on Designing Font Styles: If you aren't sure of the effects of your style changes, don't make them. You should create styles so that you can apply them consistently throughout your Web. However, changing fonts and colors just for the sake of doing something different is likely to be confusing to your site visitors. When you select a font, it should be because you feel that it is the most appropriate font for that particular use. You also need to remember that a font selection only works when your visitor has the same font installed on his or her system. Otherwise, the visitor sees the default browser font.

As you begin to design styles for your Web, here are some typographic hints:

- Select a serif font for body text. Good text fonts are
  - Times
  - Times New Roman
  - Garamond
  - Century Schoolbook or New Century Schoolbook
  - Stone Serif
  - Goudy Old Style
  - Bookman
  - Book Antigua
- Just about everyone has some form of Times or Times New Roman.
- Select a sans serif or a display font for headings. Good choices for a sans serif font are
  - Arial
  - Helvetica
  - Kabel
  - Comic Sans
  - Century Gothic
  - Futura
  - Verdana
- Just about everyone has some form of Arial or Helvetica installed.
- If you want a bold weight font, using a font that is already bold or black looks better than using the <b> tag (i.e., making it bold onscreen). Folks might not have a bold version of the font, but they can always see a font that has been made bold, so you need to make a conscious decision to trade quality for availability.

- You may select more than one font for an element, but only if you type it into the style sheet yourself. You'll do that in Chapter 9 on HTML.

With these thoughts in mind, try this example to build your own style sheet:

1. Launch FrontPage and make sure that no Webs are open.

2. Choose File | New | Page. Select the Style Sheets tab and select the Normal style sheet. This creates a blank style sheet with the default name of new_page_1.css.

3. Click the style toolbar. Select the Body element from the list of All HTML styles. Click the Modify button.

4. Click the Format button and choose Font.

5. In the Font dialog box, select Bookman Old Style (or whatever else you prefer). Select Regular as the font weight and 12pt as the font size. (When you write styles for your Webs, of course, you can select whatever you want as the font, the weight, and the size.)

6. Select navy as the color and click OK. Click OK until all of the dialog boxes are closed. FrontPage writes the new Style on your page like this:

```
body          { font-family: Bookman Old Style; font-size: 12pt; color: #000080 }
```

7. Click the style toolbar again. Change the "User-defined styles" list to the "All HTML tags" list and select h1. Define it as Shotgun BT (if you have that on your system, or whatever else your prefer if you don't), Regular weight, 24pts, Green. Click OK until all dialog boxes are closed.

8. Define h2 as you did h1, but change the color to red and the weight to 18pts.

9. Define h3 and change the color to blue and the size to 14pts.

Your style sheet isn't quite done yet, but it is time to talk about some of the other controls that you have when you create styles. Read the next section and then you'll finish creating the style sheet.

Tabs, Margins, Indents, and Spacing

You use the Paragraph settings to change the alignment, spacing, and indents for your text. You really don't have tabs in an HTML document, so you can simulate them for a first line indent by setting the exact number of pixels by which you want to indent your first line of text. As you can see in Figure 5-16, you have a large number of items that you can set.

The p tag is used to define paragraphs in HTML. If you read the HTML code that FrontPage writes for your Web, you'll notice a <p> in front of every text paragraph and a </p> after every paragraph. Therefore, it makes sense to modify the p tag in a style sheet if you want to change the global way in which paragraphs are displayed.

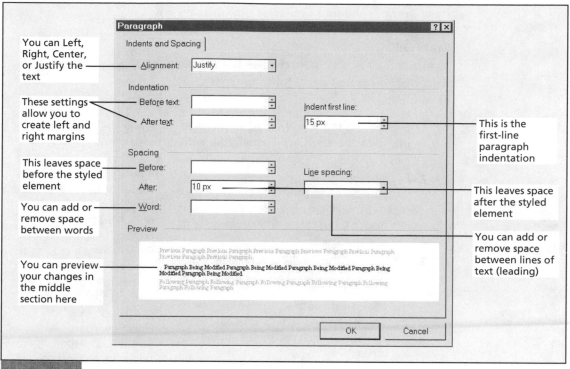

The Paragraph style settings dialog box

When you modified the Body tag, you set the font characteristics for everything that is displayed in the Web page. You then changed the fonts used for the Heading 1, Heading 2, and Heading 3 styles. This style definition makes the top three headings use a different font from the rest of the body text. Now, you can change the specifications for paragraph text by using the Paragraph settings. These changes won't alter the font or type characteristics at all.

You can use the Paragraph settings to create an indent for each paragraph. When you indent your paragraphs, "good typography" states that there should be no extra text left between the paragraphs (i.e., you can indicate paragraphs by indenting or by leaving space, but you should not do both). The Space settings in the Paragraph dialog box work *in addition to the space* normally left by HTML. Therefore, if you want to create paragraphs that have no extra space between them, you need to remove space (i.e., enter a negative number). On my system for the style sheet that we started above, this number is -19 pixels. You will need to experiment using the fonts and font sizes every time that you make a font change. An indent of +35 pixels also works well.

Here's how to add these changes to the style sheet that you started above (or to any style sheet of your own):

1. Select the p tag from the "All HTML tags" list. Click Modify. Click Format and select Paragraph.

2. Follow the guidelines in Figure 5-16. Change the Alignment field to Justify (this makes the text line up at both the right and left margins, but it has nothing to do with the spacing issues).

3. Enter **35** in the "Indentation: Indent first line" field, and enter **-19** in the Spacing: After field. The preview shows the last line of the paragraph overlapping the first line of the next paragraph. That's what you want to see. Click OK until you close all of the dialog boxes.

4. Save your style sheet as access.css.

If you want, you can also change the paragraph styling for the headings to leave more room before or after the lines. You might want to center-align the heading text, but that really only looks good when the text that is under the heading occupies the entire width of the page. It will work in this example, so go back and modify the h1, h2, and h3 paragraph styles to use center alignment. Save the style sheet again. Don't close it.

Let's try out this style sheet with a page from the Access-Ability Web site. You can download the document londonaccess.txt from the Osborne Web site for this book.

1. In FrontPage, choose File | New | Page and open the Normal page.

2. Choose Insert | File and navigate to the londonaccess.txt document. Select it and use Normal paragraphs.

> **Tip:** The paragraph after spacing shows up properly in Microsoft Internet Explorer 5.0. It doesn't make any difference at all in Netscape Communicator 4.5.

> **Tip:** If you are told that the file is "read only" and your site is not using the source control that is built into FrontPage, try closing the file and opening it again. Sometimes that helps. You can turn source control on or off by selecting Tools | Web Settings. On the General tab, click to turn on or off the "Use document check-in and check-out" checkbox. If you are using Visual SourceSafe (a separate administrative package from Microsoft), you need administrator authority to change the settings.

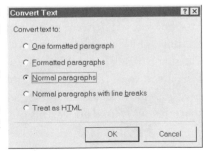

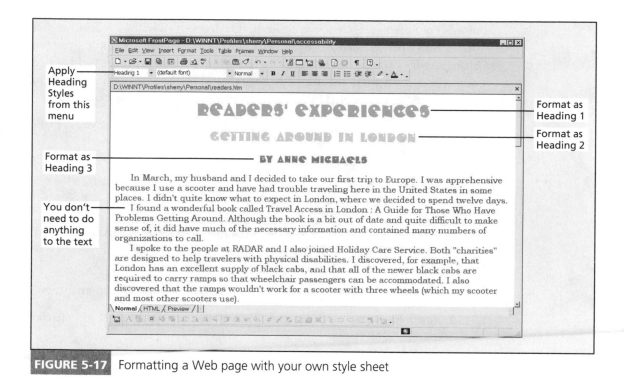

Apply Heading Styles from this menu

Format as Heading 1

Format as Heading 2

Format as Heading 3

You don't need to do anything to the text

FIGURE 5-17 Formatting a Web page with your own style sheet

3. Choose Format | Style Sheet Links and select the access.css document that you just created. Follow Figure 5-17 and apply the styles shown.

When you want to apply an original style sheet to your own pages, just select your style sheet and apply the styles from the Style menu to the text on your page.

Classes and ID Selectors

You might discover as you design your Web that you have several different types of paragraphs that you want to create. In many publications, for example, the first paragraph under a heading is styled differently than the remaining paragraphs. When you create cascading style sheets, you can build all of these different paragraph styles. If you have several different possibilities for a specific tag, you can create several different *classes*. A class takes the format p.first (i.e., the tag, a period, and a class name). If you want to create a specific style that you can use with a

> **Tip:** If you are wondering why you don't see the paragraphs justified, justified alignment only shows up in the preview of the page.

number of different tags, you can create an ID selector (this is just an identifier that begins with a period, such as .smallcaps). Using the ID Selector .smallcaps, you can change either a standard paragraph or a heading into small caps. Let's add both a new class and a new ID selector to the style sheet. You'd use the same methods to create any type of class or ID selector that you want. Follow these steps:

1. Make the access.css document active (or whichever style sheet you are currently creating).

2. Select Format | Style.

3. Click the New button. If you want to create a class, you need to type the element tag plus the class name. Type **p.first** as the name for the new style (p is the tag and first is the class).

4. To make the first line of this special paragraph show up with no indent, click Format. Select Paragraph. Enter **0** in the First Line Indent field. Click OK until all dialog boxes are closed. Save the style sheet.

Now you can create an ID selector that only changes the font effect to small caps:

1. Make the access.css document active (or whichever style sheet you are currently creating).

2. Click Format | Style.

3. Click the New button. If you want to create an ID selector, you need to type a period plus the ID name. Type **.smallcaps**.

4. Click Format and select Font. Click the "Small caps" checkbox. Click OK until all dialog boxes are closed. Save the style sheet.

You can apply these new styles to your page. Make the Web page active. To add the p.first style to your first paragraph, click the first paragraph in the document and select Normal.first in the Style menu.

If you want to use only small caps for the byline heading (the Heading 3 text that says "By Anne Michaels"), you can apply it by selecting the .smallcaps style from the Style menu.

Small caps are also frequently used for just a few words at the start of the first paragraph in a section. However, if you try to select the first line of the first paragraph and apply the .smallcaps style to it, your paragraph indent reappears and the entire paragraph changes to small caps. The reason is that FrontPage will only redefine an entire tag using the styles from the Style menu. You cannot format only part of a line.

Creating Inline Styles

"You cannot format only part of a line." That's a wonderful segue into the topic of inline styles. If you can't format part of a line using a style, then how can you do it?

You need to select the text that you want to style (for example, the words "In March, my husband and I" in the first paragraph of the Access-Ability document). Right-click the mouse and choose Font from the drop-down menu. You'll see the same Font dialog box that you've used all along. Click the "Small caps" checkbox to select it. Click OK. The words that you selected are now in small caps.

You can make any changes that you want to selected text in this manner. You can change the font, font size, font weight, font color, or font effect. This is a powerful feature, so use it sparingly.

Embedding Style Sheets

If you have styles that you want to define for only one page of your Web, you can place the style definitions directly into that page (i.e., *embed* them). If you select the Style command from the Format menu while a Web page is open in Page view, FrontPage automatically writes the style definition that you create into the <head> section of the page.

Cross-Reference: Chapter 9 describes the parts of an HTML page.

The embedded style sheets work exactly the way that the linked style sheets do, but you can only use the definitions in that one page. You create the styles exactly as you did the linked style sheets.

Here's a way to redefine the Citation tag for this one page so that you can use it to style the title of the book mentioned in paragraph 2 of the Access-Ability document you've been creating. You will first create the style definition and then use it to change the way that the Citation effect is applied to text in this page.

1. Make the Access-Ability document about London active in Normal Page view.

2. Choose Format | Style. In the "All HTML tags" list, select Cite. Click Modify. Click Format and select Font. Figure 5-18 shows the changes that you need to make.

3. Back out of all of the dialog boxes.

4. Select the text "Travel Access in London: A Guide for Those Who Have Problems Getting Around" in the second paragraph.

5. Right-click the mouse and choose Font from the drop-down menu. Select the Citation checkbox. The preview won't show your changed style. Click OK. Your title is italicized and changed to all caps.

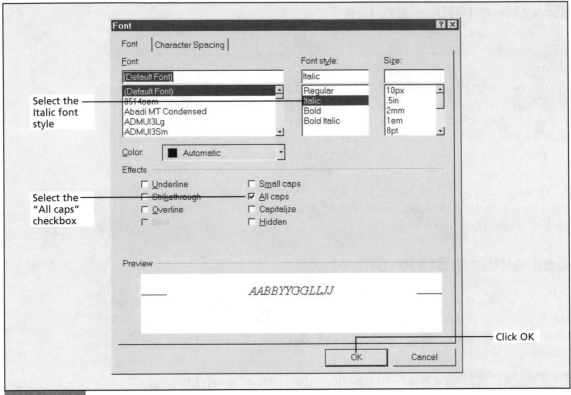

Select the Italic font style

Select the "All caps" checkbox

Click OK

FIGURE 5-18 Redefining the Citation effect

As you can see in Figure 5-19, you have more choices for effects in this dialog box than you have when you are creating a style (as in Figure 5-18). Most of the Effects checkboxes that aren't shown on Figure 5-18 (but which are on Figure 5-19) are actually HTML tags that you can redefine using CSS.

Themes and Style Sheets

So far, you've been applying styles and cascading style sheets to pages that don't contain themes. When you apply a theme to a Web or to a page, you need to modify the style sheet for the theme if you want to make style changes.

When you apply the theme, click the Apply Using CSS checkbox to select it. To modify the text styles in the theme, click Modify and then Text. The dialog boxes should all be familiar by now, and you modify the styles the same way that you have done before.

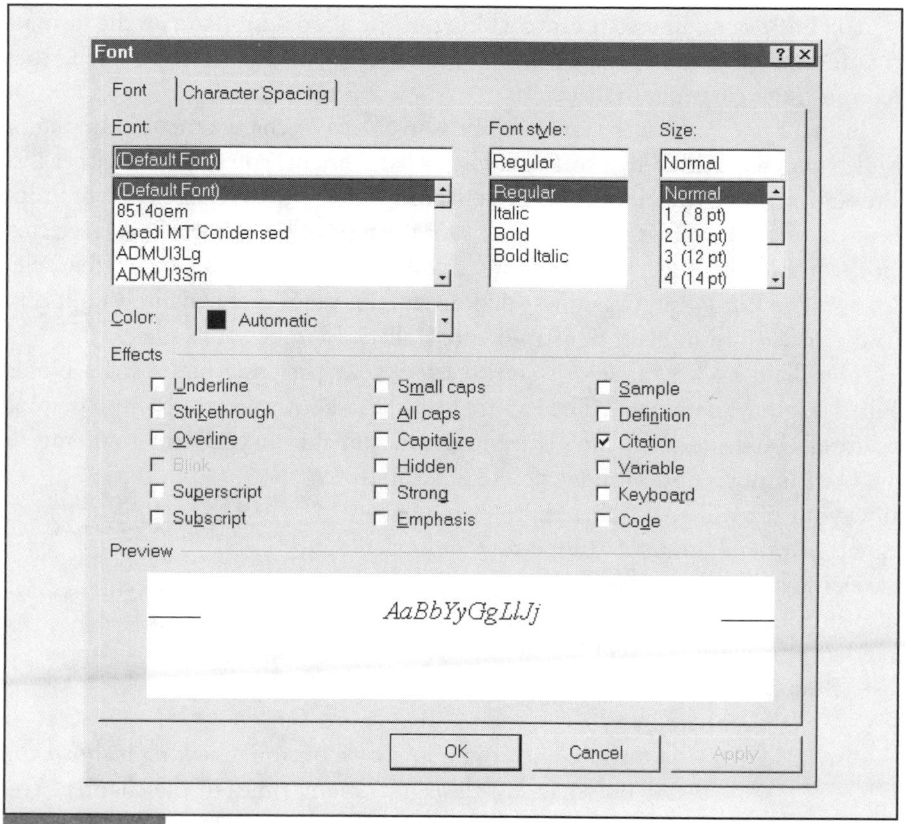

FIGURE 5-19   Selecting the Citation effect

When you've made your changes, save the theme itself under a new name so that you don't overwrite the settings for the original theme. I generally just add a number to the altered theme when I save it (such as Clear Day 2).

List Management 101

Another major element in page layout is the list. While this can be a seriously misused and overused element, the list is very handy element to have available. A list can help you to organize the page and add structure to your document. You can use a list to present a numbered series of items (*an ordered list*), a series of bulleted points (*an unordered list*), or even a specially formatted set of definitions (*the definition list*). The most commonly used lists are the numbered and bulleted lists.

Tip: If you find that the Apply Using CSS checkbox in the Theme dialog box is grayed out, you need to change your Compatibility option to Internet Explorer Only (Tools | Page Options | Compatibility). I'm not sure if this is a bug or a feature. Since Netscape Navigator 4.5 supports CSS in a somewhat different manner, it could be Microsoft's way of trying to shield you from mistakes.

You create a numbered list by clicking the Numbered List icon on the formatting toolbar (shown in Figure 5-6). You can create bulleted lists by clicking that icon in the formatting toolbar.

FrontPage gives you the same ability as in Word to change the numbering or bullets on your lists. When you right-click a list element, you can select either List Properties or List Item Properties from the drop-down menu. The List Item Properties choice only shows you the options for the type of list element that is selected (for example, the Bulleted List options if you have right-clicked a bulleted list element). The List Properties shows you four different tabs that contain list options. You can select from Plain Bullets, Picture Bullets, Numbers, or Other.

The Plain Bullets tab allows you to select your preferred bullet style (None, Filled, Hollow, or Square). The Picture Bullets tab allows you to specify a graphic to use as a bullet or allows you to use the graphic bullet from your current theme.

The Numbers option allows you to determine how your list will be numbered. You can use ordinals, Roman numerals (uppercase or lowercase), or letters (uppercase or lowercase). You can also turn off numbering completely. The Other tab lets you specify the HTML definition of the list (Bulleted, Definition, Directory, Menu, or Numbered).

Tip: When you have a theme selected for a Web, the bullets used are those that come from the theme unless you specifically change the settings.

Tip: Many browsers don't understand the Menu or Directory lists, so test before you use these.

Each of the tabs also contains a Style button. Clicking it shows the same dialog box that you've seen so many times in the chapter. You can click Format and specify the font or the paragraph (or the border, numbering, or position). You can create styles for your lists directly from within the Style dialog box.

Cross-Reference: Chapter 7 contains more information about graphic bullets. Chapter 13 contains more information about creating collapsing lists.

Some Thoughts on Page Design

As you lay out your page, keep in mind the visual appearance of the text. Text is a graphic element when you look at it rather than try to read it. Stand a few feet away from your preview and see if the shape and color of the text is pleasing to the eye. Notice if anything on the page jumps out at you.

If you use a lot of bold or italic, those elements will stand out from the page. It is **really** *distracting* to read a *sentence* where the *author* feels it *necessary* to create **emphasis** *every* few words. (See what I mean?)

Colors can also be distracting. Try to change text colors only where there is a structural reason to do so. If you make every word a different color, the page might look lovely, but no one will want to read it.

Watch your margins. If you allow the text to go from edge to edge in the browser, you might feel as if the text is screaming for more room. Use your white space (the empty space on the page) to allow the text (and your graphics) to breathe.

Also watch your page length. You can treat your Web site as if it were a book (with short pages) or an unfolding scroll that rolls and rolls. A book metaphor forces your user to make constant decisions about which page to view next, but it keeps the mousing around down to a minimum (since the viewer doesn't need to scroll in order to read the material on your page). The scroll metaphor removes the need for the site visitor to make viewing choices, but by the time that the visitor reaches the end of the page, he or she might have forgotten what was at the top! Would you enjoy reading *War and Peace* in one long scroll? You need to find the right balance. Because this balance changes based on the material on the page itself, I really can't give you any definite guidelines.

An old typographical maxim states that "If people notice your typography, you've overdone it."

Professional Skills Summary

You really jumped into FrontPage with this chapter, and if you've completed all of the exercises in the chapter, you should feel quite pleased with yourself.

In this chapter, you've learned to place text on your page. You've learned how to enter text, read text from a file, drag and drop text, and check your spelling. You've learned how to use search and replace.

You've learned how to tell FrontPage about the browsers that your site visitors are expected to use. You've learned how to format a page using plain HTML features that are supported by every browser. You can select a style from the Styles menu on the formatting toolbar, and change the font, font size, font effect, and font color. You can create indented text and text with line breaks but no paragraph breaks. You can create numbered and bulleted lists.

You've also learned how to create linked, embedded, and inline cascading style sheets. You can modify the styles in a theme.

In the next chapter, you'll learn how to create hyperlinks.

chapter 6

Using Hyperlinks

In this chapter, you:

- Learn to create hyperlinks between text and graphics

- Learn how to create bookmarks to link to a specific location on a page

- Learn how to select links to pages in your Web, pages on your local system, or pages on the Web

- Learn how to create and select custom colors for links

- Learn how to edit and remove links

- Learn how to design your navigation system

Links provide the glue that holds the Web together. If you couldn't get from here to there, the Web would not be a web. It would have no real function, and you would not be able to "surf." It really is the hyperlink that weaves the Web.

In this chapter, you'll learn how these hyperlinks work.

A Hyperlink Primer

Back in my high school days, I took public transportation to school. To change bus lines required a transfer pass. So long as I had a transfer pass, I could ride the city of Philadelphia's buses all day long. Hyperlinks are your transfer pass to the World Wide Web. They allow you to cross between sections in a Web page, pages in a Web site, and sites all over the globe.

You have only two ways to reach a page on the Web. You can directly type in the exact Uniform Resource Locator (URL)—the address of the Web site. Your other alternative is to use your "transfer pass" and click on a hyperlink. The URL will take you where you tell it to go; the hyperlink can send you on a journey whose serendipitous route can lead you on a path that you couldn't possibly predict.

Hyperlinks allow you to "transfer" on either text or graphics. You can define almost any element in a Web page as a hyperlink. Basically, a hyperlink is something that you can click to get somewhere else.

Hyperlinks have great power, but they need to be used with thought and care. The earliest form of hyperlinks were text links—hypertext.

What's Hypertext?

The first hyperlink-type material that I ever used was "programmed instruction." It was print-based. As the students read a self-study course, they were asked a question on the material that they had just read. If they got the question right, they were instructed to read the next portion of the course. If they got the answer wrong, they were sent to another location to read the material again presented in a slightly different way. This was an early form of hypertext in that it changed the normal, linear way in which books have been read for centuries.

You can also purchase adventure books that give you places where you need to make a decision. Do you go one way or another? Does the monster hide in the grove or come down from a tree? Your decision sends you to another part of the story, and by your decisions you actually change the outcome of the tale. Although this form of nonlinear reading is also in print, it, too, is a precursor of hypertext.

Hypertext is an online technique that allows you to get immediate information about something that the site author thinks is of interest. If you read an article on the presidents of the United States, you can follow links to learn more about George Washington, Abraham Lincoln, or even James Buchanan.

The World Wide Web abounds with hypertext links. It is one of the most common (and most poorly used) elements on the Web. A typical paragraph of text on the Web might look something like this:

> HomeNClosures is proud to announce a new variety of **greenhouse** rooms. The rooms use a new **honeycomb material** developed by **Craft-Built** that resists moisture and provides an outstanding new **insulation** capacity. These rooms cost much less than the **traditional greenhouse** additions and …

The paragraph above shows the use of hypertext links. It also shows a selection of the problems with using hypertext links, some of which are listed here:

1. In purely visual terms, the paragraph is dreadful. The bold, underlined text (which would be colored and underlined on the Web) jumps out at you and makes it difficult to concentrate on the message that you're reading. All you can see is the links.

2. You have no clue where a link will take you. You don't know if it takes you deeper into the site or sends you somewhere else entirely.

3. As the site designer, why would you want to immediately send someone to another site when you just managed to get his or her attention at this one? If you send your visitors away, you have no guarantee that they will return.

4. If you follow each link as it is presented and then return to this site to finish reading the paragraph, will you have any clue at all what the original paragraph said?

Since you need to use hypertext as one of your most frequent linking devices, you need to learn to use it well. Perhaps the most basic question that the designer forgot to ask when writing the "bad example" above is "What is the purpose for providing this link?" If the answer is "Because I can," then the link should be removed.

You need to provide links that both enhance your visitor's experience with your site and serve your purpose for having the site. It can be a delicate balance. Wherever possible, you should avoid sending your readers away in the middle of a paragraph. You can provide the links in the margin of the article, or you can provide the links at the end of the article. Either way can work. Let's look at the paragraph, shown in Figure 6-1, again.

You can now read the paragraph without feeling compelled to jump all over the known universe. The text now talks to you rather than screaming at you. The margin is a bit loud, but you can ignore it if you want. It was very hard to ignore the links in the original paragraph. The one problem with the margin links is that you still don't have a good idea where the links will lead. In Figure 6-2, you see that placing the links under the text allows you more room for explanation, but

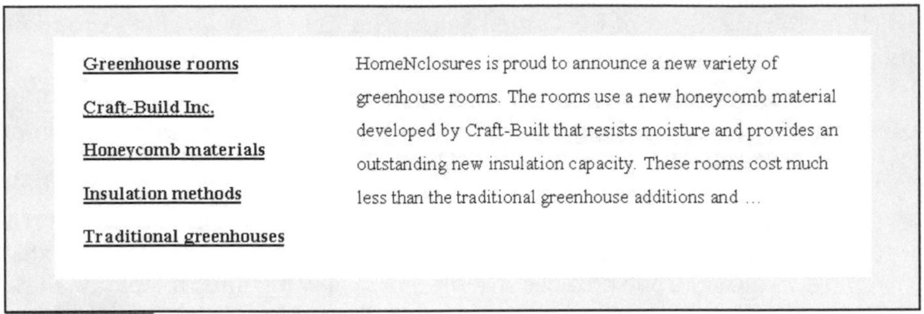

Greenhouse rooms

Craft-Build Inc.

Honeycomb materials

Insulation methods

Traditional greenhouses

HomeNclosures is proud to announce a new variety of greenhouse rooms. The rooms use a new honeycomb material developed by Craft-Built that resists moisture and provides an outstanding new insulation capacity. These rooms cost much less than the traditional greenhouse additions and ...

FIGURE 6-1 Hypertext links placed in the margin

now the links look as if they are more important than the text and dwarf the paragraph about your great new product.

Figure 6-3 shows another possible solution. You can make the links much smaller and less conspicuous. Placing the links inside of a sentence, however, still causes a distraction as you read the paragraph. Of course, another solution is to decide which links you really have to have. In the example paragraph, the only one that is really going to be of great interest to the readers is the one that allows them to view the new greenhouse products. Once they like the greenhouses, they might want to learn more about the honeycomb material that would help to insulate the room addition to cut down on the heating bills. In very few cases would the reader care to learn more about the company that manufactures the material. To send the readers to learn about traditional greenhouse design is counterproductive to the purpose of

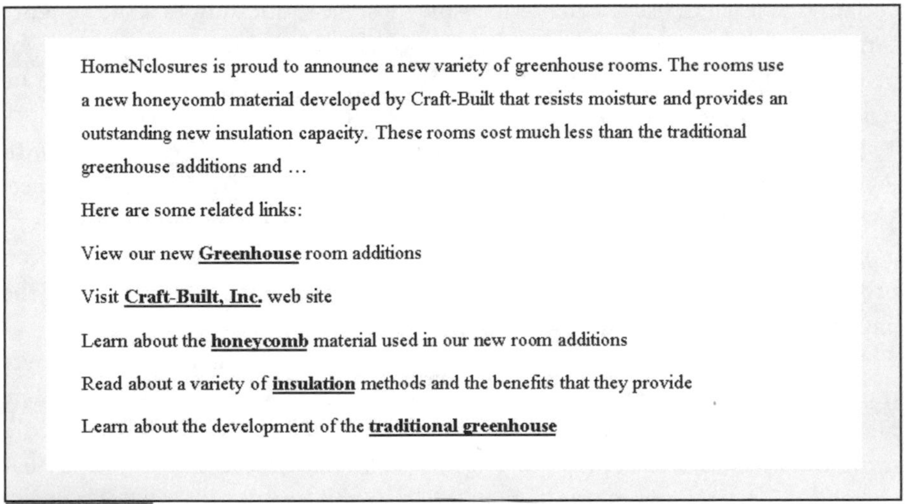

HomeNclosures is proud to announce a new variety of greenhouse rooms. The rooms use a new honeycomb material developed by Craft-Built that resists moisture and provides an outstanding new insulation capacity. These rooms cost much less than the traditional greenhouse additions and ...

Here are some related links:

View our new **Greenhouse** room additions

Visit **Craft-Built, Inc.** web site

Learn about the **honeycomb** material used in our new room additions

Read about a variety of **insulation** methods and the benefits that they provide

Learn about the development of the **traditional greenhouse**

FIGURE 6-2 Hyperlinks placed at the end of the paragraph

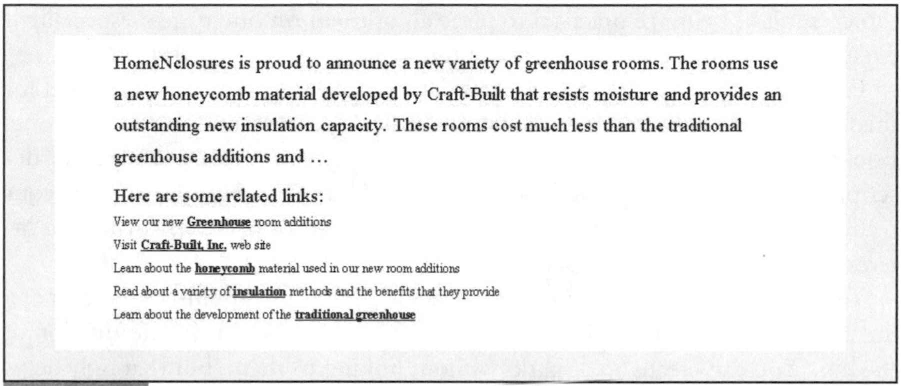

HomeNclosures is proud to announce a new variety of greenhouse rooms. The rooms use a new honeycomb material developed by Craft-Built that resists moisture and provides an outstanding new insulation capacity. These rooms cost much less than the traditional greenhouse additions and …

Here are some related links:

View our new **Greenhouse** room additions

Visit **Craft-Built, Inc.** web site

Learn about the **honeycomb** material used in our new room additions

Read about a variety of **insulation** methods and the benefits that they provide

Learn about the development of the **traditional greenhouse**

FIGURE 6-3 The links can be made smaller so that they don't overwhelm the paragraph

selling them the new greenhouse addition unless the selection compares the two and points out the reasons why the new product is better.

Once you learn about JavaScript, you'll learn about a simple way not just to list the links but to place a description of the link in the status area of the browser. Instead of displaying the URL to which the link will go, you can show the site visitor a text description of the link. This solves the problem of having the links overshadow the original material.

Cross-Reference: Learn about JavaScript in Chapter 13. *Hotwired Style: Principles for Building Smart Web Sites* by Jeffrey Veen (Hardwired, 1997) is an excellent resource if you want to learn more about the creative and clear use of links. Another excellent resource is *Web Navigation: Designing the User Experience* by Jennifer Fleming and Richard Koman (O'Reilly and Associates, 1998).

Creating Basic Links and Bookmarks

FrontPage makes linking text and images easy. You can link to something on the current page, something on your site, or something on a site anywhere else on the Web. FrontPage distinguishes between links on the same page and links anywhere else. Links to the same page are called *bookmarks*.

Creating bookmarks

If a bookmark is a link to the current page, what purpose is served by creating one? After all, you're already on that page!

Pages on the Web can be of any length. Although you are usually advised to keep your pages short, if you have a long list of items that belong to a specific topic, it might be more practical to place all of them on one page—especially if what you need to say about each topic is not long.

Figure 6-4 shows a page taken from the Village Flowers Web site created for this book. Here, a list of seasonal bouquets leads to a description of each one. Bookmarks are an appropriate way to deal with this type of information. The descriptions are too small to merit their own page, but it is awkward to make your reader actually wade through every description to find the bouquet that's of interest. The bookmark is the perfect compromise.

You need to perform two different steps in order to use bookmarks as part of a link. You need to first create the bookmark, and then use it as the destination of the link. You can create bookmarks without linking to them, but that only helps you as the page designer. Your site visitors cannot use the bookmarks that you create unless you link to them.

You can use the example shown in Figure 6-4 (flower.htm to be found on the Web site for this book) and follow along to create linked bookmarks, or you can use any page of your own. You will first create the bookmarks, and then you'll use them as the link destination. Follow these steps:

1. To create a bookmark, select the text that you want to bookmark. Since the bookmark will be the link destination, the selected text should be the location where you want your site visitor to end up after they've clicked the link. If you're using our example, select the text "A January heart-warmer" that is under the bulleted list (not in the list).

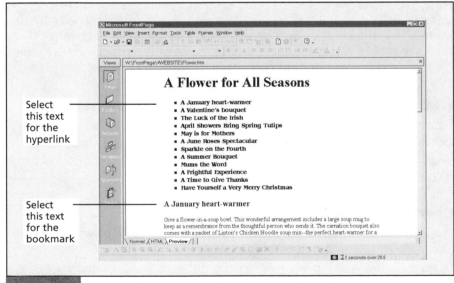

FIGURE 6-4 A page of product descriptions from Village Flowers

2. Choose Insert | Bookmark. The selected text appears as the bookmark name. Click OK.

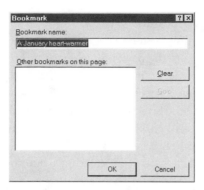

3. Repeat Step 2 for all of the bookmarks that you want to define on the page. In the Village Flowers example, you would define each Heading 3 in front of a description as a bookmark. The "Other Bookmarks on this page" section lists the already created bookmarks so that you can remember what you've done.

4. Now you can create the link. When you link to a bookmark, FrontPage helps you. Choose Insert | Hyperlink. Figure 6-5 shows you the Bookmark drop-down menu. Select a bookmark from the list and click OK.

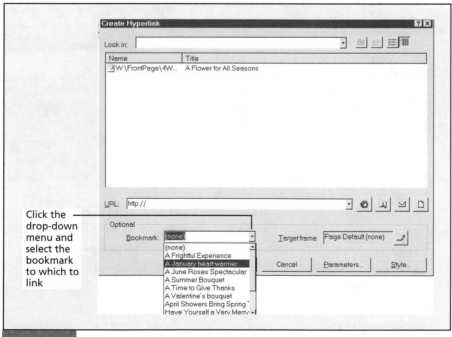

FIGURE 6-5   Defining a bookmark as a hyperlink

5. Define the rest of the bulleted list as hyperlinks to the appropriate bookmarks.

Linking to a new page

Tip: You can create a hyperlink using the keyboard shortcut of CTRL-K.

You can also link from one page in your Web to another. Even if you choose not to use the navigational features of FrontPage, you can create links that take your site visitors from one page to another. If you want to follow a specific example, download the Candyman Web from the Osborne book site using the Import Web Wizard (File | New Web | Import Web Wizard) and follow along. If not, you can use your own example to link pages together.

This example is actually easier than creating a bookmark, because it only requires one step:

1. Open the page that you want to link from. If you want to use our example, open the news.htm page in the Candyman Web.

2. Select the text that you want use as the link. In our example, select the word "Bracset" near the bottom of the news article.

3. Choose Insert | Hyperlink. Figure 6-6 shows the same dialog box as Figure 6-5, but your choices now include all of the pages in the active Web. Select the page that you want to link to. If you are following our example, select bracset.htm. Its name appears in the URL box as shown. Click OK to make the link appear. Your selected text will change color and become underlined—which is the Web convention for hyperlinks. Figure 6-6 also explains the other buttons of the dialog box, and you'll refer back to this figure later.

Linking to another site

Finally, you can link to any other site on the Web or to a file on your hard drive (although that is not a practical option to use because all of the files need to be available all of the time for a Web site to work properly).

Of the example sites created for this book, the "My Skate Web" site is designed to feature links from the Web site to a variety of skating sites across the world. You can download the MySkate Web from the Osborne Web site for this book (again, if you download it, do so by selecting File | New Web | Import Web) and follow the directions below, or you can use any page that you've created as an example.

When you link to another site, you need to enter the exact URL of the page or you need to locate the specific document interactively online. The now familiar Insert | Hyperlink dialog box allows you to choose either method of linking.

1. Open the link1.htm page in the MySkate Web that you downloaded or open a page of your own on which you want to create an external hyperlink. Figure 6-7

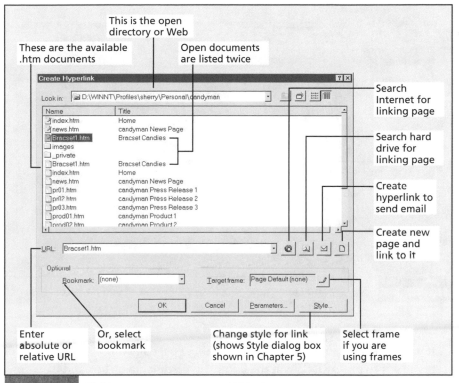

FIGURE 6-6   Linking to a page on your Web site

shows the Skating Links page and the text that you should select if you are following our example. If you are using your own, select the text that you want to turn into a link.

2. The dialog box shown in Figure 6-6 appears. Make sure that you are connected to the Internet and then click the button shown as "Search Internet for linking page" on Figure 6-6.

3. Switch to your browser and use your Favorites folder (or the URL) to navigate to the linking location. The URL of the USFSA (United States Figure Skating Association) is http://www.usfsa.org. Type this into your browser if you're using our example; if not, type in the URL of the page to which you want to link.

4. Switch back to FrontPage. The URL in your browser has been transferred to the URL field in the Create Hyperlink dialog box.

5. Click OK to save the link and exit the dialog box.

Tip: After you've created the link, save the page. I found that sometimes FrontPage "forgets" a link that it has just created this way. Saving the page seems to improve its memory.

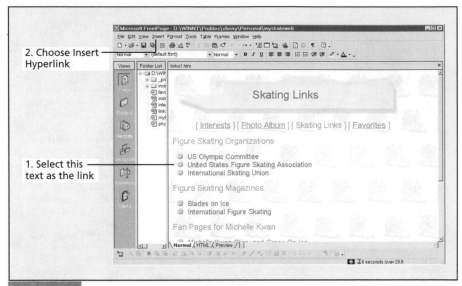

2. Choose Insert Hyperlink

1. Select this text as the link

FIGURE 6-7 The Skating Links page shows the text that needs to become a link

If you have to type in the URL of the linking page in your browser, why not just type it into the URL field in the Create Hyperlink dialog box and have done with it? Frankly, that's just what I usually do. However, if you make a typing mistake, you're stuck with a broken link whereas if you search the Web for the link, you know you've got a valid URL. Again, this is your choice.

Cross-Reference: You can also use FrontPage to check the validity of all of your links. You'll find out how in Chapter 9.

Remember, when you link to an external site, you have no guarantee that the page will always be there. You need to periodically check all of the links in your site to make sure that they remain valid.

The Color of Links

By default, the color of linked text on the Internet is blue. Some books on Web creation advise that you not tamper with this color because many users think that all links are supposed to be blue and that if something is not blue, then it is not a link. Personally, I feel that most users are intelligent enough to figure it out. I see the underlining as the clue to "click here." I prefer to change the colors of the link to coordinate with my screen décor.

Some Web designers have decided to go fairly far in the other direction and they will not change the color of a link or differentiate it from the text in any way.

They feel that the site visitors can find a link by running their cursors over the text to see what pops up on the status bar. I think that that attitude creates a lovely unified page that is almost actively user-hostile. However, you need to make your own decision for your pages.

You can change the color and the style of the text link using many of the same dialog boxes that you used in Chapter 5 to alter the color, font, and font size. Just as you learned in Chapter 5, however, you have several ways in which you can change your link colors depending on whether or not you are using cascading style sheets or whether or not you are using a theme. If you use CSS and no theme, you can click on the Style button at the bottom of the Create Hyperlink dialog box.

Your least efficient procedure is to select the linked text and use the Font and Font Size menus on the formatting toolbar to change the properties of the link. This is inefficient because you need to select the links one at a time to make the changes this way (unless they are all bunched together and can be selected as a group).

A much better procedure to define link colors is to use the Page Properties dialog box. You haven't seen this one discussed before. It only works when the page contains no theme. To try it, close all of your open Webs and follow these steps:

1. Create a new Web page (File | New | Page | Normal Page) or open a page in a Web that has no theme attached.

2. If the page appears with a theme attached to it, choose Format | Theme and select the No Theme option in the list of possible Themes. Close the Themes dialog box.

3. Right-click on the blank page. From the menu, select Page Properties. Click the Background tab. Figure 6-8 explains the Background dialog box options for choosing hyperlink colors.

Although you did change some colors in Chapter 5, you didn't see an in-depth look at the dialog boxes that FrontPage uses to set color. These dialog boxes are consistent throughout the entire application, even if the color selections appear on a variety of different dialog boxes. Let's take a few moments for a closer look at selecting colors (for text, for graphics, or for anything in FrontPage that needs a color).

Selecting standard colors

FrontPage contains three different color selection methods. They are the Standard colors, the Custom colors, and More colors. The standard colors appear when you first choose to change a color property.

Tip: Keep your links colored consistently. You have three types of links—normal (you've never clicked on it), active (your mouse is on top of it or it is the currently selected link), and visited (you've been there)—and each type may have a different color. For the sake of your users, however, you should not use more than one color for any type of link. If normal links can be red, green, or pink and visited links are yellow or purple, your user quickly loses all sense of color as a clue to site behavior. You may be a little less careful about size consistency in links. If you need to have links that use more than one size of text throughout the site, it should not cause confusion. The link should conform to the size of the surrounding text.

Tip: When you want to change the hyperlink style for a page that uses a theme, you need to modify that theme. You'll learn how in Chapter 7.

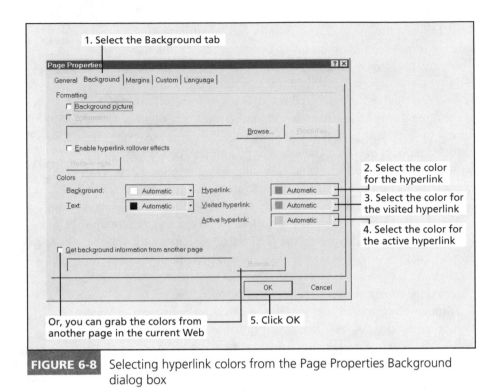

FIGURE 6-8 Selecting hyperlink colors from the Page Properties Background dialog box

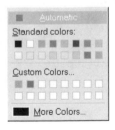

This is the main menu for color choice. Simply pick the color that you want by clicking on it. If the standard colors don't contain the color that you want, you can select one from the Custom Colors group if you see one that you like. The custom colors are colors that you have defined. When you first install FrontPage, there are no custom colors in the Custom Colors palette. However, you can easily create one. I'll show you how after we look at the More Colors option.

Selecting more colors

The More Colors dialog box appears when you click on a More Colors button in a color dialog box. Figure 6-9 shows the More Colors dialog box and all of its options.

The main feature of the More Colors screen is that it contains a hexagon filled with many colors. This is the Web-safe palette. The colors in this hexagon can be displayed in any browser on any 256-color computer without dithering (i.e., as a solid color rather than as a color that is made up of different-colored pixels). The colors might not look the same on every computer, but they will look better on

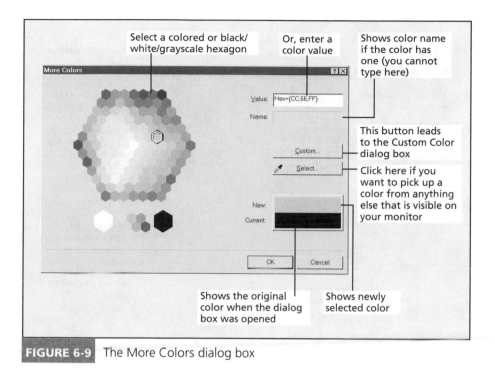

Select a colored or black/white/grayscale hexagon

Or, enter a color value

Shows color name if the color has one (you cannot type here)

This button leads to the Custom Color dialog box

Click here if you want to pick up a color from anything else that is visible on your monitor

Shows the original color when the dialog box was opened

Shows newly selected color

FIGURE 6-9 The More Colors dialog box

monitors that only display 256 colors than any color that is not in this list. If you think that your target audience will be using standard VGA colors, then pick most (or all) of your colors from this window.

The other notable feature in this dialog box is the Select button (the one with the eyedropper on it). The eyedropper is a common symbol in graphics programs that means you can click on a color anywhere in the screen and make that color the selected one. The benefit is that by choosing the Select button, you could set your link color to the color of a pixel in an open graphic anywhere on your screen, and make a better match for your text. Simply click the button and then move the cursor over your window. The New button changes as you move your cursor. When you see the color that you want, click the left mouse button. That "sucks up" the color into the eyedropper. Then, click the OK button to exit the dialog box.

Selecting custom colors

If you don't want/need to select a Web-safe color or select a color from an open document, you can create a custom color. You can reach the Custom Colors dialog box from within the Standard Colors palette or the More Colors screen by

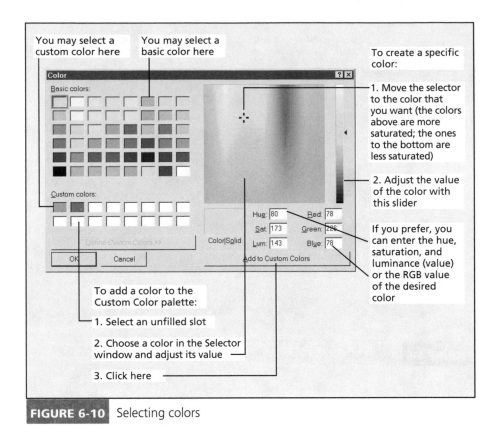

FIGURE 6-10 Selecting colors

clicking the button or text that says Custom. Figure 6-10 shows the Custom Color dialog box and explains its options.

FrontPage makes it fairly easy to select a custom color, and quite easy to add the first custom color to the palette. But creating a family of related custom colors is almost diabolical. If you simply create the color that you want and then click the Add to Custom Colors button, you always replace the *first* color in the Custom Colors palette. That's less than helpful.

For example, you might want to create your links so that you use three shades of green (dark for a hyperlink, bright for an active link, and light for a visited link). You want the colors to be from the same green family. Therefore, you need to create the colors in several steps, as follows:

1. After you have saved your first custom color, you need to create the second custom color by adjusting the value slider.

2. Make note of the new color's RGB values. *Don't* add the color to the Custom Colors palette.

3. Now, click an unused slot in the palette. The color changes immediately to white (and clicking your original color will only select that custom color slot).

4. Type in the RGB value that you noted.

5. Now you can click the Add to Custom Colors button and you will fill the selected slot instead of replacing your previous color.

Editing Links

You can edit a link by right-clicking the link and selecting Hyperlink Properties from the drop-down menu.

You'll see the same dialog box as shown in Figure 6-6 (but it will be titled Edit Hyperlink). You can make any changes that you want.

You can change the linking text without changing the link. To do this, select the underlined link text and type in the changes that you want.

> **Tip:** When you want to create related colors that only differ in value, create the first one and jot down its hue and saturation. The new color should use the same hue and saturation with a different luminosity (or brightness) value as the only change.

Breaking Links

Sometimes, you might want to get rid of a hyperlink entirely. If you cut the link, that certainly removes it, but it also removes the associated text. If you want to leave your text unchanged but remove the link from it, right-click the link and select Hyperlink Properties. In the URL field, completely remove the link reference and leave the field blank. Click OK. The text reverts to normal text and the link is removed.

Cross-Reference: Chapter 7 discusses the difference between linking text and linking graphics.

Creating a Mailto Link

You can also create a link that sends an email. It is common Web courtesy to place a contact email at the bottom of every page. You can use the Shared Borders feature so that you only need to create your email link once per Web.

Here's a fast way to try out this feature:

1. Create new Web page (File | New | Page | Normal Page). It doesn't need to be part of a Web, but you could use any page that you want, themed or not.

2. Type **Contact:** and your email address (or whatever text you want to use to describe the person to whom the email will go). You don't need to have the specific email address listed, but site visitors usually like to see it.

3. Select the text and choose Insert | Hyperlink.

4. From the Create Hyperlink dialog box, click the Envelope icon as shown in Figure 6-6. The Create E-mail Hyperlink dialog box appears.

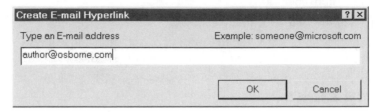

5. Enter the desired email address (yours, if you entered your own name into the link text), and click OK. If the site visitor clicks that link, their default mail program will open ready to compose a new message.

Navigating Your Site

Hyperlinks are usually thought of as the text links that allow you to move through the Web site and connect to other sites to "surf the Web." However, you also need to create the internal page-to-page linking that glues your site together. In Chapter 4, you saw how FrontPage could automate that entire process.

The FrontPage-specific features that are used for navigation are the Navigation view (to create the site hierarchy), the navigation bar (which specifies the automatic links to show), and the Shared Borders feature (which standardizes the list of links shown on each page). Together, the three features create a very strong package to weave your Web into a seamless cloth.

The basic tenet of Web site navigation is that every page in the Web needs to be linked to something. You need a way to get to the page and to get off of the page (without having to use the Next and Back browser buttons). You especially need to have a way to access the page. A page that has no incoming links is like a house with no doors and windows. It could be very cozy inside, but you'll never find out because you can't get inside the house.

Cross-Reference: Chapter 9 talks about the reports that you can use to locate unlinked files.

Navigation Philosophy

One of the best categorizations of Web sites that I ever read appeared in the *Hotwired Style* book recommended at the start of this chapter. The authors divided Web sites into a continuum of library vs. gallery sites. A library site is a site that exists for the purpose of obtaining information. This can be a list site like about.com or a shopping site or a corporate presence site. The critical thing about a library site is that the site visitor wants to read or use the information that it contains. A gallery site, on the other hand, is a site where the surfing event itself is the important thing. Your site visitor is interested in the puzzles and "gee whiz" effects and the whole gestalt of "experiencing" the site.

To the degree that you are creating a library site, you need to make the navigation of the site as straightforward and simple as possible. It's not supposed to be a guessing game. Use buttons or standard underlined and colored hyperlinks, and create a simple hierarchical structure. If you are creating purely a gallery site, you can do anything you want. If you want to fly your visitors in on a virtual spaceship and have them hunt for flying objects that contain the links (or look word-by-word to see if anything happens if you click the word), it's your site—go for it! Just don't be surprised if you lose as many visitors as you enchant. In my examples, I have mostly created library sites rather than "user experiences" because that is usually what most site developers want.

Building a Navigation System

In Chapter 4, you learned the completely automated way to build your navigation system. The system was easy to create because you used a theme. Many of the pieces, such as the buttons and banners, were already created for you and in place.

You don't need to apply a theme or even use graphics, however, in order to be able to build an automatic navigation system. (What do I mean by "automatic"? It's a system that FrontPage automatically maintains when you add or delete pages.) All you need to do in order to create this system is

1. Enter all of your Web pages in the Navigation view and create the hierarchy.
2. Turn on your desired shared borders.
3. Determine the levels that you want on your navigation bars.

(You learned how to do all of this with a theme in Chapter 4.) If you don't use a theme, the graphics will not automatically be there for you, but in Chapter 7 you'll see how you can attach graphics to use your buttons and bars (and build your own theme if you prefer). You can, however, select Text buttons in the Navigation Properties dialog box and that solves the problem.

If you find the idea of creating a totally blank Web a bit daunting, you can create a Web using one of the templates and remove the theme that is automatically added to the template. Your basic navigation remains in place.

Tip: If you don't use a theme—or if you significantly modify a theme—FrontPage doesn't always clearly show the shared borders. If you discover that text on one page is showing up on another page, you're not hallucinating. FrontPage has just decided that you entered that material in a shared border. Coax it out of the shared border area and all will be well.

Tip: To remove the theme from a Web, choose Format | Theme. In the list of themes on the left side of the windows, select No Theme and click OK.

Shared Borders and the Navigation Bar

I have very mixed feelings about FrontPage's shared borders and navigation bar feature. I really like the power that they give you to easily control the main navigational links in your site. I also get the feeling that they often use too much space.

Many of the theme buttons are too big. That is certainly one problem with it (however, you can use text links or create your own graphics). Another problem is the issue of flexibility. You might find that it makes more sense to specifically list the links that you want on each page.

One of the more awkward moments in creating a navigation system occurs when you reach the last page in a hierarchy. For example, in the Smythe's Web, the individual link pages are the ends of the hierarchy. They have no "lower-level" pages. If you define your navigation bar so that it shows the child level and there is no child level, what shows up on the navigation bar? Figure 6-11 shows this situation with the top border, and it's ugly. The notice to edit the navigation bar properties doesn't disappear when you preview the page. Removing the notice removes the bar from the entire shared border for the whole Web site.

The navigation bar properties are an all-or-nothing proposition when they are used in a shared border. If a page uses a shared border, the information that appears in the shared border is the same for every page.

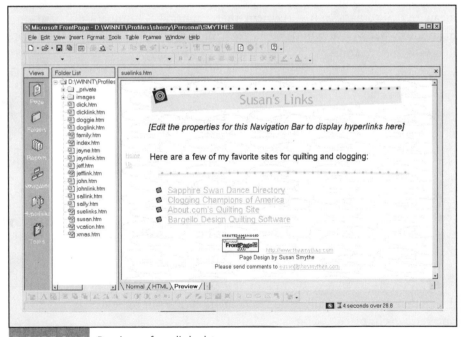

FIGURE 6-11   Preview of suelinks.htm

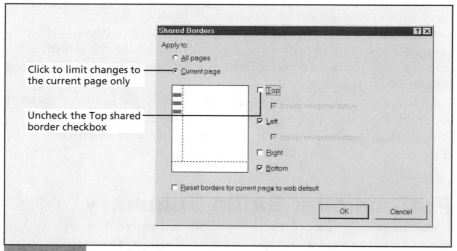

FIGURE 6-12   Removing a shared border for the current page

How, then, can you fix the problem? In the example shown for Susan's link page, if you added the home page or the parent page to the top shared border navigation bar, every page would have at least one button, and the error message would disappear.

You can also remove the shared border for the page. You need to open the Shared Borders command (Format | Shared Borders). Figure 6-12 shows you how to remove the Top shared border for just the current page.

Once the border is gone, you can insert a navigation bar that makes sense for the page. When you remove the shared border on Susan's link page, the page banner as well as the navigation bar disappears. Therefore, you would need to create a new page banner (Insert | Page Banner)

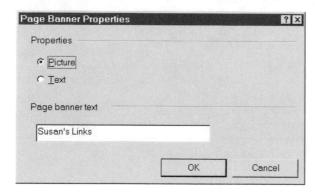

Click Picture to use the graphic that is part of the active theme.

You can also insert a new navigation bar that contains a better selection of links. Choose Insert | Navigation bar. Figure 6-13 shows the new choice for Susan's link page. You can certainly use whatever selection of buttons you feel most appropriate for your page.

Because the page is no longer part of a shared border, you can choose any set of buttons that you want. Figure 6-14 shows the Susan links page with a new navigation bar that uses the parent level (instead of the child level selected for the rest of the site).

Professional Skills Summary

In this chapter, you learned about hyperlinks and navigational systems. You learned how to create links that move within a Web page. You learned to create links that linked together the pages in your site. You also learned to specify links to pages over which you have no control (external pages).

You learned about selecting colors for links and about the need to be consistent in your color choices. You also learned about the need for consistency in creating your site navigation system. You revisited some of the material in Chapter 4 and learned how to add navigation to sites with no themes or sites with shared

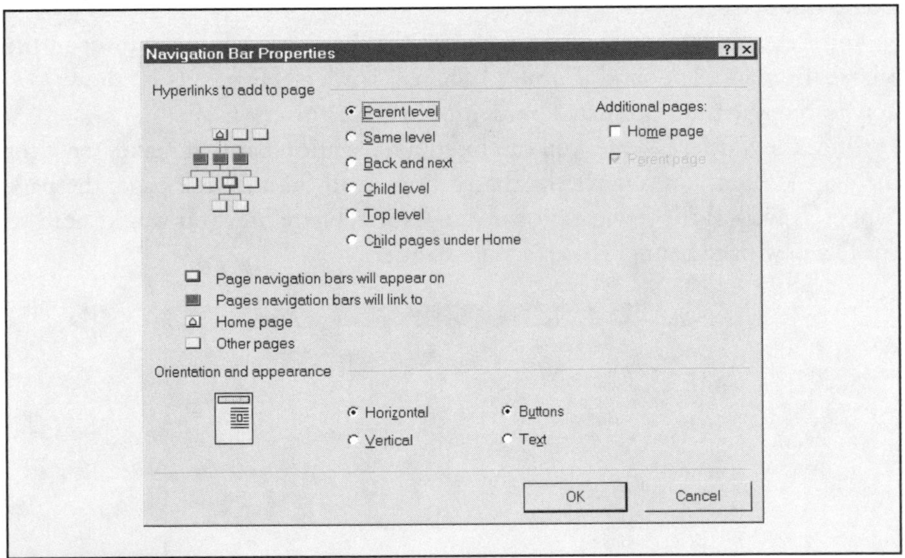

FIGURE 6-13   The Navigation Bar Properties dialog box

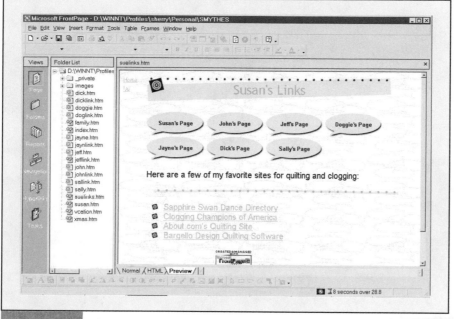

FIGURE 6-14 The new navigation bar

borders where the shared border selection on the navigation bar was not appropriate for a specific page. You learned how to add a new page banner and a new navigation bar.

In Chapter 7, you'll learn about adding graphics to your pages.

chapter 7

Great Graphics

In this chapter, you:

- Learn about the graphic formats available for use on the Web

- Learn what makes a graphic download quickly

- Learn about the Web-safe palette

- Learn to gracefully degrade sites with text alternatives for your graphics

- Learn how to position images on the screen precisely

- Learn ways to make text wrap around graphics

- Learn how to create links using images

- Learn about image maps

- Learn how FrontPage allows you to manipulate images

- Learn to create thumbnails for graphics-heavy sites

- Learn techniques for using background images and patterns

If I say that graphics makes the Web go 'round, I know that I'm showing my prejudice as a graphic designer. However, the Web without graphics is like a book on a monitor, but it isn't as easy to turn the pages electronically.

Graphics bring color and energy to the Web, and give it an excitement that it would not otherwise have. In this chapter, you'll learn how to use FrontPage to display graphics to add life to *your* Web pages.

An Introduction to Web Graphics

You are surfing the Internet and you reach a site that promises a rich graphics experience. You sit while the images begin to load, and you wait patiently for the first image to appear. And you wait…and you wait…and you wait…and when the page finally loads, it is glorious to behold—rich in color, music, and interactivity.

Is this your idea of heaven or hell?

Most Web surfers won't stay at a site beyond an initial brief period of waiting. The graphics rule #1 is that users want their images *fast*. On the Web, speed is everything.

Even if you never create a Web graphic, you will still need to acquire graphics for the Web and, perhaps, even prepare them so that they will download quickly. Although many of the topics on producing graphics for the Web (such as how to use a graphics program) are beyond the scope of this book, the problem of making graphics load quickly is very much within its domain.

As you learned in Chapter 3, you have many places from which you can acquire graphics. In the color pages, you can see a sample of the many sources available to you. You can create the images yourself in a painting program, create them in an illustration program, purchase conventional clip art, or purchase stock photographs. You can use a graphic from the FrontPage Clip Art Gallery, purchase graphics designed specifically for the Web, or download a variety of free artwork or linkware from the Web. You can scan photos that you've taken and prepare them for Web use, get photos developed onto PhotoCD, take photos and have them loaded automatically onto the Web for you, or take photos with a digital camera or a video camera and acquire them into your computer.

For all of the graphics, in any format and regardless of how you acquire them, you need to make sure that they are optimized for the Web.

Think Download Time

Good Web graphics are graphics that download quickly. Many Web users have old, slow machines at home and will not wait around for your dazzling graphics to load.

One of the keys to keeping users happy is to build a site that degrades gracefully. To *degrade gracefully* is Web jargon for a site that can accommodate all classes of users. If you first build your site for the lowest-common-denominator user, you can then add features that work on the newer browsers but leave the original HTML alone (cascading style sheets, for example).

For graphics, you can help your site to degrade gracefully by creating several types of placeholder files. You can make your downloads faster and smaller by limiting the number of colors used in an image. You can make life easier for folks who keep their graphics options turned off (or who are visually impaired and must have the site read to them by machine) by including text descriptions of your images as well as the images themselves.

Creating Low-Bandwidth Images

A low-bandwidth image is one that doesn't take much time to download. You can keep your site visitors interested while complex graphics download by giving them something to watch.

FrontPage allows you to create a preview image that loads first—while the "real" image is slowly being downloaded. You create this preview image in a graphics program. The preview image provides an interim image while the larger one downloads, which means that the preview image needs to load very quickly and be much smaller in file size (though identical in physical dimensions) than the real one.

You can create a black-and-white version of the image, a structure, or a totally unrelated image and use it as the preview image. Figure 7-1 shows four views of an image that is meant to fill the left side of the article for Access-Ability about getting around in London with a wheelchair. The image simply displays a narrow strip of images about London. The "real" image takes about 10 seconds to download on the 28.8-Kbps connection. The center two images download in about 2 seconds and the image grid downloads in less than 1 second. Any of the three preview images can keep the viewer interested as the full-resolution image downloads.

L▶ Tip: The Low-Res feature only works with Netscape Navigator. It uses the HTML attribute "lowsrc=" in the generated code, and that is a Netscape-only addition to standard HTML. If a site visitor's browser doesn't understand the tag, then it will show the intended full-resolution image. Therefore, you have no penalty to pay for using the Low-Res feature, even if some of your audience can't see it.

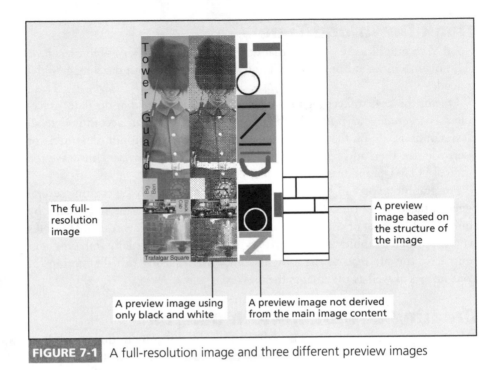

The full-resolution image

A preview image based on the structure of the image

A preview image using only black and white

A preview image not derived from the main image content

FIGURE 7-1   A full-resolution image and three different preview images

Here's how you tell FrontPage to use your preview image once you've created it:

1. Position the image on the page where you want it to go (I'll show you how to do that a bit later in this chapter).

2. Open the Picture Properties dialog box by right-clicking on the image and selecting Picture Properties from the menu. The General tab should already be selected.

3. Type in the location of the preview file or click on the Browse button to locate it on your hard drive. Click OK when you are done.

Alternative representations

Low-Res: file:///W:/FrontPage/images/guardline.gif   Browse...

Text:

Limiting Your Palette

You can also create low-bandwidth, fast-loading images by preparing your graphics properly and optimizing them for the Web. To help make an intelligent choice of file format, you need to understand a little bit about Web graphics formats. The Web has three graphics formats that it likes or tolerates. They are GIF (pronounced as either "gif" as in "green" or "jif" as in peanut butter), JPG (pronounced "J-Peg"), and PNG (pronounced "ping").

In order to make an image suitable for the Web, you need to do two things:

- Reduce its number of pixels to something that can physically be seen at full size on your screen

- Reduce the colors in the file or compress it to shorten the download times

A photographic image should be compressed as a JPG file. Even if the GIF file version of a photograph actually looks better than a JPG image with heavy compression, the JPG image will download faster.

JPG (or JPEG) stands for Joint Photographic Experts Group (/www.jpeg.org/ public/jpeghomepage.htm). This standard is a *lossy data* compression scheme (which means that it doesn't keep every pixel in the original image). When you JPEG an image, the process looks at the image as if it were on a grid. Within each grid of 8 × 8 pixels, the colors are averaged based on the quality setting that you select. The higher the quality setting, the less the color is blended within the grid squares. In all cases, however, the saved JPG image contains pixels that are changed from the original. The lower quality settings produce images with visible damage; the higher quality settings produce images that are changed but do not display the artifacting that is so typical of a JPEG image.

The JPEG compression scheme makes an awful mess of images that contain text. For those images, or for images that contain large areas of solid color, the GIF file format is the better choice. The small sample shown here

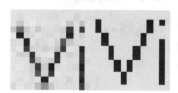

shows the left part of the image compressed at a low JPG quality setting and the section on the right saved as a GIF file. Both sections are enlarged here for easier viewing so that you can see the pattern of pixels. The JPG image is full of noise, but the GIF image is clean and clear.

GIF images cannot use more than 256 colors. The 256 colors that you use in the GIF file are known as the image's "color table." The Web-safe palette that is mentioned in so many books as being the color table of choice is a 216-color palette that contains colors that both Netscape Navigator and Microsoft Internet Explorer can display as solid colors on both the Mac and the PC. A color that is

> **Tip:** Don't use PNG files (yet). The support for this type of file is slow in coming and it creates a much larger (though potentially better looking) file than either the GIF or JPG format. Its main strength is that it permits up to 256 levels of transparency in an image. However, most of the browsers won't display the multiple levels of transparency properly. Give this file format more time to mature.

not in the Web safe palette will be displayed as a series of ugly dots if the site visitor's system can only display 256 colors.

You can use a GIF file format to reduce your images to fewer than 256 colors. You can create images that are only black and white. However, the fewer the colors you use (especially if the image is photographic in nature), the lower the quality of the image. Of course, if the image only had five colors when you created the GIF image, it won't look any different at all.

Creating Picture-Text Placeholders

You can create text that displays when the browser first tries to load an image. The text should be descriptive and allow your site visitor to decide if he or she wants to stick around to see the whole image. If you want to create alternate text for the London image that we used above, you can type it directly in to the Alternative Representations Text field in the Picture Properties | General dialog box.

That way, reading machines for the blind can read a useful picture description, users who keep their graphics options turned off in their browsers can get an idea of what the pictures contain, and impatient site visitors can click on your links without waiting for the graphics to display.

Into Your Web and onto Your Page...

Once you have the graphics prepared for the Web, half the battle is over. However, you still need to import the image into the Web, place it on a page, and get it to look right. FrontPage gives you a number of options for managing the storage and retrieval of images on your Web.

Any graphics that you use on your Web should be stored in the Web folder itself. You need to have everything in one container when you publish it on the Web.

Once your graphics are in place, you need to place your images on a Web page one at a time in order to use them. You can place single graphics into your Web page by selecting the Insert | Picture command from FrontPage's top menu bar.

You already tried this command in Chapter 4. The Insert Picture command allows you to place a picture either from a file or from the clip art collection.

Using the Clip Art Collection

When you purchased Microsoft FrontPage, you also gained access to a large collection of clip art. The best thing about this clip art is that the collection is constantly growing. You not only have an entire library on your hard drive, you can access—at no charge—the online update service for the Gallery. Each month, more images are added and you may download as many as you wish into your own Gallery. Here's how the system works.

Perhaps you are looking for some figure-skating clip art to add to the My Skate Web site. In your open Web page, you could select Insert | Picture | Clip Art.

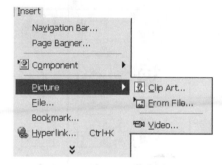

The Clip Art Gallery opens to reveal all of the available categories of image, as shown in Figure 7-2.

You could look for clip art about figure skating in the People section, or in the Sports and Leisure section, or, possibly even in the Seasons section. An even better way to try to find an appropriate image is to type in the request in the "Search for clips" field. However, trying this only shows a hockey player—not quite right for a site about figure skating.

You have several choices at this point. You can click on the Keep Looking button and FrontPage will see if it can find anything close to the terms that you requested.

Another choice is to search the online Gallery to see if something has recently been added. Before you search online, you either need to connect to your Internet service provider or make sure that a request for a URL will launch your browser and connect to the Net. Once you know that you can connect, you simply click on the Clips Online option.

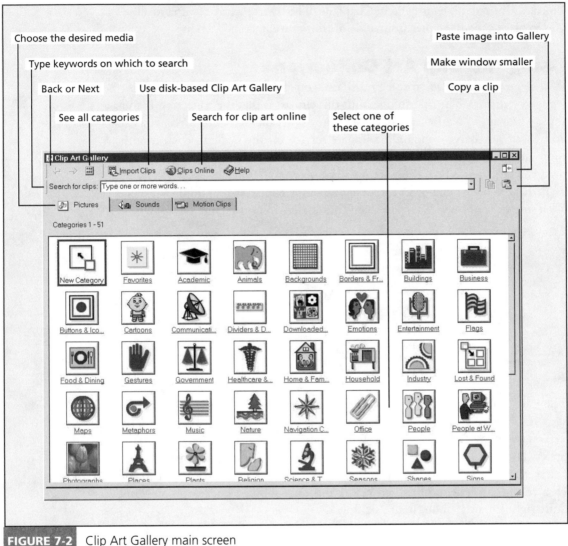

Choose the desired media

Type keywords on which to search

Back or Next

See all categories

Use disk-based Clip Art Gallery

Search for clip art online

Select one of these categories

Paste image into Gallery

Make window smaller

Copy a clip

FIGURE 7-2 Clip Art Gallery main screen

If you enter the term figure skating in the Search box, you will find an entire page of clips. Figure 7-3 shows what to do with the clip art that you locate.

As soon as you click on the images that you want to download, a link appears on the screen. It is not there unless you decide that you want to save some of the online images. Just as if you were using a shopping cart at an e-commerce site, you can continue "shopping" the Gallery site until you are ready to download all of the images. To "check out," you simply click on the Download link and then on the Download Now link on the screen. The clips are automatically placed in the Clip Art Gallery on your hard drive. Now, you need to get them from the Gallery onto your page.

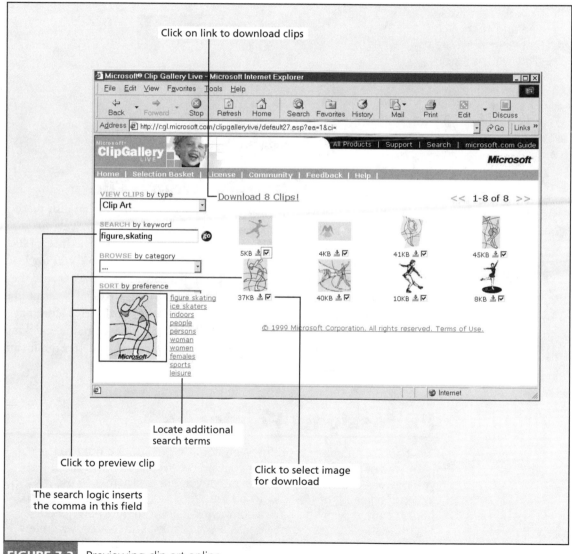

FIGURE 7-3 Previewing clip art online

Tip: You can
add your own images to
the Clip Art Gallery by
pasting them into the
page that you want. You
can also add, delete, or
modify the categories
under which items can
be filed and change the
categories in which items
are filed (right-click on
a picture and choose
Clip Properties). That
allows you to perform
a keyword search that
is customized to your
needs. You can include
any image in multiple
categories, but it is only
stored on your hard drive
one time—which makes
this a very efficient
storage holder for your
miscellaneous clip art.

To place the clip art that you downloaded onto your Web page,
you need to switch back into the Gallery. Select the clip that you want
to use (all of your downloaded images are in the Downloads category).
Right-click the mouse button and select Insert.

The image is added to your Web page.

Inserting Graphics from a File

When you select the Insert | Picture command, you can also place a
picture onto your page from a file located in the current Web, on your
local hard drive, or on the Internet. Figure 7-4 shows the Insert | Picture | From File dialog box. The symbols to search the Web or load
from your hard drive should be familiar to you by now, because they
are used consistently throughout the FrontPage dialog boxes. To select the
michelle.jpg image, you would click on the Search Your Hard Drive icon, navigate to the directory where the image is located, and select the file name. Clicking
on OK in the File dialog box closes both open windows and transfers the image
to your page.

Professional Pointer

Just because an image is on the Web doesn't give you the right to use
it on your own Web site. Most images on the Web are copyrighted. If
you download an image, make sure that you are legally free to use it.
You can find a lot of free clip art on the Web. Much of it is licensed for
personal use only. If you have a commercial site, you must negotiate a
fee to use the images. Some images are available as linkware—you may
use the image if you include a link back to the artist's home site. Always
check the terms of use. "Free" rarely means "do whatever you want
with this."

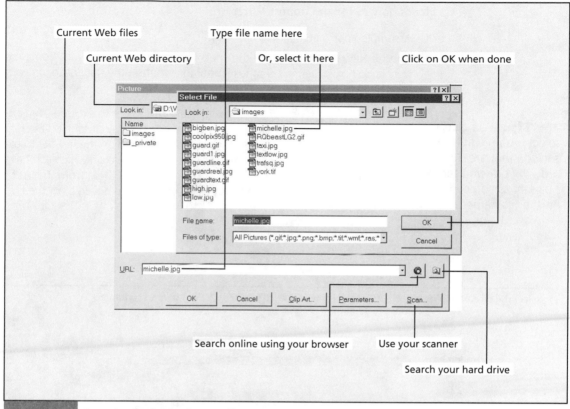

FIGURE 7-4 Inserting a picture from a file

You can use your Web browser to search for an image online, but that is surprisingly tricky. The good news is that you can right-click on your found image and select View Image from the pop-up menu if you are using Netscape Navigator as your browser. The bad news is that you can't do this with Microsoft Internet Explorer at all. Internet Explorer can only link to the *page* containing the graphic, and cannot create a link to the graphic itself. In Internet Explorer, the easiest way to get the picture is to copy it and then paste it into your page.

Importing Graphics Using the Import Wizard

If you already have a collection of images that you want to use, you can use them as the basis of your Web. You can create the Web around them, as it were. The Import Web Wizard allows you to use any one folder as the start of the Web. This is especially useful if you have content material that is also already prepared.

Here's how to use the Import Wizard:

1. Assemble your materials in a common folder.

2. Choose New | Web and select the Import Wizard. Name the Web. Complete the dialog box in Figure 7-5 to tell FrontPage whether the folders are on your hard drive or on the Web.

3. Select the specific files within the selected folder to *exclude* from import. You can exclude multiple files at one time by clicking on the first file and then pressing the SHIFT key and clicking on the last file to exclude. This selects all of the files between the two on which you have clicked. Click on the Exclude button to remove them from the list of files to import. Click on Finish when you have removed all of the files (or folders) that you *don't* want to import.

> ▶ **Tip:** You can select multiple files to exclude that are not in order by pressing the CTRL key as you click on the file names.

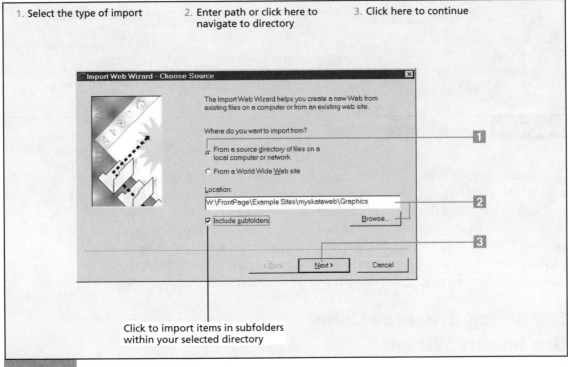

1. **Select the type of import**

2. **Enter path or click here to navigate to directory**

3. **Click here to continue**

Click to import items in subfolders within your selected directory

FIGURE 7-5   The Import Wizard dialog box

The Import Web Wizard is a great time-saver if you have a large number of resources in one location that you want to turn into a Web. You cannot combine the Import Wizard and a Web template, so when you've imported all of your graphics, your Web has no pages and no structure.

Copying Folders into Your Web

How else can you copy folders full of graphics into FrontPage? The flippant answer would be "carefully." Actually, the File | Import command (which can bring in both entire folders and/or individual files) is the easiest method of all. Here's how:

1. Click on the folder in the Folders list that you want to use to hold the imported files. This tells FrontPage where to put the files that you are importing. Leave the folder selected.

2. Choose File | Import.

3. The dialog box that appears gives you the option to import a file, a folder, or from the Web. Select your preferred option (the From the Web option uses the Import Wizard discussed above). If you select File or Folders, you can navigate to that location on your hard drive. In the Select File or Folder dialog box, you may select multiple files or subdirectories in one location. Press the SHIFT key to choose contiguous files or folders and press the CTRL key to select noncontiguous files or folders in the same directory.

4. Click on Open when you've found as many items as you want in the one location. You can continue to add additional files and folders that are in other locations, all during the same Import session. When you are ready to import, click on OK.

Moving Individual Images

When you place images that aren't stored in your Web onto a page, you are asked to save the files ("embedded" files) when you save the page. If you agree to save the files to your Web, you can select the file folder in which to store them. FrontPage doesn't care where you put them so long as it can find them again, but it is easier for you to remember where they are if you make sure that all of your graphics files go into the Images folder that is automatically created with every FrontPage Web. That way, if you are the type of person who can't find a pair of shoes in the morning (as I am), you'll always be able to locate your graphics because they've been put away in the "right place."

> **Tip:** You can use the Import Web Wizard to import an entire working Web from the Internet. However, don't use it to import a Web site that was already created with FrontPage. When you import a FrontPage Web, you lose all of the navigation information for the Web as well as the shared borders and navigation bars. If you need to make a copy of your Web to a different location, *publish* the Web to that location. (See Chapter 9 for how to publish your Web.)

Professional Pointer

FrontPage allows you to link to "internal" graphics that are not imported into your Web. *Don't do it*. You need to upload all of the images in your Web to your Web site eventually. You cannot have site visitors attempting to access your own hard drive. If you use a graphic taken from a remote Web site (with permission, of course), you need to make sure that that image is also copied onto your hard drive. There are two main reasons for this. If the location of the original graphic were to change, you site would be "broken." It is also considered very rude to create the traffic on someone else's site that would be generated by forcing a visitor's browser to go to a remote site to access a graphic. This is known as "bandwidth theft" and is a major Web "no-no."

Using Images

Once you have imported all of the graphics that you need and chosen the graphics that you want on a page, how do you arrange the graphics so that they look good? Page layout with graphics can get quite complex. You need to be able to place graphics into text areas or to place graphics one after another. In this section, you'll learn some basic techniques for arranging graphics.

Cross-Reference: Chapter 10 shows you how to arrange graphics using tables, and Chapter 13 shows you how to use absolute positioning (a feature of DHTML and CCS2) to layer and float your graphics.

Positioning Your Images

By default, all graphics that you place on your pages are assumed to be *inline* graphics. That means that the graphic appears at the location of the cursor in your window. If you have text on your screen and are in the middle of typing a line when you decide to show an image, the image appears right in the middle of the line (as you can see in Figure 7-6).

The original problem with Figure 7-6 is that the image is inserted in the wrong location regardless of how you want to arrange the screen. You should not insert an image into the middle of a line of text unless it is tiny. When you place an image in the center of the text, it acts like a "bumper" and it "bumps" the text above, creating this extremely unattractive use of space.

FIGURE 7-6 Image of Michelle Kwan appears inline at cursor position

You do have other options for aligning your images. If you right-click on a graphic image, you'll reveal the Shortcut Options menu. Selecting the Graphic Properties option and choosing the Appearance tab in the dialog box gives you a list of alignment options for your graphic.

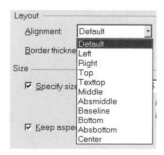

Let's look at those before we correct the image position for Michelle's page. Here is another image that's been inserted inline. The image is in the default location. This image belongs inline because it is being used as a logo for the MYSKATEWEB site. The image is located in the bottom shared border area.

Figure 7-7 shows what happens to it if you change the position using some of the choices on the Appearance Alignment menu. You'll notice that the default and bottom alignments are the same. The alignment is in relationship to the surrounding text.

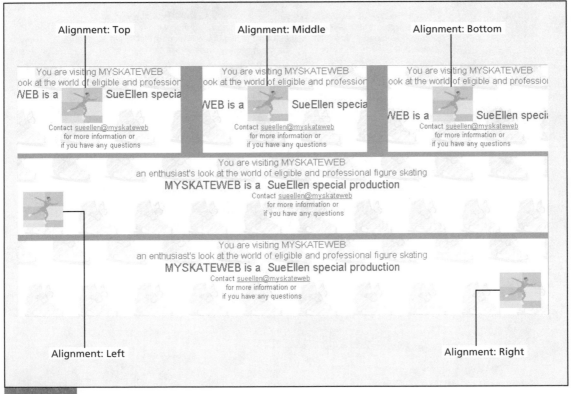

FIGURE 7-7   A variety of alignment options

Baseline and Absbottom do much the same thing as Bottom. Top and TextTop are the same. Middle and Absmiddle are identical. Center is the same as Middle in this example, but it would not be the same if the image had been inserted at the beginning of the line. If no other text were on the line, the Center alignment would have brought the image to the vertical center of the page. The Top, Middle, and Bottom alignment options work in relation to height of the text line surrounding the image.

When you use Align Left or Align Right, the image moves to that side of the line—regardless of where it was inserted in the text. The Align Left and Align Right settings allow you to begin to organize your page and integrate text and graphics.

Images and Text—An Uneasy Alliance

Let's go back to Michelle Kwan's page on the MYSKATEWEB site and see if we can get the text to wrap along the right side of the image. You can download the page with the text and Michelle's picture (michelle.htm) on it from the Osborne Web site. If you want to use your own image, all you need to do is to place an image in the middle of a bunch of text. Then you will be able to follow along as well.

This example shows you how to make text align along the side of an image:

1. Open michelle.htm in FrontPage or create a new page and add some text and an image.
2. Click on the image. Control handles surround it. Cut the image (CTRL-X).
3. Place the I-beam cursor's insertion point at the beginning of the paragraph of text. Paste the image (CTRL-V).
4. Right-click on the image and select Picture Properties.
5. Click on the Appearance tab. Change the Alignment to Left. Click on OK.

Tip: The alignment options only specify how the image is aligned in relation to the text on a page. If you want to keep your image centered on the Web page and the image appears without text around it, click on the Center button in the formatting toolbar. The image will appear in the center of the page (in whatever line position it was given) regardless of the size of the site visitor's browser window.

Although the text now lines up nicely at the left edge of the image, it is much too close to the image. The text really needs some breathing room. You can set this "keep-away" distance for either the horizontal or vertical borders or both, but you cannot assign different margins to each side of the image. For example, if you create a 16-pixel keep-away area for the horizontal border, the image moves 16 pixels to the right and pushes the text to the left of it another 16 pixels away. You cannot choose a 0-pixel left margin with a 16-pixel right margin. Figure 7-8 shows you how to set margins and text alignments in the Appearance tab.

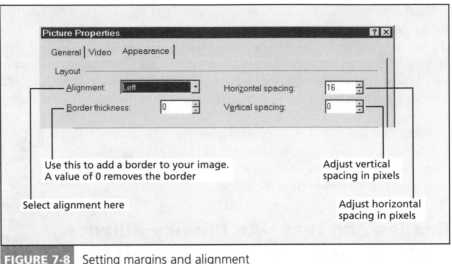

FIGURE 7-8   Setting margins and alignment

When you set a border for an image that uses spacing as well, the border doesn't display properly in the Normal view. It looks as if the image has a border around the image and a second one around the spacing. However, the border displays properly in the Preview mode and in Preview in Browser. In the color section, you can see the properly placed image of Michelle Kwan.

Once you understand how the various alignment options can change the way text and graphics interact, you can begin to use it to your advantage. You can perform a large number of "tricks" on your layout using nothing more than images with various alignment options. Figure 7-9 uses three differently sized images to create an arch that frames a paragraph of text.

Here's how to create the arch:

1. Create three images that relate to one another in size. Mine were sized at 200 pixels wide, 100 pixels wide, and 50 pixels wide. If you want to duplicate my example, you can download the three images (villflr1.jpg, villflr2.jpg, and villflr3.jpg) from the Osborne Web site for this book.

2. Open a new, blank page in FrontPage. Type a headline for the page and set it to Center alignment and Heading 1 style. Press the ENTER key to begin a new paragraph.

3. Choose Insert | Picture | From File and select the first image that you want to use. I used villflr1.jpg.

4. Right-click on the image and choose Picture Properties. Select the Appearance tab. Change the Alignment to Left. Click on OK to exit.

5. Place your cursor to the right of the image and click the mouse button. The insert point for the lines "snaps" to the next place in line. Open your next image (villflr2.jpg) and choose the same Left alignment in the Picture Properties | Appearance tab that you did in Step 4.

6. Repeat Step 5, but use the third image this time (villflr3.jpg).

7. Repeat Steps 3–6 using the same images as called for in each step, but aligning them to the right. The key trick here is to keep clicking to the right of the leftmost images on the top line if you want your pictures to line up the way I've shown. At this point, you have built the complete arch.

8. Click once more in the center of the top line, between the two sets of images. Type your text. Set the text to Center alignment by clicking on the Center button in the formatting toolbar.

9. Press the ENTER key after your paragraph to begin your next paragraph.

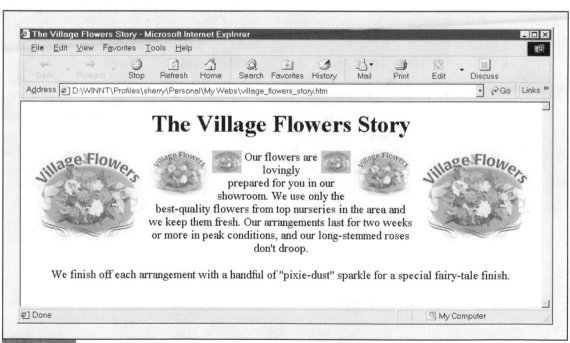

FIGURE 7-9   Picture "arch" for text in a page from the Village Flowers Web site

This technique gives you a "quick and dirty" formatting for your page that holds up well unless the site visitor displays the page in a very narrow window. The text usually stays between the two sets of images, but when the distance between the two sets of images narrows, the text begins to get cut off.

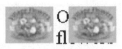

are lovingly

After the images begin to overlap, all formatting bets are off, and the page deteriorates rapidly.

Images as Links

In Chapter 6, you learned about hyperlinks. You can use an image as the link source as easily as you can use text. You can also create links from an image to a number of different locations by turning your image into an image map.

Using Images as Hyperlinks

You have many situations that lend themselves to using images as links. All of the navigation buttons that send site visitors from one page to another are links. The Web abounds with buttons of all types. Of course, you can create links from images where the picture is not really a glorified button—it is just a picture that happens to also be a link. You can link tiny images to their large siblings (the Auto Thumbnails feature that you'll use later in this chapter) so that the page loads faster and the user has more control over how long to wait for images. You can also use images as a "front door" to your site with a link to the home page.

You use a graphic as the source for a link exactly as you would text. Chapter 6 contains all of the information on creating links, and no difference exists when you link a graphic instead of text to another page on your site.

Image Maps

FrontPage can also create image maps. An image map is a single image that can link to multiple images. You link to multiple images by creating hotspots—areas that are clickable and are linked to other URLs.

One of the advantages of using an image map is that you can place graphics exactly where you want them within the image map and not worry about the spacing of the graphics. Because they are a single image, the spacing can't be changed.

The image(s) that you use in an image map will probably fall within three categories: Figure 7-10 shows these three image types from top to bottom:

- A fused image made up of other images but joined as one.
- A series of separate images with white space in them that are combined to optimize spacing. The button bar from PrancingPixel's Web site is really an image map.
- A single image that contains clickable regions made up from the normal flow of the photograph like the Vidalia onion site's fruit stand. This type of image map can also be a "treasure hunt" for links.

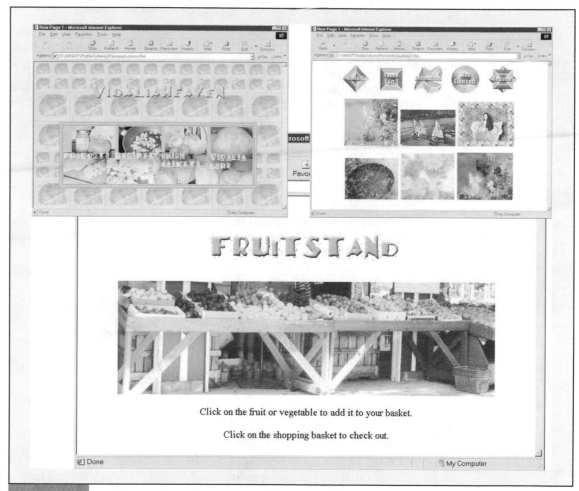

FIGURE 7-10   VidaliaHeaven's main page is a fused image map, while the PrancingPixel site uses an image map as a button bar, and the Fruit Stand in the VidaliaHeaven site just puts clickable regions over a photograph

After you create (or purchase) the artwork to use as your image map, you need to add the hotspots. Hotspots can be rectangular, circular, or polygonal. The tools to create them are on the pictures toolbar. The only "trick" to creating the hotspots is to make sure that you leave enough room for each hotspot so that it is easy to click. You may overlap hotspots, but the one on top is the "winner" in the overlapping region. Here's how to create an image map. You may download VidaliaHeaven's home page from the Osborne Web site for this book, or you may use your own image.

1. Open the file that you want to use. Place the image that you want for the image map or select the image. If you are using our example, select the picture of the onion products on the home page of the VidaliaHeaven Web.

2. Once the image is selected, the pictures toolbar (shown in Figure 7-11) becomes active. So that I don't need to repeat the toolbar in later examples, all of the functions are commented. Select the Polygonal Hotspot tool.

3. To use the Polygonal Hotspot tool, you place your cursor at the start of the shape that you want to draw and click. Drag the cursor from point to point around the area that you want to make clickable and click at each corner. Click on the original point to close the shape.

4. As soon as you close the shape, the Link To dialog box appears. This is the same dialog box that you've used before to create links. For this example, if you don't have pages already created, simply choose the "Create Page and Link to it" icon.

5. When you've created all of the hotspots, you can see them by clicking on the Highlight Hotspots icon. You'll see just the outline of the hotspots without the image itself.

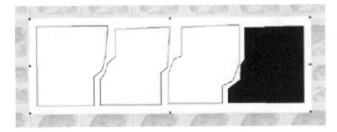

6. Choose Preview mode to test out your links.

If you prefer to use the Rectangular Hotspot or Circular Hotspot tool, the procedure is the same. Those tools are easier to use, however. If the site visitor clicks on an area that isn't in a hotspot, no linking occurs. Try to select the largest area possible without causing confusion. If you need to move a hotspot, you can use the Select tool and drag the hotspot to its adjusted location.

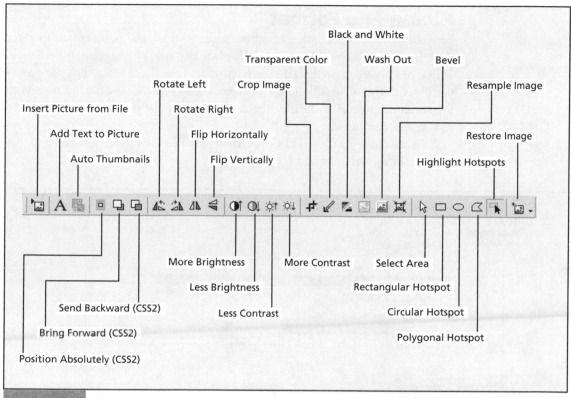

FIGURE 7-11   The pictures toolbar has a number of tools on it to create hotspots

Manipulating Images

When you select or create the images that you want to use on your Web, that image might be "not quite ready for Web time" as yet. Images in clip art collections, unless they are specifically purposed for the Web, are not usually optimized for use on the Web. An optimized file is one that is designed to download quickly.

You might also want to reduce the size of your image, crop it to use only a portion of the image, rotate the image, or change either the image contrast or its brightness. FrontPage can make all of these adjustments to your image plus a few more. It enables you to create bevels, wash out an image, or change the image to black and white.

Pick a File Format

FrontPage imports a number of different file formats and permits you to place these into a document. However, if you place any type of image other than GIF, JPEG, or PNG, you need to change the format of the file to make the image compatible with the Web. Although FrontPage allows you to save a file in a non-Web format, it can't preview the file, nor can you see the file if you select the Preview in Browser command.

You can change a file to JPEG or GIF via the Picture Properties | General dialog box, as shown in Figure 7-12.

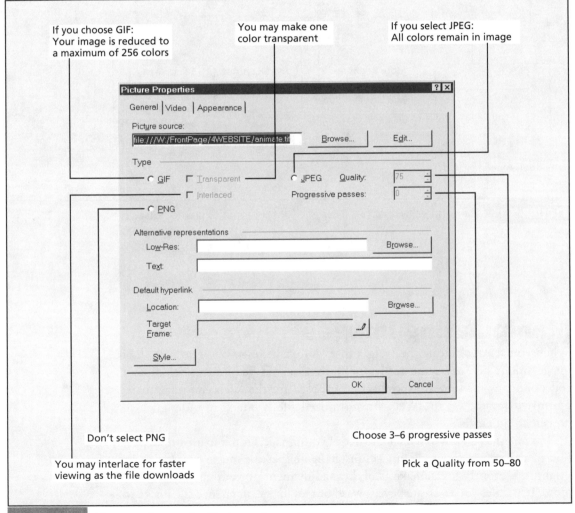

FIGURE 7-12 You can change the file type of your image

Deleting Images

You may delete any image that you have placed on a page by selecting it and pressing the BACKSPACE key. This removes it from the page, *but not from your Web if it has already been saved.* If you want to get rid of the picture from the Web itself, you need to select it in Folder list or in Folders view and right-click on it to delete it.

Setting Display Dimensions

FrontPage can change the dimensions of the image that you display in two ways. It can resize the image or it can resample the image. If you *resize* the image, you only change the way the image is displayed. You do not change the size of the file that is downloaded. Resampling actually changes the number of pixels in the file so that the image contains fewer pixels. In this example, you'll walk through the process of both resizing and resampling a file:

1. Insert a picture into a page (Insert | Picture | From File). If you have a fairly large sized TIF file in your stash of files, use that. You may also download the image fruitstd.tif from the Osborne Web site for this book.

2. Right-click on the picture and select Picture Properties from the context-sensitive menu. Choose the Appearance tab. Figure 7-13 explains how to change the size of the image as it is displayed on your page.

3. Once you have changed the size of the image on the page, you can click on the Resample icon on the pictures toolbar. This is a one-step process—a simple click and you're done. If you don't get an error message, the resampling worked.

When you save the page, you'll be prompted to save the picture again.

You can also resize the image interactively. When you click on a picture to select it, FrontPage places a bounding box around the image. This box contains small rectangles (called *control handles*) in each corner and at the midpoints of each side. To resize an image interactively, select the image. Place your cursor on top of a control handle. It changes to a double-pointed arrow that shows the directions in which you can drag the control handle. A control handle on the sides of an image may be dragged to the right or left. The control handles on the top and bottom of an image may be dragged up or down, and the control handles at the corners of the image may be dragged diagonally to resize the image and keep the aspect ratio constant.

L▶ Tip: For the best optimization of your images, you ought to use Photoshop, Equilibrium deBabelizer, or Macromedia FireWorks (or a special-purpose optimization program, of which many exist). FrontPage doesn't give you the control over which colors appear in the GIF file or how many colors to use. It doesn't let you select Web-safe colors when you convert your file. It also doesn't contain the world's greatest compression routines for JPEG images. I have been able to create acceptable JPEG images in Photoshop 5.5 with only 23-percent quality, but I recommend using a higher quality setting if you let FrontPage compress your image.

L▶ Tip: Don't make an image larger. Although nothing prevents you from doing so, the image will not look good enlarged because FrontPage has to "invent" the extra pixels.

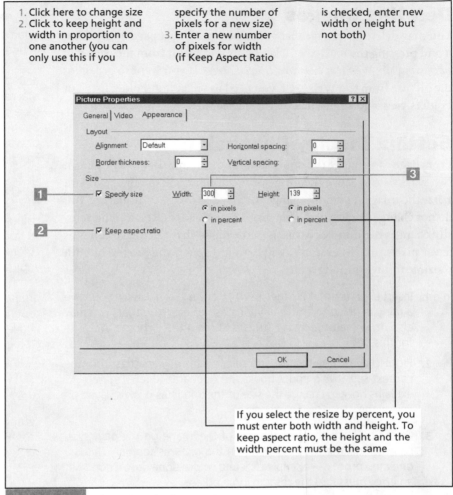

1. Click here to change size
2. Click to keep height and width in proportion to one another (you can only use this if you specify the number of pixels for a new size)
3. Enter a new number of pixels for width (if Keep Aspect Ratio is checked, enter new width or height but not both)

If you select the resize by percent, you must enter both width and height. To keep aspect ratio, the height and the width percent must be the same

FIGURE 7-13 Changing the image size

Cropping an Image

You might want to use only a part of an image that you find for your page. FrontPage allows you to crop the image to isolate the part that you want to use. To crop an image, you first select the image. You then click on the Crop button in the pictures toolbar. FrontPage places a bounding box with control handles inside of the image. Drag the box corners so that it encloses the part of the image that you want to keep. Click on the Crop button in the pictures toolbar again to execute the Crop command.

What Else Can You Do to an Image?

FrontPage is not an image editor. It doesn't permit you to change individual pixels in an image. However, it does have some limited image manipulation features on the pictures toolbar. The buttons for these features are located in the three center sections that we haven't yet discussed on the pictures toolbar. These sections contain the orientation tools, the tone tools, and the effects tools.

The orientation tools

FrontPage enables you to change the orientation of your image. You may rotate it to the left or right in 90-degree increments, or you may flip it either horizontally or vertically. The buttons are shown on Figure 7-11. Each button is a one-step process. No dialog box is associated with the button. Click on the desired button and you can see the immediate result. These images have been rotated left, rotated right, flipped horizontally, and flipped vertically.

Tip: If you place multiple copies of an image on a Web page and change the orientation of one of them, you will change the orientation of all of them on that page. You can get around this by saving the same image multiple times with different names.

The tone tools

The four tools that I've lumped together as "tone tools" enable you to control the brightness and the contrast of the image. They are also one-step tools. Again, if you have multiple copies of an image on a page and change one of them, all copies change.

Brightness makes the image darker or lighter. You cannot change the amount by which the picture is brightened or darken, but you can click on the More Brightness or Less Brightness button multiple times until you like the results. Contrast makes the image colors more similar or farther apart. As you lessen the contrast by clicking on the Less Contrast button, your image becomes muddier. If you click on the More Contrast button, you make the lights in the image lighter and the darks darker.

You cannot "revert" an image to its original state but you can click on the reverse operation or use the Undo command.

The effects tools

The tools that I've named "effects tools" enable you to select a transparent color in a GIF image, change the image to grayscale (i.e., "black and white"), wash out the image, and create a bevel. Like the other tools, what you do for one copy affects all of the copies on the page. All of these commands are one-step click-and-change buttons with no dialog boxes attached. Figure 7-11 shows the location of these buttons.

The GIF file format enables you to select a single color in the image to be transparent. This is usually the background color of an image, and you would want to make it transparent so that you can place the object in the image on a different color background. Figure 7-14 shows how you can change the green background of the image to make it transparent so that only the button appears on the page. The same technique works for any other color background or any other single color in an image.

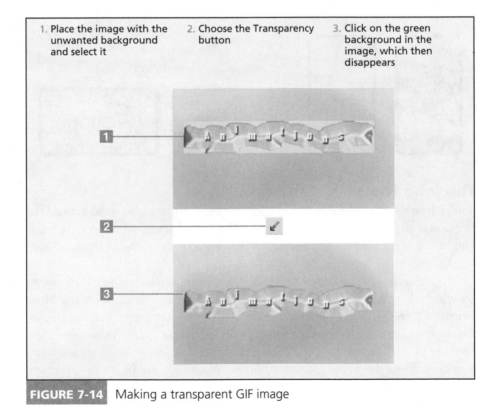

FIGURE 7-14   Making a transparent GIF image

When you remove the background color to make the image transparent in that area, you need to be sure that your "transparency" color is only used where you want the pixels to vanish. If I had used a white background on the Animations button and then made it transparent, the lettering on the button would also have disappeared.

You can also change an image to black and white. Just click on the Black and White button in the pictures toolbar. The Washout button enables you to fade the image to make it less noticeable on the page. You cannot control the amount of fading, however, nor can you apply it more than once. However, if you are using the absolute positioning in CSS2 (which you will learn about in Chapter 13), it can be useful to fade out an image if you want to place text on top of it.

The Bevel button creates a raised edge along an image for a 3-D effect. You have no control over the bevel that FrontPage creates. Therefore, you should choose an image that has a medium-toned background. If you try to bevel an image with a black or a white edge, you will not see the beveled effect. All of these effects change all copies of an image and are one-step processes. Simply select the picture that you want and click.

You can also add text directly onto an image. If the image is not a GIF file, it will be changed to one as soon as you try to type on it.

Auto thumbnails

One of FrontPage's more wonderful features is its ability to create auto thumbnails. If you have a site that relies on using many images for content—such as an art gallery site or a store with a large visual inventory—then the Auto Thumbnails feature is going to be one of your favorite program features.

What are auto thumbnails? A thumbnail shows a tiny preview of an image. It takes the place of the larger image. FrontPage can automatically create tiny versions of your image when you place the larger version on the page. If you want to display a thumbnail for a selected image, FrontPage automatically creates one for you when you click on the Auto Thumbnail button in the pictures toolbar. FrontPage also creates a link to the original (larger) image. You can see an example of auto thumbnails in the color section.

You can create the auto thumbnail by selecting an image and clicking on the Auto Thumbnails button (shown in Figure 7-11) to replace the larger image with a tiny version that links to the original one.

You can right-click on the page and select Page Options and then click on the Auto Thumbnails tag to change the thumbnail characteristics. You can change the width of the thumbnail, select the number of pixels to use as a border, and either bevel the thumbnail or leave it plain.

Page Graphics

If you do not use a theme, you have control over the colors used on your page from the Page Properties context-sensitive menu. You've already used the General tab in the Page Properties dialog box to change the titles of your pages. You can both change the colors used on your page and change or select the background image or color to be used.

Changing Colors and Backgrounds

To change the colors on a nonthemed page, you right-click on the page, choose Page Properties, and select the Background tab. Figure 7-15 displays the Background tab and shows you how to select new colors for your page.

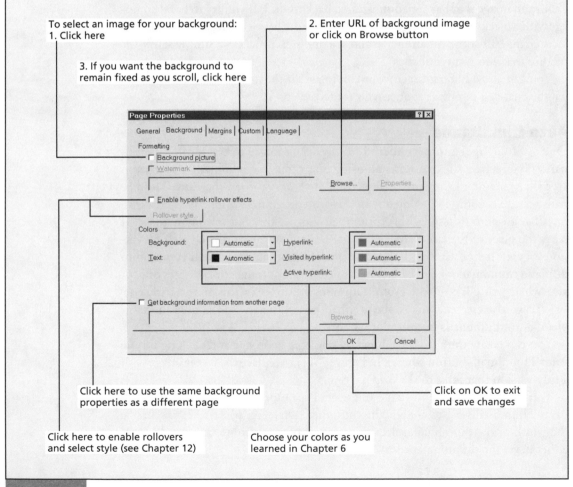

FIGURE 7-15 Selecting page colors

You'll learn more about page layout and choosing images for page backgrounds a little later in this chapter.

The Single-Pixel GIF Trick

I've tried to stick to fairly straightforward techniques so far, but designers have been using the following technique to achieve page layout control that works on any browser. The technique is both ingenious and simple. If you are not familiar with it, you should be.

Cascading style sheets only work on newer browsers. The single-pixel GIF trick (first popularized by David Siegel in his book *Creating Killer Web Sites*, Hayden Books, 1997) works everywhere.

If you create a GIF file that contains only one pixel and save it as a transparent GIF, it is both invisible on the page and fast to download. You can change its size to make it as large as you want without harming anything—you won't lose image quality by scaling it up in size because the file is invisible.

Of what possible use is an invisible image? Remember how an image file that is embedded in text causes the text to rearrange itself around it? You can use a single-pixel GIF file to create leading in your text by placing one copy of the file every five words. Size the image so that it is one pixel wide, but it can be as many pixels high as you want for your leading. The copy of the file that is placed every five words will keep the lines of text spaced regardless of the size of the browser window.

You can use an invisible GIF file to indent your text or to create a margin for graphics. Anywhere you need to precisely space something, you can use an invisible single-pixel GIF file scaled to the size of the needed space. You can use the same image file multiple times on the page, and you can set each copy to be its own size. Unlike the effects buttons in the pictures toolbar, image size changes are coded into the HTML that FrontPage generates so that each instance of the file can be sized differently.

Designing Page Backgrounds

If you don't use a theme, you need to decide whether your pages will be plain or patterned. In the early days of the Web, many Web designers went as crazy with patterns as early desktop publishers did with fonts.

To use patterns wisely, you need to understand what they do and how they work.

Patterns

A pattern is an image that is repeated multiple times across a surface. When you choose a background image in FrontPage, you are not given the choice of the number of times to use the image. (FrontPage is not being difficult; it is following the coding conventions in HTML for the use of background images.) If you select an image that is 100 × 100 pixels square, the picture will repeat six times across the width of a 600-pixel-wide browser screen.

If you have any interest in the science or art of creating repeating images, you can find many reference materials. The design and use of patterns is beyond the scope of this book. However, if you decide to use patterns for your backgrounds, you need to be very sure that they don't cause your text to be unreadable. One way to do this is to wash out the background pattern tile so that it becomes very light and subtle.

The current "trend" in Web site design seems to be toward the clean crisp look of unpatterned white backgrounds. When patterns are used, they are typically seen in the borders on one or more sides of the Web page.

Creating one-sided page borders

You can create a one-sided border for a Web page and use it as a background pattern fairly easily so long as you have access to a paint program. The tile shown here was created in Photoshop.

If you used that small tile as your background image, your page would have a hard edge and the scallop would repeat ever the entire surface. You can make the scallop repeat only down the left edge of the page, however, if you add to the scallop enough white space on the right side that the tile will not be able top repeat regardless of the page size. The highest-resolution monitors available today do not usually exceed 1,600 pixels across. Therefore, if you expand this tile so that, instead of being 100 pixels square, it is 1600 pixels wide and 100 pixels high, the tile is very unlikely to form a pattern on anyone's monitor. Of course, this preparation work needs to be done in a painting program. You make this change to your tile by expanding the canvas so that the width of the image becomes 1,600 pixels but the actual image does not change in size—only white space is added.

If you change this image into GIF format, the white areas of the image will compress very nicely and the download times will still be low. According to Photoshop's Save for Web command, this large scallop tile saved as a 16-color GIF file will download in 3 seconds under ideal conditions on a 28.8-Kbps modem. Figure 7-16 shows the start of a page for the StockChatter Web site.

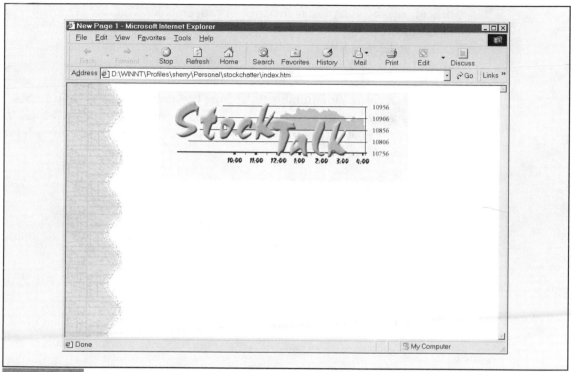

FIGURE 7-16 Scallop border pattern for StockChatter Web site

Creating background images that don't repeat

You can take this a step further and create a background for your page that covers the entire page and will not repeat because it is larger than the largest page size on your Web. You need to calculate this size quite differently. This technique is only practical on short pages.

Professional Skills Summary

This ends our look at placing graphics. It's a journey that has brought us from the simplest "How do you place graphics on your Web?" to the issue of "How do you create complex graphics for background images?"

Along the way, you've learned how to decide which graphics format to use, and how the various formats compare for download time. You've learned about the Web-safe palette and how to use it to best advantage, and how to gracefully degrade sites by using text alternatives for your graphics. You've also learned how to use the File | Import command to bring graphics into your site.

You've learned how to position images on the screen and make text wrap around graphics. You've also learned to link graphics to other pages.

You have created image maps, and seen how to delete images, crop images, set image sizes, create auto thumbnails, and use background images and patterns.

You'll learn how to modify themes and to create your own in Chapter 8. You'll learn new ways to format your graphics in Chapter 10, when you learn about using tables.

Customizing and Creating Themes

Themes are one of the features that make FrontPage special. A professional graphic designer can create incredible interfaces for a Web page. However, the interface needs to be placed manually on every page. FrontPage's themes allow you to "design once, apply once, use many times." This type of automation is a real time-saver.

Most time-savers come at a price, but this price you can afford to pay. Even if you don't like the themes that ship with FrontPage, you can design your own and use those. Because of the flexibility of being able to remove a theme from an individual page, you're not locked in to creating your entire site in a theme when it makes no sense for a specific page.

This chapter is about themes, and how to make them your own.

Customizing Themes

You already had practice creating Webs and applying themes to them. Themes are a wonderful facility that allows you to create pages that present a consistent look and feel to the site visitor. However, they are also somewhat like buying "one size fits all" clothing. Though they fit just about everybody, they might fit nobody particularly well.

Microsoft has therefore decided to allow you to modify the themes that come with the program. You can buy additional themes from third-party vendors such as WebSpice (www.webspice.com). You can also find themes available for free download as linkware (you link back to the designer if you use the theme). Chris Dimaano created such a site (http://www.dwwd.com/graphics/themepreviews/theme_previews.htm). PixelMill (http://pagemill.net) has themes from many designers for sale for $8.00–$12.00 per theme. You can find others if you search under "FrontPage Themes" in a Web search engine such as www.altavista.com.

You can modify any theme. To create a new theme, you need to start with a previous theme and modify it. Once you've created the theme, if you know where it is stored on your hard drive (and I'll tell you in a few minutes how to find it), you can package your new theme and distribute it to other FrontPage users.

Anatomy of a Theme

Themes contain three types of information that can be modified or changed. You can change the colors used in a theme, the graphics used in the theme, or the text used in the theme. In addition, each theme contains two sets of colors (Normal colors and Vivid colors) and two sets of graphics—one for normal graphics,

and a different set of graphic elements for active graphics.

Each theme also contains a cascading style sheet definition that is used if you chose the Apply Using CSS checkbox.

New in 2000: This version of FrontPage allows you to modify the themes inside of FrontPage. In earlier versions, you needed an add-on program to modify themes or create new ones.

You can modify your theme by selecting Format | Theme and clicking the Modify button. Three new buttons appear that enable you to select which facet of the theme you want to change.

If you click Colors, the dialog box shown in Figure 8-1 appears. Although changing the colors in the Color Scheme view is quite simple (as you can see by reading the instructions embedded in the figure), the results are not predictable. It is quite difficult to deduce from the five swatches shown for each theme the exact element that changes if you modify the colors. While the center swatch seems to predictably control the color of the background, the button text does not change based on a specific location in the swatches. However, you can quickly change some of the colors in your theme using this method.

You gain a bit more control over the colors used in your theme if you choose the Color Wheel method of selecting colors. To use the Color Wheel, click the moving spot within the wheel. This spot sets the colors of the fourth swatch in the palette. Even if the fourth swatch is not used for the Horizontal Navigation button colors when you enter the dialog box, it will be after you have moved the dot in the color wheel. You have direct control over the fourth color swatch in the group, but all of the other color swatches change in relation to the fourth color as you move it around the color wheel. Figure 8-2 shows how to use the color wheel to make changes to the colors of your theme text. You can brighten or darken all of the colors in your theme

Tip: You cannot change the colors of the graphic elements. The graphics are stored in "real" image files and FrontPage cannot perform a pixel-level edit on them. A blue button will remain blue no matter what else you change in the theme. Be careful about changing the background color of an image. Many of the graphics in the themes have white space around the edges that looks quite ugly when placed against a colored background.

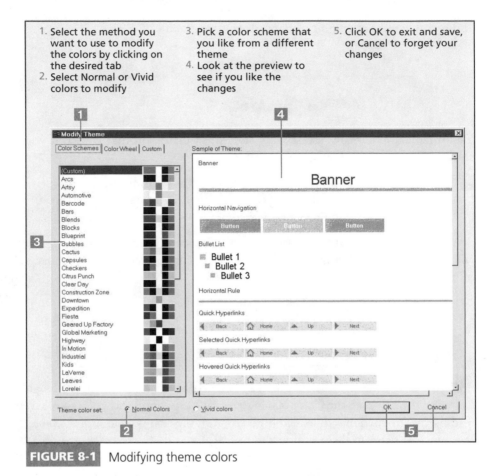

1. Select the method you want to use to modify the colors by clicking on the desired tab
2. Select Normal or Vivid colors to modify

3. Pick a color scheme that you like from a different theme
4. Look at the preview to see if you like the changes

5. Click OK to exit and save, or Cancel to forget your changes

FIGURE 8-1   Modifying theme colors

at one time, which is really the only unique feature of this dialog box. None of the changes that you make affect the color that appears over the Global Navigation buttons in the theme. Nothing that I've discovered in any dialog box seems to be able to change this color at all.

The best way to change your colors is to change every element directly using the Custom tab. You can select the actual colors as you learned in the previous chapters. However, the unique and wonderful thing about the Custom tab is that it names the element that you are changing so that you don't have to play guessing games. The only element that is not named in the list is the Global Navigation button color. Figure 8-3 shows how to use the Custom tab options to select new colors.

You can change the text style used over your graphics by selecting the Font tab in the Modify Theme dialog box as shown in Figure 8-4. You cannot change the

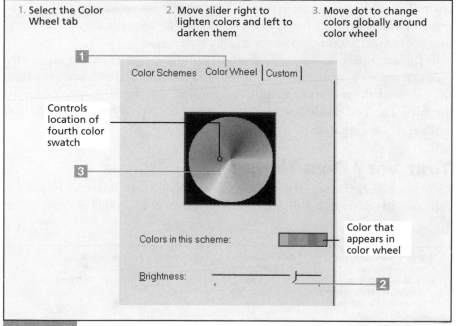

FIGURE 8-2 Using the color wheel

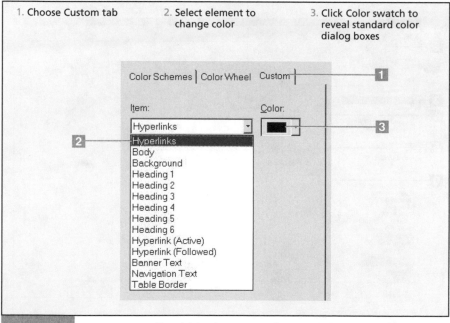

FIGURE 8-3 You can specify which element to change in the Custom tab
dialog box

color of the text on the buttons this way, however. Those colors are set by modifying the colors in the theme. However, you can alter both the size and the alignment of the text within the various graphic elements.

If you are using cascading style sheets in your theme, you can also modify the style sheet by clicking on the Text button. However, this option is best for setting the colors of the text styles in your image—not the text that appears on the graphics. The Text dialog box enables you to set the type style for the body font and the six heading styles.

Your Very Own Theme

Once you have experimented with changing the themes that come with FrontPage, you are ready to try to build your own. The only way to do this is to modify an

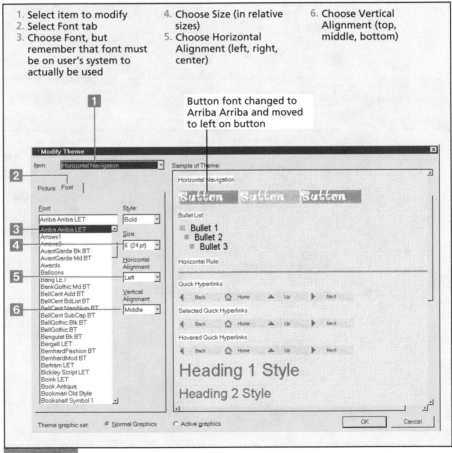

FIGURE 8-4 Modifying the text display on the graphic elements

existing theme and add new graphics to it. In this section, I'll show you how to build a new theme for the MySkateWeb site, but the principles apply to any new theme that you can create. If you want to work along with me, download the graphics.zip file on the Osborne Web site for this book. If you don't want to use my example, then gather together your own graphics and follow along. We're going to build a wrap-around interface that goes across the top of the page and down the left side. None of the Microsoft-supplied themes do this, but the effect is common on the Web and quite attractive. In addition, the awesome power of the shared borders in FrontPage make an easy task out of a major chore.

You will need to use the graphic elements listed in Table 8-1 to build a new theme (Note: The sizes are Microsoft's recommendations only; you may use your own discretion as to dimensions):

Element	Description	Size
Background picture	This is the tile that is to be repeated across the background of the image. It can be a "traditional pattern" file, a border pattern, or a full background image.	Varies
Banner	The navigation banner uses the structure in the Navigation view to display the page name. It can be inserted anywhere on the page, but is most often used at the top of a page (and frequently within a shared border).	600w × 60h
Bullet list	You need three graphics to be used for bullets: Small (level 3) Medium (level 2) Large (level 1)	12w × 12h 14w × 14h 20w × 20h
Global navigation buttons	These buttons are the top-level navigation buttons. You need three states for active graphics and two states for normal (static) graphics. All states should be the same size.	140w × 160h
Horizontal navigation	These buttons appear in the automatic navigation bars when you select Horizontal Buttons in the Navigation Bar Properties dialog box. You need three of these (Normal, Hovered, Selected) for active graphics and two of these (Normal and Selected) for normal graphics.	140w × 60h
Vertical navigation	These buttons appear in the automatic navigation bars when you select Vertical Buttons in the Navigation Bar Properties dialog box. You need three of these (Normal, Hovered, Selected) for active graphics and two of these (Normal and Selected) for normal graphics.	140w × 60h
Quick Home, Next, Back, and Up buttons	You need three of each of these buttons (Normal, Hovered, Selected) for active graphics and two of each these (Normal and Selected) for normal graphics. (Yes, that's a total of 20 different button states.)	100w × 20h
Horizontal rule	This is the divider line that appears when you select the horizontal rule. Your theme automatically uses the included graphic line.	300w × 10h

TABLE 8-1   Elements Needed to Create Custom Themes

After reading the table above, you're probably thinking "*How* many elements do I need to create???" It isn't quite as bad as it sounds. Although you need two full sets of graphics in theory, in practice you can reuse your Active graphics for the Normal graphics scheme if you want. Also, because you are modifying an existing theme (as that is the only way to create a new one), you can make use of any of the original theme graphics that you like. If the theme is for your own use and you intend only to use Active graphics, then you don't need to bother changing the elements that you don't intend to use. (Of course, if you want to package your theme for resale, you need to replace all of the elements in the theme). Figure 8-5 shows the graphics that I've designed for the MySkateWeb site.

Once you have created or collected the needed graphics, the process of creating the theme is fairly easy. Here's what you need to do:

1. Select a theme that you want to modify. It can either contain graphics that you want to reuse or simply be selected at random if you want to replace everything. In this series of instructions, I'm going to modify the Cactus theme (see Figure 8-6) because I like the fonts that it uses. I am also going to select the "Vivid colors," "Active graphics," and "Background picture" checkboxes. You

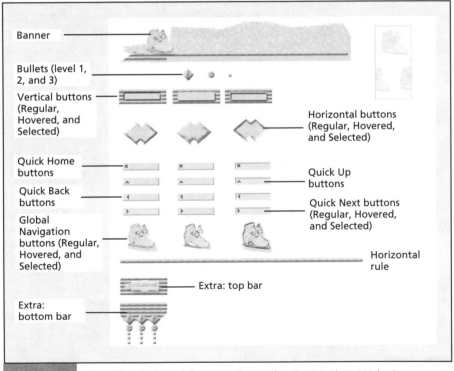

FIGURE 8-5   Graphics designed for new theme for the MySkateWeb site

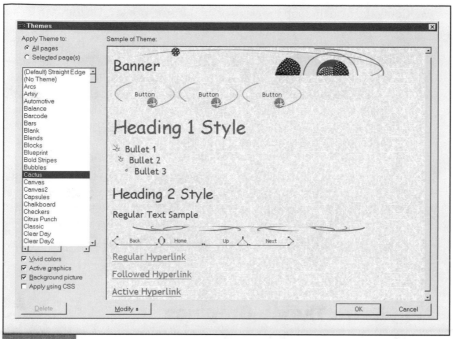

FIGURE 8-6   Modify the Cactus theme to build a new theme

would repeat this entire procedure for Normal graphics, and also reselect your colors if you want another scheme for regular colors.

2. Click on the Modify button and then select the Graphics button. Let's get the new graphics in place first. With the Picture tab selected, you can see all of the elements that need to be changed. The list begins with the background picture. Click the Browse button to locate the image that you want to use for the background picture. If the images are on your hard drive, then you need to select the Hard Drive icon in the Browse dialog as you did when you inserted an image.

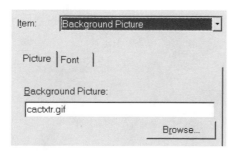

3. Continue to go through the elements in the drop-down list in turn and locate the graphic to use for each one by clicking the Browse button. If you have all of your graphics in one location, it becomes a fairly quick procedure to link each of them into the theme.

4. In this example, the banner text is aligned to the bottom left of the banner. That won't work for this banner, so you need to select the Font tab and change the banner alignment to Center, Middle. On your own sites, you will have adjustments that you either want or need to make. Here is where you would change the font used on the graphics as well. Click OK when you're finished adjusting both the graphics and fonts for the graphics.

5. The one thing left for you to do is to select colors for the various elements. Use the Custom button. Create new custom colors as you need to. Wherever possible, use Web-safe colors so that the text color won't dither on a monitor with only 256 colors.

6. Finally, choose Save As on the Theme dialog box and give your theme a new name. I selected MySkateWeb as the theme name.

7. Click OK to apply the new theme to your Web.

Using Extra Theme Graphics

You can create wraparound interfaces with your themes using planning and a bit of ingenuity. Here's how to use the two extra theme graphics that I created shown in Figure 8-5. Although these steps are based on my particular design, once you understand the process, you can create all types of wonderful interfaces. Paul Vineburg (http://www.vineburg.com.au) created a sunflower that uses all of the vertical navigation buttons as its leaves.

1. Design your interface to wrap around one or more corners and cut the graphics into component pieces. Look at the horizontal navigation buttons in Figure 8-5. They contain the relevant parts of a panel in addition to the object that looks like the button. Because the button consists of background as well as a live button, these graphics form their own panel when they are stacked one on top of the other.

2. Choose Format | Shared Borders. Select a top border with no navigation buttons and a left-side border with navigation buttons.

Chapter 1: **So What Do I Need to Do?**

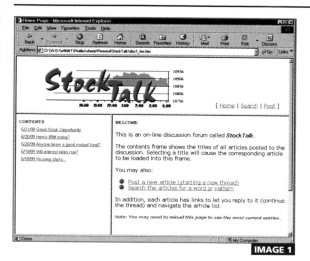

IMAGE 1

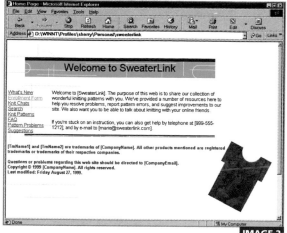

IMAGE 2

Microsoft FrontPage can help save development time by allowing you to use and customize themes. These three home pages from our example sites use variants of themes included with FrontPage. The "Cases Studies" section describes these example sites.

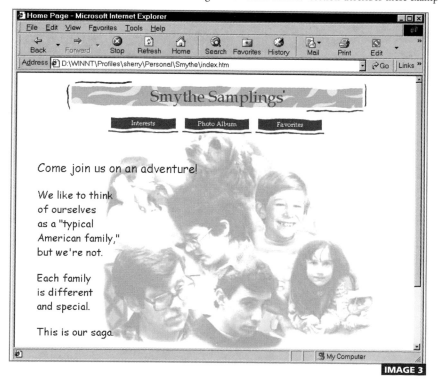

IMAGE 3

Microsoft FrontPage allows you the flexibility to use your own graphics and design your own site to whatever standards you need. These three example sites sport home pages that are custom designed. The "Cases Studies" section describes these example sites.

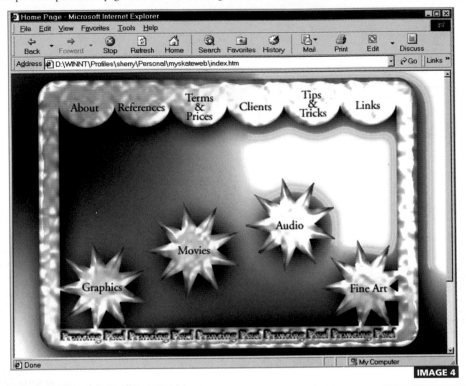

IMAGE 4

IMAGE 5

IMAGE 6

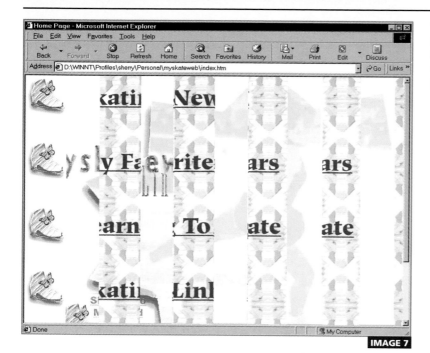

You can add effects easily to your Web site like the Window Shade transition shown here. "What Is a Web Site?" describes the elements needed to create professional-looking Web pages.

IMAGE 7

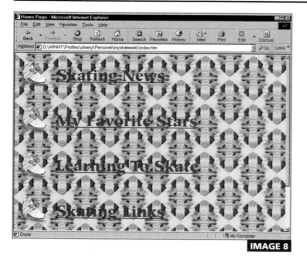

IMAGE 8

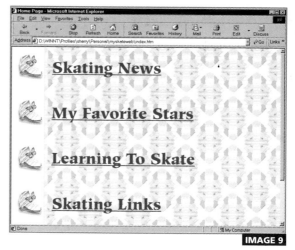

IMAGE 9

You can create colorful Web pages that are hard to read and navigate (Image 8) or you can tone down the use of background patterns so that the page, though still colorful, is much easier to read. "What Makes a Good Web Site?" has many more techniques for creating professional-looking sites.

Chapter 2: **Creating a Framework**

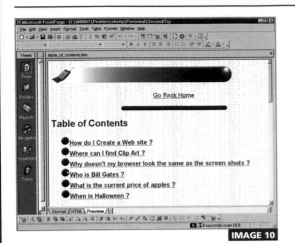

IMAGE 10

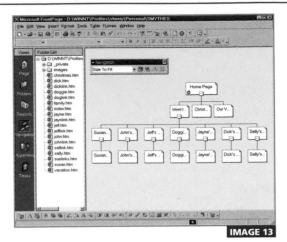

IMAGE 13

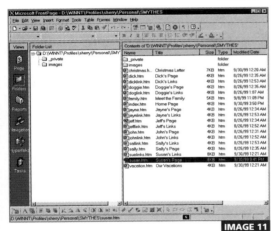

IMAGE 11

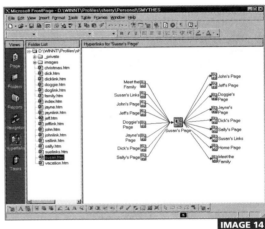

IMAGE 14

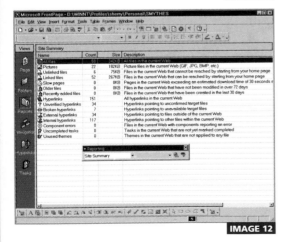

IMAGE 12

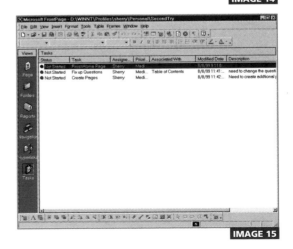

IMAGE 15

FrontPage gives you six different ways to look at your Web site. Although you do most of your work in Page view (Image 10), you can also manage your files in Folders view, see a large number of reports in Reports view, create a framework for the logic of your Web in Navigation view, check your link in Hyperlinks view, and see how much is left to develop on your Web in Tasks view. "A View from the Bridge" describes all of these views.

Chapter 3: **Gathering Documents and Graphics**

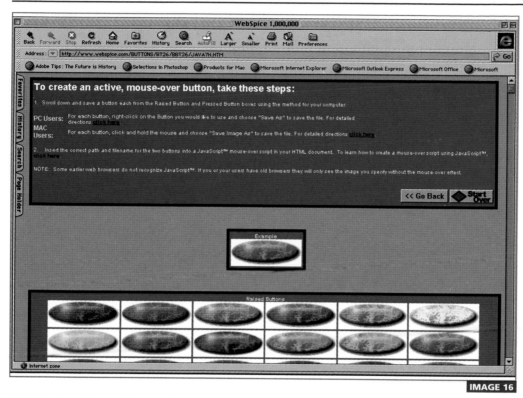

IMAGE 16

WebSpice is a collection of images designed specifically for the Web. The collection includes buttons, objects, animations, and additional FrontPage themes. Read about this and other clip art resources in "But I Can't Draw!"

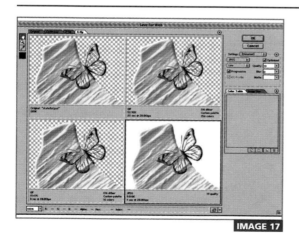

IMAGE 17

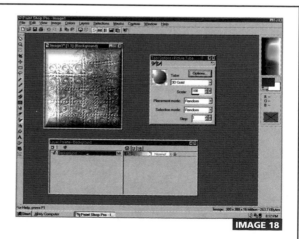

IMAGE 18

Photoshop (Image 16) is the "gold standard" of painting programs. It is the popular high-end program used by graphics professionals. You can use it to prepare images for the Web and make speed vs. quality decisions as you save a file. PaintShop Pro (Image 17) is a popular shareware program. At a fraction of Photoshop's price, you can acquire a program that allows you to create wild effects and perform many of the same functions as its more expensive rival. Learn more about your options for preparing Web graphics in "Paint and Drawing Programs."

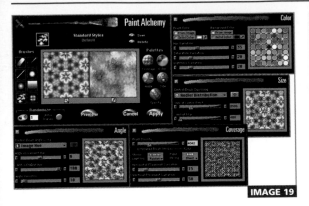

IMAGE 19

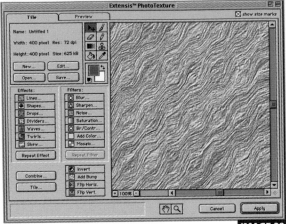

IMAGE 20

An almost endless selection of wild filters and effects exists for you to use to create buttons, bevels, interfaces, and any other Web element that you can imagine. Learn more about what's out there in "Graphic Utilities and Plug-ins."

IMAGE 21

Chapter 4: **Site Building**

IMAGE 22

FrontPage can automate the process of placing navigational buttons at the top and sides of the screen, and can make the navigational display consistent. Learn how in "Creating a Navigation System."

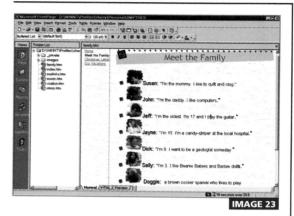

IMAGE 23

Once you've built the Web structure, you can add lists with bullets and graphics to your pages. You can create links to other pages. Learn the basics in "Adding Text" and in "Adding Graphics."

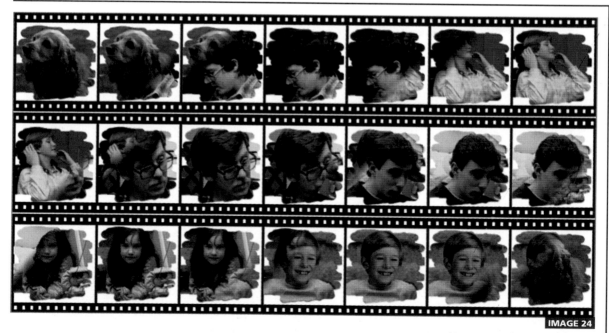

IMAGE 24

Gif animations can add interest to your site and yet be quick to load and compatible even with the older browsers. Learn how to attach a gif animation to a page in "Adding an Animation." Chapter 11 also tells you more about the topic.

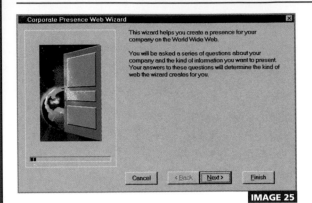
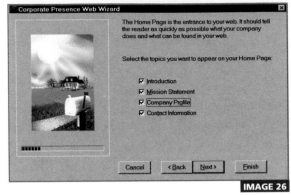

IMAGE 25

IMAGE 26

You can build Web sites for any size business. The Corporate Web Presence site has so many options that a Wizard walks you through the process. You only need to answer the questions asked to build a complex site. Learn how in "Using the Wizards."

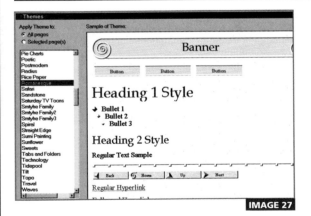
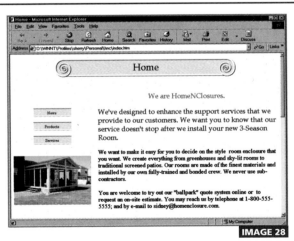

IMAGE 27

IMAGE 28

When you create a new Web site, you can select your own interface, or you can use one of the many themes that come with FrontPage. Image 27 shows the Romanesque theme in the process of being selected, and Image 28 shows the completed home page. Learn how to select and apply a theme for your Web in "Creating the Web." You can find additional references to selecting themes in both Chapter 1 and Chapter 7.

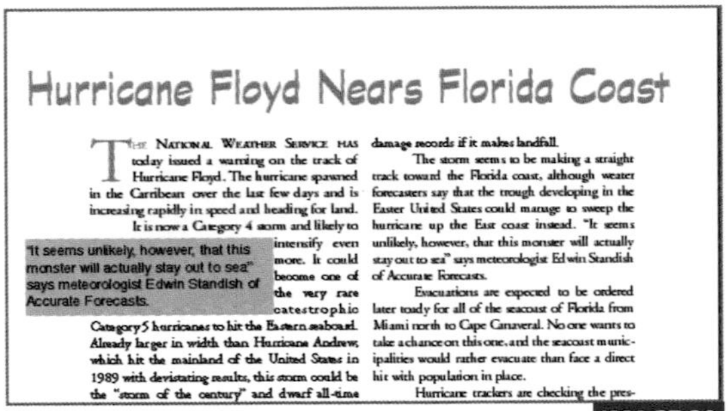

Chapter 5: **All About Text**

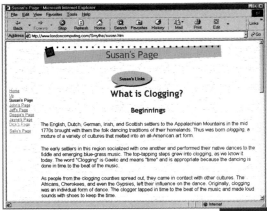

IMAGE 29

HTML doesn't make it easy to produce pages that contain elements like callouts and drop caps, which are common elements in the world of printing. However, you will learn a number of techniques to help you to produce good-looking pages in "Cascading Style Sheets."

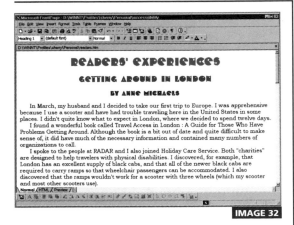

IMAGE 30

In "Adding Content," you'll find out how to import a Word file and format it to give your Web site a professional look. FrontPage 2000 gives you many of the features of Microsoft Word to help you to produce pages that do you proud.

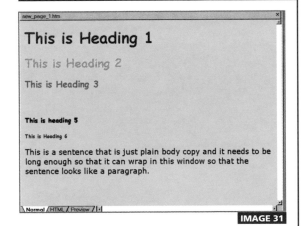

IMAGE 31

"List Management 101" shows you how to use the various levels of headings available in FrontPage 2000. You'll also learn how to change these formats in "Cascading Style Sheets." "Fonts (and Other Web Layout Annoyances)" tells you how to change the fonts used in your pages.

IMAGE 32

Once you've learned how to format text and use cascading style sheets, "Some Thoughts on Page Design" helps you to put it all together to create harmonious pages.

Chapter 6: **Using Hyperlinks**

IMAGE 33

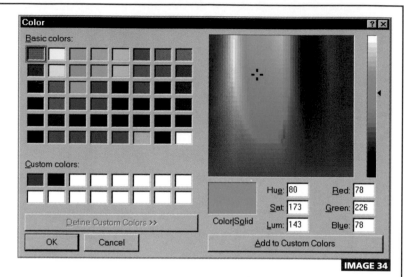

IMAGE 34

Microsoft FrontPage enables you to select colors by a variety of methods. The Font dialog box (and many other dialog boxes) allows you to select colors from a group of standard colors, document colors, or theme colors. You can also create custom colors. "The Color of Links" shows you how to use the various methods that FrontPage provides for color creation and selection.

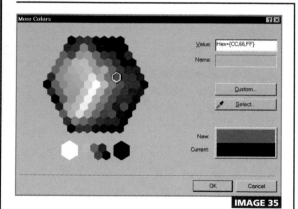

IMAGE 35

"The Color of Links" also shows you how to use the hexagonal color picker to select colors that are Web-safe. You can select any color using its hexadecimal number or you can simply click on the hexagon to select it.

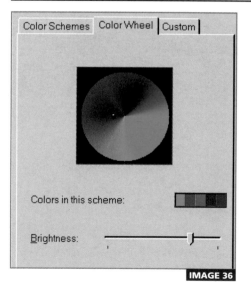

IMAGE 36

You can vary the colors in a theme as well. Chapter 8's "Anatomy of a Theme" shows you how to use the Color Wheel picker to globally alter the colors in a theme. You can "push" the colors toward a specific range on the color wheel, or you can change their brightness.

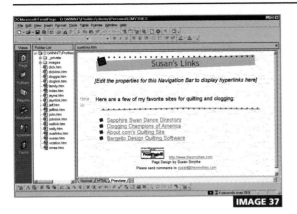

IMAGE 37

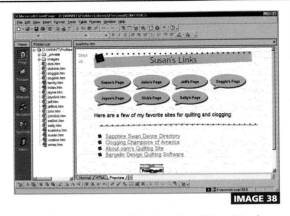

IMAGE 38

The Navigation Bar and Shared Borders feature is one of the most powerful Web site creation tools in FrontPage. "Shared Borders and the Navigation Bar" shows you how to turn off shared borders and insert a navigation bar so that the image on the left turns into the image on the right. With one command, you can automatically generate all of the button graphics and HTML code to make links to all of the relevant pages in your site.

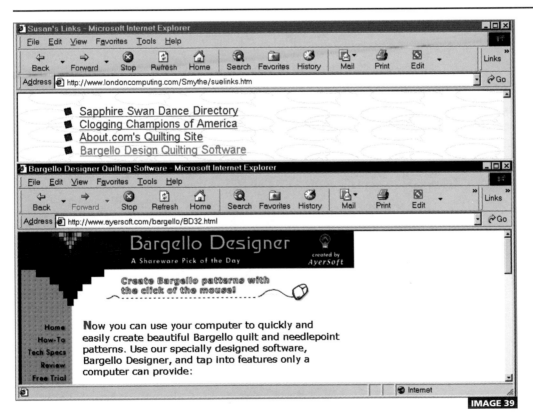

IMAGE 39

"Creating Basic Links and Bookmarks" tells you how to create the standard "click on the text" hyperlinks that enable your site visitor to surf your site and surf from your site to external links. By clicking on a link in your site, your visitor is able to access information in another site located elsewhere on the Web.

Chapter 7: **Great Graphics**

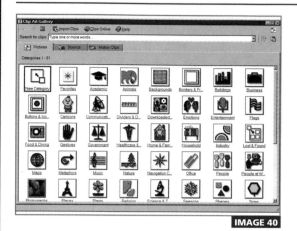

IMAGE 40

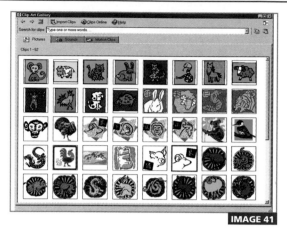

IMAGE 41

FrontPage includes access to Microsoft's clip art collection. This is a combination of on-disk images that you can search by category (as shown on the left) and online images that you can also search for by category and download onto your system. For each category, you can find many different examples (as shown on the right). "Using the Clip Art Collection" shows you how to find, retrieve, and place these images in your pages.

IMAGE 42

FrontPage gives you many different means by which you can acquire images to decorate your site. "An Introduction to Web Graphics" shows you how you can create your own images in a painting program or vector drawing program, grab an image from a PhotoCD, develop your photographs directly to a Web-based service, or use a digital camera to take the picture. In addition, you can use clip art from a Web-based collection (the pink button is from the Ultimate Symbol Web Elements collection) or a stock image (the rose at top-left from Vivid Details), use clip art from a vector collection (the gorilla from Art Parts), or find free images on the Web (the Celtic graphic—RqbeastlG2.gif—created by Bradley Schenck at www.webomator.com).

IMAGE 43

"Image Maps" shows you how to create multiple hyperlinks from a single a image. The buttons are created and placed as a single image onto your page. You can use FrontPage's Image Map tools to draw hot spots around each button and link each hot spot to a different page.

IMAGE 44

"Image Maps" also shows you how to create hot spots in a photograph that contains a number of "natural" areas that can be used as individual links, like the fruit stand shown here. Each vegetable bin can be linked to page that allows the site visitor to purchase or learn about the produce pictured.

IMAGE 45

Finally, you will learn in "Image Maps" how to create a collaged image map like the one pictured here. Each of the different onion products pictured has been made into a hot spot that when clicked on takes the site visitor to a different page in the Web site.

IMAGE 46

In "Images and Text—An Uneasy Alliance," you'll learn how to place graphics to force text into different shapes. Here, several different sizes of graphic elements are used along with different alignment options to create a tree-like shape out of the text.

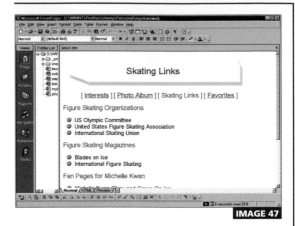

IMAGE 47

You can also use graphic elements as bullets on a list. You can learn more about lists and graphics in Chapter 5's "List Management 101," Chapter 6's "Creating Basic Links and Bookmarks," and Chapter 7's "Images and Text—An Uneasy Alliance."

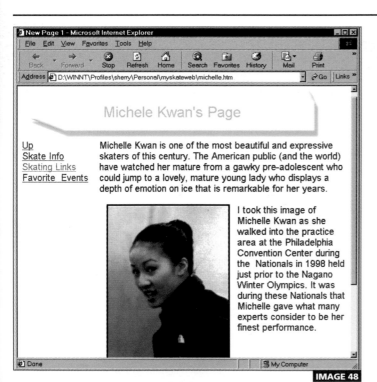

IMAGE 48

"Inserting Graphics from a File" demonstrates how to place an image and align it so that it makes the text wrap around it. The example shown here is a good illustration of the professional-looking results that you can obtain.

The images on this page all illustrate graphics effects that are possible with FrontPage.

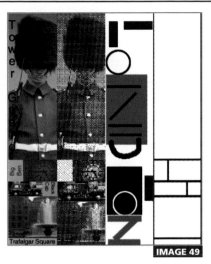

IMAGE 49

FrontPage allows you to create low source images. These are images that load quickly and are displayed while the "real" image loads (if your site visitor is using Netscape Navigator to browse the Web). "Creating Low Bandwidth Images" shows you how to create placeholder images for the original image (the left-most image) that are (from left to right) black and white, a text-based graphic, or a structure of the cut-up graphic that is loading.

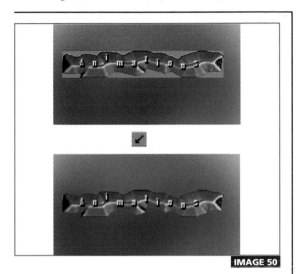

IMAGE 50

"The Effects Tools" section helps you to create transparent GIF images—images where the background (selected in the top part of this image) can be dropped out so that the image appears to sink into the background color of your page.

IMAGE 51

This page shows the ability of FrontPage to create thumbnail images—small images that act as placeholders for larger images. The "Auto Thumbnails" section describes how to create and use this feature of FrontPage. When you click on one of these tiny, fast-loading images, you can see the full-sized image. This is a way to enable your visitor to wait only for the images that she/he really wants to view.

IMAGE 52

"Designing Page Backgrounds" shows you how to create some fancy as well as plain backgrounds and repeat patterns. Shown here is a scalloped effect that is actually only a small-but-wide repeating pattern that creates a one-sided border on your page.

Chapter 8: **Customizing and Creating Themes**

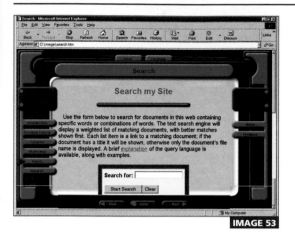

IMAGE 53

IMAGE 54

"Customizing Themes" gives you several sources for purchasing or developing themes from already-created art work. The image on the left shows a theme (MEGA) created by Paul Vineburg and available for purchase at PixelMill (www.pixelmill.com) or from Paul's Web site (http://www.vineburg.com.au). The image on the right shows elements of Kelly Loomis's artwork (available as linkware at www.7rings.com) being used in the Modify Theme dialog box to create a new theme. Kelly is an incredibly talented artist and her images are a privilege to use. Although you can create custom themes with her images, you still need to display her link icon whenever you use the images.

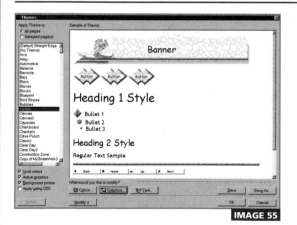

IMAGE 55

IMAGE 56

"Your Very Own Theme" shows you how to create a theme for yourself that you can package and distribute as you wish. On the left, the image shows a variety of elements being defined as a theme. The image on the right shows these theme elements being used in a page. Notice how you can create graphics that form both the button and part of the bar behind the buttons. That allows you to automatically generate a bar/border as large as you need to hold the links that you specify for the page.

Chapter 9: **Publishing, Maintaining, and Troubleshooting Your Web**

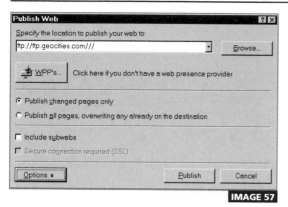

IMAGE 57

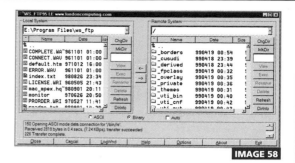

IMAGE 58

You can publish your Web to your server using the Publish dialog box in FrontPage. This works even if you don't have FrontPage Server Extensions on your server. The only thing that you won't be able to do is to immediately view your site if you haven't got Server Extensions installed. You can learn how to this and more in the "Publishing Your Web" section.

In the "FTP" section, you'll find out how to use an FTP program to upload your changes to the Web. This image uses WS-FTP95 LE, a shareware FTP program.

IMAGE 59

IMAGE 60

These are two images from a Web site that I maintain as a support site for an online Photoshop course that I teach. Using FrontPage, I was able to develop the basic site in less than an hour (with a standard Theme and shared borders). When a student has a question that requires an image to explain the answer, or when an image is missing from the course site, I can quickly update this site at www.geocities.com/prancingpixel to make the needed changes. Chapter 9 shows you a number of ways to keep your site up-to-date.

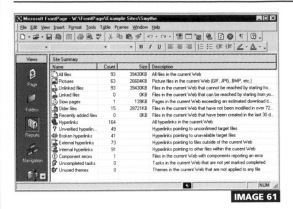

IMAGE 61

IMAGE 62

The report of images used in a Web is only one of the possible reports that you'll learn about in "Reports 'R Us." You'll also be able to make changes directly inside of some of the reports.

You might even begin to think of FrontPage as "Reports 'R Us" when you've read about all of the reports that FrontPage produces. This image shows most of the list of reports. Behind each report line is another full report.

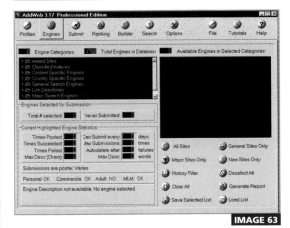

IMAGE 63

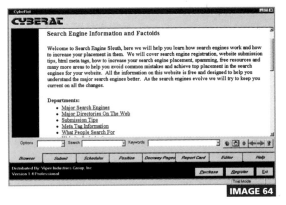

IMAGE 64

You want your site to be visited, so in "Getting Noticed," you'll learn how to create META tags and offer your site to a search engine. You'll learn about programs such as AddWeb, that specialize in making search engine submissions.

You'll also find references to pages on the Web that keep you updated on the latest ways to get search engines to recognize your site and to better the placement that your site receives on search engines.

Chapter 10: **Using Tables**

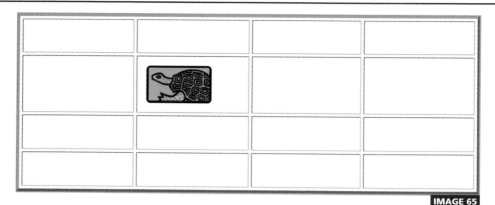

IMAGE 65

You can learn how to create tables from the simple to the complex in Chapter 10. In this simple table, a single image is embedded in a grid. While this table's borders are visible, you'll learn how to create tables with invisible borders as well.

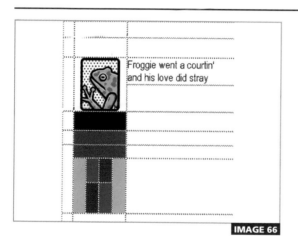

IMAGE 66

IMAGE 67

In "Drawing Your Table," you'll learn how to break up the space in a table and create interesting shapes. No rule says that the table cells need to filled with either image or text. You can create some very interesting effects simply by changing the background color on a table cell, as you can see here. In these images, you see how the table is constructed, and you can see the table as it is finished.

IMAGE 68

In "Tables as a Layout Device," you'll learn how to use a table to hold the buttons that you used originally as an image map. You can see the structure of the table in this image.

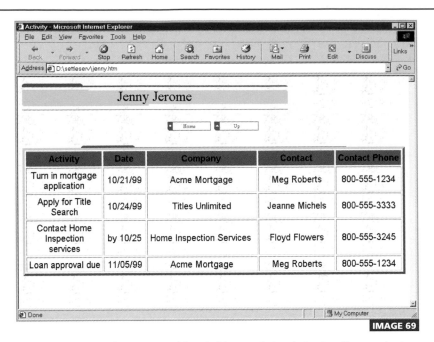

IMAGE 69

"Creating Traditional Tables" teaches you how to use a table to hold—surprise!—tabular data. You can also import tabular data from other programs or from database or spreadsheet programs. Any text that you can store in comma-delimited files can be directly placed into a table in FrontPage.

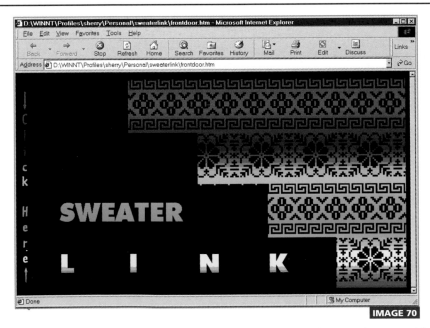

IMAGE 70

You can also use tables to hold cut-up images. As such, the table is one of the most powerful layout devices possible on the Web. In this example, using a table saves many bytes of data because the solid portion of the image is nothing more a group of cells with a black background.

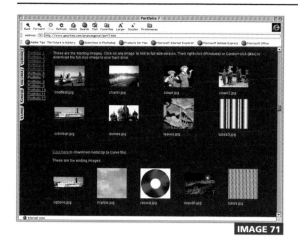

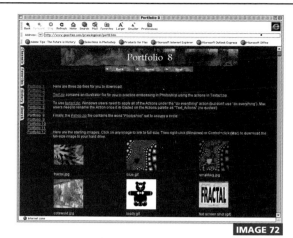

IMAGE 71

IMAGE 72

Here are two more pages from the PrancingPixel site (my real one). In both cases, I used tables to hold and organize the images. A table allows you to effortlessly combine text and data.

IMAGE 73

Tables can also become quite complex. Here, you can see the structure of the MEGA template created by Paul Vineburg and available for purchase at PixelMill (www.pixelmill.com) or from Paul's Web site (http://www.vineburg.com.au). The image is cut up into many pieces. Storing pieces in a cell makes it easy to swap graphics and create rollovers.

```
<p align="center"> 
<div align="center">
  <center>
  <table border="0" cellpadding="0" cellspacing="0">
    <tr>
      <td><img border="0" src="1.jpg" width="257" height="119"><img border="0" src="2.jp
    </tr>
    <tr>
      <td>
        <table border="0" cellpadding="0" cellspacing="0">
          <tr>
            <td bgcolor="#000000"><img border="0" src="3.jpg" width="46" height="166"><i
            <td bgcolor="#000000"><img border="0" src="5.jpg" width="28" height="38"><br
              <a href="javascript:" onmouseclick="return 1" onmouseover="changeImages('i
              <a href="javascript:" onmouseclick="return 2" onmouseover="changeImages('i
              <a href="javascript:" onmouseclick="return 3" onmouseover="changeImages('i
              <a href="javascript:" onmouseclick="return 4" onmouseover="changeImages('i
            <td bgcolor="#000000"><img border="0" src="6.jpg" width="58" height="166"><i
          </tr>
          <tr>
            <td colspan="3"><img border="0" src="9.jpg" width="46" height="39"><img name
          </tr>
          <tr>
            <td colspan="3"><img border="0" src="12.jpg" width="257" height="15"></td>
          </tr>
        </table>
      </td>
```

IMAGE 74

When you create a table, FrontPage writes the HTML code for you. The code shown here is needed to make the table shown below display properly in a browser.

IMAGE 75

This jukebox interface by Kelly Loomis of www.7rings.com shows another complex use of a table as a layout device. The interface "lives" in a table of many cells. The buttons down the center of the image actually contain rollovers. You'll learn how to work with complex tables in "Tables as a Layout Device."

Chapter 11: **Frames**

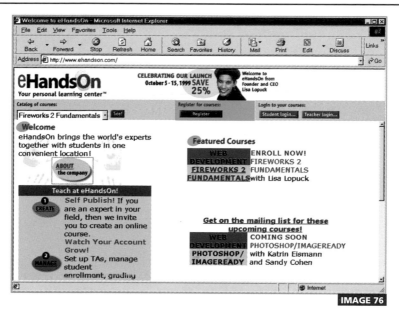

IMAGE 76

In "Frames and When to Use Them," you'll learn about good examples and bad examples of frames. This page from ehandson.com, an online training company, shows a good (and subtle) use of frames. The top portion of the screen is a frame that functions as a menu.

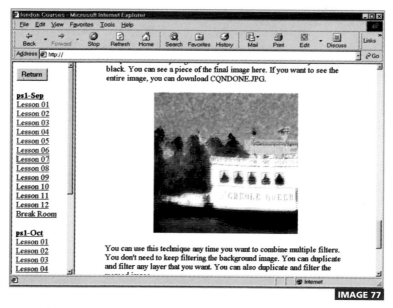

IMAGE 77

This framed page, from a tutorial site, also shows a good use of frames. The left-side of the screen contains a menu that gives you constant access to all of your options and enables you to jump to any lesson or message board available simply by clicking on the ever-present table of contents in the left-hand frame.

IMAGE 78

You can also use frames to keep a graphics-heavy design from having to be downloaded on every page. This example from the fictional PrancingPixel site uses a frame as a border on the top and side of the page. Only the content changes. However, the page displays quite quickly.

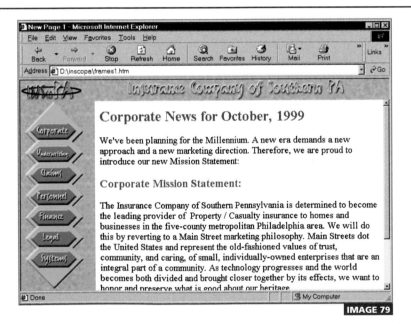

IMAGE 79

"Adding Content" shows you how to create the imagery and text that you want to place inside of a frameset. This example shows you how to create a frames Web site for a fictional insurance company. You'll learn how to measure the area, define the content, and display and edit it.

Chapter 12: **Using HTML**

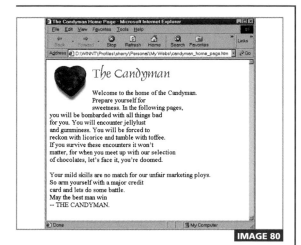

IMAGE 80

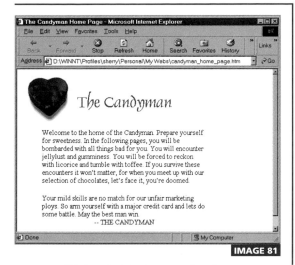

IMAGE 81

Even though FrontPage generates HTML code for you, you might want to learn how to write your own. It can help to solve problems or it can allow you to include multiple fonts. In "A Simple HTML Page," you'll learn how to change text that just wraps around an image and sits there (like this image)…

…into a well-behaved table where everything lines up.

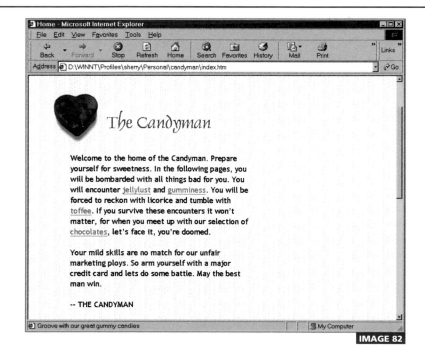

IMAGE 82

Chapter 13: **Adding Life to Your Page with DHTML**

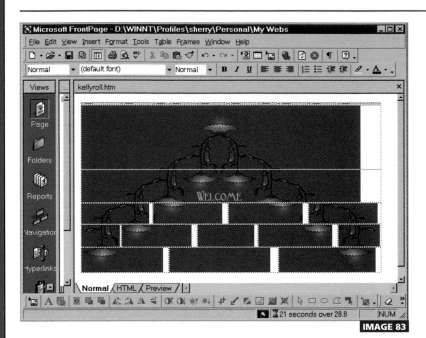

IMAGE 83

In "Text Rollovers," you'll take this simple HTML document a bit farther and learn how to create text rollovers. A text rollover is an area of regular HTML text that changes color, font, or style (or all of the above) when your site visitor's mouse is on top of it.

You can place a cut-up image into a table and have FrontPage generate the code that swaps images inside of a cell when the mouse rolls over that cell. You'll learn how to create the rollovers in "Traditional (Image) Rollovers." Although this table looks particularly odd in Page View…

IMAGE 84

…it displays properly in preview mode and in a browser. You'll use all of your table skills from Chapter 10 in building this cut-up table where planning is the key to success. The real trick is to determine exactly how many cells you'll need before you begin to combine them. As you can see, you need to leave room for the text that informs your site visitor of their choices. The image used here is the Tiffany's Light Set by Kelly Loomis of www.7rings.com.

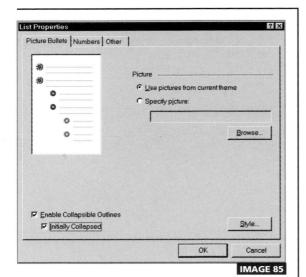

IMAGE 85

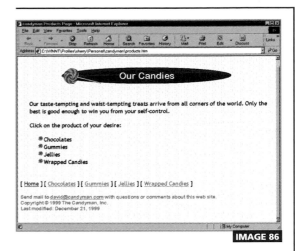

IMAGE 86

In "DHTML Collapsible Lists," you'll learn how to create lists that expand to show the site visitor a more complete list of items or links. You can use the graphic bullets that are part of a theme to show the hierarchy of your list.

You can specify that you want the list to display in its collapsed state when the page opens.

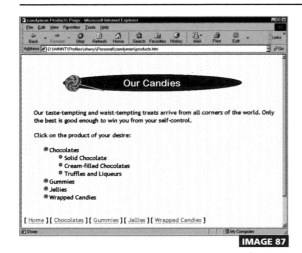

IMAGE 87

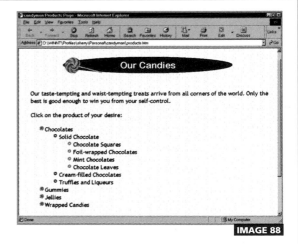

IMAGE 88

When the site visitor clicks on an item in the list, the list opens up. If they select an item in the expanded list and more information is available, the next level of the hierarchy appears.

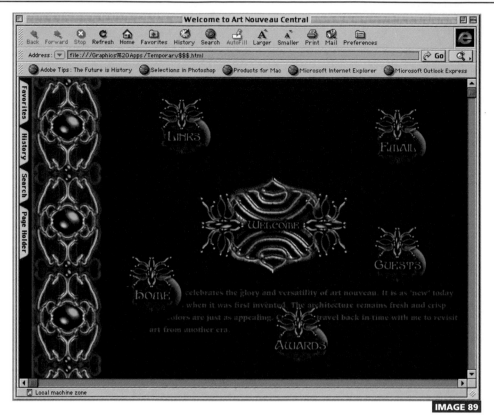

IMAGE 89

Dynamic HTML enables you to layer text and graphics and to position them precisely. In "Floating Content," you'll learn how to create effects similar to this one where text sits behind the buttons in the page. This example again features the artwork of Kelly Loomis from www.7rings.com. The set is called "A Touch of Nouveau."

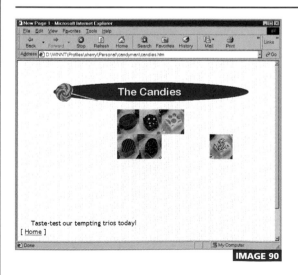

IMAGE 90

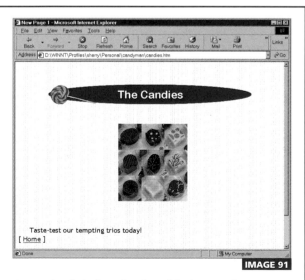

IMAGE 91

"Other Effects from the DHTML Toolbar" shows you how to create images that fly in from the edges of the image as the page loads. You could also make the images fly out when the site visitor leaves the page.

Chapter 14: **Movies and Audio**

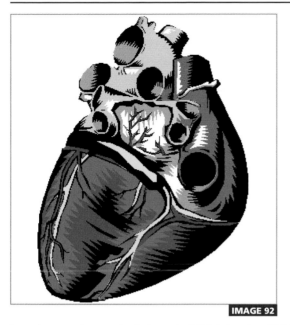

IMAGE 92

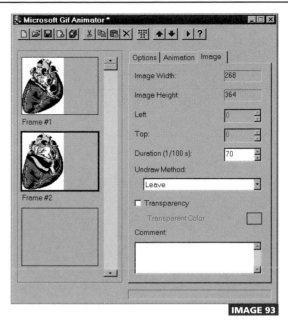

IMAGE 93

Learn how to animate a simple image in "GIF Animations." This heart image, which begins as Microsoft clip art downloaded from the online clip art library site, becomes a living, beating thing. It only requires two different images. When you attach a sound clip, you can even hear the heart beat.

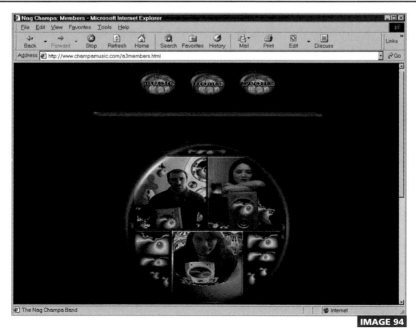

IMAGE 94

In "Adding Audio to a FrontPage Web," you'll learn how to embed audio files like the ones on the site pictured here. This image is one of the pages on the site of the band Nag Champa (www.champamusic.com). The site contains a variety of original music in MP3 format. In this section of the book, you'll also learn about the various music formats and how to use them.

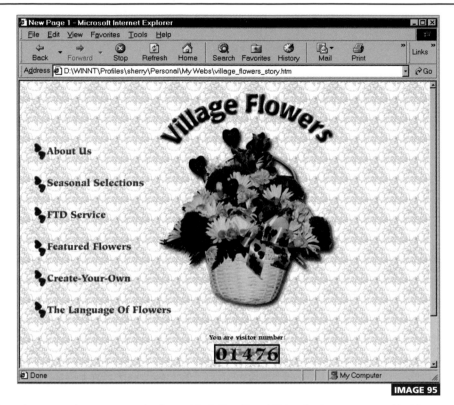

IMAGE 95

A *hit counter* shows how many times your page has been visited. FrontPage 2000 makes it very easy to add a hit counter for your page, and to use any of several styles to display it. You'll learn how in "Hit Counter." You can use any of the included styles of numbering for your hit counter or you can create your own, as I did here.

IMAGE 96

The "Include Page Component" section tells you how to add sections that update to your pages. This page can be added …

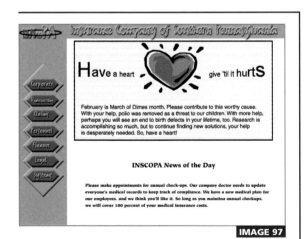

IMAGE 97

…to another page or can be included in every page on the site as a reminder to contribute to the March of Dimes. You can easily update news flashes or even schedule both pictures and images to appear at certain times.

IMAGE 98

In "Banner Ads," you'll learn how to make a graphic that can display multiple images and link to another location. These four images are all the same size and are to be used in a banner ad for the Village Flowers site. Only one image is displayed at a time, and you can decide how you want to transition from one to another.

IMAGE 99

Here, you can see how the banner ad is displayed on the Village Flowers Web site. It links to the "Seasonal Flowers" page.

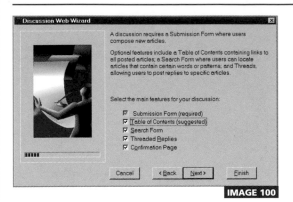

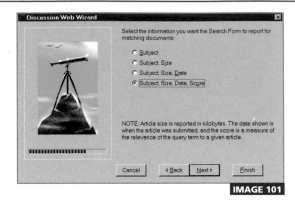

"Discussion Groups" helps you to use the FrontPage Discussion Group feature. This is a component in that it requires the FrontPage extensions in order to work. You can create a discussion group by creating the Web using the Discussion Wizard. These two images show some of the options that you need to specify in the Wizard.

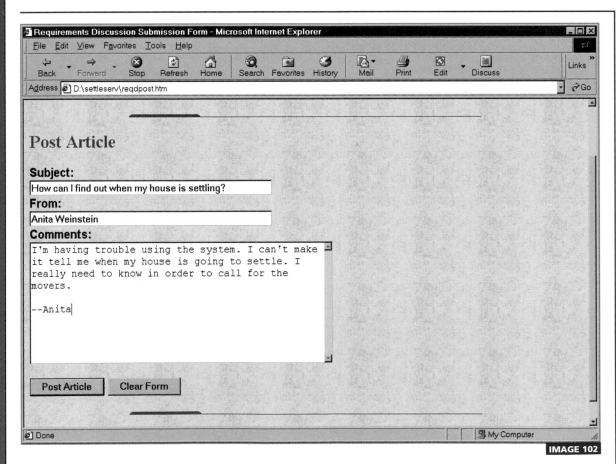

The Discussion Wizard actually creates a form that your site visitors complete in order to post questions and to answer questions that others have posted. Chapter 15 contains a section on designing your own forms.

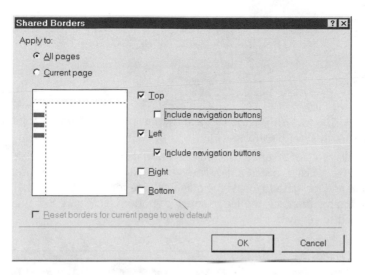

In the top shared border, choose Insert | Page Banner.

3. Then, right-click on the left-side shared border and choose Navigation Bar Properties. Add the Child level to the hyperlinks on the page and select Vertical Buttons. Click OK. If you don't remember how to do this, reread the section in Chapter 5 that discusses the navigation bar properties.

4. If the dotted line between the shared border and the page top is not right underneath the page banner, you need to remove the extra space. Place your cursor at the bottom of the shared border area and press the BACKSPACE key until the space is removed.

5. You need to insert the top and bottom extra graphics above and below the navigation bar in the left-side shared border. This is the only really tricky part of the entire process. Place your cursor under the left-side navigation bar and click. The cursor will "cling" to the next possible insertion point in the border. Press the left arrow key one time. This moves the insertion point to the beginning of the navigation bar.

6. Choose Insert | Picture | File and navigate to locate the graphic to use for the top of the bar. If you are using my graphics, the file to select is bartop.gif. The new image moves the first button on the navigation bar toward the right.

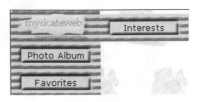

7. Press the SHIFT-ENTER keys to force the navigation button back into position (without leaving extra space).

8. Place your cursor under the left-side navigation bar and click again. Press the SHIFT-ENTER keys to start a new line with no extra space. Choose Insert | Picture | File and navigate to locate the graphic to use for the top of the bar. If you are using my graphics, the file to select is vbottom.gif. Figure 8-7 shows the finished screen with the new theme in use.

FIGURE 8-7   Finished home page for MySkateWeb

Packaging Your Theme

Where does FrontPage store the altered themes? The answer depends on the operating system that you're using. Windows 95 and Windows 98 store the templates in C:\Program Files\Common Files\Microsoft Shared\Themes\ (unless you've installed to a different disk). If you don't see the themes there, try C:\WINDOWS\Application Data\Microsoft\ Themes\. If you are using Windows NT, the default directory is C:\winnt\Profiles\"username"\Application Data\Microsoft\Themes\.

If you navigate to the correct directory and look at the themes stored there, you'll see a folder for each theme. Inside the folder are the actual theme files. If I had applied the new theme using CSS, a .css file would also have been present in the folder.

If you want to share your altered themes, all you need to do is copy these files to another disk and then have the person using them place them into the same folders in their installation of FrontPage.

All of the graphics that you use in the theme are stored in your Web in a hidden directory. To view the hidden directories in your Web (these directories begin with an underscore character), choose Tools | Web Settings | Advanced. Click the "Show documents in hidden directories" checkbox.

Tip: If the bar does not preview correctly, make sure that your insertion point is to the right of the bottom graphic. Press the left arrow key to bring the insertion point to the left of the graphic, and press the BACKSPACE key. This messes up the navigation bar again, but it removes any invisible space. Now, press SHIFT-ENTER again and the preview should be fine.

All of your graphics are stored in the _themes folder. You can navigate to this directory to place theme elements into your pages.

Professional Skills Summary

This ends our look at modifying themes. You've learned how to modify themes and how to create your own. Themes are among the most powerful of FrontPage's features for easy Web creation. When combined with the shared borders and navigation bars, Web sites almost assemble themselves.

If you look at prices for site design on the Web, you'll find a wide variety. I recently located a company that advertised a simple FrontPage theme-based Web for $125. How could it make money doing this? A simple five-page Web site using an already-created theme probably takes no more than an hour to create and it uploads (as you'll see in Chapter 9) like a dream. If you want top-notch graphics and cutting-edge design, of course your site will take longer to assemble.

The beauty of FrontPage is that it gives you the flexibility to be "cookie cutter" or trendsetter. You've seen an example of a very complex interface that can be used as a FrontPage theme.

You'll learn how to publish and maintain your Web in Chapter 9.

Part III

Advanced Options

chapter 9

Publishing, Maintaining, and Troubleshooting Your Web

In this chapter, you:

- Learn how to publish your Web on the Internet

- Learn about the various configurations of the FrontPage Server Extensions

- Learn what functions the FrontPage Server Extensions can perform

- Learn how to use FTP to upload your Web to the Web

- Learn how to make changes to published material

- Learn how to use the FrontPage reports to manage your Web

You're Live at Five!

Finally. You've managed to learn the basic features of FrontPage and are ready to publish your Web site to the world. FrontPage is really a program with a split personality. It is a very capable Web layout program—which is the part of FrontPage that you've used so far—but it is also a superior site management application. FrontPage gives you extensive management reports, power to protect and secure your sites, and multiple ways to keep your site updated and current.

Getting Ready to Publish

What does it mean to *publish* your Web? Publishing your Web means copying the files from FrontPage to a server on the World Wide Web. When you develop your Web, you are most likely working on your own computer. You create your content, add your graphics, and get everything ready to go. However, everything is still only on your computer. Before anyone else can see it, it must be moved to the World Wide Web. That's what publishing your Web means.

Before you can publish, there are certain things that you need to do. You need to know where to send your site—i.e., you need to know the name of the Internet service provider (ISP) that will host your Web pages. You also need to get any user IDs or passwords necessary to let you add your code to the host computer.

You need to know whether the host site supports the FrontPage Server Extensions. The process of moving your Web pages to the host computer is different if the host computer is or is not running the server extensions. You actually need to know this very early on because the Server Extensions provide extra functionality to your Web. If you used any of the components provided in FrontPage, you need to publish to a site that supports the extensions. You can look on the Microsoft FrontPage Web site to find a list of ISPs and Web Presence Providers (WPPs) who support the FrontPage extensions.

You need to check over your Web to make sure that everything works properly:

- Preview your Web using a browser like Internet Explorer or Netscape Navigator to make sure that everything works.
- Look for broken hyperlinks—i.e., hyperlinks that point to nonexisting destinations. The reporting functions (described later in this chapter) can help.
- Look at each page and make sure that it displays the way that you want it to.

Once you have everything working and looking the way that you want it to, it's time to publish. Before we talk about publishing, we'll describe two different sets of tools that might be required: The FrontPage Server Extensions and FTP.

FrontPage Server Extensions and You

Many Web layout programs exist today. FrontPage doesn't have a monopoly on good layout tools. Programs such as Adobe's GoLive and Macromedia's DreamWeaver provide more visual means of layout for Web pages. No other program, however, combines as much power into one package as does FrontPage. No other Web design package has its own set of extensions for automating features once a Web site is operational. FrontPage's themes, shared borders, navigation bars, and the Server Extensions combo add up to an unbeatable array of brute force. The Server Extensions are the final coup de grace on the competition.

The FrontPage 2000 Server Extensions give additional functionality to FrontPage-created (or imported) Webs. They provide improved functions that help you administer, author, and browse your FrontPage Webs. The Server Extensions use Common Gateway Interface (CGI) or the Internet Server Application Programming Interface (ISAPI) and are available for Web servers from Microsoft, Netscape, Stronghold, O'Reilly and Associates, Apache, and NCSA. This means that you are not limited to using a WinNT machine as your Web server and you can find an ISP who uses different operating systems than "Windows Standard."

The Server Extensions enhance the browsing, authoring, or administrative functions of FrontPage.

Browsing function additions

The extensions listed below allow you to implement the following functions on your Web site without requiring any special coding. You don't need to be a programmer or learn to program to use them. These features will *not* work if your server doesn't have the Server Extensions installed (although some of them can be programmed to work using JavaScript or CGI functions):

- Banner ad manager
- Confirmation fields
- Discussion form handler (which allows interactive discussion groups)
- Email form handler
- Include Page support
- Interactive discussion groups
- Hit counters
- Hover buttons
- Marquee
- Scheduled picture

- Search forms
- Substitution properties
- Table of contents
- Superior integration of Office 2000 documents.

Cross-Reference: You'll learn about many of these components in Chapter 15.

Authoring function additions

If you have the Server Extensions, you will be able to complete the following authoring tasks online. Without them, you need to work on your own hard drive and then publish your changes to the Web:

- Create/modify/change your Web pages.
- Develop your Web on a local computer and then *automatically* publish your Web to a Web server on the Intranet or Internet.
- View all the FrontPage Webs on a server.
- Open a FrontPage Web for authoring.
- View, create, and delete directories.
- View, create, delete, edit, save, and rename files.
- Create and configure FrontPage components.
- Apply shared borders.
- Add META information to your Web pages.
- Add a document to a Microsoft Visual SourceSafe project, check it out, and check it in. Visual SourceSafe simplifies collaborations between Web authors by identifying multiple changes to a Web page. Check out and check in allow authors to each work on a different part of a site.
- Recalculate the hyperlink map of the FrontPage Web showing all of the links on your Web.
- Create a full-text index of your Web.
- Add, modify, or delete an item from Tasks view.
- View and modify the navigation structure of your Web.
- Add predefined database queries to your Web pages.
- Change an author's password.
- Give Web authors the ability to refresh their FrontPage site definitions from the actual Web site.

- Identify when more than one author is attempting to open a page and ensure that only one author has write access to a Web page at any one time.

Administrative functions

These extensions simplify Web site administration while connected to a live FrontPage-managed site:

- Set authoring, administering, and site-browsing permissions
- Create, delete, and rename FrontPage Webs
- View user and group lists on your Web
- View Windows NT domains
- Add new authors, administrators, and site visitors (UNIX only)
- Use a Microsoft Visual SourceSafe project

You need to install (or have someone install) the extensions on your Web server before you can use them. Many, but not all, Web presence providers (WPPs) and Internet service providers support the Microsoft Server Extensions. If you are using a commercial WPP or ISP, you will need to determine whether the extensions are available for your use. Sometimes, Server Extension support requires an additional fee. If you are using an in-house Web server, you must speak to your Webmaster to determine whether you have the extensions installed or to arrange to have them installed.

The FrontPage Server Extensions for all servers are available for downloading at:

http://msdn.microsoft.com/workshop/languages/fp/2000/winfpse.asp

The extensions (for Windows NT 4.0 and later/IIS 3.0 and later) are also available on:

- The FrontPage 2000 CD-ROM (run servext.exe to install)
- As part of the Office Server Extensions in Microsoft Office 2000 Standard, Professional, and Premium
- Windows 2000

The extensions are available for the Web servers and platforms listed in Table 9-1. This information is current as of Fall 1999 and is based on information from the Microsoft FrontPage Server Extensions Resource Kit. Note that not all Web servers may be available for all operating systems shown.

Platform	Operating System	Web Server
Intel X86	Microsoft Windows NT Server 4.0 and later	IIS 3.0 and greater
Intel X86	Microsoft Windows Workstation 4.0 and later Microsoft Windows NT Server 4.0 and later	Microsoft Peer Web Services FrontPage Personal Web Server Netscape Enterprise Server 3.x, 3.51 Netscape FastTrack 2.0, 3.01 O'Reilly WebSite 2.0
Intel X86	Microsoft Windows 95/98	Microsoft Personal Web Server 2.0,4.0 FrontPage Personal Web Server Netscape FastTrack 2.0, 3.01 O'Reilly WebSite
Intel X86	BSD/OS 3.1, 4.0 Red Hat Linux 4.1 and above Solaris 2.6 SCO OpenServer5.0 SCO UnixWare 7	Apache 1.2.6, 1.3.3 NCSA 1.5.2 (not 1.5a or 1.5.1) Netscape Enterprise Server 3.x, 3.51 Netscape FastTrack 2.0, 3.01 StrongHold 2.3
Compaq Alpha	Microsoft Windows NT Server Microsoft Windows Workstation	IIS 3.0 or later (NT Server 4.0 or later) Microsoft Peer Web Services (Workstation)
Compaq Alpha	Digital UNIX 3.2c, 4.0 Linux 2.0.34	Apache 1.2.6, 1.3.3 NCSA 1.5.2 (not 1.5a or 1.5.1) Netscape Enterprise Server 3.x, 3.51 Netscape FastTrack 2.0, 3.01 StrongHold 2.3
PA-RISC	HP/UX 10.2, 11.0	Apache 1.2.6, 1.3.3 NCSA 1.5.2 (not 1.5a or 1.5.1) Netscape Enterprise Server 3.x, 3.51 Netscape FastTrack 2.0, 3.01 StrongHold 2.3
Silicon Graphics	IRIX 6.2, 6.3	Apache 1.2.6, 1.3.3 NCSA 1.5.2 (not 1.5a or 1.5.1) Netscape Enterprise Server 3.x, 3.51 Netscape FastTrack 2.0, 3.01 StrongHold 2.3
RS6000 / Power PC	AIX 4.x	Apache 1.2.6, 1.3.3 NCSA 1.5.2 (not 1.5a or 1.5.1) Netscape Enterprise Server 3.x, 3.51 Netscape FastTrack 2.0, 3.01 StrongHold 2.3
Sun SPARC	Solaris 2.5.1, 2.6	Apache 1.2.6, 1.3.3 NCSA 1.5.2 (not 1.5a or 1.5.1) Netscape Enterprise Server 3.x, 3.51 Netscape FastTrack 2.0, 3.01 StrongHold 2.3

TABLE 9-1 List of Servers for Which FrontPage Server Extensions Are Available

FTP

FTP (File Transfer Protocol) is a standard part of the TCP/IP protocol suite. It provides a method for copying files between two machines running TCP/IP. Microsoft supplies an FTP client in both Windows 95/98 and Windows NT, which will allow you to copy files to another TCP/IP machine (e.g., your Web Server).

If your Web server does not have the FrontPage Server Extensions installed, you must use FTP to move files between your workstation and your Web server. Your ISP or WPP or LAN administrator will be able to provide you with instructions for using FTP to move Web pages up to your Web server.

The FTP client provided by Microsoft is basically a command line tool. It runs in a Command Prompt window and, while help is available, it is not really all that easy to use. FrontPage 2000 will use FTP automatically to move a page to a Web host without your needing to learn the command lines. Unfortunately, this may not work in all cases.

If you must use FTP, I suggest downloading a GUI FTP client, which makes using FTP much simpler. I prefer to use WS-FTP, which has a simple interface that shows directories on both the client and server and allows you to click on the files that you want to move. You can download a trial version of WS_FTP at www.ipswich.com.87.

Publishing Your Web

The publishing process differs slightly based on the presence or absence of Server Extensions from your Web server.

Publishing your Web using the server extensions

When the server extensions are installed, publishing is easy. FrontPage knows what it needs to copy to the host system and can talk to the extensions to see that everything is moved easily. Before you publish your Web, you need to do the following:

1. Pick the files that you want to publish. You can publish only selected files or publish everything that you have worked on (except for files marked Don't Publish).

2. Decide if you want FrontPage to copy only changed files or replace all files. With the extensions installed on the server, FrontPage can compare the pages on your computer with the pages on the Web server and only send changed pages. Of course, the first time that you publish, the Web server doesn't have any of your pages so that all will be sent up.

3. Decide if you want FrontPage to publish subwebs. FrontPage can either publish the specified Web or it can look for subwebs and publish them as well. If a subweb has a subweb of its own, this too would be published if you select the "include subwebs" option. (We'll talk about subwebs a bit later in the chapter.)

4. Decide if you want FrontPage to use a secure connection. With the extensions installed, FrontPage normally uses HTTP to move the files from your computer to the Web. When you use a secure connection, FrontPage uses Secure Socket Layer (SSL) to move your files. This provides added security and should be used when the Web pages contain sensitive information.

When you are ready to upload your Web to your Web server, connect to your ISP and then choose File | Publish. Figure 9-1 shows how to complete the Publish Web dialog box.

Although you can always publish all of the files every time, it is not always a great idea. Some files should only be published once. If you place a hit counter on your site, for example, you shouldn't change or update it again (unless it breaks); otherwise, you'll set the hit count back to zero each time you update your site (a not-very-useful thing to do to a running count).

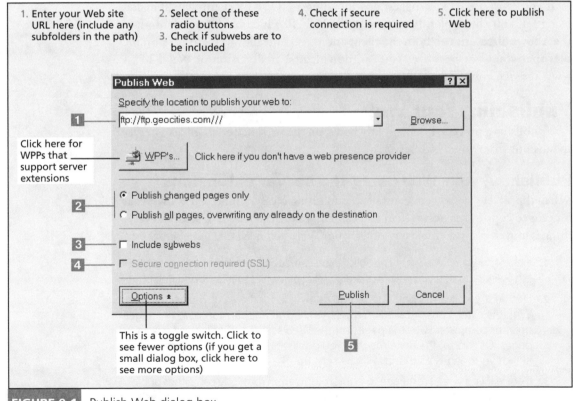

FIGURE 9-1   Publish Web dialog box

Not publishing specific material

You also might want to omit certain files from update when you're making modifications to Web pages or you have incomplete pages in progress. Suppose that you see some problems on the existing site when you log on to add new content.

You want to fix your problem, but you don't want to update any of the new material. You can mark the pages that you were working on as "Don't Publish." Here's how:

1. Right-click on the file name in the Folder list. Select Properties from the context-sensitive menu.

2. Click the Workgroup tab to display workgroup information. Checkmark the "Exclude this file when publishing the rest of the Web,"

> ☑ Exclude this file when publishing the rest of the Web

then click OK. This file will not be copied to your Web site when you publish.

If/when you are ready to publish this file, just repeat Steps 1 and 2 and remove the checkmark.

Publishing your Web using FrontPage and FTP

Even if your ISP or WPP doesn't provide the FrontPage extensions, you can still use FrontPage to upload your Web to the net via FTP. If you select File | Publish and specify an FTP site for your Web, FrontPage will upload using FTP. As described above, you can select the pages to publish and decide to publish only changed or all files.

In order to publish your files using FTP, you need to know the name of your FTP server, the user ID (or logon name) you need to use during the upload, and the password you need for the upload.

Most ISPs and WPPs are set up so that their FTP servers can write to your Web site. FTP is the mechanism used to upload new Webs and pages. In order to protect your pages, your ISP usually insists on a user ID and password to ensure that only authorized users can upload data. You can use the same File | Publish command as the folks who have Server Extensions. To publish your Web using FTP, follow these steps:

1. Connect to the Web.

2. Select File | Publish.

Tip: Before you upload everything inside of your Web, check to see if there are file types that your ISP cannot accept. Geocities, for example, will not accept native Photoshop-formatted files (.psd) and if these files are accidentally uploaded, they stop the transfer in midstream. If you need to clutter up your Web with non-Web-safe formats, then make sure that you mark them "Don't Publish" before you try to publish your Web.

Tip: Some Web servers, like Geocities, don't give you the directory names. Geocities is a very popular ISP that offers free personal site Web hosting. Microsoft Technical Support is quite familiar with getting FrontPage to upload to Geocities. You need to add four forward slashes after the FTP address. So, the full path to upload to if you use Geocities is ftp://ftp.geocities.com////.

3. Enter the name of your FTP site. For example, to upload a site to Geocities, you'd enter **ftp://ftp.myISP.com** (replace *myISP* with yours, please, but don't press the ENTER key yet).

4. You also need to know the name of the directory on the Web server where you will store your files. The Smythe site that we've been using throughout this book might be stored in the Smythe directory. If the directory does not exist, FrontPage will create it for you. To upload to the Smythe directory, you'd type **ftp://ftp.myisp.com/smythe**.

5. Click the Publish button. (Don't click the Browse button—it probably won't work correctly.)

6. If your FTP site requires a user ID and password for authentication, you will be prompted with this dialog box.

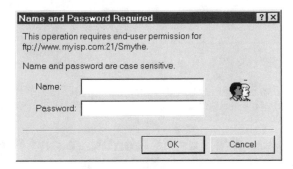

Enter the user ID and Password and click OK to continue. FrontPage then begins to upload your data.

Uploading your pages can take a while. FrontPage first creates the list of files to upload, then it begins moving files. As files are moved, FrontPage displays a message box showing the upload status. It should look something like this:

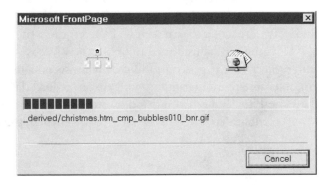

When the upload is complete, FrontPage displays the completion message.

The message gives you the option of visiting your site to check things out, but don't take FrontPage up on its invitation. Click on Done instead. You shouldn't select the "Click here to view…" option because you are pointing to an FTP site, not an HTTP site. In order to test your Web after you upload via FTP, start your browser and enter the URL for your home page.

Publishing your Web manually using FTP

You can publish your Web by yourself without any help from FrontPage using FTP. You first need to install a friendly FTP client, like WS_FTP from www.ipswitch.com. This utility contains a graphical user interface (GUI—pronounced "gooey") that makes it very simple to copy files. Once you have installed the FTP client application, you'll be able to use it over and over again.

You also need to set up an entry for your Web hosting service to allow you to connect to the site via FTP. Here's how to create a connection entry. Bear in mind that I'm using WS-FTP, so if you use a different FTP client, you need to look for similar options. You will definitely need to know the user ID and password that will allow you to upload data to the Web.

To create a new entry, follow these steps:

1. Click on New to create a new entry.
2. Fill in the Profile Name, Host Name/Address, User ID, and Password as shown in Figure 9-2.
3. Checkmark the Save Password (Save Pwd) checkbox.
4. Don't select the Anonymous option. It's generally used to download data from an FTP site, not upload data. Most sites require a specific user ID and password.
5. Press OK to create your entry.

Once you have the entry, you can use it every time you need to make a change to your site. With everything set up, here's how a typical FTP session is conducted:

1. Connect to the Web through your ISP.

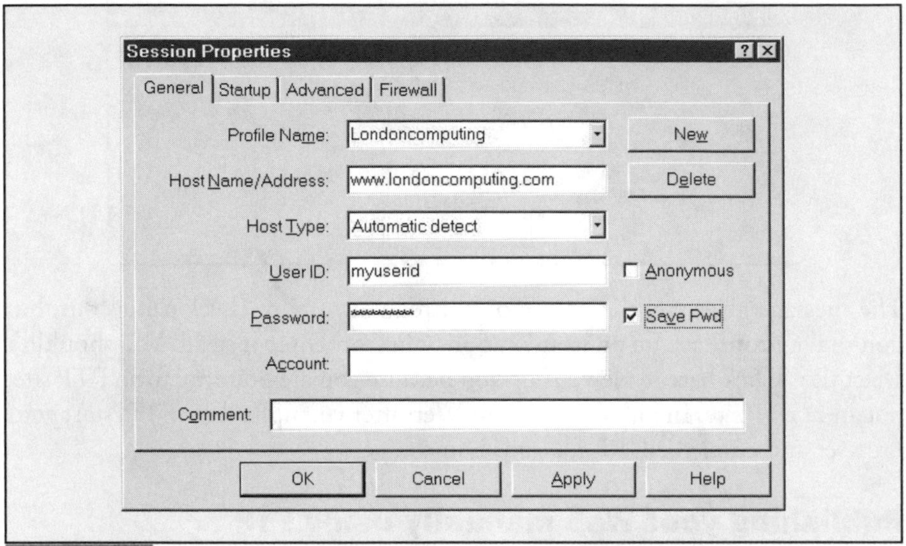

FIGURE 9-2 Setting up the FTP client

2. Start the FTP client program. Because there are various versions of WS_FTP with slightly different interfaces, you may not be able to completely reproduce the samples below. When my copy of WS_FTP starts, this is what I see:

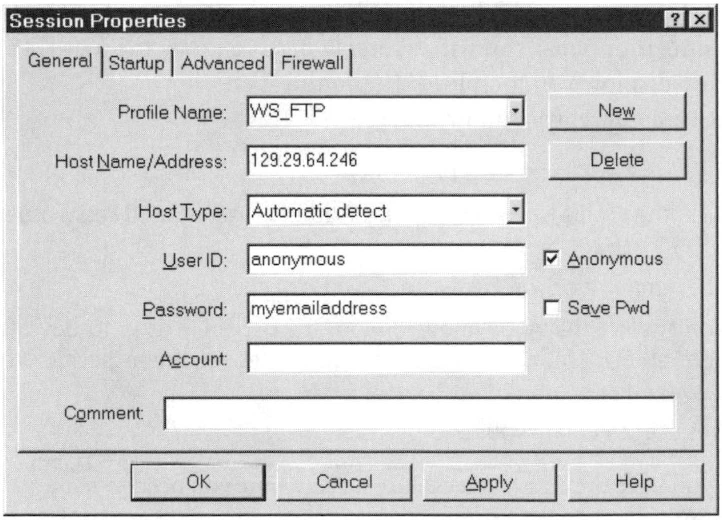

If you already have a connection defined for your host, click the arrow on the Profile Name entry and select your location. If you don't have a connection already, you will need to create one (as was shown above).

3. When you click OK, WS_FTP connects to your site and displays two panels that show the files on your local machine and the files on the host. It looks similar to Figure 9-3.

4. Once you have connected, you need to navigate in the left-hand menu until the Local System file list displays the files in your Web.

5. Now, do the same thing for the Remote System listing. If the directory that you want to copy your Web to does not exist, click the Mkdir button to create a new directory, then position to it. In our example, this is what you see:

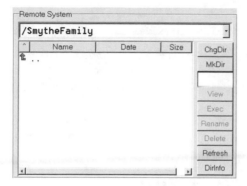

6. Click on all of the directories and files that you need from the left-hand panel. If this is the first time that you are uploading to your site, you can click on everything. Click on the first entry, hold the SHIFT key down, scroll to the last entry and click again. The entire set of files and directories should be

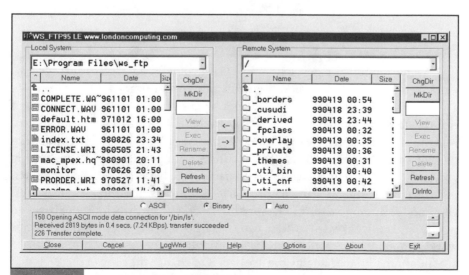

FIGURE 9-3 The FTP Session dialog box

highlighted. (You have actually selected more than you need, but this is the easiest way to proceed.) If you are just updating an existing site, just click on the files to upload. Because WS_FTP does not give you the option of only selecting changed files, you have to know which files have changed.

7. Click on the right arrow. You'll be asked to confirm the transfer.

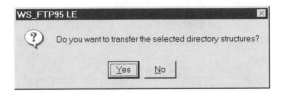

8. Click on Yes and wait for the Web to upload. As data uploads, the panel contents change, showing what has happened and the upload status displays in the message box located immediately above the bottom buttons of the FTP dialog box.

9. When you're done, click the Exit button. You've now uploaded your files to your site. As you can see, it is much easier to use FrontPage.

Making Changes

Once your site is operational, it cannot be static if you want it to be a success. Unless your only purpose is to have your business location on permanent display so people can find you, you need to keep adding new and fresh content to your Web. (Of course, even with a static site, things like area codes on phone numbers need to change on occasion.) FrontPage shines when it comes to making frequent updates.

Maintenance Strategies

If you have the Server Extensions available on your Web server, FrontPage provides several alternative methods for maintaining your pages.

You can make changes directly on your Web server. FrontPage allows you to edit the data on the Web directly. However, this is generally not recommended. Making changes on the live site is rarely a good idea. You have no way of turning off access to your site, so that anyone looking at your pages while you are making changes would see only partially created pages—so that everything looks broken or doesn't work right. Changing pages live also means that you can't really test your modifications to ensure that everything works properly before your pages go public. It usually takes me at least two tries before any type of complex change works properly, and I prefer to make my mistakes in private.

The alternative to changing the live data is to change the copy of the Web that is stored on your local computer. This is the site that you initially created with FrontPage and then copied to your Web server. You can make all of your changes locally, test them out, then copy the changed pages to the Web using FrontPage's Publish feature (publishing changed pages only). This is a much better approach. No one will see your half-completed pages. You can easily try various alternatives until you are happy with the result, and because you have tested your pages first, they are much more likely to work when copied to the Web.

What do you do if your local machine no longer has the latest version of your Web site? This can happen if you develop on more than one machine, if more than one person has created the site, or if you have accidentally erased this information. If you need to bring the site back down to your hard drive, you can use either FrontPage to import your Web or use FTP to transfer the site from your Web server to your local machine.

Don't let your local copy of the site get out-of-date. Neither of the solutions above is good. If you have used shared borders, themes, and navigation bars, the Import Web feature will misfire and not update your copy properly (unless you are very lucky). FrontPage even warns you that there is a major potential problem.

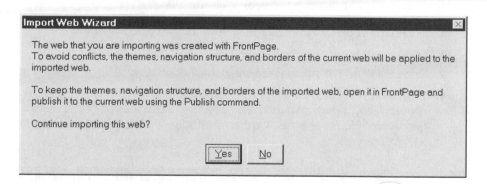

Tip: For corporate sites, you may want a development server to avoid these problems, and do all development on the development server, then publish to the production server.

If you just use the FTP program to move your entire Web in-house, the navigation works better but any subfolders that use different themes get creamed. You lose your themes and all of your navigation information.

However, if you are using the Server Extensions and can open your Web directly while it is on the Internet, you can use the Publish command to place a copy on your hard drive. The Publish command will preserve all of the functions of your site. (But it is still easier to make sure that your site doesn't get out of synch, and one of the best ways to make that happen is to always update your local copy and publish to the Web from that.)

What do you do if your local machine *does* have the latest version of your Web site but you think that it would be smarter to make changes to a copy of your site? That is fairly simple. Create a second copy and make your changes to the new copy. There is one glitch, however. You can't just copy the directory containing your Web to a new subdirectory and go on from there. If you do, all of your links will point to the wrong places. What should you do instead?

You need to create a new subdirectory for your new Web and use FrontPage to publish your existing Web to the new directory. A simple example might help. You have completed work on the Candyman site and published it to your Web server. Everyone loves the site, but you now need to make some major enhancements. You decide to create a CandymanV2 directory and place the Candyman site into it. Once you have everything in place, you'll make all of your changes on the CandymanV2 site.

This is a good strategy for making major changes. It leaves the original data unchanged and untouched, so that it provides a backup and a "fallback" if you do such a good job of "fixing" that you can't make anything work anymore. It also acts as a reference for you as you make the changes. In addition, it's useful if you find a bug in the original site that needs to be fixed. Finally, all of your original data is on your local machine and you can avoid importing from your Web server.

Here's how to publish a copy of your Web site:

1. Create a new directory on your hard drive for the copied Web.

2. Open FrontPage (if not already opened).

3. Open the Web that you want to copy. (File | Open Web).

4. Choose File | Publish. The Publish Web dialog box (that was shown in Figure 9-1) appears. Click the Browse button and navigate to the directory that you created. Click Publish. You'll see a message that asks if you want to convert your folder to a FrontPage Web.

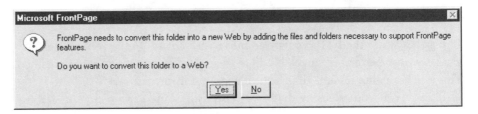

5. Click Yes. FrontPage will begin publishing your Web. While it works, you will see a dialog box showing the current status.

6. If you see a message box saying that dynamic components are used, just click on Continue and wait for FrontPage to finish publishing.

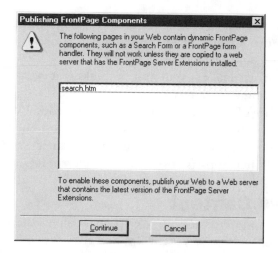

7. When FrontPage has finished, it shows the message telling you that it has successfully done as you asked. Click Done. You now have a new copy of your Web suitable for making changes.

If your Web site contains custom scripts or accesses a database, you might not be able to complete all of your testing on your local machine. In this case, you should create a staging Web server. This is a Web server that runs locally on your intranet and contains a copy of your site. You can configure this server so that it can run scripts, access databases, etc. After you make your changes locally, move your Web pages to the staging server. Once your data has been moved to the staging server, you can test all of your modifications. It is generally a good idea to test the pages that haven't changed as well. Sometimes things break accidentally when you make changes in a supposedly unrelated area.

Adding New Content to Your Web

Do you need to do anything special when you add new pages, graphics, or descriptions to your Web? No. It is amazingly easy to keep your site updated with the changes that you have already made—and tested—on your local machine.

All you need to do is to modify the Web on your local computer and then publish your changed files only. As long as you use FrontPage to publish your data, you can either use the Server Extensions or FTP to publish your changed files. The FTP transfer appears to be much slower than using the extensions. FrontPage must first pull data back from the Web server in order to determine what files have changed. This can take longer than you'd like it to, although I've been uploading small changes to a personal Web site that I maintain in about three minutes per change.

You can also use manual FTP to transfer the changed files. This is actually faster for servers that do not contain the Server Extensions. If you originally put up your site using manual FTP transfer, try not to use the FrontPage publish feature. When FrontPage looks at your host, it thinks that every file that is on the host has changed and will ask if you want to overwrite it.

When FrontPage's Publish command compares your local Web with the Web on the host, it will also find any files that exist on the host but not on your Web and give you the opportunity to remove them from the host. Be careful, especially if you have different parts of your site on different local computers.

Repetitive Content

FrontPage allows you to include one Web page on top of another (this requires Server Extensions), which is very useful if you need to place the same information on every page and you don't want to make the changes on each page. All you need to do is create your duplicate content in a single page and then include that page in all of your other pages. When any of the standard content needs to change, you only have to make changes to the page holding the repetitive content. You will see examples of this technique (called the Include Page component) in Chapter 15.

This technique is well suited to single pages, too. If you have a page that needs to be updated daily (to contain the latest news, for example), you can keep the content of this "included" page current and repost it every day. Because the page within a page is self-contained, nothing else in your Web page layout needs to change.

Time-Sensitive Content

FrontPage extends the include process described above and allows you to place time-sensitive content on your Web. For example, starting on October 15, you might want to remind everyone that daylight savings time is ending on the last Sunday in October at 2:00 A.M. On that Sunday, after 2:01 A.M. (see how nicely we have avoided trying to determine which 2:00 A.M.), you want to put up a message reminding people that the time has changed. You want to keep that message until Monday at 5:00 P.M., then remove it from your Web.

You can use a variant of the Include Web Page component (described above) called Schedule Include Web Page. You need to create the two messages as Web pages. Use the Schedule Include component to include the page containing your first message at 12:01 A.M. on October 15 and to remove the include at 2:01 A.M. on the Sunday when daylight savings time ends. Use the Schedule Include component to include the page containing your second message at 2:02 A.M. on Sunday and to stop including it at 5:00 P.M. on Monday.

You can also schedule graphics to appear and disappear in the same way.

Creating Subwebs

You may need to break up your Web into smaller pieces to make it easier to have several people work on individual parts. For example, your Web describes an organization with several divisions. You want each division to be able to create and maintain its own information. You do not want them to maintain anyone else's information and you want to make sure that all of the pieces have the same look and feel. A simple solution to this problem is to create a number of subwebs, one per division.

A subweb is a Web nested inside another Web. The Web that contains a subweb is called the parent Web. Each subweb is a child of the parent.

For example, the Insurance Company of Southern Pennsylvania (INSCOPA) has several divisions: Underwriting, Claims, and Personnel. You might want to create a Web for INSCOPA and let the various divisions populate and maintain their own sites. You would create a parent Web, called INSCOPA. In this parent Web, you'd define the styles to be used as well as define the overall look and feel of the site. The parent site contains links to the Underwriting, Personnel, and Claims divisions.

For each division, you create a subweb. When the subwebs are created, they inherit certain Web settings (themes, permissions, etc.) from the parent. Each subweb can have its own set of permissions limiting who can author, browse, or administer the subweb. This allows you to give Sally Brown from Claims the permissions for the Claims subweb, Angela DePasquale from Personnel permissions for the Personnel subweb, and Joe Lyons from Underwriting permissions for the Underwriting subweb.

You can also use subwebs to limit access for security reasons. Because each subweb can have its own set of permissions for designating who can author, browse, or administer it, you can set up individual subwebs with different levels of permissions and different groups of users.

You can create a subweb by converting a folder to a Web, by importing a Web into a folder and then converting the folder into a Web, and by publishing one Web to another as a subweb. A subweb initially inherits certain Web settings (such as theme information and permissions) from its parent Web. Use subwebs to organize your intranet logically based on your organizational model.

Here's how to create a subweb:

1. Open the Web that contains a folder that you want to make into a subweb.

2. Right-click on the folder in the Folders list. Select Convert to Web from the context-sensitive menu.

L▶ Tip: For some peculiar reason, FrontPage allows you to convert any folder (or even your entire hard drive) to a Web. Other than the warning that it puts up, it makes no attempt to stop you from doing something extremely dumb (like making a subweb out of your hard drive). When you convert a folder to a Web, FrontPage changes items in the folder. Believe me, you only want to convert a folder to a Web when the folder needs to be a Web. You can render your hard drive useless if you convert it to a Web, so be careful!

3. You will see a warning label.

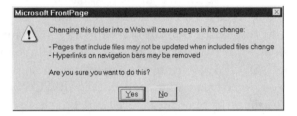

When you convert a folder into a subweb, there's a fairly good chance that you will have substantial cleanup and repair to do. If you still want to make a subweb, click OK.

If you have a subweb, you can convert it back to a plain folder by right-clicking and selecting Convert to Folder. Expect to have to do more cleanup on it, however.

Reports 'R Us

FrontPage provides a large number of reports that help you organize and manage your Web. These reports are all available by selecting View | Reports on the menu bar to display the Reports list. In order to view a specific report, place a checkmark next to the desired report. You are automatically transferred to Reports view.

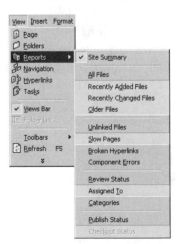

You can see the same reports by directly selecting the Reports View icon in the Views panel to the left of the window. When you look at your reports in Reports view, the reports toolbar appears. It also contains a drop-down menu that enables you to select the report you want to see.

Viewing Reports

The site summary report view looks at your Web and provides summary information about your Web. A sample summary for the Smythe family site is shown in Figure 9-4. As you can see, the summary shows file counts and file sizes for all files, pictures, unlinked files, linked files, slow pages, older files, and recently added files. The site summary also shows counts and descriptions for total hyperlinks, unverified hyperlinks, broken hyperlinks, external hyperlinks, internal hyperlinks, component errors, uncompleted tasks, and unused themes. If the site summary shows that there are problems, you can search further using the other detail reports. (The report shows a number of errors in the site—but remember, I never really finished it!)

The All Files report displays all of the files in your Web in a table that shows the file name, the file title, the folder containing the file, the file size, file type, the date that the file was last modified, who modified the file, and any comments added when the file was created or modified. The All Files report shows all files. In Figure 9-5, you can see an All Files view of the Smythe site.

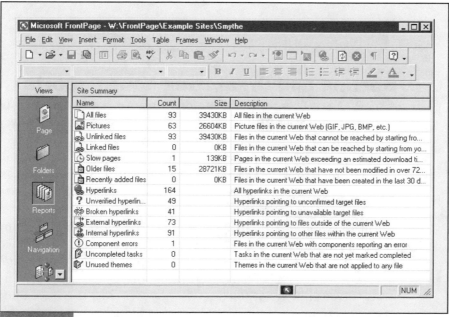

FIGURE 9-4 All Files report

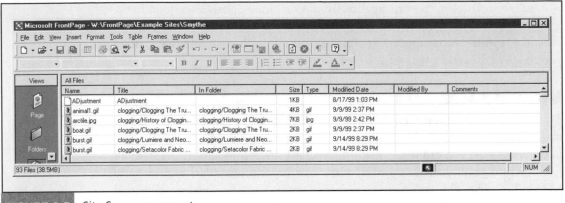

FIGURE 9-5   Site Summary report

In addition to all files, you can view recently added files, older files, or unlinked files. You can change the criteria to decide what constitutes an "old" or "recently added" file.

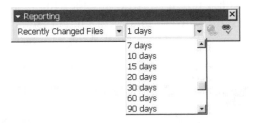

Sorting and Organizing Your Reports

A static report is not always the most informative thing to see. A list of all of the files in your Web can be overwhelming to look at and convey very little real meaning. In order for you to *use* the reports as a tool for managing your Web, you need to be able to rearrange the columns and sorting orders so that the reports show you useful information. FrontPage will not allow you to rearrange columns. However, it does allow you to select a report column on which to sort.

You can customize FrontPage's reports to sort the file display on any of the column names (Name, Title, In Folder, Size, Type, Modified Date, Modified By, or Comments). When you first click on a column header, you'll show all of the files sorted on that column, in ascending order. If you click again, you'll reverse the sort order to a descending one. You can open a file shown in a report by right-clicking on a file name and choosing Open.

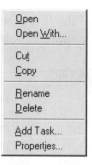

If the file is not one that can be edited in FrontPage, you can choose to open it with another program. You can also cut or copy data, rename the file, delete the files, add a task for the file, or display file properties.

Why would you want to view a report in a particular order? You might want to know how many .htm files you have in your Web. To see this, you would select the All Files report and sort on File Type. By reading the list of files that congregate around the .htm area in the report, you can quickly find the answer.

Although you can't rearrange the columns in a report, you can resize the columns. If you place your cursor on the dividing lines between the columns, you'll see the resizing cursor (a double-headed arrow) that allows you to move the columns closer together or farther apart (behavior that works in Excel to resize columns as well). You can move a column so close to another one that it is completely hidden—which is a good way to remove unneeded columns from view. Here,

All Files		
Name	Size	Type
text.zip	40KB	zip
pinkcactus.jpg	39KB	jpg
pshop.zip	36KB	zip
opal.zip	34KB	zip
riverdn.jpg	29KB	jpg
cactusdn.jpg	29KB	jpg
vector.zip	23KB	zip
sunset.gif	23KB	gif

I've created a report to show me which files on my site are larger than 20KB. A large file is indicative of a slow page, so I can check for file sizes first.

I can also request to see a list of slow pages, as shown here:

Slow Pages			
Name	Download Time	Size	Type
port1.htm	15 Seconds	4KB	htm
port11.htm	11 Seconds	4KB	htm

Viewing the report, I discover that I have two pages that take more than 10 seconds to load. I can change my display criteria from 0 seconds to 600 seconds.

(Tools | Options | Reports View Tab). Were I to view my report at 0 seconds, every HTML page would be listed, so that I could compare download times of all of the pages.

You can obtain reports that let you:

- List broken hyperlinks
- List unlinked files
- List errors in components
- List files by assignment
- List files by category

Sometimes, the reports that FrontPage displays don't give you all of the information that you need to manage a complex project. Because of this, FrontPage allows you to categorize your files using any system that you like. When you select the List files by Category report, you'll see the list of files organized by category (obviously). You can categorize your files when you add them to your Web or at any time thereafter. You can add and delete custom categories so that the Category report becomes useful for your particular task. Adding categories allows you to group files with similar properties.

Here's how to associate a category with a specific file:

1. Choose a report that displays all or most of the files (e.g., the All Files report).
2. Right-click a file and select Properties. You'll see the Properties dialog box.
3. Click on the Workgroup tab and select a category from the Categories list, as shown in Figure 9-6.

You can add or delete categories in this list as well. To add a new category, click on the Categories button in the dialog box shown in Figure 9-6. In the Master Category list that appears,

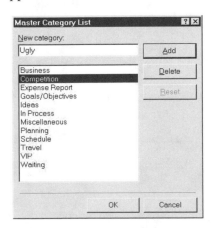

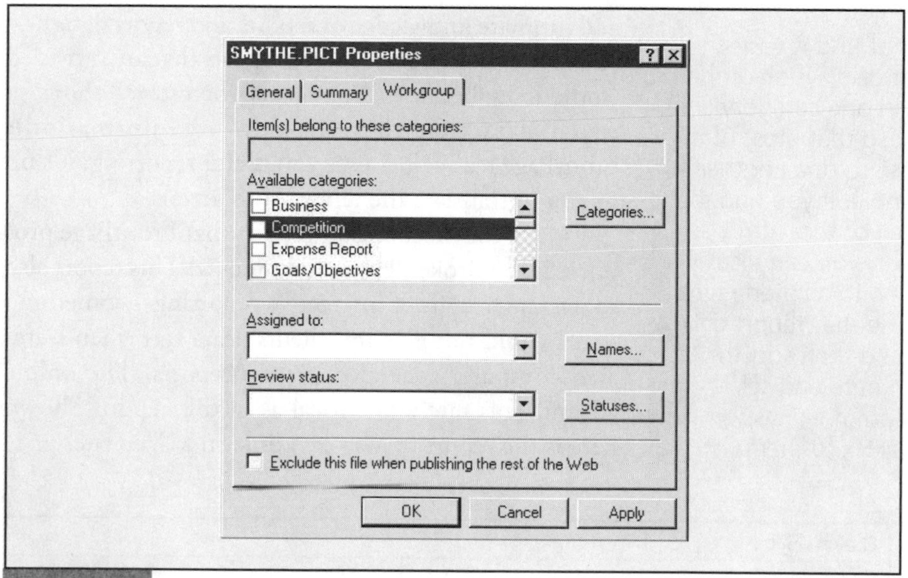

FIGURE 9-6 Selecting a category

type the name of the new category. (Here, I'm adding a category called "Ugly" to remind myself which pages I think are unattractive enough to warrant a "redo.") Click the Add button. You may add and delete as many categories as you want to make the system work for you.

If the thought of adding categories to a huge number of files one at a time is about as appealing as having a root canal, you can categorize multiple files at one time. Select all of the files you want to be in the same category, right-click to display the context-sensitive menu, and choose `Properties`. Click the `Workgroup` tab and then select the categories for the selected files (you can choose more than one category at a time, but the categories selected apply to all of the files that you selected at the same time).

Using the FrontPage Reports

In the section above, we began to discuss ways to use the copious reports that FrontPage provides. Although I am currently a full-time graphic designer and writer, I have been a database programmer and systems analyst in my checkered career (I actually have a master's degree in information science with a specialty in management information systems—which I taught for 12 years). I have a long

Tip: You might find it easier to pick a report that displays all of the files that you want in one category and then sort the report so that most of the needed files fall close to one another in the report. For example, if you find that you want to revise all of the .htm files created in September, you can display the Slow Pages file (with a criteria time of 0 seconds) because that report only shows .htm file. You'd then sort the files by modification date and select the grouping for September. Assign a category of Priority Fix to them.

and intimate knowledge of reports and report design—and of the pitfalls of not using reports that are provided (sometimes because the reports themselves show so much data that they provide no information). FrontPage really does give you useful reporting; it's up to you to translate the reports into action.

One of the most critical reports that FrontPage produces is the Broken Hyperlinks report. This report also shows the benefit of interactive reporting—something that I could not give my clients years ago when I created computer-generated *printed* reports. The online advantage is rarely as critical as in this report. Shown here is the report of a broken link on a Web site.

Broken Hyperlinks				
Status	Hyperlink	In Page	Page Title	Modified By
? Edited	http://www.microsoft.com/fron...	index.htm	The Prancing Pixel	Sherry

By double-clicking on the entry of the offending hyperlink, you display the Edit Hyperlink dialog box. In this instance, the suspect hyperlink is in the Microsoft FrontPage log that is placed by default on every home page created in FrontPage. I am fairly certain that this hyperlink is not really broken.

If you think that the hyperlink is actually correct, you can verify the external hyperlinks listed as broken in the report. The reporting toolbar contains two icons at the right side.

The leftmost icon is the Edit Hyperlinks button and the one on the right is the Verify Hyperlinks button. If you are fairly sure that you have nothing to edit, you can connect to the Internet and click on the Verify Hyperlinks icon. You have the choice of verifying all hyperlinks in your site (not a bad idea at least once a month) or only selected hyperlinks. In the report that indicated my broken hyperlink, as soon as I asked FrontPage to verify the hyperlink, it found Microsoft's site and changed the status of the link to OK.

I teach an online course in Photoshop for Education to Go (http://www.educationtogo.com). For each of the lessons in the Photoshop course, I need to keep a list of helpful Web sites for the students to visit. The Verify Hyperlinks feature is so easy to use that I have all of my links stored as an HTML document and I can verify the over 200 links in this document (which, of course, is not shown online in this way) quite easily and quickly. You could, if you wanted, keep your bookmarks file updated by making a page of links and using the Verify Hyperlinks feature on it.

Getting Noticed

Once you've created your fantastic Web site, how do you tell people to come and visit you? Spam certainly isn't the way—at least not for me. If you have a small target of interested prospects, you might send them an email. However, for most Web sites, the best way to get noticed is to submit the site to the various portals and search engines that crawl (and index) the Web.

The key ingredient in getting your site listed so that it is included in *relevant* searches is to embed a list of keywords into your pages that can be used by the search engines to point potential visitors in your direction.

The keywords for the search engines are stored in a META tag in your page. Especially if you are creating a commercial site, it makes sense to ensure that you set up a useful set of keywords. Many of the search engines use these keywords to list your site. Start with the most relevant keyword first. Create approximately nine keywords (between five and fifteen is a decent range). Although you may create many more keywords, the folks on the Web who have made a career of trying to help you get a better search engine "placement" recommend nine as an optimum number of keywords.

You can create keywords for your home page by using the Page Properties command. Here's how:

1. Open your home page.
2. Right-click in the page to show the context-sensitive menu. Select Page Properties.
3. Click on the Custom tab. The Custom dialog box shown in Figure 9-7 appears.

Once you have the keywords properly listed, you're partway there. The trick when trying to get hits from search engines is to somehow manage to get your site listed in the top 10–30 links that a search engine finds when someone enters a search term. The techniques used to try to secure this placement seem to be part science and part voodoo.

You can pay a consulting firm large sums of money to list your site with the search engines, or you can do it yourself. In preparation for this chapter, I

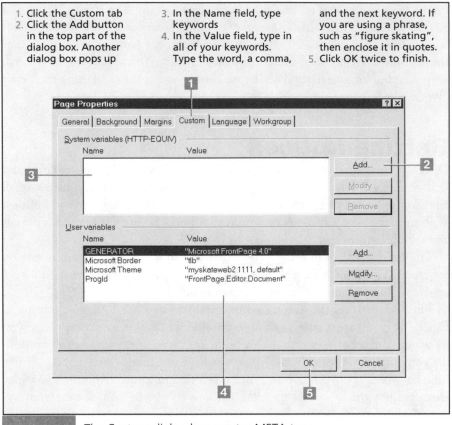

1. Click the Custom tab
2. Click the Add button in the top part of the dialog box. Another dialog box pops up
3. In the Name field, type keywords
4. In the Value field, type in all of your keywords. Type the word, a comma, and the next keyword. If you are using a phrase, such as "figure skating", then enclose it in quotes.
5. Click OK twice to finish.

FIGURE 9-7 The Custom dialog box creates META tags

searched the Web trying to find software that would allow you to automate the submission process. I found a number of packages, but two of them were rated five stars by ZDnet.

AddWeb, by CyberspaceHQ (www.cyberspacehq.com), helps you to submit your site to many different search engines. The product is available in three versions to suit a variety of business sizes and needs. This program walks you through the entire submission process and can even generate the keywords as part of the HTML on your page. In addition, it can simultaneously submit to hundreds of search engines at one time. However, you can also select just the search engines to which you want to promote your site (the interface for this is shown in Figure 9-8). You can download a free trial version of the product. Also available in the product are tips and tricks for improving your placements, live program updates, and

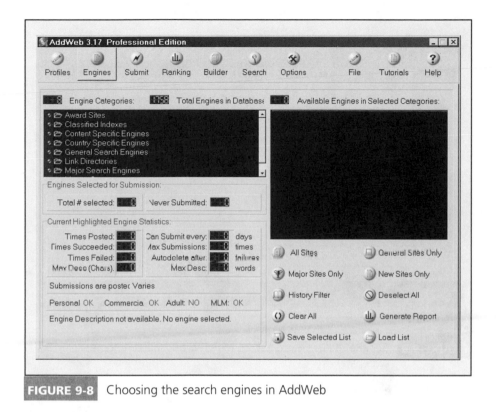

FIGURE 9-8   Choosing the search engines in AddWeb

real-time access to the most current list of categories and subcategories of search terms on Yahoo, Snap, and other sites that require custom categories.

CybeRat, from Viper Industries Group (www.viperinc.com), is a combination Web site (see Figure 9-9) and submission engine. The Web site contains fascinating and copious information about how to improve your ratings in the search engines. The program concentrates on the major search engines only—and explains its reasoning to you. You can download a free trial version of this as well. The interface to the program is interesting in that it mirrors the Web site.

Both applications (CybeRat and AddWeb) give you large numbers of reports, track the number of submissions made to which engines on which dates, and allow you to do a keyword search on your terms to see how well your site rates.

What else can you do to promote your site? You can exchange links with similar or complementary sites. This is an excellent way to build up a visitor base. You can join a Web ring or start one so that people interested in the items in your site can

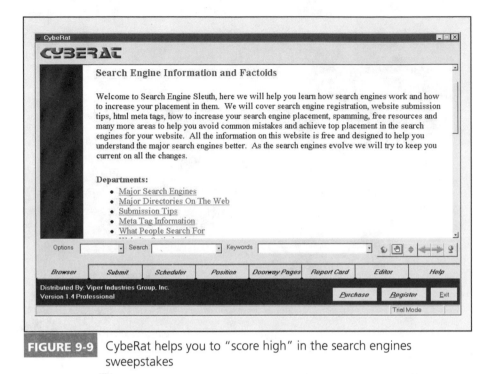

FIGURE 9-9 CyberRat helps you to "score high" in the search engines sweepstakes

follow a ring of sites across the Web. I've seen figure skating rings, bead store rings, rings for a specific piece of graphics softw

are, needlework rings, and many other types of Web rings (though you can get an idea of my favorite things in that list!).

You can also register your Web site so that you get a unique URL. A site named www.myskateweb.com is much easier to remember than www.isp.com/members/sites/five more slashes/~myskatepage. You can check to see if the name that you want is already taken by visiting http://rs.internic.net. The site maintains a list of all domain names in use. Once you find an available name, your ISP can help you to register it.

Professional Skills Summary

In this chapter, you've learned how to publish your site and how to maintain and manage it. Putting up a site is just the beginning of the necessary work. You need to be able to post changes and keep your links current and working.

The chapter also introduced you to the FrontPage Server Extensions and explained how to obtain them and why they are a valuable thing to be able to use. You learned which features the Server Extensions will help you to implement.

You also learned how to use the reports and Report view to learn about your site. You can customize the way the reports are displayed and take action to fix any problems identified by the reports.

You learned how to search for and fix broken links, and how to create keywords for your site and submit to the search engines.

In the next chapter, you'll learn how to create tables— a very useful layout device to learn.

chapter 10

Using Tables

In this chapter, you:

- Learn three ways to create a table
- Learn how to use the table toolbar to edit tables
- Learn how to create traditional grid-based tables
- Learn how to create free-form tables with varying rows and columns
- Change cell characteristics such as borders, cell padding, and colors
- Learn how to add and delete rows and columns
- Learn how to rearrange cells
- Learn how to insert text and pictures into tables
- Discover ways to use tables as layout devices
- Learn how to build a table around previously-created text

Tables: An Introduction

One constant theme that runs throughout this book is "How do I create a Web site that looks professional?" A professional-looking Web site has several characteristics:

- It is easy to read.
- The text and graphics are arranged on the page in an orderly and pleasing fashion.
- It looks well planned and well-thought-out.
- The navigation method is logical and easy to use.

Another theme that has run through this book is the knowledge that the HTML, the "native" language of the Web, does not make it easy to achieve professional results. Using HTML, it can be extremely difficult to control the layout of a page so elements appear where you want them to be.

In Chapter 7, you learned one important layout trick—using a single-pixel gif image to create precise spacing of elements. In this chapter, you will learn about the other important technique for precise layouts—using tables. Both of these techniques work with standard HTML and older browsers, and therefore have universal application for site design.

Although you also learned how to format pages precisely using cascading style sheets, only the newest browsers can see the style sheets and Netscape and Microsoft have not implemented style sheets the same way. The browser inconsistencies make using cascading style styles a major challenge.

Tables were added to HTML as a way to display tabular data such as spreadsheets or timetables, or the periodic chart of elements. Because table cells can contain any type of data (including other tables), graphic designers eagerly began to use tables as a way of gaining control over the display of their pages. In this chapter, you'll learn how to create both traditional tables (i.e., tables for tabular data) and tables for page layout control.

Manufacturing Tables Three Ways

Microsoft FrontPage has three techniques that enable you to place tables into your page. You can use the Insert Table button on the formatting toolbar, the

Insert Table command on the Table menu, or you can draw a table using the Pencil tool on the table toolbar.

The Insert Table Button

The Insert Table button provides the easiest and fastest way to create a table.
To add a table using the Insert Table button, follow these steps:

1. Click on the Insert Table button in the standard toolbar.

2. Drag your cursor through the desired number of rows and columns. You can select from 1–4 rows or 1–5 columns.

The table is created at the full width of the window. You can change any of the table characteristics after the table has been created. Figure 10-1 shows a three-row, three-column table created using the Insert Table button.

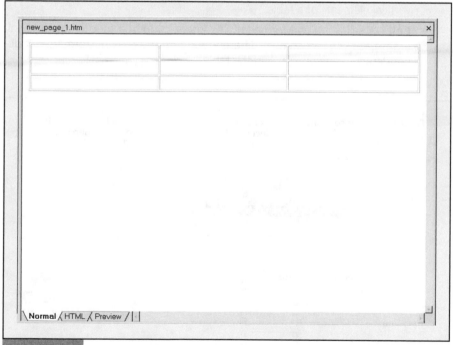

FIGURE 10-1 A simple table structure created by using the Insert Table button on the standard toolbar

The Insert Table Command

The Insert Table command that is found on the Table menu of the top menu bar gives you a bit more control over the original creation of the table. To create a table using the Insert Table command, follow these steps:

1. Choose Table | Insert | Table.

2. Enter the number of rows and columns, the alignment, border size, cell padding, cell spacing, and absolute or relative size, as shown on Figure 10-2.

Let's take a closer look at the elements that the Insert Table command enables you to set. Figure 10-3 shows the anatomy of a table. Let's look at each element:

- **Row**   Rows are the horizontal elements in the table. They go across the table from left to right.

- **Column**   Columns run from the top of the table to the bottom. They are the vertical elements of a table.

- **Cell**   A cell is the unit formed by the intersection of a specific row and column. Each cell can contain different content and may be formatted independently of any other cell in the table.

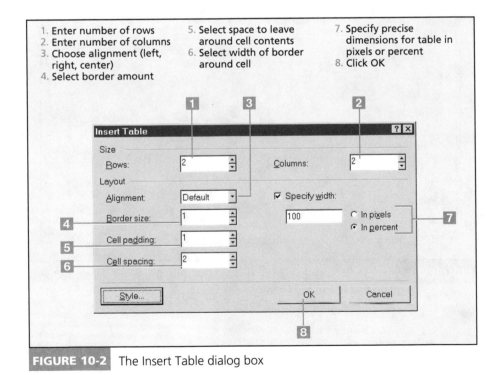

1. Enter number of rows
2. Enter number of columns
3. Choose alignment (left, right, center)
4. Select border amount
5. Select space to leave around cell contents
6. Select width of border around cell
7. Specify precise dimensions for table in pixels or percent
8. Click OK

FIGURE 10-2   The Insert Table dialog box

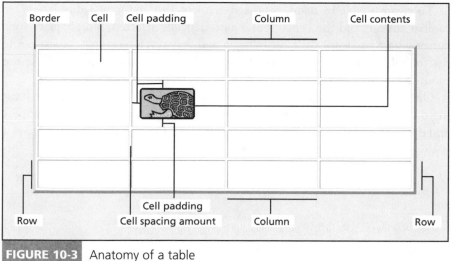

FIGURE 10-3 Anatomy of a table

- **Border**   The border is the area of that surrounds the outer edge of the table. It can be flat, 3-D, or invisible.

- **Cell spacing**   The Cell spacing amount controls the visible width of the dividers between the cells. The amount that you specify for cell spacing can form horizontal and vertical lines or, if you select 0 as the cell spacing amount, they can be invisible. When cell spacing is 0, you can cut apart images and place them seamlessly into cells to reconstruct the original image. The cell spacing is set in the Table Properties dialog box and is a single amount for the entire table.

- **Cell padding**   The cell padding amount determines the amount of space or "breathing room" left between the contents of your cells and the cell perimeter. If you want sliced images to touch one another, this amount needs to be set to 0. The cell padding is set in the Table Properties dialog box and is a single amount for the entire table. If you need to pad the contents of a single cell, you can either use the single-pixel gif trick or, if you have an image in the cell, set the image alignment and/or the spacing from the Picture Properties dialog box.

Drawing Your Table

The third method of drawing a table is both the most fun and the most complex. You can select the Table | Draw Table command and use the Pencil tool to create the table and the rows and columns in it. The thing that makes this complex is that you don't need rows or columns to continue through the entire length of the table.

To create a table by hand, you need to select Table | Draw Table. The table toolbar appears and the Pencil tool is automatically selected. Simply place your cursor where you want the table to begin and drag out a rectangle the size of the desired table. Figure 10-4 shows the start of a hand-drawn table. Release the mouse button when the table is as large as you want it to be.

Once you have the outline of the table, you can add rows and columns to it using the Pencil tool. Place the pencil where you want the row or column to appear and drag the pencil in the direction that you want. Dragging left or right leaves a new row and dragging up or down leaves a new column.

The dotted line that appears while you are using the pencil turns into a cell-spacing line when you release the mouse. You can continue drawing new rows and columns, and, as you can see, they don't need to extend the length and width of the table. (However, a new row needs to extend the width of its column and a new column needs to extend the width of the row in which it is drawn).

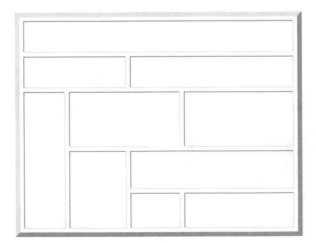

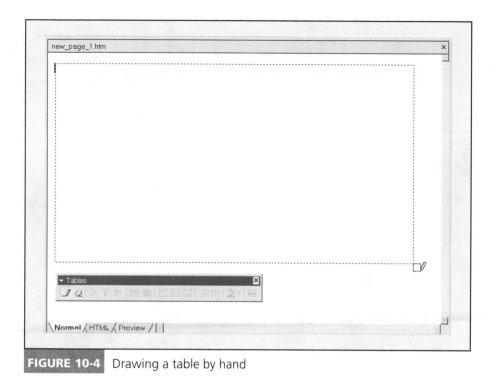

FIGURE 10-4   Drawing a table by hand

You can continue to add rows and columns as often as you want. However, you will discover that the Pencil tool has a mind of its own when it comes to where some of the dividing lines should go. Figure 10-5 explains the logic of the Pencil tool and shows how new dividers can be placed in some locations and not in others.

Figure 10-5 shows how the Pencil tool determines where it will allow you to add a new row or column divider. Because a row divider already exists under cells B and C, you can only add a new row divider into cell A if it is parallel to the divider under cell B or C. You can't add a new row between cells C and B inside of cell A. The Pencil tool refuses to snap to that location. However, if you added a new row divider to cell D, then you could place a divider parallel to it in cell A.

Sometimes this feature doesn't work consistently and a new row or column will simply be autocentered and you must drag it where you want it to go.

The Draw Table feature works nicely, but it points out a serious need for planning if you want to draw the best table for your page. It's

Tip: Even if I don't want to see cell spacing in my finished table, I find it easier to draw the table with cell spacing on.

Tip: The Pencil tool doesn't want to go away after you've used it. To get rid of it (and get the arrow or I-beam cursor back again), press the ESCAPE key or click on the Pencil Tool icon in the tables toolbar again.

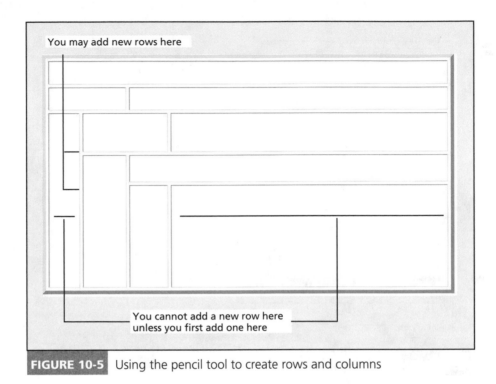

You may add new rows here

You cannot add a new row here
unless you first add one here

FIGURE 10-5 Using the pencil tool to create rows and columns

a lot of fun to simply draw cells into a table, but you should really have an idea what type of table you want to draw before you begin.

Creating Traditional Tables

Once you have created the basic table (with or without rows and columns), you can edit it in many different ways. All of the editing commands are on the Table menu command as well as on the tables toolbar. Figure 10-6 identifies all of the tables toolbar icons.

With the exception of the Split Cells icon, none of these buttons have dialog boxes. They are click-and-go. The Split Cells icon, however, asks you to determine how many rows or columns you want to create from the selected cell.

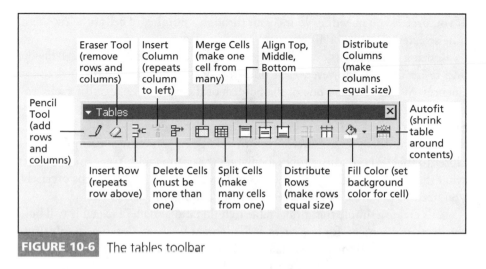

FIGURE 10-6 The tables toolbar

Selecting and Adding Cells

FrontPage tables can be sized interactively if you know what to look for. The shape of your cursor is your guide to what may be done. If you place your cursor over the edge of a table, you'll see one of two possible cursor shapes. The short, chunky single arrow indicates that you may click to select an entire row or column. The longer, thinner double-pointed arrow indicates that you can hold the mouse button and resize the table, row, or column. You will see the double-pointed arrow if you hold the cursor over a cell divider as well as over the outer border.

Tip: If the table toolbar annoys you by sitting in your work area, you can dock it by dragging to the right edge of the bottom of your window, next to the pictures toolbar.

You may select cells by clicking on the table outline when you see the single arrow cursor. However, the cells that are selected might surprise you if you are selecting in an uneven table. If you have cells selected and you press the SHIFT key and click somewhere else along the edge of the table, you will select the entire table.

You can also select the cells, rows, columns, or the entire table by choosing Table | Select and picking the option from the side drop-down menu.

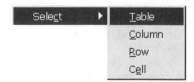

If you prefer, you may drag your cursor through a number of cells to select them. The selected cells turn a different color.

Resizing a table has its own challenges. It is perfectly easy to pull on a cell divider and resize the cell. However, each time you do so, there are unexpected consequences. When you drag one of the borders of the table to enlarge the table, you don't enlarge the table proportionally. You simply make the cells at that end of the table bigger.

When you drag on an interior cell to enlarge it, sometimes it simply moves closer to the next cell; other times it enlarges the entire table. You cannot predict what the effect will be. If you need to set the size of rows and columns precisely, you need to use the Cell or Table Properties commands.

Let's create a simple traditional table to hold tabular data. This table will hold the dates and contacts for one client at Settlement Services. Feel free to substitute your own information. You'll create a table, create a header, and then add data to it. You'll also make some changes to the table by adding a new column.

1. Open a new page (File | New | Page | Normal Page). You may also simply press the New Page button on the toolbar. If you are working in a Web that uses shared borders, choose Format | Shared Borders. Click the Current Page radio button and remove all of the shared borders for the page. (You can turn them on again if you want after you create the table. If you want to duplicate my steps, create a new Project Web named "SettleServ" and format it with the Tabs and Folders theme. Add a new page to it and remove the shared borders.

2. Choose Table | Insert | Table. Create a table with five rows and four columns as shown. Use the border size, cell padding, and cell spacing settings shown.

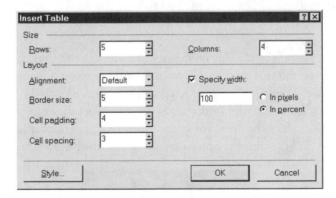

3. The first row of the table can be used for header data. When you mark a row, column, or cell as "header," the text inside is made bold to stand out from the rest of the table. Select the first row (place your cursor on the left margin of the table by the first row and click, or, with the insertion point located in the first cell of the table, choose Table | Select | Row). With the row selected, right-click the mouse and select Cell Properties.

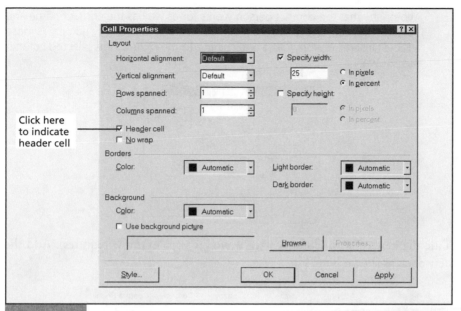

Click here to indicate header cell

FIGURE 10-7 Selecting Header cells in the Cell Properties dialog box

4. In the Cell Properties dialog box, click the Header checkbox to select it as shown in Figure 10-7. Click OK for now.

5. Type some heading into the top row. Then, type some data into the columns. Figure 10-8 shows the table with data entered. You may use my data or your own.

6. Now that you have data entered, you might realize that you forgot a column. In this case, it would be more useful if the client could see the name of the

Activity	Date	Contact	Contact Phone
Turn in mortgage application	10/21/99	Meg Roberts	800-555-1234
Apply for Title Search	10/24/99	Jeanne Michels	800-555-3333
Contact Home Inspection services	by 10/25	Floyd Flowers	800-555-3245
Loan approval due	11/05/99	Meg Roberts	800-555-1234

FIGURE 10-8 Table with data entered

company that the contact person works for as well as the contact name and phone number. Select the column that contains the Activity names. Choose Table | Insert Column. Insert one column to the right of the selected column as shown.

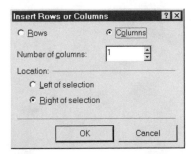

Title the new column Company (or whatever your example requires). Add the new data, as shown here:

Activity	Date	Company	Contact	Contact Phone
Turn in mortgage application	10/21/99	Acme Mortgage	Meg Roberts	800-555-1234
Apply for Title Search	10/24/99	Titles Unlimited	Jeanne Michels	800-555-3333
Contact Home Inspection services	by 10/25	Home Inspection Services	Floyd Flowers	800-555-3245
Loan approval due	11/05/99	Acme Mortgage	Meg Roberts	800-555-1234

Cell Sizing

You can assign set sizes to your table and to the cells within the table. These sizes can be set using either pixels or percentages. There are advantages and disadvantages to either method.

If you set a specific size for the cells in the table, then you know how they will display on any monitor. If you place images inside of the cells, you know in advance exactly how large you need to make the image. However, the table will not expand and collapse as the size of the browser window changes. The table remains fixed, which means that site visitors might need to scroll their window in both directions in order to read the entire table. Many site visitors don't bother scrolling. If something isn't immediately visible, many visitors are not going to see it—or they will scroll and complain. If you decide to design a fixed-width table, you might want to consider limiting it to 640 pixels wide as a maximum (or certainly no more than 800 pixels wide if you think that most site visitors will have monitors that at least display 800 × 600 pixels).

If you choose to size your cells using percentages, then the table will fit on most monitors but you lose all of your careful spacing to make the table look good. The choice is yours, and there is usually no "right" choice.

You set the size of the individual cells or of a group of cells in the Cell Properties dialog box. Shown here is the section of the Cell Properties dialog box that concerns the sizing of cells.

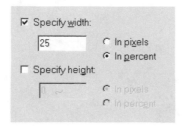

As you can see, all you need to do is to checkmark the "Specify width" or "Specify height" box and then enter the precise dimensions in either pixels or percentages.

You may select multiple cells at one time and use the Cell Properties dialog box to set all of the characteristics for the selected cells.

Table Properties and Cell Properties

The Table Properties and Cell Properties dialog boxes allow you to control the appearance and setup for both the entire table and individual cells. The Table Properties dialog box sets global characteristics for your table and the Cell Properties dialog box sets properties for a single cell (or a group of selected cells).

Tables have *inheritance*. Settings that exist for your entire page are also used for the table, and settings for the table are used—in the absence of more specific instructions—for the individual cells. In Figure 10-8, for example, you'll notice that the background of the table is the same as the background of the page. You can change that, but if you don't your background will default to the same color or image as your page. This is an example of inheritance.

Let's take a closer look at the items that you can set in the Table Properties dialog box. You'll notice that many of the items on Figure 10-9 could also be set in the Insert Table dialog box shown in Figure 10-2. Figure 10-9 describes the items that you could not set on the Insert Table dialog box.

Tip: When you click the Apply button, you've applied the change—even if you press Cancel afterwards. The only thing that the Apply button does that the OK button does not is to leave the dialog box open.

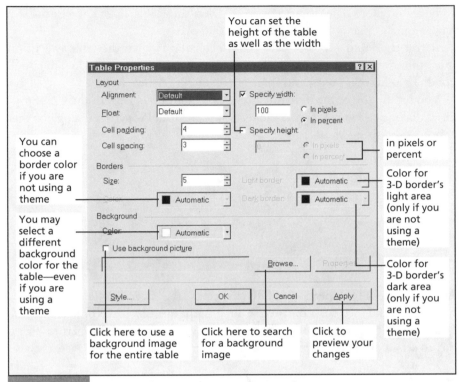

You can set the height of the table as well as the width

You can choose a border color if you are not using a theme

You may select a different background color for the table—even if you are using a theme

in pixels or percent

Color for 3-D border's light area (only if you are not using a theme)

Color for 3-D border's dark area (only if you are not using a theme)

Click here to use a background image for the entire table

Click here to search for a background image

Click to preview your changes

FIGURE 10-9   Using the Table Properties dialog box

Tip: FrontPage help says: "You can adjust a cell's width or height by setting the number of rows and columns that it spans. Adjusting the cell spanning allows you to have cells of varying heights or widths in a table."

The Cell Properties dialog box also lets you select sizes and background colors. However, the background color or image that you select in this dialog box takes precedence over the one set in the Table Properties dialog box. Let's take a look at the dialog box.

Nothing in the Cell Properties dialog box prevents you from mixing pixel and percent dimensions. However, you need to exercise a bit of caution that your numbers are internally consistent. You also need to test your table in every available browser.

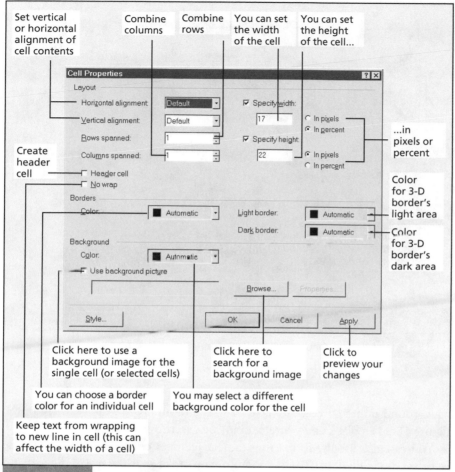

Set vertical or horizontal alignment of cell contents

Combine columns

Combine rows

You can set the width of the cell

You can set the height of the cell...

...in pixels or percent

Create header cell

Color for 3-D border's light area

Color for 3-D border's dark area

Click here to use a background image for the single cell (or selected cells)

Click here to search for a background image

Click to preview your changes

You can choose a border color for an individual cell

You may select a different background color for the cell

Keep text from wrapping to new line in cell (this can affect the width of a cell)

FIGURE 10-10 Cell Properties dialog box

Formatting Your Table

You can use all of the standard formatting devices that you've learned. The formatting options on the formatting toolbar all work within tables. You can use the background color in the Cell Properties dialog box to change the color of the

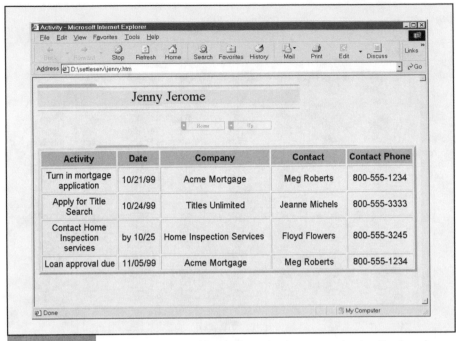

FIGURE 10-11 Using a change of background color to emphasize the headers

background in header cells to make them stand out, as you can see here in the Figure 10-11 in black and white, and in color in the color section.

You can also use the formatting toolbar icons to center the text within the cells, as I did in Figure 10-10. If you want, you can change the size of the text and its color, font, or other typographic properties.

Tables as a Layout Device

Now that you've learned the basics of using tables to create—surprise!—tables, you're ready to meet them again as the most powerful layout tool available without the use of any special facilities such as cascading style sheets or XML (Extensible Markup Language—a more flexible subset of SGML, the markup language from which HTML is also derived).

One Solution to the Precise Layout Problem

Tables are the mainstay of graphic design for most of the professional Web sites today. In a year or so that might not be the case, but for now, if you surf the Web and know what to look for, you'll see tables everywhere. You will even see tables in the templates that come with FrontPage. If you create a new page, you'll be presented with a selection of templates. The templates that use columns—such as the preview for the three-column template shown here—all use tables for their formatting.

The lovely feature of this is that these templates are blissfully easy to modify to your own uses. Figure 10-12 shows the same document from Village Flowers that was used as the Bookmarks example in Chapter 6. It has been placed into a two-column page template and is now a thing of beauty.

You can open any template and rearrange the table that it uses for formatting to suit your needs. You can also create your own layout table and then save it as a template. Graphic designers have used grids for layouts for years. A table is nothing more than a grid. A grid-based layout gives your pages an underlying structure while retaining flexibility.

If you need ideas for tables and layouts, look in the national magazines and newspapers. All mainstream magazines have a grid structure underneath their pages. Often, the grid structure is based on three columns. This allows the page layout person to use any combination of:

- Three columns for text
- Two columns for text and one for images
- One column for text and two for images
- All images
- All text
- Any other combination of text, images, and white space

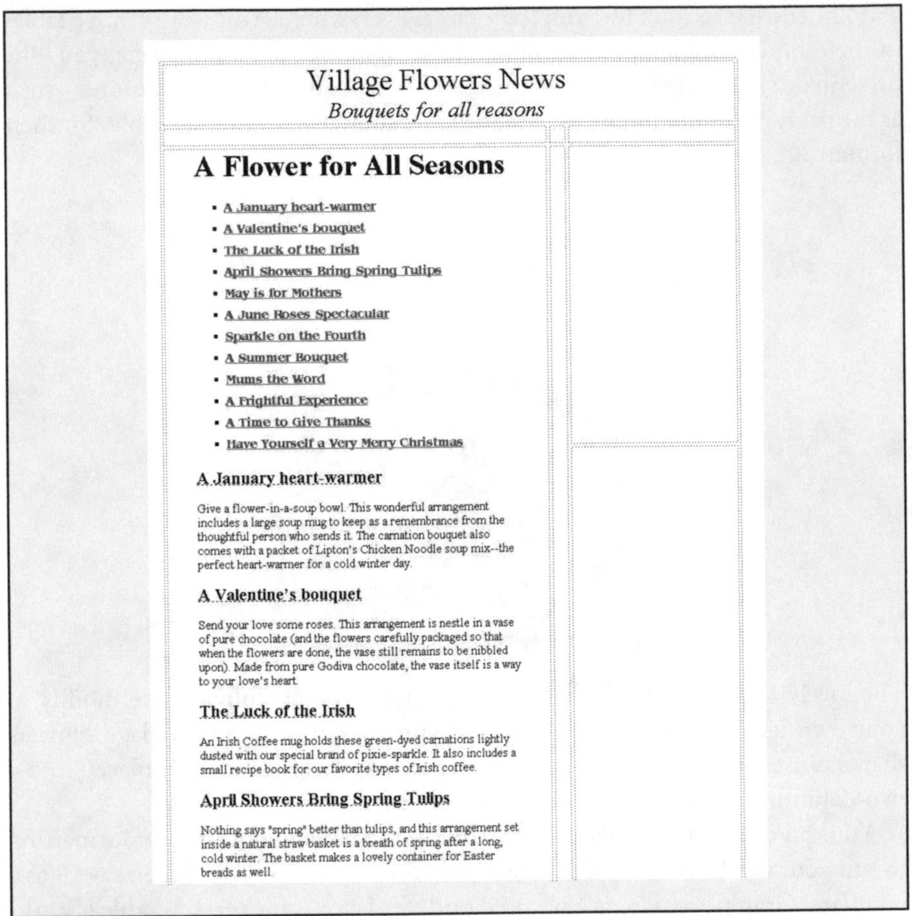

Village Flowers News

Bouquets for all reasons

A Flower for All Seasons

- A January heart-warmer
- A Valentine's bouquet
- The Luck of the Irish
- April Showers Bring Spring Tulips
- May is for Mothers
- A June Roses Spectacular
- Sparkle on the Fourth
- A Summer Bouquet
- Mums the Word
- A Frightful Experience
- A Time to Give Thanks
- Have Yourself a Very Merry Christmas

A January heart-warmer

Give a flower-in-a-soup bowl. This wonderful arrangement includes a large soup mug to keep as a remembrance from the thoughtful person who sends it. The carnation bouquet also comes with a packet of Lipton's Chicken Noodle soup mix--the perfect heart-warmer for a cold winter day.

A Valentine's bouquet

Send your love some roses. This arrangement is nestle in a vase of pure chocolate (and the flowers carefully packaged so that when the flowers are done, the vase still remains to be nibbled upon). Made from pure Godiva chocolate, the vase itself is a way to your love's heart.

The Luck of the Irish

An Irish Coffee mug holds these green-dyed carnations lightly dusted with our special brand of pixie-sparkle. It also includes a small recipe book for our favorite types of Irish coffee.

April Showers Bring Spring Tulips

Nothing says "spring" better than tulips, and this arrangement set inside a natural straw basket is a breath of spring after a long, cold winter. The basket makes a lovely container for Easter breads as well.

FIGURE 10-12 Village Flowers newsletter in two-column layout

Within each page, you can change the placement of images in one column or another—they don't need to stay in the same location. The use of a grid/table for layout becomes a subtle but potent force for developing an online identity because it gives your site a consistent look that site visitors soon come to identify.

You can visit Web sites such as *Byte* magazine (www.byte.com) and *Wired* (www.wired.com) to see this principle in action. *Byte* magazine has gone the additional mile to format their pages so that they print nicely to standard 8.5 × 11 paper. The site looks like a magazine both online and in print.

Creating an Uneven Table

When you use tables for the sole purpose of layout control, you can begin to play games with them. For example, the little ditty shown here,

is actually a table made up of uneven cells and filled with different background colors, a bit of text, and an image. The border, cell spacing, and cell padding are all set to 0. You can see in this view how the table was constructed.

Some Examples

The frontdoor page for SweaterLink acts as an introduction to the Web site. It is constructed from a table. Figure 10-13 shows the Web page as it looks in Internet Explorer.

Let's take a closer look at the mechanics of constructing this table, shown in Figure 10-14. The basic table has four rows and six columns. I removed the column

FIGURE 10-13   SweaterLink front door page

Tip: if you are going to insert graphics that are sliced to fit their locations, keep your dimensions in pixels and read the dimensions off of the Cell Properties dialog box before you slice your images. You need to cut you larger images into smaller ones in a graphics program. You can't do that in FrontPage. (Caveat: You can if you make separately named copies of the image and individually place and crop each one—but the effort really isn't worth it. Learn to use a graphics program.)

dividers (using the Merge Cells button on the tables toolbar) from all of the cells so that I got cells A, B, C, D, E, F. I left the dividers on the bottom row that formed the LINK. I used the "Distribute Rows Evenly" tool to make all four rows the same height. I used the "Distribute Columns Evenly" on everything but the first column to make them all the same size. I needed to slice the Click Here graphic into four exact pieces in order to make the rows stay the same height when I inserted the graphic (originally, the center two rows expanded in height throwing off the rest of the table.). The final table can download in 2 seconds on a 28.8 modem under ideal conditions. True, the image is all black and white, but a full-page graphic would take much longer to download, even in black and white.

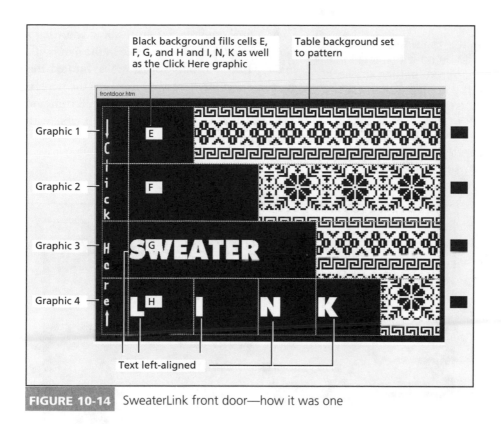

FIGURE 10-14 SweaterLink front door—how it was one

You can also use a table to take the place of an image map. The same button bar that was used in the PrancingPixel site as an image map is shown next. This time, the buttons are placed in a table. Each cell in the table can have its own link. The table keeps the elements precisely aligned and the table cannot collapse on the buttons. A graphic inserted in a table keeps the table from collapsing.

Tip: You can use the single-pixel gif trick within a table if you have text in a table that you want to keep from getting smaller than a certain size. If you place a transparent gif image sized to the minimum acceptable size into the cell, your table, even if it is all text, can still move with the browser size, but won't be squeezed into a disaster if the browser window gets too small.

As a final example, I want to show you what a table can do for the site interface in the hands of a master. Paul Vineburg, of Australia, created this awesome user interface as a FrontPage theme. It is available for purchase at www.pixelmill.com and uses, as you can see in Figure 10-15, a table with sliced graphics to work its magic.

FIGURE 10-15 Paul Vineburg's Mega 2000 template for FrontPage

Creating a Table from Text

You don't always need to create a table before you can use tabular data. FrontPage allows you to convert text into a table—and a table back into text. If you have data that is in comma-delimited format (rows of data with each field separated by a comma), you can easily convert this text into a table.

If, for example, you have a database program or a spreadsheet that can export a comma-delimited file, all you need to do is to save the data and place it onto a page. Then, choose Table | Convert. Figure 10-16 shows the original data exported as a .cvs file from Microsoft Access.

The Convert Text to Table dialog box allows you to enter the type of conversion. Because commas separated the fields in the file, when you tell FrontPage to use commas as the separator, it can place the data into the correct table positions.

Tip: If you have text that you later decide that you would rather show in a table, you can add commas and then convert the text into a table. This can avoid a great deal of cutting and pasting or retyping.

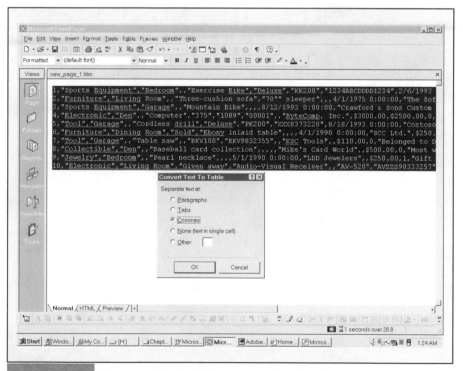

FIGURE 10-16 Comma-delimited file placed onto a blank page

With a bit of manipulation (header formatting, mostly), you can change the plain lines of text into a quite acceptable and professional-looking table.

Performance Issues

Are tables as efficient a method as can be found? Should you ever use multiple tables? Are there any problems using tables?

Tables are generally an efficient way to package graphics and text. They can be much smaller and faster to download than a single background image. Using tables, you can slice up an image that has a lot of blank areas in it and place small pieces of it (the pieces that actually contain image data) into a table. This makes the image display much more quickly.

However, a table cannot be displayed until all of it has loaded. If you fill your table with too many little pieces, the download time can become longer than using one large image. The only way to be sure that you have acceptable download times is to test the page on the Web. Use the oldest, slowest machine that you can find. You need to see how the table reacts under all conditions.

Try your table in multiple browsers as well. It appears to be different sizes in Netscape Navigator and Microsoft Internet Explorer. You need to be certain that the table looks good at whatever size is used to display it. Your browser view of the table will also differ from the view that you see in the Normal workspace.

Professional Skills Review

This chapter concentrated on tables in all of the various ways they can be used. You learned how to create a plain table for tabular data and a fancy table to hold text and graphics, and how to use tables for precise layout.

You learned that it is important to plan your table before you develop it and that tables can give structure and identity to your Web site. You learned how to change comma-separated data from Access or another database or spreadsheet program into an attractive table.

In Chapter 11, you'll learn how to use frames on your Web pages.

Frames

This chapter is about frames. Frames are the love-em-or-hate-em feature of Web page design that allows the Web designer to show multiple pages at one time. Clicking on a link in one page usually changes something in another part of the screen. Often, frames allow you to scroll different parts of the screen individually. However, the feature has been controversial since its birth.

Frames and When to Use Them

Netscape introduced the technique of frames onto the Web in the days of Navigator 2.0. Since that time, many designers have used frames in their sites. The reaction of the users to frames has been mixed. Some like frames, and many loathe them.

How Do Frames Work?

Frames are a technique for dividing monitor real estate into partitions. Each partition is an independent entity and can display its own separate content. In many ways, you can think of frames as a special type of table. Instead of placing images or text into the table cells, you place entire HTML pages in the cells.

While you can also place an HTML document into a table, that document becomes part of the page on which the table resides. When you use frames, it doesn't. The page that you place into a frame retains its own name as an independent entity but *appears* inside of the "cell"—the frame is really only a container for other HTML pages. It has no permanent content of its own.

Figure 11-1 shows a page that uses frames to display a stationary header area and scrolling content area. This site keeps the fixed logo and some links in the top frame. This allows for easy navigation to the various site areas at all times. This site uses frames in an interesting manner because the frame border isn't visible. You might not know that you are looking at a framed page until you watch the top portion stay still when you scroll the lower area. The only "giveaway" that the page is framed is that the scroll bar on the right side doesn't occupy the entire right side of the window.

Figure 11-2 shows another framed site. This one allows you to scroll both frames, but the links area on the left of the window doesn't change. Its content remains fixed to allow easy navigation to all of the linked areas. This site splits the window vertically and uses a visible divider between the areas (of course, it has to because of the scroll bar on the left-hand frame).

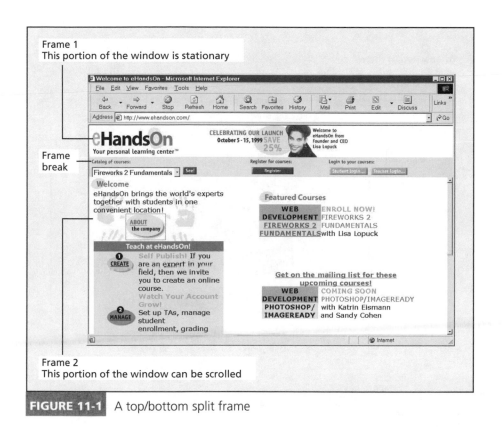

FIGURE 11-1   A top/bottom split frame

As you can see, not all frames look or work the same way. You have a wide variety of options in how you create your frames. Although both examples show the use of two different frames within one window, you aren't limited to using only two frames. You may divide your screen into as many frames as you want. Of course, given that the "typical" monitor is only 14–15 inches, and the "typical" viewing resolution is 800 × 600pixels, the practical maximum number of frames on a page is three.

What Are Frames Good for?

Frames allow you to keep one or more navigational windows or image windows in front of the site visitor at all times—regardless of the content through which

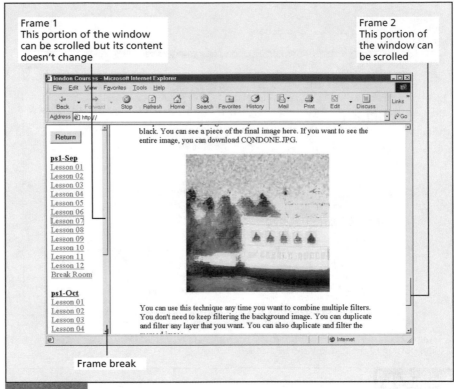

FIGURE 11-2 A site that uses visible frame breaks and two scrolling frame windows

the site visitor is scrolling. Of course, you can place whatever you want into frames, but frames should really be used for a specific purpose rather than simply because they are available.

If you have a site that contains a number of areas through which to navigate and you want that list to be present on the screen at all times, then frames provides a good way of reaching that goal. You can allow the site visitor to scroll and browse in the smaller links window without having to create long, scrolling content on the screen as well.

Recent research has suggested that more Web surfers are willing to use the scroll bars when the content of a site doesn't fit on their screen. However, a survey taken two years ago indicates that 50–80 percent of all content in locations not immediately visible on screen is never seen. Therefore, you want to make your site visitor do as little scrolling as possible.

Another good reason to use frames is when you want a graphics-heavy interface or log to be visible at all times. If you place the page in frames, then it only needs to be downloaded once. Otherwise, it becomes a bandwidth hog on every page. Consider the image shown in Figure 11-3. This interface for Prancing Pixel is quite graphics intensive but works beautifully as a framed page.

Figures 11-1 and 11-2 are also quite appropriate uses of frames. In Figure 11-1, the top logo contains enough imagery in it to warrant being used in frames, and the navigational information is useful to keep up at all times. The scrolling links window in Figure 11-2 also justifies its use in a frame.

Do Frames Cause Any Problems?

If frames seem like such a good idea for site navigation, shouldn't you use them all of the time? No...not really. Frames are problem-prone for several reasons.

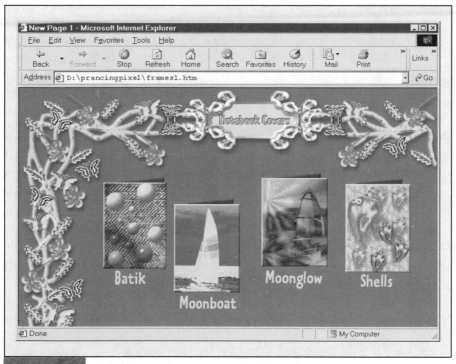

FIGURE 11-3 Framed page from Prancing Pixel

General concerns

Many people despise frames. I'm not a very big fan of having to use them myself, even though they can be extremely useful to have. However, using frames can cause the following problems:

- It is difficult to bookmark a site that uses frames. The bookmark usually sees only the name of the frame "container" or of the top frame and not the HTML documents that are displayed within the frame, so you can't easily return to your position in a set of frames.

- Because the browser can often only read the frame "container" name (called, by the way, a *frameset*) or the frame at the top of the screen, the Back button will frequently not work as expected to take you back to your last page.

- Some very old browsers cannot see frames at all. This is much less of a problem than it used to be. Browsers from Netscape and Microsoft that are more recent than version 2.0 can see frames. Some older proprietary browsers from Prodigy or AOL cannot read frames, but they, too, are becoming much less common. However, some site visitors will not tolerate being "framed," and will desert your site unless an alternate means of viewing your pages is provided.

- Automatic Web search engines also have a problem with frames and might not be able to penetrate your site to index your contents. If you have a graphic as your top frame, this problem is particularly acute. One way around it is to add meta information to the top level of your pages using HTML (something you'll learn more about in Chapter 13).

FrontPage navigation issues

You also need to be careful with setting up frames using FrontPage. FrontPage gives you excellent frame support. However, if you try to display within the frames pages that use the shared borders and navigation bar features of FrontPage, these features are apt not to work the way that you want them to.

Because the frames can take up so much of the screen real estate, you really do need to carefully design your pages. The shared borders and navigation bars also eat up screen space. They also contain fairly inflexible rules about where and how they show up on a page.

Your only option is test, test, and test again. Test every page that you frame in all available browsers. Preview your pages often when you design them.

Can I use a frameset for my home page?

You can use a frameset for your home page if you want to. You need to name the frameset default.htm. However, because many users hate frames and many Web search engines cannot penetrate beyond your initial frames page, you need to think this through carefully before deciding to create a site based totally on frames.

Frames, Tables, Shared Borders, and the Navigation Bar

You might be wondering if frames can do anything that using a table or using FrontPage's shared borders and navigation bars cannot. Frames are really very different than tables, although you can use a table inside of a frame (you can also use another frameset inside of a frame, but don't—unless you can find no other way to accomplish your objective). Frames need to be redisplayed every time that the HTML source document changes.

You can accomplish many of the same ends as frames, however, using the shared borders and navigation bars. If you choose to use the "Level under Home" option in your shared border navigation bar, then you don't need to repeat the links on every page. They are automatically produced for you and "Level under Home" won't change. Therefore, the navigation bar does stay fixed in place on your screen. Your site visitors might not be able to tell the difference between frames and the mechanism that FrontPage uses if you use a page that looks like Figure 11-4. This page (for the Insurance Company of Southern Pennsylvania) is one that you will see again in this chapter. I'll use it to show you how to create a

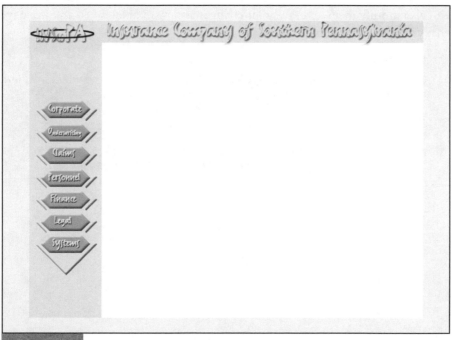

FIGURE 11-4   This page could be implemented as frames or as a shared border and navigation bar

frameset. However, it could also be implemented as a top and left shared border with a navigation bar in the left border. However, the background behind the links is not a pattern; it is a full graphic that doesn't repeat. Because of that, the images in this figure do not download rapidly.

You would need to develop the page both as a normal page and as a three-set framed page (top, side, and content). You could then upload the pages to your Web site and test the download speed under varying conditions to determine which was the most efficient way of working.

Creating Frames

Now that you've seen the reasons why and why not to use frames, let's talk about how you create a framed site.

Using the Frame Templates

You create a frames page by creating and saving a frameset. A frameset is the container page for the material that you wish to display. You need to create the structure before you can fill it with content.

FrontPage has a number of templates available for you to use as framesets. You can also modify them and save your changes as new templates. To create a page that contains frames, follow these steps:

1. Choose File | New | Page.

2. In the New Page dialog box, click the Frames Pages tab as shown in Figure 11-5 and select the template that you want to use.

Here is a list of the templates and what they do:

- **Banner and Contents**   Three frames—banner on the top, contents on the left, and main frame page to the right of the contents. Hyperlinks in the banner change the links showing in the contents, which changes the display in the main frame.

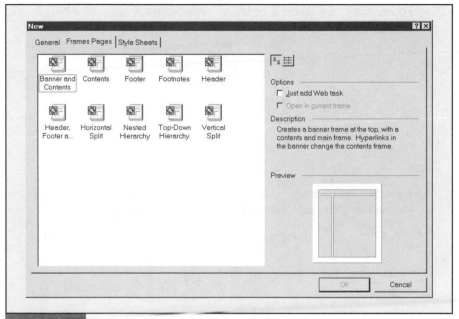

FIGURE 11-5 The Frames Pages dialog box allows you to select a template

- **Contents**   Two frames—contents frame on left contains the hyperlinks that change the page on the right.

- **Footer**   Two frames—large main page with small footer area for links. Links in footer change material in main frame.

- **Footnotes**   Two frames—looks like the footer frameset but the default links are set so that the links in the main page show the footnotes at the bottom.

- **Header**   Two frames—small header area for links and large main frame. The header links cause the display to change in the main frame.

- **Header, Footer, and Contents**   Four frames—header and footer frames for navigation. Stationary side panel. Links in header or footer change material in main frame.

- **Horizontal Split**   Two frames with independent content in each frame.

- **Nested Hierarchy**   Three frames—general hyperlinks on left change links in top. Top links change main frame display.

- **Top-Down Hierarchy**   Three horizontal frames—general links at top change more specific links in next frame, which changes the content of the main frame.

- **Vertical Split**   Two frames. The left and right frames contain independent information.

The basic ways in which the frameset templates differ from each other are in number of panel (frames) on the page, the arrangement of the frames, and the order in which the frames are used (i.e., which frame calls what).

After you have selected the specific frame template to use, and clicked OK in the New Page dialog box, your screen looks like Figure 11-6 (if, of course, you've selected the same template as pictured here—the Banner and Contents template).

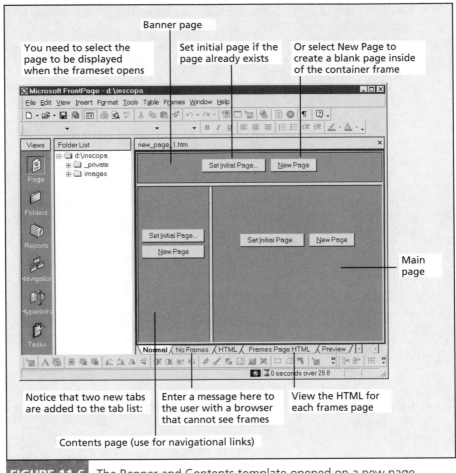

Banner page

You need to select the page to be displayed when the frameset opens

Set initial page if the page already exists

Or select New Page to create a blank page inside of the container frame

Main page

Notice that two new tabs are added to the tab list:

Enter a message here to the user with a browser that cannot see frames

View the HTML for each frames page

Contents page (use for navigational links)

FIGURE 11-6 The Banner and Contents template opened on a new page

Setting Frame Properties

With a frames page created, what next? Your next step is to indicate which page is to be used as the initial page—that is the page that is displayed automatically inside of each frame when the frames page opens. You must select an initial page for each frame if you want to be sure that all frames-capable browsers will open your frameset properly.

You can either select an existing page by clicking on the Set Initial Page button or create a new page using the New Page button. The Set Initial Page option allows you to select an HTML document to open from your current Web, your hard drive, or any valid World Wide Web URL. The New Page option gives you a blank HTML document.

The Frame Properties Dialog Box

After you've set your initial pages, you need to decide exactly how your frames page will work. You have a number of choices to make about the appearance of the frames pages, and most of them can be implemented via the Frame Properties dialog box as shown in Figure 11-7. Right-click and select Frame Properties to see this dialog box.

If you have two rows or columns next to one another in the frameset and you change the row height or the column height of one of them, FrontPage automatically changes the frame next to it to match.

The Resizable in Browser checkbox determines if the site visitor can dynamically resize the frame the same way you did when you created it. If the checkbox is

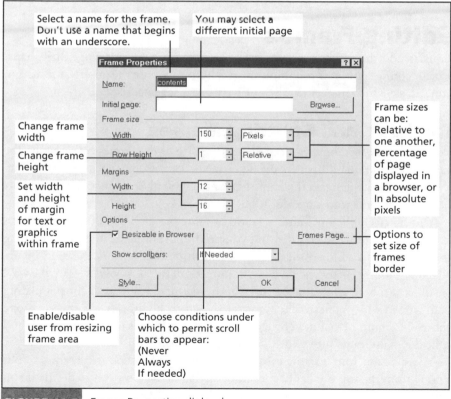

FIGURE 11-7 Frame Properties dialog box

selected, a double-pointed arrow cursor appears in the browser when the cursor is on top of the frame divider. If you don't select the checkbox, then the site visitor will see the frame at the size that you specified in the Frame Properties dialog box.

When you click the Frames Page button in the Frame Properties dialog box, you are able to change the width of the border between the frames and determine if you want the borders to be visible or not.

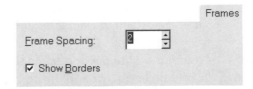

Although it seems as if the Frames Page button is a shortcut to the Frames tab on the Page Properties dialog box, there is no other way to access the Frames tab. If you go directly to the Page Properties dialog box (right-click, Page Properties) the Frames tab will not show.

Editing Frames

You can edit the frames at any point in the design process to change their shape, size, or configuration. If you think you might like to reuse the same frame design, you can save the arrangement as a new template for later use.

Resizing and Splitting Frames

You've already seen how you can change the size of the frames by changing the values in the Frame Properties dialog box. You can also change the size interactively, just by dragging on the frame borders. As you place your cursor over a border, you can drag it to a new location.

You can also split any frame into two or more pieces. This is the same process as dragging to resize the border, but you need to press the CTRL key as you drag the border. This adds another frame to your frameset, as you can see in Figure 11-8. The arrangement shown here isn't practical, but it is possible. (By the way, let me again urge you to make sure you have a practical reason for populating your screen with frames!) The frameset shown in Figure 11-8 is the same one shown in Figure 11-6, but I changed the size of the frames by dragging them and split the main frame into two additional partitions.

You can also split a frame into rows or columns by choosing Frames | Split Frame from the top menu. The resulting dialog box allows you to decide if you want the split to be horizontal or vertical.

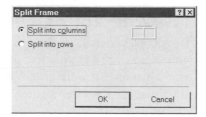

The rows or columns created are equal in size and you can move them as you wish.

Deleting Frames

You can also delete a frame that is in your frameset so long as it isn't the only frame left (although you really have no use for a frameset with only one frame container in it). To delete a frame, follow these steps:

1. Select the frame on the page by clicking in it. It acquires a blue selection rectangle around its perimeter.

2. Choose Frames | Delete Frame from the top menu.

An adjacent frame expands to fill the area left.

Tip: When you delete a frame from the page, you do not delete the page that the frame contained. The page is no longer shown in the frameset, but it remains in your Web.

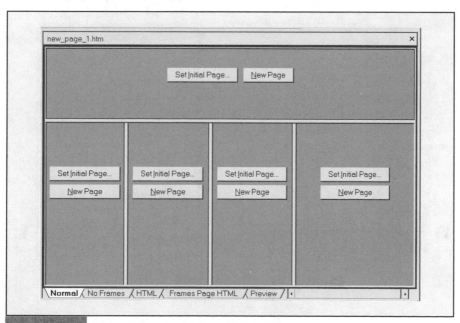

FIGURE 11-8 Altered Banner and Contents frameset

Designing and Saving Your Own Templates

You can save any of the changes that you make to a new frameset template so that you can use it again. A frameset saved as a template appears in the Frames Page tab (under File | New | Page) just as if it were an original part of FrontPage. Here's how you can save a frameset as a new template:

1. Save the frameset you are working on before starting.

2. Right-click on each frame within the frameset and make sure that the Initial Page option is blank. (If an initial page is set, then that page will be the default initial page every time you choose the new template.)

3. Choose File | Save As.

4. Change the name of the file in the dialog box and select FrontPage template (.tem) as the file type, as shown in Figure 11-9.

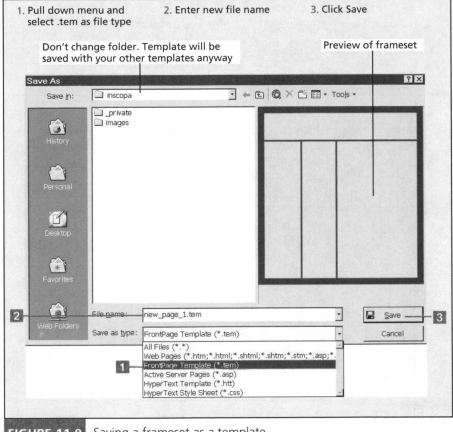

FIGURE 11-9   Saving a frameset as a template

When you click on the Save button, you'll see another dialog box.

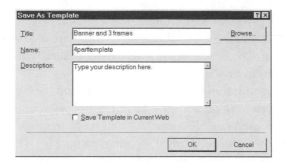

You'll need to enter the title of the new template. This is the "descriptive name" that appears under the template in the File | New | Frames Page dialog box. You'll also want to enter a description so that you can remember the purpose for which the template was created. Unless you specifically checkmark the Save Template in Current Web checkbox, your template will be saved to the same folder as the rest of the templates that come with FrontPage.

Implementing a Frames Page

After you have created the frames page, set the initial pages for the frames, and fiddled with the template to adjust it to meet your needs, it's time to look more carefully at how the frames page works and how you can use existing content within a frame.

You have some major decisions that you need to make:

- How will the frame's navigation work? (Which frame calls what?)
- What am I going to put in each frame?
- Will my pages fit inside of a frame?
- How large should each frame be?
- Do I want frames to use actual or relative dimensions?
- How do I get rid of frames if I have a page that can't use them?
- Should my whole site be based on frames?

Looking carefully at the questions listed, you see that they fall into three basic categories—navigation, content design, and site design. Let's look at the content first.

Adding Content

In principal, adding content should be as easy as designating an initial page for each frame in your frameset. In reality, few things are ever as easy as they should be.

Certainly, it is quite easy to indicate a starting page for each frame (or to create a blank page inside of each frame).

If you are using pages that were created using a full screen, you might need to re-design them to live happily in a smaller space. If you have used built-in FrontPage features such as shared borders, you will need to remove them because they will conflict with the frames technology.

To display a page inside of a frame container, click on the frame container that you want and (if you have already set a default initial page but want to change it) right-click and choose Frame Properties. Navigate to the page that you want to open. That part of the process is easy. Preparing graphics to show at absolute sizes (if you want stationary graphics in your frames) is not. Frames are often used to keep a logo or graphic stationary visible at all times, so you will need to determine the size frame needed to fit your graphics (or size your graphics to fit the dimensions of the browser as well as the frames).

Figure 11-4 showed a page that was displayed using shared borders and a navigation bar. If you wanted to use that figure as a frames page, you would first need to cut it apart. The cutting, slicing, and dicing of graphics images requires an image editor such as Photoshop, Fireworks, PaintShopPro, or Corel PhotoPaint. You could also use either Microsoft Image Composer or PhotoDraw.

If you want your page to display completely without scrolling in an 800 × 600 screen resolution, you need to make allowances for the browser interface itself. If the monitor can only show 800 × 600 pixels, your frames page must be smaller than that. How much smaller it needs to be depends on the browser that the site visitor is using, so it is unlikely that you will ever find a "perfect" solution for every possibility. However, if you take a screen shot of all of the common browsers, you should be able to reach a compromise.

If you capture a screen image of a page displayed in Internet Explorer 5.0 for Windows, you'll discover that the top area on the browser is exactly 128 pixels high (by the full 800 pixels across, of course).

The bottom portion of the screen is 29 pixels high. This means that your top banner plus menu graphic can be no higher than 600 pixels minus 128 pixels minus 29 pixels (443 pixels). The top banner shown in Figure 11-4 is 44 pixels high. That leaves 399 pixels in height for your menu bar graphic.

Taking Screen Shots and Measuring Image Areas

You can capture the entire screen to the Windows Clipboard by pressing the PRINTSCREEN key on your keyboard. If you want to save just the top window on the screen, you can press the ALT key plus the PRINTSCREEN key. You then transfer into a painting program (Photoshop, Corel PhotoPaint, PaintShop Pro, etc.) and create a new document (File | New works in most graphics programs). The programs that I mentioned will automatically default to the size of the image on your Clipboard and will create a new document at exactly the right size. You then need to paste your Clipboard image into the new image document (Edit | Paste in most graphics programs). The programs that I have suggested all have some type of Info palette that will tell you the size of a selection. You need to place a rectangular selection marquee around the interface sections of the browser whose picture you took (i.e., the part of the captured screen that "belongs" to Internet Explorer or Netscape Navigator). The size of the selection tells you how much room you need to subtract from the 800 × 600 pixels to correctly size your graphics.

The sides of the browser window each measure 6 pixels, so the widest that your top banner can be is 788 pixels (800 possible pixels minus 12 pixels for the sides). The original menu bar graphic was 146 pixels wide. Since the menu bar graphic doesn't stretch across the width of the browser window, it can remain at 146 pixels in width.

Before you can decide how to size each frame, you need to decide if you will permit a frame to scroll. Before you answer yes or no to the question, consider carefully. You are building this page for an 800 × 600 browser. What happens if the site visitor has a 640 × 480 monitor? You might want your site to degrade nicely for that monitor size. By showing you the calculations that I made on the Figure 11-4 graphic, you should be able to see how to figure out the necessary dimensions for any of your own projects.

Look at the left menu bar in Figure 11-4. While you would prefer that it doesn't scroll at all, it is better if it has to scroll up and down than if it needs to scroll from side to side. We've already determined that its dimensions without scrolling are 146 pixels wide by 399 pixels high. If you permit the frame to scroll up and down if needed on a site visitor's browser, then you need to add the width of the scroll bar to the width of the graphic to determine the necessary size of the left menu bar frame. The scroll bar in Internet Explorer 5.0 adds 14 pixels to the width of the frame.

L▶ Tip: One reason that I created an example using INSCOPA as the company is that you can control your viewing conditions if you design a site for an intranet. The designers at the fictional company of INSCOPA would already know that everyone in the organization has a 15" monitor and is running at 800 × 600 resolution. No one else will ever be able to view the site, so you can design in complete confidence of your design being seen as intended. In most instances, you're not so lucky, which is why I took the time to show you how to degrade your design for a 640 × 480 display.

L▶ Tip: If you don't want to use the INSCOPA pages, just select any example of your own to follow along with.

This gives you the frame's dimensions of:

- Top banner frame: 788 pixels wide by 44 pixels high
- Left menu bar frame: 399 pixels high by 160 pixels (146 pixels for the graphic + 14 pixels for the scroll bar) wide
- The remaining "main" frame can then be 399 pixels high and 628 pixels wide (800-12 border pixels-160 left menu bar pixels).

It would be very unattractive to need to scroll the top banner graphic for a 640 × 480 monitor size. You can either allow the top logo of the company to be cut off, or you can break your graphic apart so that you use a background image and make the text logo that says "Insurance Company of Southern Pennsylvania" into another graphic. If you make the text logo free-floating, then it can center itself as the browser size changes.

If you want to follow this example, you can download the already-cut images from the Osborne Web site for this book. They are banner.gif, logo.gif, and menubar.gif. Let's work through the steps of setting up a frames example so that you can see how to create, size, and set options for a "real" page. Once the framework is built, you'll then learn how to link your new frames page and make it work.

1. Either start a new, empty Web or open an existing Web.
2. Choose File | New | Page and select the Frames Page tab. Choose the Banner and Contents template (or whichever template you need).
3. In each of the three frames in the new frameset, click the New Page button to create a new page as the initial page for the frame.
4. Make the top frame active (click it).
5. Right-click in the top frame and select the Frame Properties option. Name the page "INSCOPA banner" (if you are following this example). Change the Height to 44 pixels. Set the Scrolling to Never. Set the Margins to 0. Make sure that the Resizable in Browser checkbox is not checkmarked.

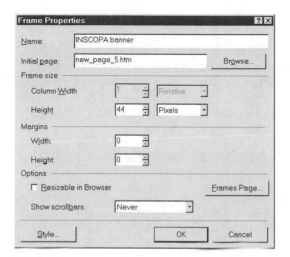

Do not click OK just yet.

6. Click the Frames Page button and set the Frame Spacing to 0 and uncheck the Show Borders checkbox. Click OK twice—once to exit the Frames Page dialog box and once again to exit the Frame Properties dialog box.

7. Now you can place the graphics. First, apply the background image (right-click in the frame and choose Page Properties. Click the Background tab (be sure you are not using a theme or the Background tab will not be visible) and select the image for your background. Choose topbkg.gif if you are following our example).

8. Place the logo file in the upper-left corner of the top frame (Insert | Picture | From File. Right-click the image and select Picture Properties. In the Appearance tab, select Left as the alignment).

9. Place the site title in the top frame (Insert | Picture | From File. Use inscopa.gif if you are working our example. With the picture selected, click on the Center alignment button in the formatting toolbar). That finishes the top frame.

Tip: If you forget how to access the Page Properties or Picture Properties dialog boxes, or forget how to choose options in them, flip back through Chapter 7.

Tip: To make it easier for you to download the image for the left frame from the Osborne Web site, I didn't cut up the buttons into all of the pieces that are needed to make the navigation work. I just placed a single file there. We're not really going to make the buttons clickable in this exercise anyway, and if you really want some navigation in the left menu bar, you can always create an image map around it.

Here's how to set up the left frame that contains the navigation:

1. Make the left frame active. Right-click in it and choose the Frame Properties dialog box. Set the Width to 160 pixels and the Height to 399 pixels. Change the Name to Buttonbar (or whatever you want to title it). Set the scrolling to If Needed. Set the Margins to 0. The Frames Page properties (the border size and the Show Borders checkbox should automatically be set correctly from the first frame). Click OK.

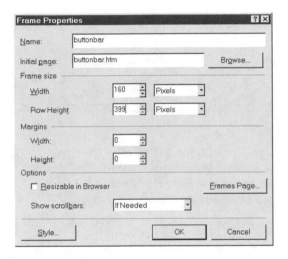

2. Select a background image. Use bkgpat.gif if you are following our example.

3. Place the button bar into the page (Insert | Picture | From File. Select buttonbar.gif if you are using our example. Right-click on the image and choose Picture Properties. Then, click on the Appearance tab and select Center alignment. After you've closed the Picture Properties dialog box, click on the Center alignment button in the formatting menu.

Tip: Even though you might see scroll bars on the bottom of the frame as well as the side of the frame in Normal view, you should not see the bottom scroll bar in Preview mode or when you Preview in Browser.

Now you have both the top and the side frames in a mostly operational state. You need to set the properties for the main frame of your frameset as well. The key thing that you need to set there is to enable scrolling so that a site visitor can read the text that you place in the main frames area.

Your next task is to tell FrontPage in which frame you want to display the link when someone clicks on a button in the button bar.

Linking Frames

Frames work by allowing you to keep all of the needed navigational links in one frame while you view the material in another frame. In the example that you've been working (shown first in Figure 11-4), the buttons that you click in the left window will display the requested material in the main frame to the right of the button bar frame.

In other words, you expect that by clicking the button labeled Corporate, you'll see information about what's new in the corporation. Furthermore, you expect that that information will show up in the frame to the right of the buttons.

The frame that is used to display the results of the link is called the *target*. When you set a target to be used for all of the links in a given frame, you are setting the *default target*. Setting a default target frame makes your life easier because you can create your links and know that unless you change your mind, they will appear in the expected frame.

Here's how to set the default target for a frame:

1. Select the frame by clicking on it.

2. Right-click in the frame. Select Page Properties from the context-sensitive menu.

3. In the dialog box, click on the tiny Pencil icon at the end of the "Default target frame" line in the General tab.

4. When you select the small Pencil icon, you see the Target Frame dialog box (as shown in Figure 11-10). The "Common targets" listed in the dialog box need some additional explanation.

If you don't want to use one of the frames in your frameset as your target, you have a few additional choices. You may choose one of the following as your target:

- **Same Frame**   This uses the HTML tag "_Self" and places the new information from your hyperlink into the same frame that contained the link. Essentially, this is the behavior of a normal, nonframes page. If you weren't using frames, when a site visitor clicked on a link in your Web, you would want to display the new page in the same window to replace the page that was linked from. The new page would need to carry its own navigation information because all of the navigation and links in the original page are lost when the new page displays. When you use frames, you need to be very careful about writing over your links. Don't leave the site visitor stranded on a page with nowhere else to go but away from your site.

- **Whole Page**   This option uses the HTML tag "_top" and breaks out of the frames environment. When you use the Whole Page option, your frameset disappears and the site visitor sees the "normal" single window again.

- **New Window**   This option inserts the "_blank" HTML tag and opens a new browser window for your linked material. This is actually a decent way to allow site visitors to leave your site and still remain attached to it. A new browser window appears and presents the new material that can be on your Web site or a totally different one anywhere else on the World Wide Web. The problem with creating a new browser window is that many users object to multiple windows being open. Also, because there is no "back" for the Back button on the browser to go to, new Web surfers tend to get confused. They often don't realize that (1) a new browser window has been opened or (2) they can get back to the original window by closing this one. So, this is a good technique, but you need to think through its consequences before you use it.

- **Parent Frame**   This option displays the linked material inside of the parent frame of the document that contains the link. This is probably the least common of the special targets.

Once you have set the default target for a frame, you can always change either the default target for the frame itself or the target for any specific link. You can get to the Target Frame dialog box through the Page Properties dialog box or through the individual hyperlinks in a frame. When you create a hyperlink for an item in a frame, the target frame in the Hyperlink dialog box is automatically set to the target default. As you can see here,

you can always change it by clicking the Pencil icon next to the Target Frame field.

If you are following our example (or even your own using the Banner and Contents template), you need to make sure that the default target page is set properly. Right-click the button bar frame, select Page Properties, and click the Pencil icon next to the Set Default Target Frame field. Select the main area of the frameset (whatever you have named it). Click OK.

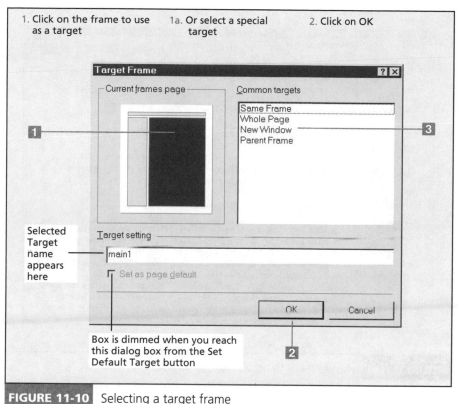

1. Click on the frame to use as a target
1a. Or select a special target
2. Click on OK

Selected Target name appears here

Box is dimmed when you reach this dialog box from the Set Default Target button

FIGURE 11-10   Selecting a target frame

Editing Framed Content

We've discussed ways to edit the frames containers, but how do you edit the actual content of the frame? You've done that too, if you followed the exercise above to create a frames page for INSCOPA. Once you open the desired document in a frame, you can edit one frame at a time as if it were a "normal" page.

You can also create the document in a full-page environment if it is easier for you to work that way. If you set a new page called corpinfo.htm as your initial page for a frame, for example, you can also edit that page by closing your frameset and opening the corpinfo.htm page directly in the FrontPage Normal Page view window. It is no different than creating any other page except that you should not use FrontPage's navigation systems around it. You may, however, attach a theme to the page.

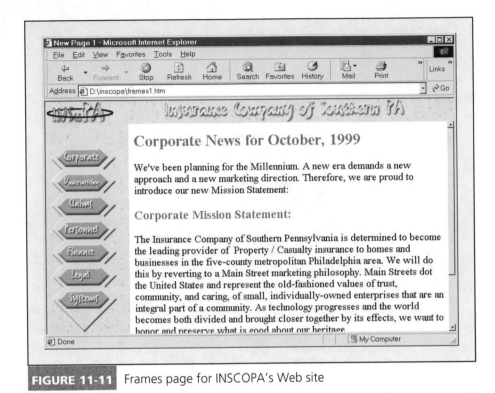

FIGURE 11-11 Frames page for INSCOPA's Web site

Figure 11-11 shows the final result of our efforts in the INSCOPA site. It shows the frames page displayed in Internet Explorer 5.0 at 800 × 600 pixels. The images fit perfectly and the scroll bar for the button bar frame is not needed.

Special Tabs

When you open a page containing frames in the workspace, FrontPage adds two additional tabs to the available viewing modes. One tab allows you to edit the HTML for the frames page itself, and the other tab allows you to display a message to the users whose browsers cannot view frames.

Editing HTML

The Frames Page HTML tab shows you the HTML code that is used to make your frames operational. You can add additional code into the HTML for the frameset if you want. One common addition to the generated HTML is a simple JavaScript to make two frames change their content when a link is clicked.

Creating No Frames Options

The other tab that is added is the No Frames tab. The No Frames tab allows you to add a message (or an entire Web site if you want) to handle the site visitors who cannot see your frames. Shown below is the HTML code that is placed by default into the Frames page code. It is this text area that you change when you edit the No Frames tab.

```
<noframes>
    <body>
       <p>This page uses frames, but your browser doesn't support them.</p>
</body>
 </noframes>
```

The default message that your site visitor would see is "This page uses frames, but your browser doesn't support them." It's a fairly polite message, but not terribly helpful. It completely cuts off the site visitor from being able to see your pages.

You can change the message to anything that you want. You can also create a link in that set of code to take the site visitor to a no-frames version of the page. While it is double work for you to design your site in multiple ways, it is another service that you provide in the name of "degrading gracefully."

Taking the time to place text-based links to your site also helps your site's chances of getting hits from search engines. If you add text links to your main pages from within the No Frames tab, the search engines will be able to access your site.

Professional Skills Summary

In this chapter, you've learned how to create a frame-based page and edit the frames so that they break up the space the way that you want them to. You have learned how to set initial pages by either creating a new blank page or by linking to an existing page. You've learned how to use the Frame Properties dialog box to set the sizes and attributes of the frames page, to determine if the frame sizes are absolute or negotiable, and to decide if you will permit scrolling to occur. You've also seen how you can show or hide the dividers in between the frames.

You've learned how to add content to your frame, add graphics and buttons, and link them so that the links appear in other frames in your frameset. You also learned how to instruct FrontPage to show a linked file in the same page that invoked the link, in a new window, in an unframed page, or in the parent page.

You learned the advantages and disadvantages of using frames and how to use the No Frames option to insert messages and/or links so that site visitors (and search engines) can find your pages.

This chapter ends Part 3 of the book. You have now seen some of the advanced functions of FrontPage. Part 4 shows you how to add interactivity to your sites. Chapter 12 introduces you to HTML, the language that provides the framework for all of the interactive magic you will learn.

Part IV

The Fun Stuff: Adding Interactivity to Your Site

chapter 12

Using HTML

In this chapter, you:

- Learn to write a basic page in HTML

- Learn the meaning of common HTML codes such as <head>, <body>, <title>

- Learn how to code a table by hand

- Learn how to structure HTML code

- Learn how to offer a choice of multiple fonts to ensure that the site visitor will have at least one of them in their system.

When you create a Web site in FrontPage, the pages can be seen by the folks who visit your site because FrontPage actually writes the HTML code that tells a site visitor's browser what to show. FrontPage "protects" you from the possibility of making HTML errors on your pages. HTML is actually quite easy to learn and can be fun to write.

In this chapter, you will learn some basic HTML and learn when it is really better for you get your hands dirty with code.

What Is HTML?

In the chapters that you've read so far, I've made a lot of semicryptic remarks about "you can fix this in the HTML" or "This feature generates an …HTML tag." Now you are finally going to discover what I was talking about. HTML is the "native language" of the World Wide Web. (It is also the "stuff" that FrontPage writes for you when it saves an .htm document. One of the reasons for learning FrontPage is so that you can usually avoid having to write your own HTML code). HTML, however, is not difficult to learn.

HTML stands for HyperText Markup Language—the key word being "Markup." I say it's key because HTML doesn't format your Web page, it just marks it up, letting the browser know how each specific piece of information should be presented. HTML doesn't work like a word processor. If you create a paragraph in Microsoft Word, for example, Word specifies how the text is displayed onscreen (according to your wishes of course). When you designate text as a paragraph in HTML, your browser (or your site visitor's browser) displays it according to its own interpretation of a paragraph.

How does HTML do this you ask? It works its magic through the use of tags. Tags are dividers that tell the browser when a specific format begins and when it ends. Tags are written within angle brackets (< and >, which are the GREATER THAN (>) and LESS THAN (<) keys on the keyboard).

Figure 12-1 shows the opening <b> tag, and the closing tag </b>. Everything within these two tags will be presented in bold format when the text is displayed in a browser.

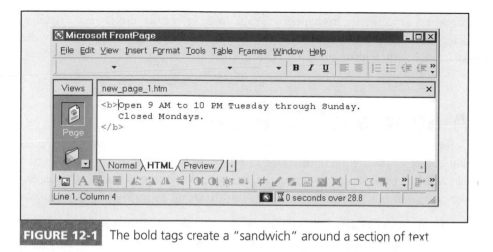

FIGURE 12-1   The bold tags create a "sandwich" around a section of text

HTML tags come in pairs (usually). For most tags, you need both a starting tag and an ending tag. The two tags are identical except for the forward slash character (/) that precedes the ending tag.

Notice that in Figure 12-1, the text was written with a hard return at the end of the first sentence (that's why the text shows up on two lines). However, here,

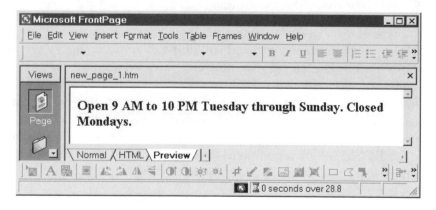

it appears as one line. This happens because to have HTML display text on a new line, you must code the line break into the page or the browser won't know the difference. You'll learn how to do this in the following examples.

A Simple HTML Page

Before you start writing the actual content, it's good practice to set up the page. In this example, you are going to create a new, blank document and write your first HTML program (for this book, at least, because I don't know what your actual experience with HTML has been). Here's how to create a simple HTML page:

1. In FrontPage, choose File | New | Page and select a Normal page.

2. Click on the HTML tab in the Page view. The page opens with all of the "standard" FrontPage HTML code already in place. Because I want to start with a totally blank document for now, select all of the text on the page (CTRL-A) and delete it (press the BACKSPACE key).

3. Every HTML page needs to start and end with the HTML tag. Therefore, type **<html>**

4. Press the ENTER key six times (to leave room in the file—although this has no significance other than ease of entry).

5. Type the ending HTML tag **</html>**.

This type of tag is known as a container tag. A container tag must be opened and closed, and everything contained within it will act according to the tag's functionality. The HTML tag states that everything between the opening and closing tag will be interpreted as HTML.

Next, you need to add the <head> tag. The head tag, or header tag, is where information about the document is stored. This information is helpful for search engines, as well as anyone viewing your code. The tag only contains the tag name (i.e., "head"). You will place additional lines of HTML code between the opening and closing <head> tags. To add the head tags, follow these steps:

1. Position your cursor to the line after the <html> tag. Press the ENTER key twice. (This just leaves a visual separator between your <html> tag and the header section of your document.)

2. Type **\<head\>**.

3. Press the ENTER key twice and type **\</head\>**.

The most important information in the head tag is the title. Titles are used for bookmarking and also appear in the title bar of a browser. Titles appear between opening and closing title tags (e.g., \<title \> The Candyman Home Page \</title \>). They are *nested* between the opening and closing head tags. You can place each opening and closing tag on separate lines, or you can write them on a single line as in the example here:

\<head\>\<title\> The Candyman – Home Page \</title\>\</head\>

I find it generally easier to read the HTML code if the empty tags are on separate lines. Here's how to enter the title tag and a title for your page:

1. Position your cursor to the line after the \<head\> tag.

2. Type **\<title\>**.

3. Press the ENTER key twice and type **\</title\>**.

4. Position your cursor at the blank line between the opening and ending title tags and type **The Candyman Home Page**.

> **Tip:** Titles should be concise, describing in as few words as possible what the page is. For our fictional candy store, a good title would be "The Candyman Home Page." If the title were just "HOME," and a user stumbled on the title somewhere, all they would know is that this was some home page, of some site, somewhere on the Web.

Other tags that go in the header are META tags, CSS tags, and Script functions, which we'll discuss a bit later.

The opening and closing header tags form a complete unit on the page. After you've written them, the next section of an HTML page is the body. This uses the \<body\> tag. This is where the *body* of your Web page goes. Anything that will be displayed for all the world to see is placed after the opening body tag. The body is also closed—just before the closing HTML tag. Here's how to add the opening and closing \<body\> tags:

1. Position your cursor so that it is on the line under the \</head\> tag.

2. Press the ENTER key twice.

3. Type **\<body\>**.

4. Position your cursor two lines above the \</html\> tag near the bottom of the document.

5. Type **\</body\>**.

Here's the HTML document so far:

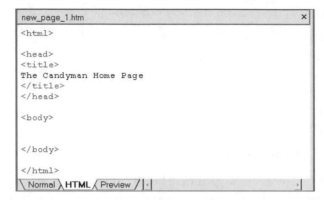

Two more quick notes about HTML. One is that it is *not* case sensitive. Whether you write **HTML** or **html**, or for that matter, **HtmL**, it will not affect your page. The other point is the way the page is written within the editor. For example, you could write all of your HTML in one continuous line, straight across the screen. Or you could write the HTML tag, hit return 10 times and write the head tag. As long as the opening and closing tags are presented in the correct order, the outcome will be the same. Having said that, it's best to write your code as clearly as possible. A clear, visual structure will make the page much easier to debug.

Now that you've prepared the page, you are ready to add some content. A very common tag to begin with is the heading <h1> tag, not to be confused with header tag. This tag specifies that whatever is contained within it will be presented in a heading format. The size of the heading is relative and goes from size 1 through size 6 (with size 1 being the biggest). You've used this tag in the formatting toolbar already, but FrontPage has written the HTML code for you. It's your turn to try writing the tag. Let's try out every size:

1. Position your cursor to the line under the <body> tag.
2. Type **<h1>The Candyman</h1>**.
3. Press the ENTER key.
4. Type **<h2>The Candyman</h2>**.
5. Press the ENTER key.
6. Type **<h3>The Candyman</h3>**.
7. Press the ENTER key.
8. Type **<h4>The Candyman</h4>**.

9. Press the ENTER key.

10. Type **<h5>The Candyman</h5>**.

11. Press the ENTER key.

12. Type **<h6>The Candyman</h6>**. Here's the way that the HTML should look.

Click on the Preview tab to see how your page looks now. You can also save your page and view in the Preview in Browser command. Figure 12-2 shows the page with all of the headings in Internet Explorer 5. Notice that each heading is a different size.

Notice that each level of the heading appears on a new line. Even if you had written the code like this,

```
<body>
<h1>The Candyman</h1><h2>The Candyman</h2><h3>The Candyman</h3>
<h4>The Candyman</h4><h5>The Candyman</h5><h6>The Candyman</h6>

</body>
```

the preview would have looked the same. Each heading line would appear on a new line. The closing heading tag (</h1>, </h2>, etc.) creates a hard return all by itself, so no further formatting is necessary to create new lines. Heading tags should be used only for actual headings, not as a way of generating larger text. This is because you can achieve more control by using the <font> tag, which will be covered shortly.

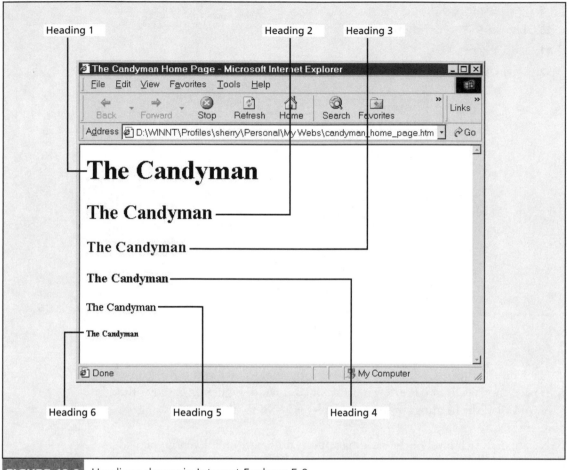

Headings shown in Internet Explorer 5.0

Let's add some information about the Candyman company to the Candyman page. First, erase all the <h> tags and their contents except for <h1>The Candyman</h1>.

Next, you'll write a brief description. Place your cursor after the </h1> tag and press ENTER. Type the following (you can press the ENTER key to start a new line whenever the typing starts to make your window scroll):

Welcome to the home of the Candyman. Prepare yourself for sweetness. In the following pages, you will be bombarded with all things bad for you. You will encounter jellylust and gumminess. You will be forced to reckon with licorice and tumble with toffee. If you survive these encounters it won't matter, for when you meet up with our selection of chocolates, let's face it, you're doomed.

Your mild skills are no match for our unfair marketing ploys. So arm yourself with a major credit card and let's do some battle. May the best man win. — THE CANDYMAN.

You need to add a bit of HTML to this. Place a paragraph <p> tag at the beginning of the first paragraph (before the word "Welcome"). Then, place one at the beginning of the second paragraph ("Your mild skills").

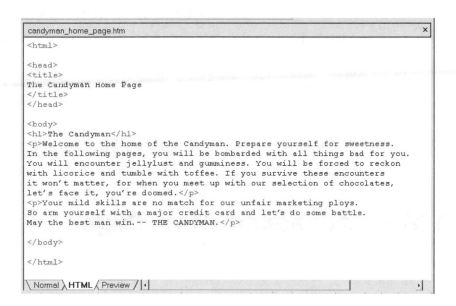

```
candyman_home_page.htm                                              ×

<html>

<head>
<title>
The Candyman Home Page
</title>
</head>

<body>
<h1>The Candyman</h1>
<p>Welcome to the home of the Candyman. Prepare yourself for sweetness.
In the following pages, you will be bombarded with all things bad for you.
You will encounter jellylust and gumminess. You will be forced to reckon
with licorice and tumble with toffee. If you survive these encounters
it won't matter, for when you meet up with our selection of chocolates,
let's face it, you're doomed.</p>
<p>Your mild skills are no match for our unfair marketing ploys.
So arm yourself with a major credit card and let's do some battle.
May the best man win.-- THE CANDYMAN.</p>

</body>

</html>

\ Normal \ HTML / Preview / | ◄ |                                    ► |
```

Paragraph tags can be closed, but do not need to be. Sometimes it makes the code easier to read, but it's up you to decide if you want to bother. When a new <p> tag appears, the browser closes the previous one, creating a hard return and a space between sentences, as you can see in the preview shown in Figure 12-3.

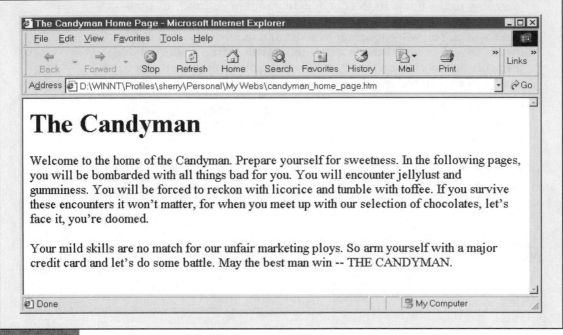

FIGURE 12-3 The HTML page shown in Microsoft Internet Explorer 5

A More Advanced HTML Page

Congratulations, you've just written a Web page. Yet somehow, you are not satisfied. This page is ugly. It's dull, and the text scrolls much too far across the screen. I understand. Let's do something about this.

One way to prevent the browser from wrapping the text only at the edge of the browser is to insert a line break tag <br>. This is not a container tag and therefore does not need to be closed. Anytime this tag appears, a line break will occur on the page, but no space is added between the sentences (this is the tag that is entered when you press SHIFT-ENTER in the document in Normal view). That's how the <br> tag differs from the <p> tag.

You can enter a <br> tag wherever you please in the text. Here are my suggestions:

```
<p>Welcome to the home <br>
of the Candyman. Prepare yourself for <br>
sweetness. In the following pages, <br>
you will be bombarded with all things bad <br>
```

for you. You will encounter jellylust \<br\>
and gumminess. You will be forced to \<br\>
reckon with licorice and tumble with toffee. \<br\>
If you survive these encounters it won't \<br\>
matter, for when you meet up with our selection \<br\>
of chocolates, let's face it, you're doomed. \</p\>
\<p\>Your mild skills are no match for our unfair marketing ploys.\<br\>
So arm yourself with a major credit \<br\>
card and let's do some battle. \<br\>
May the best man win. — THE CANDYMAN.

Figure 12-4 shows the result of placing line breaks at the end of each line. Obviously this is not the best way to achieve a readable page. That's where tables come in. But before we get to them, lets talk about images.

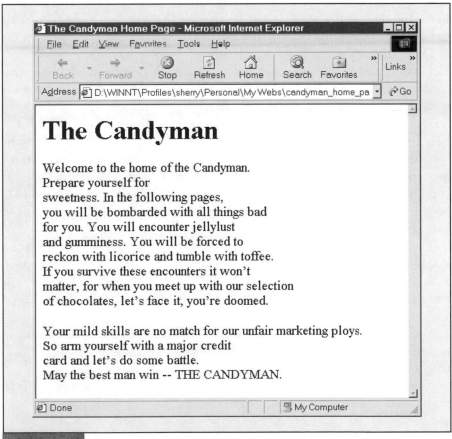

FIGURE 12-4   Placing line breaks at the end of each section of text that you want on the same line

To place an image in your page in HTML, you must use the <img> tag. Within the image tag you can specify properties that are available to the image. These properties are called *attributes*. The most important one is the source attribute (src). The source identifies the image you are using and the path to or location of the image sitting within the computer. Let's add a nice piece of chocolate to the mix. (You can download our luscious chocolate heart image— chocheart.jpg— at the Osborne Web site for this book, or you can use your own image. Import whichever graphic you select into your Web and place it in the Images folder.)

You decide that you want the candy to appear near the headline in your page. To add the HTML code for the image, follow these steps:

1. Position your cursor just to the right of the <h1> tag.

2. Click to change the insert point and type **<img src="images/chocheart.jpg">**.

This means that you are using an image entitled "chocheart.jpg" and it resides in the Images folder. The quotes are not required, but they can make code easier to read. When you place an image using Normal view and let FrontPage write the HTML code for you, it always uses the quotes.

Most container tags have properties (attributes) that can be attributed to that specific tag. An attribute extends the options for the tag. Now that we are dealing with images, let's examine some of the image tag's attributes.

We spoke of the src attribute, which we added to the tag above. Width and height are two other important attributes of the image tag. They should always be specified when placing an image. You can specify a border size on the image by using the border attribute. Here, you want a border of 0. Change the line of code that you typed to read **<img border="0" src="images/chocheart.jpg" width="122" height="122">**. (Of course, if you are using your own image, type its name and sizes rather than ours.)

You can easily determine the width and height of an image by loading it into a graphics program such as Adobe Photoshop. You could also place the image in FrontPage and discover its size by right-clicking on the image in Normal view and selecting Picture Properties. Click on the Appearance tab and read the height and width values.

You can also specify the alignment in the HTML code. Change your code again to look like this: **<img border="0" src="images/chocheart.jpg" width="122" height="122" align="left">**.

The page is getting there, but it could still use a lot of work. One thing you can do is to use a pair of <font> tags around the heading. The <font> tag has a size, color, or family attribute. Let's get rid of the <h1> all together and replace it with

<font size="6">. With font sizes, the larger the number, the larger the font. It's the opposite of the heading tags, where <h1> is larger than <h4>.

You can also change the font itself with the use of the tag <font face="">. Because fonts are not embedded into the page, but exist in a user's computer, it's good practice to list the font you would most like to use and then a few substitute fonts that are common to all systems, separated by commas—for example: <font face ="Dauphin, Helvetica, sans serif">. This way, even though you prefer Dauphin, you know the other two fonts will work as well.

Finally, let's change the color of the Candyman heading to red. Color is also an attribute of the font tag. Colors are best listed using their hexadecimal equivalents (that makes them quite specific because each hex value uniquely specifies the color).

Your HTML code should now look like this:

```
<html>
<head>
<title>
The Candyman Home Page
</title>
</head>
<body>
<img border="0" src="images/chocheart.jpg"
height="122"
width="122" align="left">
<font color="#FF0000"
     face="Dauphin, Helvetica, Sans Serif"
     Size="6">
     The Candyman
</font>
```

Figure 12-5 shows the "new look" on the page as a result of the changes you've made to the HTML code.

HTML Tables

The page is improving, but the text could be better placed. The Candyman heading and the graphic take too big a bite out of the text. The text blurb is much too close the left margin of the window. The best way to fix this is with the use of tables. You need to create a one-row table with two columns: the left column to hold a margin so the text moves to the right, and a right column to hold that actual text.

Tip: The only way to specify multiple fonts in FrontPage is to add the font list directly to the HTML page. This is one of the major reasons to understand HTML and to know how to add something to the code that FrontPage writes.

Tip: You can find the hexadecimal value of a color by selecting its hexagon-shaped swatch in the More Colors dialog box in FrontPage. (You can get the More Colors dialog box by choosing Font from a context-sensitive pop-up menu and then selecting Color | More Colors.) If you know the RGB value and want the hexadecimal value of a color, a fast way to find it is to use the free, interactive RGB-to-hex converter at http://www.creativepro.com. You enter the RGB value and click the button next to it, and you'll be shown the hexadecimal value.

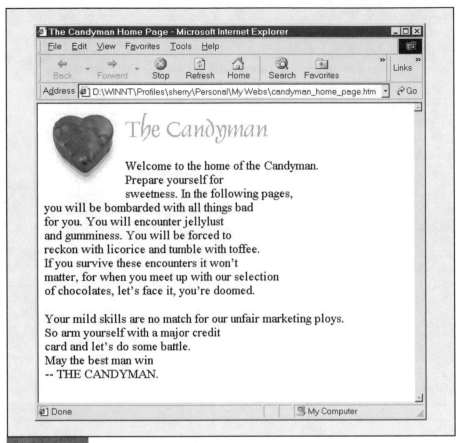

The page is starting to look more organized

You have already created a table with FrontPage's built-in features. Tables in FrontPage and in HTML act just like they do in a word processor program. They are currently the best way to position text or images. Style sheets can give you absolute positioning, but they are unreliable between browsers (that doesn't mean don't use them, it just means check it out in every browser you can find!).

To start an HTML-coded table, you begin with the table tag (<table>). It's always good to set the border attribute of the table. Eventually, you'll set yours to zero. This will hide the table from the viewer. Sometimes it helps to work with the border of 1, so you can see what the table is doing. The other two main attributes are cell padding and cell spacing. You'll set these to zero. Here's how to enter the code for the basic table:

1. Position your cursor at the start of the <p> tag that begins the text describing Candyman.

2. Press the ENTER key to create a new line, and move your cursor to the new line.

3. On the new line, type **<table border="1" cellpadding="0" cellspacing="0">**.

4. Look at the HTML code in Preview mode. You will see a table immediately appear, even though you've not finished the full definition yet.

Welcome to the home of the Candyman. Prepare yourself for sweetness. In the following pages, you will be bombarded with all things bad for you. You will encounter jellylust and gumminess. You will be forced to reckon with licorice and tumble with toffee. If you survive these encounters it won't matter, for when you meet up with our selection of chocolates, let's face it, you're doomed.

Your mild skills are no match for our unfair marketing ploys. So arm yourself with a major credit card and let's do some battle. May the best man win.

-- THE CANDYMAN

To create table cells, you need to use the table row tag, <tr>. This states that you are creating a row. Nested within the row are your cells, which are represented by the <td> tag, which stands for table data. Place the <tr> tag on the line after the table definition.

Creating a left margin will offset the text from the edge of the browser. The left margin is actually the first column in the table. Create a left margin by using a blank table data tag with only the width attribute in it. Type this line below the <tr> tag:

**<td width="50">
 </td>**

Hard-coding the exact number of pixels in a cell allows an absolute positioning of it, no matter what size the browser window appears. If you want your page to move with the window, use relative positioning with the % sign. This method will let you see the whole table as you re-create the browser window, but sometimes your text will collapse and the results aren't always pleasing. So, experiment with both methods and see what you like.

Now that you've closed the first cell, let's open a new one that will surround the text. On the next line in the HTML view, type

<td width="400">

You can now remove the <br> tags that you originally inserted. The width attribute now controls the text wrap within the cell, stopping it from scrolling across the screen. The page looks cleaner and easier to read.

Let's fancy up the text a bit as well. Another attribute of the <td> tag is valign, which stands for "vertical align." The code <valign="top"> will align the text to the top of the cell. Type this code after the <td that you just entered, but before the width="400">. The whole line now reads: <td valign="top" width="400">.

Center the tag line "--THE CANDYMAN" by placing the <center> tag in front of it and </center> tag after it. To keep the text type small, add a <font size="2"> tag before the <p> tag in front of the text and close it after the final </p> tag after the text.

Finally, close the row with the </tr> tag, and close the table with the </table> tag. Put these tags after all of the text but above the </body> tag.

Let's create another table above this one. You'll use the same method as before. Put a set of td tags around the image and another one around the Candyman logo. Here's the finished code for the entire page:

```
<html>

<head>
<title>
The Candyman Home Page
</title>
</head>

<body>
<table>
<tr>
<td width="122">
<img border="0" src="images/chocheart.jpg" height="122"
width="122" align="left">
</td>
<td width ="250">
<font color="#FF0000"
      face="Dauphin, Helvetica, Sans Serif"
      Size="6">
      The Candyman
</font>
</td>
</tr>
</table>

<table border="0" cellpadding="0" cellspacing="0">
<tr>
<td width="50"><br></td>
<td valign="top" width="400">
<font size="2"><p>Welcome to the home of the Candyman.
Prepare yourself for sweetness. In the following pages,
you will be bombarded with all things bad for you. You will
```

```
encounter jellylust and gumminess. You will be forced to
reckon with licorice and tumble with toffee.
If you survive these encounters it won't matter, for when you
meet up with our selection of chocolates, let's face it,
you're doomed.</p>

<p>Your mild skills are no match for our unfair marketing
ploys.
So arm yourself with a major credit
card and let's do some battle.
May the best man win.</p>
<p> <center-- THE CANDYMAN</center></p></font>
</td>
</tr>
<table>

</body>
```

Figure 12-6 shows how much the layout of the page has improved.

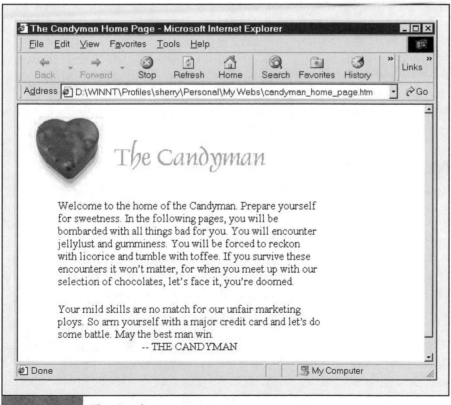

FIGURE 12-6   The Candyman page

When Should I Hand-Code the HTML?

You have probably purchased FrontPage as much to avoid having to hand-code HTML as to help you with site management tasks. Why, then, would you ever want to place HTML code into a page yourself?

Selecting Fonts

One reason for hand-coding HTML is to give the site visitor the benefit of your knowledge of fonts. You may create a list of font choices as long as you want in the hopes that something on the list will appear in the user's system. The browser will try every font on the list until it finds one. In the Candyman exercise, you inserted the code <font face="Dauphin, Helvetica, sans serif">. The Face attribute allows you to list the fonts in order of preference. If the site visitor doesn't have Dauphin, the browser will look for Helvetica. If it doesn't find that either, it will pull any sans serif font it finds (that's the kind without feet). Typically, on Windows machines, the default sans serif font is Arial. Most Mac computers have Helvetica installed (unless the user has removed it, Helvetica is always installed on a Mac).

FrontPage doesn't allow you to create sets of fonts. Therefore, the only way to specify multiple choices is for you to enter the list into the HTML code manually. Your safest strategy is to locate your preferred font on Windows, on the Mac, and then specify either sans serif or serif if neither of your other font choices is available.

META Tags

You might also want to edit the META tags in your document. The META tags are tags that are not visible to the site visitors but are used by either the browser or by Web search engines. META tags, as mentioned in Chapter 9, can hold all of the keywords needed to index your site.

You can use the Page Properties | Custom tab to enter keywords into you page, or you can type them in by yourself. To enter them yourself, type the following tag into the list of other META tags in the head of your page:

<meta http-equiv="keywords" content="...">

Replace the three dots with your keywords separated with commas. If FrontPage can do this for you, why do it yourself? I think it's actually easier to write it in. Also, if you use a program such as AddWeb to manage your keywords, it will write the HTML code for the keywords. All you need to do is to cut and paste.

Unsupported Multimedia or DHTML Commands

FrontPage has an annoying, though not unexpected, trait of writing HTML code that can only be used by Internet Explorer. As you will discover in Chapter 14, you can only add .avi formatted video in a FrontPage Web if you want to use the commands present in FrontPage for working with video. If you want to use a QuickTime movie on your page, you will need to find another way of getting it there. One of the easier ways is to just tinker with the HTML code and put it where you want it to go. This same annoyance encompasses both audio formats and a variety of dynamic HTML techniques. You will also need to add JavaScript commands to your HTML by hand. You will probably also want to add <br> tags by hand, set borders to zero, and check out (and fix up) messed up bulleted lists. More of these techniques are discussed in Chapters 13 and 14.

Professional Skills Summary

So, is HTML as much of a foreign language as you thought? I certainly find it easier to learn than high school French or Spanish. It is also a lot easier to learn than C++ or COBOL (two computer programming languages).

You've learned how to create an HTML page from scratch. This should also make it easier to read the code that FrontPage generates. You have learned the difference between opening and closing tags, and how to write a properly structured HTML page.

You've also learned how to specify fonts, colors, alignment, headings, and tables in HTML. You can create font sets and embed the code for them directly into your HTML.

In the next chapter, you'll learn about dynamic HTML and how to create sites that move.

Adding Life to Your Page with DHTML

In this chapter you:

- Learn about dynamic HTML

- Learn how to create button or image rollovers without using theme graphics

- Learn how to create text and text-link rollovers

- Learn how to create collapsible outlines

- Learn how to position your graphics and text exactly where you want them to be

- Learn how to fly in text and graphics

- Learn how to create page transitions such as wipe and venetian blind

- Learn how to add a simple JavaScript rollover that shows a description in the status bar of your browser

What Is DHTML?

Dynamic HTML (or DHTML) is a name for a combination of technologies that let you create a page that *changes after you write it.* The changes that occur may include:

- Animations (having text or graphics "fly in" from off the page or move around on the page)
- Page transitions (having pages "dissolve" or "wipe" as they enter or leave the screen)
- Rollovers (changes to text or images as the mouse is moved over them)
- Collapsible outlines
- Form field extensions (adding tab ordering and hot keys to forms)

DHTML effects, when used judiciously, can add a good deal of interest to a page without adding a lot of size to the page download.

DHTML is implemented through a combination of HTML, cascading style sheets, positioning, and scripting (usually JavaScript because it is the most widely implemented of the scripting languages).

You should be aware, however, that all is not ideal in the DHTML world. This is one of those places where browser incompatibilities rear their ugly heads. In the first place, DHTML is only fully implemented in the level 4 browsers (Netscape 4.0, Internet Explorer 4.0) and above. In most cases, there's no penalty for those with older browsers except that they won't see your dazzling effects. The problem with the level 4 browsers is that, while they all implement DHTML, they do so differently, and not all of the effects work on all of the browsers.

FrontPage Support for DHTML

FrontPage 2000 supports all of the DHTML effects listed above *for browsers that support them.* FrontPage tries very hard to limit your choices of DHTML effects to those that are applicable for the browser(s) you have specified as your targets for the page. Table 13-1 will give you some idea of the DHTML effects supported for each of the standard browser types in FrontPage 2000. You may notice that other effects may be shown in the menus for a specific browser type, but these are the ones I've found to actually work.

Netscape and IE Support for DHTML

As you can see from Table 13-1, both Netscape and Microsoft browsers at level 4 and above do support some form of DHTML, but the support differs. Both support DHTML, but....

Effect	IE4+	NS4+	IE3	NS3	WebTV
Text Animation Effects:					
Fly in	Y	Y	N	N	N
Drop in by word	Y	Maybe	N	N	N
Hop	Y	N	N	N	N
Spiral	Y	Y	N	N	N
Wave	Y	N	N	N	N
Wipe	Y	Y	N	N	N
Elastic	Y	N	N	N	N
Zoom	Y	N	N	N	N
Text Rollovers	Y	N	N	N	N
Image Rollovers	Y	Y	N	Y	N
Page Transitions	Y	N	N	N	N
Collapsible Outlines	Y	N	N	N	N

TABLE 13-1   DHTML Effects Supported for FrontPage Browser Types

There Are Major Differences

The two browsers use different Document Object Models (DOM). DOM specifies the page elements that are "exposed" to scripts. Internet Explorer 4+ makes nearly everything on the page accessible to scripting, while Netscape Navigator 4+ exposes relatively few elements. Netscape uses layers heavily while Microsoft prefers CSS-standard elements.

The browsers use different CSS implementations. Page elements with the same style sheet definitions may (and probably will) look different in Netscape Navigator 4+ than in Internet Explorer 4+. Internet Explorer 4+ is closer to the standard as specified by the World Wide Web Consortium, but neither is ideal yet. For example: font size specification is not consistent (fonts appear smaller in Netscape than in Internet Explorer for the same point size) and list formatting differs (vertical spacing of list elements is problematic in Netscape).

There Is Hope for Cross-Browser Solutions, but Not in FrontPage

FrontPage 2000 support focuses on Internet Explorer 4+ capabilities and doesn't bother much with cross-browser implementations. Generally, FrontPage provides only the Microsoft solution for DHTML, which means that you need to be very careful about the effects that you decide to use unless you know that your audience is going to browse your site using Internet Explorer. (The INSCOPA site that we've created, for example, would be a good place to implement DHTML techniques because all of the site visitors are members of the same corporation and will be using Internet Explorer on the intranet that accesses the Web site.)

You can find cross-browser solutions if you're willing to roll up your sleeves and do your own scripting. If you really want to include dynamic effects that work the same in both major browsers, try DHTMLLIB or Dynamic Duo, or a variety of other available code libraries. (More information on these code libraries later in this chapter.) This solution assumes, of course, that you are a programmer or can find one to code the effects for you.

Rollovers

Rollovers are probably the most commonly used of the dynamic effects. A rollover is a change that occurs when the mouse pointer moves over an object on the page. The most typical use of rollovers is to change the appearance of a button when the mouse moves over it, to indicate the selection that will be made when the mouse button is clicked. FrontPage 2000 also supports text rollovers for links (in Internet Explorer 4+ only). Text rollovers allow the appearance of text to be changed when the mouse moves over the text. Although the selection to create such rollovers is available when Netscape 4 is selected as a target browser, text rollovers don't seem to work in Netscape.

Traditional (Image) Rollovers

The image rollover simply swaps a new image (the *over* image) for the original image whenever the mouse pointer moves across it. FrontPage gives you two ways to implement a button with an image rollover: by Hover button or by DHTML rollover.

The Hover button is a Java applet that you can add and customize through the FrontPage Insert menu. The Hover button involves a little more overhead while loading the page, but has the advantage of working fine in level 3 browsers. The Hover button is actually a FrontPage component, so you will learn how to use it in Chapter 15.

The DHTML rollover works only in level 4 browsers, but has less overhead than the Hover button. It generates JavaScript to perform the image rollover. There are several steps that you need to perform in preparation for creating DHTML rollovers:

- Make sure that you have selected "4.0 Browsers and later" in the Compatibility tab of the Page Options dialog box (under the Tools menu).

- Create two versions of the items that you want to use in the rollover. Shown here are two button states—the normal and the over states. These buttons (and the images to be used as examples for this rollover) are the work of Kelly Loomis, the exceptionally talented genius behind www.7rings.com, a site that contains a large assortment of linkware that you may use free of charge (after displaying Kelly's link logo) on noncommercial sites.

Let's work an example to create a DHTML rollover. The end effect is really similar to the navigation buttons that contain rollovers when you use a theme. However, the DHTML version works when you aren't using a navigation bar. You may select your own set of buttons or images. I am using Kelly's Tiffany's Light Set as my example. Figure 13-1 shows the image, which looks as it if is in a single piece.

Even though this image seems to be in one piece, it is actually living inside of a table with each cell containing a single image slice. I prepared the table from the downloaded images (already sliced) from Kelly's Web site at www.7rings.com. I used Adobe ImageReady to create the table structure, and pasted the resulting code for the table into the HTML view of my FrontPage document. All of the

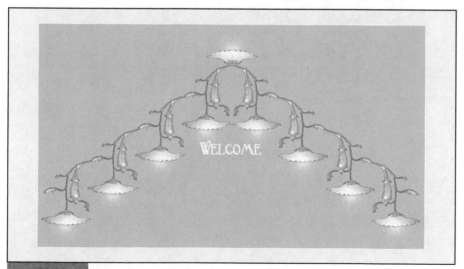

FIGURE 13-1   Tiffany's Light Set as a table in Page view

table references were nonfunctioning, but the structure was correct so I loaded each image slide into the correct cell and saved the graphics into my Web. Figure 13-2 shows the table in Page view. It previews and works correctly even though the Page view of it looks quite odd.

Professional Pointer

You can use DHTML rollovers in a table. You could define the table in FrontPage, but a complex table needs to be carefully created. In Figure 13-2, the FrontPage table would actually need to contain 11 columns. You need to merge all cells together in Rows 1 and 2. In Rows 3, 4, and 5, only some of the cells need to be merged to allow you to create the cells that you need. FrontPage is a bit recalcitrant about merging the cells that want to be placed together, which is why I finally created the table in ImageReady.

Once you have your images created, you are ready to apply the rollover effect. Here's how to create the DHTML rollover effect:

1. Insert the main (i.e., nonrollover) image by choosing Insert | Picture | From File and then selecting the image to insert. Each image is in a different table cell.

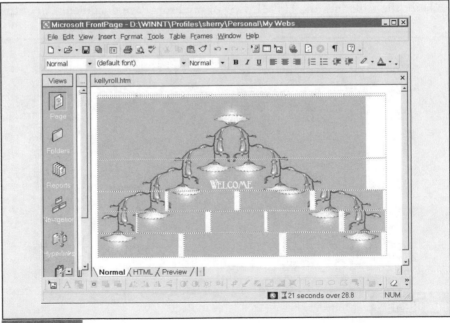

FIGURE 13-2 Tiffany's Light Set's opening screen (image by Kelly Loomis of 7rings.com)

2. Click once on the image to highlight it. (If the image is in a cell, one click will select the cell.)

3. Click on Format in the menu bar, then on Dynamic HTML Effects to display the DHTML Effects dialog box. (Or, you can right-click in the toolbar area and show the DHTML toolbar.)

4. In the DHTML Effects dialog box, click the down-pointing arrow next to Choose an Event. This will pull down the Events menu. Click on "Mouse over," as shown in Figure 13-3. The Apply section of the DHTML Effects dialog box will then be activated.

5. Click on the down-pointing arrow next to Apply to open the Effects menu, then select Swap Picture. When you select an image and then choose "Mouse over" as your event, your only possible effect is to swap an image. The "Choose settings" section is then activated.

6. Click on the down-pointing arrow next to "Choose settings" and then on the "Choose picture" option. This opens a file selection dialog box. Select the image that you want for your over state and click on OK.

7. This completes the DHTML image rollover definition process. You can now preview your button. Figure 13-4 shows the over state for the Tiffany's Light Set splash screen.

> **Tip:** FrontPage only lets you define one action for the button. If you try to add a Click action, for example, it will replace the "Mouse over" action rather than being added as a separate action.

Text Rollovers

For pages intended for Internet Explorer 4+, you can define text rollovers that change the color, font, and other style attributes of sections of text when the mouse pointer is over them. You can define a standard rollover behavior to apply to all links, or a custom rollover to apply to any section of text.

Defining Link Rollovers

To set the rollover behavior for link elements in Internet Explorer 4+ pages, follow these steps:

1. Make sure that you have selected "4.0 Browsers and later" in the Compatibility tab of the Page Options dialog box (under the Tools menu). Note that

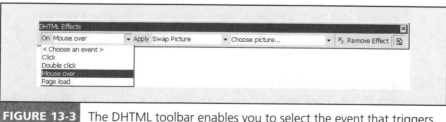

FIGURE 13-3 The DHTML toolbar enables you to select the event that triggers the effect

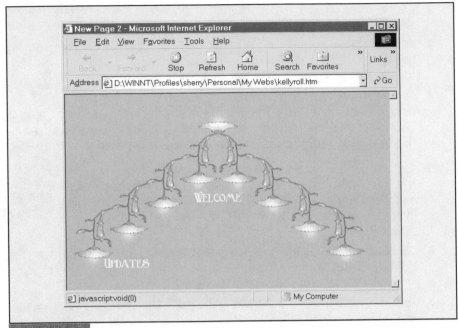

FIGURE 13-4 You can see what happens when you rollover the button

the menu options will be active even if Netscape is selected as the browser, although the effect will not actually be seen in Netscape.

2. You also need to make certain that you've defined the text as a hyperlink.

3. Click on Format | Background. This will open the Page Properties dialog box at the Background tab.

4. Click on the checkbox labeled "Enable hyperlink rollover effects." The Roll-over Style button will be activated.

5. Click on the Rollover Style button. This will open a Font dialog box in which you can select the font, font size, color, style, and spacing for the rollover effect. When satisfied with your selections, click on the OK button. Figure 13-5 shows the Font dialog box on top of the Format Background dialog box.

6. You're now ready to test your selections, which will apply by default to all links in the document. Click on the Preview tab and move the mouse button over any link to check the rollover behavior.

Defining Custom Text Rollovers

To set a rollover effect for any section of text in an Internet Explorer 4+ page, follow these steps:

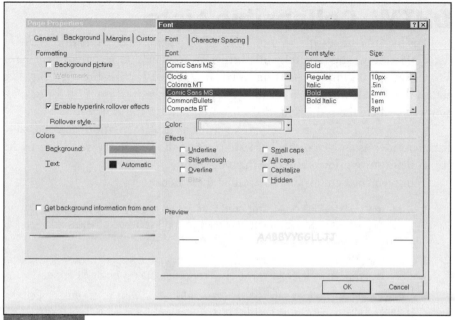

FIGURE 13-5 Selecting new styles for rollover text

1. Ensure that you have selected "Microsoft Internet Explorer only" and "4.0 Browsers and later" in the Compatibility tab of the Page Options dialog box (under the Tools menu).

2. Highlight the section of text to which you want to apply the rollover effect.

3. Click on Format in the menu bar, then on Dynamic HTML Effects in the Format menu to display the DHTML effects toolbar.

4. Click on the down-pointing arrow next to "Choose an event" to open the Events menu, then select "Mouse over." The Apply section will then be activated.

> **Tip:** The steps listed here are different from what's in FrontPage's Help. I tried it their way and it didn't work for me. This way works reliably.

5. Click on the down-pointing arrow next to Apply to open the Effects menu, then select Formatting. The Choose Settings section will then be activated.

6. Click on the down-pointing arrow next to Choose Settings to display the Font dialog box (the same font dialog box as shown in Figure 13-5) in which you can select the font, font size, color, style, and spacing for the rollover effect. When satisfied with your selections, click on the OK button.

7. You can now test your rollover in the Preview tab. Pass the mouse over the text for which you defined the rollover to see the effect.

DHTML Collapsible Lists

Collapsible lists are another "cool" effect made possible by dynamic HTML. This effect shows the hierarchy of a list when you click on it. Microsoft claims FrontPage 2000's implementation of collapsible lists is cross-browser, but I've found that it only works in Internet Explorer 4+. This effect is useful for navigation tasks where the fully expanded list would take up too much room.

If you want a cross-browser, cross-platform implementation of collapsible lists, consider using Macromedia Flash to create the list. Flash will animate the list so that it drops down any way that you want.

To implement a collapsible list, follow these steps:

1. Create a bulleted list or a numbered list containing all of the items. I've found that this works best when you leave all of the list items at the same level at this point (don't demote items to make sublists yet).

2. Highlight the entire list and right-click to show the shortcut menu. Click on the List Properties selection. The List Properties dialog box will appear.

3. Select the appropriate tab for the type of list you want to create. Check the Enable Collapsible Outlines checkbox. If you want the list to be collapsed initially, click on the Initially Collapsed checkbox. Figure 13-6 shows this action in process. Click on the OK button.

4. Now you can go back and demote the sublist items. Select a group of items that should be invisible when the list is collapsed, then click on the Increase

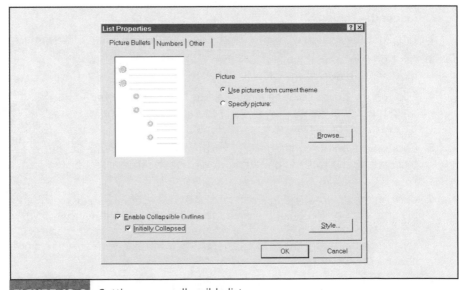

FIGURE 13-6 Setting up a collapsible list

Indent button twice to demote these items. Do the same for all items that should be below any of the main selections. You can also demote items below the subtopics, if desired.

5. Now switch to the Preview pane to preview your list. If you selected Initially Collapsed, only the main topics should now be shown. Click on any of the main topics and its subtopics will drop down. If any of the subtopics has lower-level topics below it, you can click the subtopic to display its lower-level topics. Figure 3-7 shows a partially opened list created according to the instructions above.

Page Transitions

FrontPage 2000 lets you add page transitions like dissolves, wipes, box-ins, and others to give your Web pages a cinematic feel. Page transitions work only with Internet Explorer 4+, and may be applied when entering the page, when entering the site, when leaving the page, or when leaving the site.

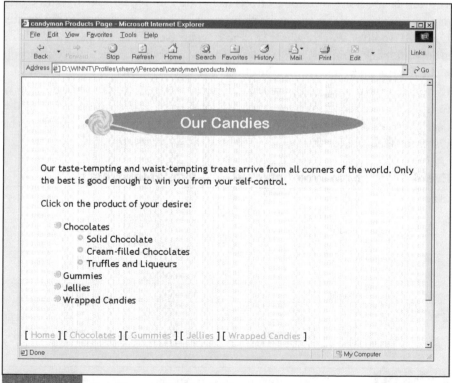

FIGURE 13-7 Creating a collapsible list

To add a page transition (remember, they only work on Internet Explorer 4+ pages), follow these steps:

1. Ensure that you have selected "4.0 Browsers and later" in the Compatibility tab of the Page Options dialog box (under the Tools menu). Note that the menu options will be active even if Netscape is selected as the browser, although the effect will not actually be seen in Netscape.

2. Click on Format in the menu bar, then on Page Transition in the Format menu. The Page Transitions dialog box will be displayed.

3. Select the event to which the transition will be applied, then the transition effect to apply. Finally, enter a duration (if desired) that specifies how long the transition effect will take to complete. Click on the OK button when finished.

You can now preview the transition effect in the Preview tab.

Other Effects from the DHTML Toolbar

You can create some additional effects using the DHTML toolbar. With either text or graphics selected, if you click on the Choose an Event menu in the DHTML toolbar, you see a list of possible events (see Table 13-2). The available events are click, double-click, mouse over, or page load. The choice that you make for the event determines the effects that are available.

You can create a page, as pictured in Figure 13-8, that contains images that fly in from various locations when the page loads. The text on the bottom of the page drops in word-by-word. You can download the page candies.htm from the Osborne Web site for this book to see how these effects appear in motion.

Event	Item Type Selected	Available Effects
Click	text	Fly out Formatting
	graphics	Fly out Swap Picture
Double-click	text	Fly out Formatting
	graphics	Fly out
Mouse over	text	Formatting
	graphics	Swap Picture
Page Load	text or graphics	Drop In By Word, Elastic, Fly in, Hop, Spiral, Wave, Wipe, Zoom

TABLE 13-2   List of Effects Available by Event and Item Type

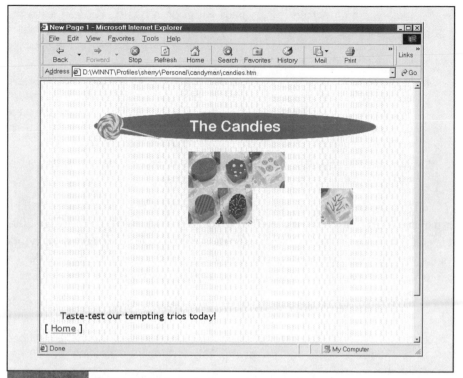

FIGURE 13-8   Each piece of candy flies in from a different location when the page loads

Floating Content

There are several ways to add content that "floats" on the page; that is, content that occupies a fixed space while the text of the page flows around it. The simplest is to use what's called a floating table. This is a table that occupies less than the full width of the page and is aligned to one side of the page or in the center. When the table is positioned like this, the text outside the table flows around it. This effect is really easy to create in FrontPage 2000 using these steps:

1. Use the Insert Table button on the toolbar to insert a table with as many rows and columns as you need (it can be one cell, if that's all you need).

2. Right-click anywhere inside the table and select Table Properties from the pop-up menu. A Table Properties dialog box will appear.

3. In the Layout section at the top of the dialog box, you can specify the float, which specifies which side of the page that the table will appear on, and the

table width (in percent of the page width or in pixels). You can leave the alignment set to Default. The table will appear on the side of the page set in the float attribute, and the text outside the table will appear on the opposite side, neatly aligned along the table edge.

4. In the Table Properties dialog box, you can also specify the size of the table borders (0 means the table will have no borders), two colors for the borders, and the color of the table background, which can be different from the page background color. Setting the background color different from the page color is useful for setting the table off from the rest of the text.

5. Put whatever you want inside the table. This may be a "sidebar" of text, a picture, or anything else that will go in a table cell.

You can also create floating content through the use of absolute positioning. This generally works well only with level 4 browsers, and Microsoft's FrontPage 2000 Help also warns against using it in conjunction with DHTML. It does have the advantage of allowing you to position one page element on top of another (to display text over a picture, for example). Here's how to absolutely position a page element:

1. Enter the page element (a section of text, a picture, a table, etc.) on the page and highlight it.

2. If the positioning toolbar isn't displayed, click on View in the menu bar, then on Toolbars, then on Positioning. This will open a floating positioning toolbar.

3. Click on the icon at the left end of the toolbar (its ToolHelp cursor says Position Absolutely). The current position of the element will be shown in the boxes to the right of the icon.

4. You can set the position of the left side (in pixels or percent of the page width from the left side of the page) and top (in pixels or percent of page height from the top of the page) of the element. If you are specifying the position in percent, put a percent sign after the number (e.g., 50%). You can also specify the width and height of the element. Finally, you can specify its Z-index. This tells the browser where to "stack" the element on the page. A Z-index of zero means that the element will fall below all other elements on the page. An element with a Z-index of 1 will display on top of any elements with Z-index zero but beneath elements with Z-index 2, and so forth. You can also use the two icons on the right side of the positioning toolbar to do the same thing; one icon moves the element "forward" on the page (increasing its Z-index) and the other moves it backward (decreasing its Z-index). Figure 13-9 shows the results of using absolute positioning on a Web page to place buttons in positions that would not have been possible without using a table. The graphics shown are also by Kelly Loomis of www.7rings.com. This set is called "A Touch of Nouveau."

We will discuss positioning in more detail in the next section.

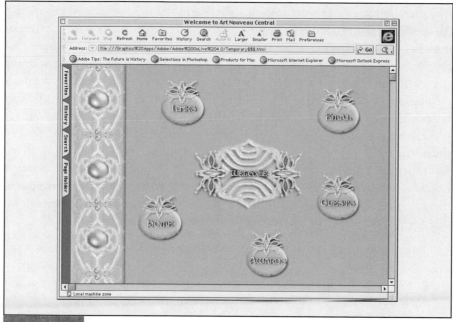

FIGURE 13-9   Positioning enables you to place buttons exactly where you want them to appear on this page using Kelly Loomis' graphic elements

Positioning—Another Partial Solution

The preceding section showed the use of absolute positioning to place an element on the page. This generally works well, but results may not be the same in the major browsers.

Drawbacks

Netscape and Internet Explorer use different interpretation of the positioning rules, and neither is 100 percent "standard" (as defined by the World Wide Web Consortium). In general, positioning only works reasonably reliably in level 4 and above browsers. Absolute positioning is a feature of CSS2.

Creating a Site Using Relative and Absolute Positioning

Absolute positioning places the positioned element at an exact location relative to the page boundaries and removes it from the flow of the document (i.e., the way the graphic or text would normally relate to the other elements around it). Absolute positioning and relative positioning also enable you to layer text over or under graphics or layer graphics on top of one another. Regardless of where your element appears in the Normal view, it will appear according to your positioning rules when the page is viewed in a browser (or in Preview view). Absolute positioning can be established by highlighting the element to be positioned, opening the positioning toolbar, and setting the element's positioning in the toolbar.

Relative positioning positions the element relative to its place in the flow of the document.

FrontPage 2000 supports relative positioning through the use of "position boxes." To relatively position an element or group of elements within the document flow, you insert a position box and then absolutely position the element inside the position box. To insert a position box, follow these steps:

1. In Normal view, place the insertion point where you want the position box and press the ENTER key twice to create a blank line.

2. Select the blank line that you just created, click on Format in the menu bar, and then click on Position in the pull-down menu. This will open a Position dialog box.

3. In this dialog box, you can choose the way text wraps and choose the positioning style. For a relatively positioned element, select the Relative positioning style.

4. You can also specify the width and height of the element and the location of its top and left sides (note that if you have chosen relative positioning, these positions are relative to the positioning box, not to the document as a whole). You can also specify the Z-index, which specifies how the element is stacked on the page.

5. Place your element inside the position box.

Layering and Z-Ordering

We've said before that the Z-order parameter controls the "stacking" of elements on the page. You can think of the page as a base layer (containing the unpositioned page elements, page background, etc.) with transparent "layers" containing positioned elements stacked above it. The higher the Z-index of an element, the higher its position on the stack of layers. Z-index 0 is the base layer. Z-index 1 is stacked above the base layer, so that any elements in it will appear in front of elements in the base layer but behind elements in the layer with Z-index 2.

Adding DHTML by Yourself

You can add your own DHTML effects, but this is not for the faint of heart because of differences between browsers in the implementation of DHTML. The browser differences often necessitate writing separate versions of the same page for the two major browsers, or using a cross-browser library.

There are a number of cross-browser libraries that allow you to use of most DHTML features in both major browsers. These include:

- DHTMLLIB 2.0 from SiteExperts.com (http://www.insidedhtml.com/dhtmllib/page1.asp)
- Dynamic Layer Object API (DynLayer) from the Dynamic Duo site by Dan Steinman (http://www.dansteinman.com/dynapi)

Each of the above sources requires you to download the library code (a JavaScript file) and link to it in your page (which will slightly increase the time it takes to download your page). Each also requires you to learn a different, nonstandard syntax and do your own JavaScript coding to set up the page elements, transitions, rollovers, etc.). Even using these libraries, you can't do everything in every browser.

You can also go to http://builder.cnet.com/Programming/Kahn/012898/toolmom.html. This is the site of the Mighty Mouseover machine. It will write JavaScript mouse overs for you and you can cut and paste the code that it generates into the HTML view of your FrontPage document.

Simple JavaScript

JavaScript is a scripting language (not related to Java, by the way) that allows you to program some interactivity into your site. Learning JavaScript is out of the scope of this book. However, you can add some JavaScript rollovers to your HTML code very easily (rollovers that FrontPage does not generate). You can do this without even understanding anything about JavaScript.

You might have noticed that when you place your mouse over a link, the name of the link appears at the bottom left of your browser. This is sometimes less than useful to the site visitor because the link name URL does not show what the link will contain. It is quite easy to change the message displayed at the bottom of the browser so that it gives a description in plain English of what the site visitor will see if the link is selected.

Creating this effect involves two changes in the HTML view. You need to add an attribute to the <body> tag that clears the message line in the browser, and then you need to add an OnRollOver attribute to the <a href> tag. Here's how to change the HTML code to create this effect:

1. Switch to the HTML view of your page.
2. Locate the <body> tag in the code. Add this statement to the <body> tag so that the body tag reads:

   <body onLoad="window.defaultStatus=' ' " >

It might be difficult to see from the text string shown, but you are typing two single quotes and one double quote at the end of the statement. If your <body> tag contains additional attributes such as bgcolor, then simply add the window.defaultStatus attribute after everything else but before the ending > symbol. This statement clears the status line so that the message disappears when your cursor is not on top of a link.

3. You next need to create your links exactly as you normally would (in Normal mode, select your text or graphics and choose Insert | Hyperlink. Then return to the HTML view.

4. In HTML view, locate the first <a href> statement. In my example, which is a continuation of the Candyman home page from Chapter 12, my first link is the word "gumminess." I want this word to link to the pages of the gummy products for site visitors to see. The original statement looked like this:

   <a href="prod03.htm"> jellylust</a>

   It contained the <a href> tag with the URL, the word that was the link itself, and the ending </a> tag. The change is placed directly after the URL in the <a href> tag. Here's what you'd need to add (but change the actual text inside of the single quotes to your own link description):

   <a href="prod03.htm" onMouseOver="window.status='Groove with our great gummy candies'; return true"> jellylust</a>

   This modification works for both text and graphics links. There is no difference.

5. Save your page and preview it in a browser. Figure 13-10 shows the screen with the cursor on the gumminess link. Notice that your message appears in the lower-left of the browser.

Another wonderful rollover effect that you can add with JavaScript enables you to pop up an image on rollover that is in a different location from the area that contains the rollover. The code to create this effect is a bit more complex, and because the effect should be seen first before you try to code it, I've placed the example on the Osborne Web site as remote.htm. See what it does and then read the instructions on how to create the effect.

Our book Web site also contains another complex JavaScript example written by Jim Mundy. This effect allows you to combine images dynamically. It was written for the Village Flowers Web site and enables the site visitor to click on a bouquet and a basket and see how the two would look as one image. View it and then download the instructions.

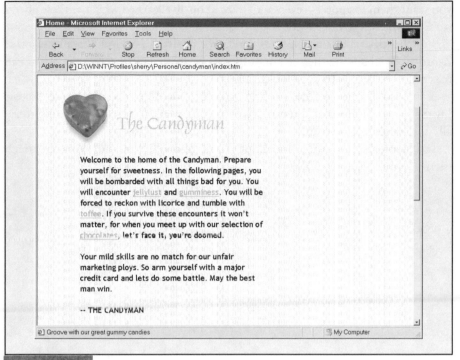

FIGURE 13-10 Adding a custom message as a rollover

Professional Skills Summary

You learned a number of different tricks that you can do to your pages using dynamic HTML. Hopefully, you also learned that this is a tool to be used carefully and tested, tested, and tested again before you "go live" with the result.

You learned how to create DHTML rollovers for both images and text. You saw how the graphics can be made to change even when they are in a table. You learned how to create rollovers for all of the text links in your page or for just a piece of selected code.

You learned how to create collapsible lists, make images fly in when a page loads, create transitions when a page appears or leaves, and position images exactly where you want them to appear—even under text. You also learned which of these effects work in which type of browser.

You learned about absolute and relative positioning, and the meaning of Z-order. By changing the stacking order of your images (the Z-order), you can rearrange the way your page looks.

You also learned where to find source code libraries and some simple JavaScript additions that you can place on your Web site without needing to really understand JavaScript.

In Chapter 14, you will learn about sounds and video and how you can attach them to your pages.

Adding Movies and Audio

Multimedia is one of the hottest "buzzwords" on the 'Net. Everyone wants to add multimedia to his or her site. Multimedia is the "cutting edge" of Web design right now and it generates a lot of excitement. Unfortunately, a lot of the heat and excitement comes from annoyed users who can't get it to work right or who are asked to spend incredibly long gobs of time waiting for the "multimedia" to download.

In this chapter, we'll take a look at multimedia in all of its gory glory. Specifically, we'll cover the various ways in which FrontPage handles audio and video, and we'll discuss the basics of each media type.

Essential Multimedia

What exactly is multimedia anyway? By definition, it's indulging in more than one media at a time. Therefore, singing while watching television is multimedia. On the Web, though, multimedia usually refers to audio, video, or graphic animation. If used with restraint, these techniques can add life to an otherwise static Web site.

In Chapter 13, you learned how to use dynamic HTML to create a variety of movement and motion effects on your page. The multimedia techniques in this chapter are a bit more traditional—though I use this word loosely. By "traditional," I mean that they have been capabilities of the browsers for a while and, in theory at least, are easier to set up and view, and are more cross-platform/cross-browser compatible, than DHTML effects.

Both audio and video clips are taxing to a user's system. They can require fast computers, heaps of RAM, tons of hard disk space, and megafast modem speeds. The lowly GIF animation, by contrast, is a little lamb in terms of resource consumption.

Before we dive into the meat of the chapter, let's take a moment to briefly define terms:

- **GIF animation**   This is a GIF file (256 colors) that has more than one image stored in it. Those browsers that can display this multiple-files-in-one variant of the GIF format show each GIF image in succession, giving the impression of movement, much like an old flip book.

- **Video**   A video clip can be one of many things. It can be a full-motion set of frames that have been imported into the computer from a video camera and prepared especially for viewing on the Web. It can even be a live real-time broadcast across the Web. It can be a set of images that are hand-drawn or somehow computer-created (and are hand-animated). In this case, the difference between video and a GIF animation is one of format and, possibly, of length. In short, a video is any type of image that moves and is saved in a recognized video format such as .avi or .mov. Another generic term for video on the Web is "movies."

- **Audio**   An audio file that contains sound that has been digitized so that it can be played over the Internet. This sound is saved in a format so that it is available on its own—without pictures attached to it (video can have sound tracks as well).

GIF Animations

If, while on the Web, you've seen a cartoon dog wagging its tail, or perhaps a glass of wine being poured, you've "experienced" GIF animations. They are nothing more than a group of images played sequentially to create the illusion of movement. Their only difference from static images is the way they are created. Once created, though, they are placed onto a Web page exactly the same way that their static siblings—GIF images—are placed. A single animation is really only one GIF file, placed into your page with the <img src="file_name.gif"> tag. Using FrontPage, you would place the GIF image by choosing Insert | Picture | From File.

Many programs are available that will allow you to create animations. Adobe ImageReady, Metacreations Painter, and Macromedia Fireworks are all popular choices. For this example, I've used GIF Animator 1.0 (which is free) from Microsoft. If you don't have this program (and want it), you can download it for free at http://computingcentral.msn.com/Topics/Graphics/DBDetails.asp?DownloadID=7894. If you already have a GIF animation program, you may use that to create an animation instead.

You can create interesting GIF animations easily from clip art. Naturally, if you want to create more "serious" animations, art skills come in handy, but you don't need to be an artist to create acceptable animations for your pages. All you need is a GIF animation program, a painting program, and a bit of imagination. In this exercise, you'll see how easy it is to create a GIF animation using a piece of clip art from the Microsoft Online ClipArt collection. You don't *have* to use these images, of course. As usual, it's the technique that's important. This example uses Photoshop as the painting program, but just about any other painting program that contains filters will have a filter that performs a similar distortion. This exercise shows you how to open the image of a heart (a "real" one—not a valentine) and create an animation that simulates a beating heart.

Here's one way to create a GIF animation from clip art and place it into a FrontPage Web:

1. First, you need to find the image that you want to animate. In FrontPage, prepare the page on which you want to place the animated GIF image. Choose Insert | Picture | From Clip Art and click the Clips Online button.

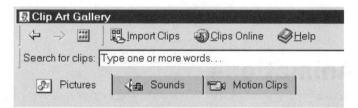

Enter the two keywords "**heart, anatomy**" into the "Search by Keyword" field. (You can review these steps in Chapter 7 if you don't remember how to do this.) At the time of this writing, there are 150 images that used the keyword "heart," but only three images had both "heart" and "anatomy" as search terms. The one that I used is the third on the list.

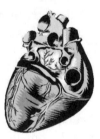

However, any anatomical heart image will work.

2. Download the image to your Clip Art Manager and insert it (temporarily) into your Web page. Copy the image to the clipboard.

3. Open both GIF Animator and Photoshop (if you have Photoshop 5.5 with ImageReady, you don't need GIF Animator). If you don't have Photoshop, open your image editor of choice.

4. In Photoshop or your image editor, create a new image (it should automatically be created at the size of the copied image) and paste the copied heart into the new image.

5. Arrange your screen so that both GIF Animator and Photoshop are visible.

6. Select the Move tool and drag the image into the top location on the GIF Animator screen as shown in Figure 14-1. If you cannot drag an image from your image editor, you can copy it and then paste it into GIF Animator. The height and width are automatically set correctly for the image.

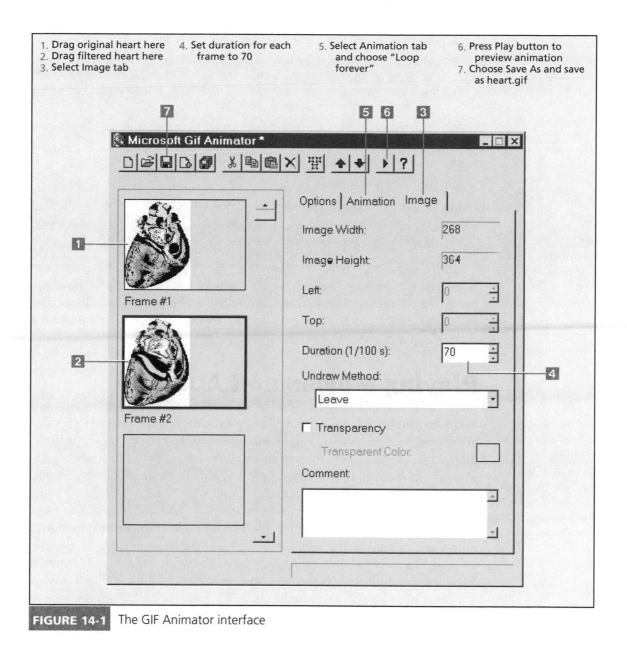

1. Drag original heart here
2. Drag filtered heart here
3. Select Image tab

4. Set duration for each frame to 70

5. Select Animation tab and choose "Loop forever"

6. Press Play button to preview animation
7. Choose Save As and save as heart.gif

FIGURE 14-1 The GIF Animator interface

7. Back in your graphics program, choose Filter | Distort | Pinch, -100. If you don't have a Pinch filter, use one that creates a sphere (Spherize). The Pinch filter makes the heart look as if it is filled and beating.

8. Drag this version into the second box in GIF Animator.

9. Select the first frame in GIF Animator. Click the Image tab, then type **70** into the Duration box. Select the second frame and type **70** into the Duration field. Because the duration is measured in 1/100s of a second, "70" keeps each image on the screen for .7 seconds.

10. Click the Animation tab, and select "Looping, repeat forever." This causes the GIF animation to play endlessly.

11. Press the Play arrow and watch this heart beat.

12. Save your animation as heart.gif.

13. Switch to FrontPage 2000 (or open it) and select Insert | Picture | From File.

14. Click on the Preview tab. If the heart is beating, you have successfully created an animation. You are now on the road to multimedia heaven.

With animations—as with images—the smaller, the better. You can create an animation with thousands of cells, and it might look great within your program. But when a user tries to download it and waits for about an hour, I doubt they will share your enthusiasm. Once again there are no little animations, only little animators. Keep it simple.

Playing Movies and Audio

These days, movies and audio are all over the Web. You can listen to unsigned bands at sights like www.mp3.com. Go to www.cnn.com and you can view video of the latest news. You can hear the World Series at www.broadcast.com. Recently, there was a live four-hour broadcast of breast cancer surgery to help raise awareness for this dreadful disease. Whatever you prefer to watch, all forms of media are becoming increasingly popular.

FrontPage makes it very simple to attach video and audio to a Web page. However, as with many things in life, there's a big catch to this ease of placement. FrontPage is a Microsoft product. Although it could be a coincidence, strangely enough, the media commands that it uses only work in Microsoft Internet Explorer. Site visitors with other browsers cannot see the video at all. All they see is a blank window with a tiny icon in it.

In addition, FrontPage cannot place a QuickTime file (Apple's extremely popular video format) in your page, although it can easily place .avi (Windows Movie format files). Before I show you how to create a cross-browser solution later in the chapter, let's see how FrontPage prefers to work.

Adding Video to a FrontPage Web

Inserting video onto a FrontPage Web is quite straightforward (unless you want to view it under Netscape Navigator or play a QuickTime movie). To add video to a page, follow these steps:

1. Choose Insert | Picture | Video. Select the video file to insert from the dialog box that appears (the same one used to insert still graphics). There are some videos that you can use on the Osborne Web site for this book, and I'll mention some other sources a bit later in the chapter. See Chapter 7 if you don't remember how to insert graphics.

2. Set the properties for the video by right-clicking on the video clip and choosing Picture Properties from the context-sensitive menu. Figure 14-2 shows the options on the Video Picture Properties dialog box.

You can set the movie loop to delay repeating for a set number of milliseconds. How long is a millisecond? Well, a millisecond contains 1,000 seconds, so 250 milliseconds is a quarter of a second.

Adding Audio to a FrontPage Web

Adding audio clips to a page is similar to adding video. It's also similar in that you can only hear it using Internet Explorer. The main difference is that you cannot add a sound file by using the Picture Properties dialog box. Instead, you need to use the Page properties dialog box.

Here's how to attach sound to your page so that it plays as soon as the page opens in Internet Explorer (of course, the site visitor also needs sound cards and speakers to be able to hear the sound clip):

1. Open the page to which you wish to attach a sound file. If you don't have a file to use, you can download the file lite.ra from the Osborne Web site for this book. This audio file contains part of a song by Nag Champa, an original rock band (www.champamusic.com).

2. Right-click on an empty area of the page and choose Page Properties from the context-sensitive menu.

3. Enter the location of the sound file and the number of times to repeat it, as shown in Figure 14-3.

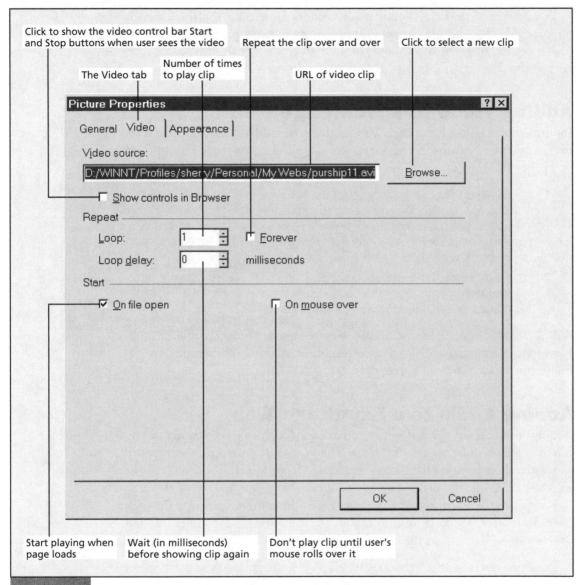

Click to show the video control bar Start
and Stop buttons when user sees the video

Number of times
to play clip

Repeat the clip over and over

Click to select a new clip

The Video tab

URL of video clip

FIGURE 14-2   The Video tab of the Picture Properties dialog box

Start playing when
page loads

Wait (in milliseconds)
before showing clip again

Don't play clip until user's
mouse rolls over it

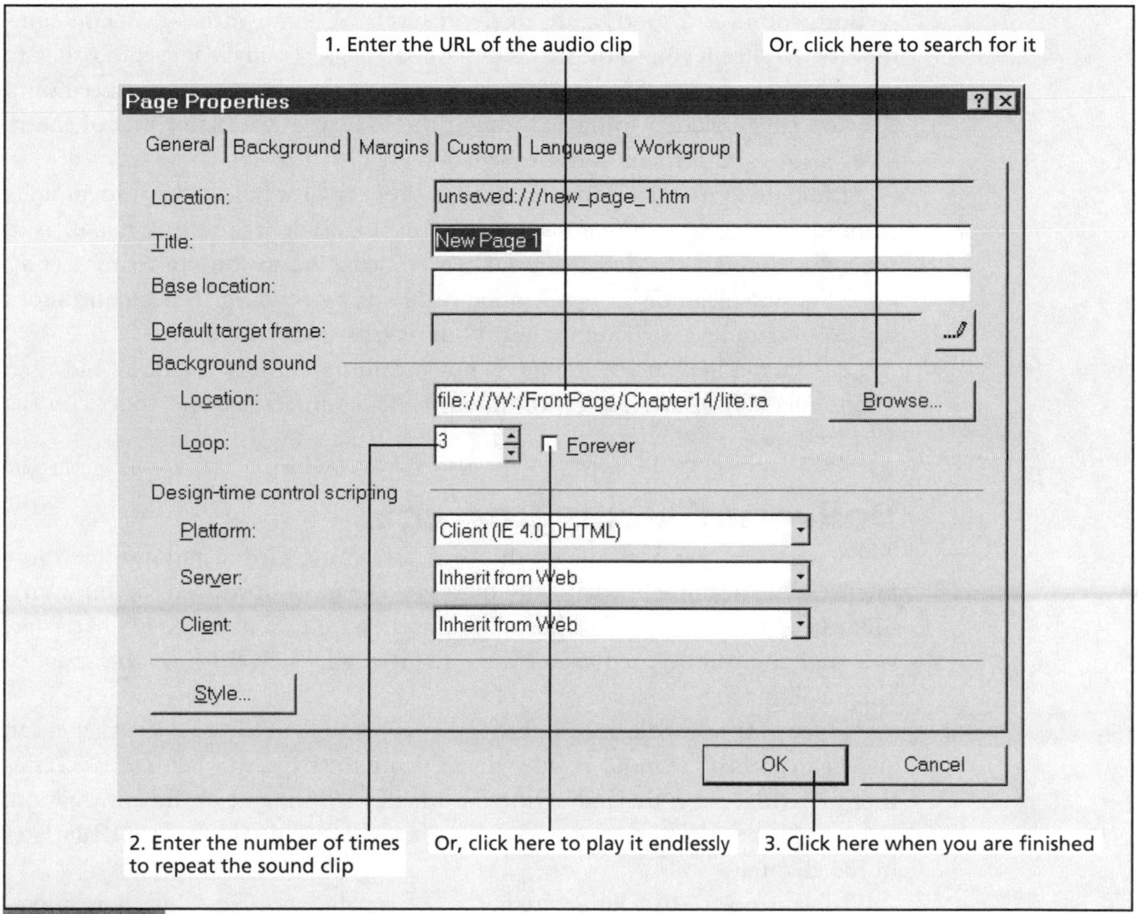

1. Enter the URL of the audio clip   Or, click here to search for it

Page Properties   [?][X]

General | Background | Margins | Custom | Language | Workgroup |

Location: unsaved:///new_page_1.htm

Title: New Page 1

Base location:

Default target frame: ...✎

Background sound

  Location: file:///W:/FrontPage/Chapter14/lite.ra   Browse...

  Loop: 3 ⬍   ☐ Forever

Design-time control scripting

  Platform: Client (IE 4.0 DHTML)   ▾

  Server: Inherit from Web   ▾

  Client: Inherit from Web   ▾

  Style...

                                                OK   Cancel

2. Enter the number of times   Or, click here to play it endlessly   3. Click here when you are finished
to repeat the sound clip

FIGURE 14-3   Setting up a background sound

The Technology of Motion and Sound

You can play sound and view movies on the Web because a number of technologies have made it possible to do so. These technologies are alternately called "file formats" or "architecture." Architecture is actually the correct word for schemes such as QuickTime and RealAudio. The format is just the way the architecture stores its data.

Both sound and motion are costly in terms of bandwidth—that rare commodity that keeps you staring at a slow-to-load page. To make it even possible to see or hear media files on the Web, the files must somehow be compressed until they are small enough to travel through the 'Net at a reasonable rate of speed. The various compression software schemes are called *codecs*.

Although a variety of different architectures exist for both video and audio, a common theme among them is the decision that each architecture makes as to the delivery method. Media content can be delivered to the site visitor's computer by downloading it to a temporary file or by sending it in a continuous stream of data that is viewed or heard but never stored.

Let's take a look at streaming vs. nonstreaming delivery methods and then briefly meet a few of the most common media architectures and codecs on the Web today.

Delivering Media Content

There are two types of media on the Web, streaming media, and nonstreaming media. Nonstreaming media is anything the user must download. If you want a link to a music video, it's just like linking to an image. Within the HTML page, you state the path to the file and when the user clicks on the link, the audio or video will play.

Nonstreaming media has properties that apply to it. With special tags, you can choose to embed the audio or video directly into the page, so when a user accesses that particular page, the audio/video will load with the rest of the information. We will go through a cross-browser example on how to do this in FrontPage later in the chapter.

Other properties include whether a file can be accessed while it is downloading or if it cannot be listened to or viewed until it has finished loading.

The advantages to nonstreaming audio are as follows:

1. You don't need a special server to house the files.
2. There is no real HTML learning curve.

The disadvantages are as follows:

1. Files, even small ones, take a long time to download.
2. Speed and quality of the file depends on many elements besides just download speed. Contributing factors include user's RAM, CPU (brand and speed), and the video or sound card in the user's system.

A newer type of media is *streaming* media. Most of the major commercial Web sites that incorporate multimedia are using streaming technology. With streaming media, the user doesn't actually download the file onto his/her local machine. The file sits on a server, one that has been specially configured for streaming. The file is accessed through a link in the HTML page and then "streamed" across the Web—i.e., sent continually. Basically, streaming media turns the users system into a "dumb" terminal, from which they can listen and or view the media.

The advantages of streaming media are as follows:

1. The file does not need to be downloaded in its entirety before the user can view/listen to it. The only lag time is the buffer time—the time needed to connect the client to the streaming serve.

2. Much larger files can be used because the user isn't actually downloading the file; only the link is downloaded.

The disadvantages are as follows:

1. The files must sit on a server specifically configured for streaming media, which makes it more difficult for the site developer to use streaming media.

2. Streaming media requires extra coding compared to nonstreaming media.

3. Modem speed still greatly affects the quality of the streamed media.

4. Because the files are not stored on the site visitor's hard drive, they must be resent every time that the site visitor wants to see or hear the media again.

Music and Video Architecture

Let's meet some of the larger players in the video and music architecture market. Both Apple and Microsoft have video/audio technologies that compete with one another, and the market has several other large players as well. One of the best sources on the Web for general information about video and audio is the Terran Interactive site: www.terran-int.com. Terran, as you will discover in a short while, is the manufacturer of Media Cleaner Pro, a product that helps to compress your files for Web viewing (or for any other viewing purpose).

Apple QuickTime

QuickTime has been around since long before the Web. It is Apple's proprietary media technology. Like Real Media (the video/audio standard that you'll meet in a minute), it is fully cross-platform. QuickTime, now in version 4.0, is once again gaining popularity on the Web because of its streaming capabilities. (Version 3.0 could perform a progressive download, but version 4.0 does "real" streaming.) It creates a higher-quality file than Real, but also, usually, a larger-sized one.

> "With a customer base of more than fifteen million Mac and Windows users who downloaded the preview release, and a growing list of online publishers— including, most recently, Fox News Online, Fox Sports Online and The Weather Channel—QuickTime 4 is the hottest streaming technology on the Internet."

This is what one reads when first visiting the Apple QuickTime Web site. Whether this is true or not, it is clear that QuickTime is used by many high-profile companies.

You can use HTML tags to embed a QuickTime movie in your page. You can find additional information about QuickTime at Apple's Web site at www.apple.com/quicktime/. QuickTime files usually end a with .mov extension. Apple's audio format is .aif.

Windows Media Technology

Microsoft is the newest major player in the multimedia world, at least as far as the Web is concerned. Microsoft's first video standard used .avi files for video, and .wav for audio. This standard was not originally designed for Web use and is now no longer supported by Microsoft, even though it was built into Windows 95. In early 1999, Microsoft finally unveiled its Windows Media Technology (previously called NetShow). Windows Media Technology promises to deliver "near FM" quality audio. Windows Media video's codec is based on MPEG 4 standards.

At Microsoft's Web site, you can read about the new technology and learn why they consider their codec to be better optimized than Real's. Only the future will tell if Microsoft can conquer the multimedia market on the Web the way it did the browser market. To find out more on this technology, visit the site at www.microsoft.com.

Real Media

Real Media consists of the Real proprietary codec, a server, a few different players, an encoder, a new technology they call "G2," and a marketing scheme that is virtually everywhere on the Web. Real was, if not the first, then the most successful company to date to take advantage of streaming media. CNN, NPR, ABC, and other media giants all feature Real audio and video.

Real creates the smallest file size of all the media types that are available on the Web. With use of the Real encoder, you can save and encode your media for 14.4 modems up through T1 lines. Most major media software support Real technology.

The Real player ships with many Windows machines, and though originally associated with the Windows platform, Real products are fully cross-platform. To stream Real media, you must purchase time on a Real server or find an ISP set up to handle it.

Real files type are .rm, .ra, and .ram.

To find out more about Real, you can go to www.real.com.

MPEG

MPEG stands for Moving Picture Experts Group. This group has created a standard for storage and retrieval of moving pictures and audio on storage media (MPEG 1) and a standard for digital television (MPEG 2). They are working on MPEG 4 version 2, the standard for multimedia applications, and MPEG 7, the content representation standard for multimedia information searching, filtering, management, and processing (to be approved July 2001).

For Web use, however, their most popular codec is used for audio, not video. MP3 (or MPEG 1 layer 3) has taken the Web audio world by storm. MP3 delivers "near CD quality audio" on the Web. This isn't quite true, but as a marketing slogan it sounds very good. By far, it's the best sounding audio available on the Web. Its file size is generally too large for streaming and it seems to take forever to download on a normal modem. But, if your site visitors generally use a cable modem or DSL, MP3 is the perfect media.

Players like Diamond's Rio allow the user to play MP3's outside of the computer environment. Because of MP3's high quality, many underground bootleg sites have appeared on the Web where you can find convincing replicas of your favorite music—all for free. Of course, this pirated music is also highly illegal. So, before posting your own audio on the Web, remember that you are basically giving up control over it. Still, MP3 promises to change the music industry itself. Watch *Court TV*, and tune into mp3.com for the latest skinny on MP3's future.

MIDI

MIDI stands for Musical Internal Digital Interface. These are sound files. MIDI files contain only information, not content, so they are very small. The output quality, however, depends on the user's sound card or MIDI setup. This method gives the author the least control of what the final result of the sound will be. MIDI files talk to the user's computer and play the appropriate instrument files that correspond with MIDI numbers. Of course, if the user has a violin sound set up where the standard snare drum should be, a simple music file could wind up sounding like John Cage instead of John Cougar Mellencamp.

Codecs

Codecs are the second piece of the puzzle. The architecture sets up the basic technology; the codec makes it work for your intended purpose.

The word *codecs* is derived from the word *compression*. Codecs are the standard by which audio and video programs "compress" their data. Each company that offers multimedia software has it's own compression scheme—proprietary codec—each promising better quality for less money.

Because the Internet is so vast, data needs to travel as fast across it as it does from your CD player to your speakers. Your site needs to be able to deliver sound and video to your site visitors as quickly as possible. To move data quickly, you need to trade off quality for speed. To send CD-quality audio or professional video as quickly as compressed audio or video, the transfer speed would have to increase by almost 1,000 times for the average Web surfer. This is why codecs are so important. You need to compress the data because, although transfer speeds are increasing, they aren't increasing enough to make uncompressed audio or video practical.

Actually, in a sense, all media is normally somewhat compressed, but the media for the Web is sometimes compressed by more than half the original information. For example, you might wake up one sunny morning and look up at what appears to be a single-colored blue sky. Yet in reality, that blue sky consists of millions of colors. What a codec will do is to decide which few colors are the most important to give the impression of that sky. Once it does that, it trashes the rest of the data and basically re-creates the missing colors from the ones it chose to keep. When the user views this picture, they will definitely know that it's supposed to be a blue sky, but they won't experience it as you did that lovely day.

Here's another example. Let's say it's that same morning. The wind is blowing gently against the turning leaves. You decide to videotape this event. The codec you choose decides how much motion is needed to preserve the image of blowing leaves. On television, it takes 30 frames per second to give a fairly accurate reconstruction of the windy morning. Yet the average video on the Web is less than half that. Therefore, the motion will be choppy, but the user should still be able to determine that the leaves were blowing, even if they cannot actually feel the wind through the screen.

You don't need to use your content-creating program as your compression program. One of the best compression programs available is Media Cleaner Pro from Terran Interactive (www.terran-int.com). Terran Interactive specializes in optimizing codecs. They can write QuickTime codecs like Cinepak, as well as Real, MPEG,

Windows Media, and a variety of other file types. They are completely cross-platform, so you can take video captured on the Mac and turn it into an AVI (video for Windows) file. Their site provides some of the video and audio background information on the Web. The address http://www.terran-int.com/CodecCentral/Architectures/index.html reaches Codec Central, a site area that Terran calls "the definitive source of information on delivery technologies." The best part of this is that this wealth of information is completely free and available to all.

When you prepare video or audio for the Web, your workflow should be as follows:

- Capture the sound or motion into a program such as Adobe Premiere (or Media 100 or Avid).

- Add effects in a special effects program (After Effects, also from Adobe, is my usual choice).

- Compress the software by applying the codec. For this step, I turn to Media Cleaner Pro.

The advantage of this workflow is that it allows me to get as clean and uncompressed a capture as I can store on my system. I can apply the correct amount of compression for my delivery method (which varies if I am creating video for a Web site or for a CD). Finally, if I need to repurpose video, I have the original high-quality version and can get the best possible new use from it.

Plug-Ins and Helper Apps

Many file types for audio or video require that the site visitor have a specific piece of software on their machine. This software attaches to the site visitor's browser and tells it how to play the audio or video. This class of software is called a "*plug-in*" or a "*helper application.*"

Plug-ins are proprietary programs that allow the user to listen to or view a specific file format. Because both audio and video can create very large files, the files are usually compressed before being placed on the Web. Each compression type has it's own standards. These standards are the codecs that we discussed above. However, to view or listen to these files, a user must have the necessary plug-in.

If you display a file that needs a plug-in, you need to create a link to a Web site where the plug-in can be obtained. The thing to keep in mind, however, is that this is another step before your information can be enjoyed. Hopefully, the time spent getting the plug-in will be worth the effort. But think twice before forcing a user to expend this much effort. Consider giving the site visitor a way to bypass the necessity of having the plug-in. Your content needs to be particularly compelling for a visitor to, sight unseen, take the trouble to go to another site, wait for a plug-in to download, quit the browser program, load the plug-in or helper app into their system, restart the browser, and return to your site.

Some plug-ins are very popular, and it might be safe to assume most people have them. Most Windows users have the RealPlayer format, QuickTime, and some kind of MP3 player on their systems.

Other types of popular plug-ins are the Flash Player and Shockwave from Macromedia. Although sites that offer Shockwave and Flash content are becoming more numerous on the Web, most of these sites also offer an alternative version of the site.

Flash is being used on sites of all varieties. Flash is used to show movie trailers, sell clothing, and advertise Chrysler automobiles. Flash is a program that allows you to create complex animations that have a relatively small file size. It has been developed specifically for the Web. The only catch is that the user must have the Flash plug-in or the site will be unviewable. The plug-in is free for download at www.macromedia.com. Most Flash sites automatically take you to the download location. Download the plug-in and then follow some of the links. See for yourself the impressive things one can do with Flash.

Macromedia's other popular plug-in on the Web is Shockwave. This enables a user to view files that were created with Macromedia's Director. Director has been around much longer than the Web itself, yet the program has gained a second life with the growth of the Web. Director enables you to create animations, create games that react to user interaction, and add other exciting effects. Shockwave enables you to transfer these files to the Web.

Shockwave is also a free download. It now has its own toolbar, which can be obtained from Macromedia's Web site. One popular use of Shockwave is for animated greetings from cartoons such as *South Park* and *Dr. Katz*.

Creating Cross-Browser Pages

Now that you know more about the way that audio and video work, it's time to talk about ways to create pages that can be seen in other browsers in addition to Internet Explorer (or at least can also be seen in Netscape Navigator).

To create cross-browser pages, you need to use a different command to insert the video or audio clips. This command is the Insert | Advanced | Plug-In command. It uses the standard HTML <embed> tag to place audio and video. (The Insert | Picture | Video command, by comparison, uses the Internet Explorer–only tag <dynsrc> and sound files that are inserted in the Page Properties dialog box use the Internet Explorer–only <bkgsound> tag).

You may try out these steps using any video or .avi file for which you have a plug-in on your system. The Osborne site for this book has an assortment of practice video files if you want to download one. You can also find free video clips for personal use at http://www.erinet.com/cunning1/avi_mov.htm, and you can watch a variety of movies (including new Hollywood movie trailers) at Apple's QuickTime site (www.apple.com/quicktime).

Here's how to use the Insert | Advanced | Plug-In command:

1. Open the page on which you want to place a movie.

2. Choose Insert | Advanced | Plug-In.

3. Complete the Plug-In Properties dialog box as shown in Figure 14-4.

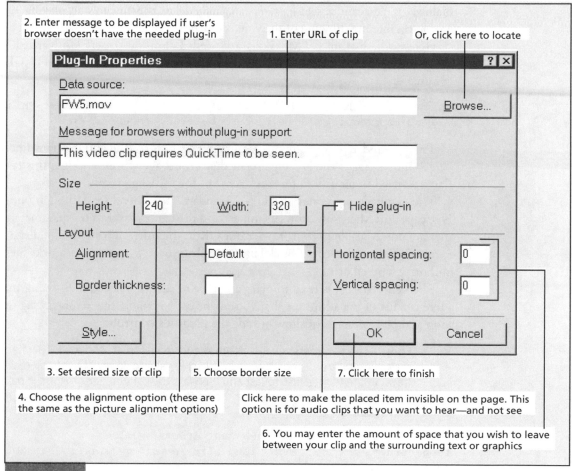

FIGURE 14-4   The Plug-In Properties dialog box

You can see that you've placed the file on your page in Normal view, because FrontPage shows the Plug-In icon.

FW5.mov

You should be able to see the actual movie clip in Preview mode.

You might notice that some of the options that you had when you used the In-sert | Picture | Video command are missing from the Insert | Advanced | Plug-In dialog box. You cannot set a loop repeat, a loop delay, the time to start playing, or enable/disable the showing of the video controls.

Here's where your HTML skills are needed. For the Insert | Advanced | Plug-In dialog box shown in Figure 14-4, FrontPage wrote this HTML command:

```
<p><embed width="320" height="240" src="FW5.mov"><noembed>This
video clip requires QuickTime to be seen.</noembed></p>
```

The <p> and </p> tags are the paragraph tags to force the clip to a new line. The <embed> tag is the key ingredient that FrontPage writes, and it is this tag that you need to modify to put back some of the missing pieces.

The <embed> tag is not an HTML standard tag. Therefore, although both Netscape and Microsoft browsers understand the tag, there are a few parameters that are not available in one browser but OK in the other. To see the full list of <embed> tags available for QuickTime, go to http://www.apple.com/quicktime/authoring/embed.html.

The <embed> tag is used to place any type of media that requires a plug-in. Here is a list of the additions that you might use to enable the <embed> tag to loop and play on start, or show or hide the plug-in's controls:

- **Loop** This parameter causes the movie to repeat in an endless loop when set to loop="true", not repeat at all when set to loop="false", or cycle through the frames first-to-last and then last-to-first when set to loop="pal-indrome". If you wanted the clip shown in Figure 14-4 to loop forever, your HTML should read:

```
<p><embed width="320" height="240" src="FW5.mov"
loop="true"><noembed>This video clip requires QuickTime to be
seen.</noembed></p>
```

- **Autostart**   The autostart parameter enables the movie to play as soon as the plug-in feels that it has enough data to sustain the motion or sound. The autostart parameter can be set to true or false. To modify the HTML tag if you wanted to enable autostart, you'd write:

```
<p><embed width="320" height="240" src="FW5.mov"
autostart="true"><noembed>This video clip requires QuickTime
to be seen.</noembed></p>
```

- **Controller**   The controller parameter determines if the start and stop controls for the movie are to be shown. The value of this parameter can be true or false. If you want to show the controller, you need to add an additional 16 pixels to the height of the movie if you are calling the QuickTime plug-in. You need to experiment with other plug-ins to see what height they require for the controller. If you don't add enough height, the movie is cut off. Here's the HTML code:

```
<p><embed width="320" height="256" src="FW5.mov"
controller="true"><noembed>This video clip requires QuickTime
to be seen.</noembed></p>
```

Another useful parameter is the pluginspage parameter. This addition allows you to point a user to the correct page from which to download the needed plug-in. Here's the HTML with all of the changes shown in boldface:

```
<p><embed width="320" height="256" src="FW5.mov"
autoplay="true"*loop="true" controller="true"
pluginspage="http://www.apple.com/quicktime/download/">
<noembed>This video clip requires QuickTime to be seen.
</noembed></p>
```

You can also create cross-browser pages by creating a link object and attaching the media item as the target of the link, just as you did with images. Using this method, you can place either a graphic or text link indicating the availability of the sound or video. You can use the linking techniques shown in Chapter 6 to link to the item to be played. The advantage is that you give the control over whether or not to view/hear the item back to the user. It could be particularly important in the case of sound to give the user control over listening to it or not. I work all day in silence, with not even a radio for company. I actually enjoy the silence, and few things annoy me as quickly as a page that I cannot get to shut up.

The final technique that I'll show you is for QuickTime. QuickTime enables you to make a poster or a reference movie to sit on a page until the user clicks on it. It is an excellent "holding" device for streaming video as well as for video that is downloaded to your hard drive.

A reference movie is a placeholder that points to several versions of the same movie—each at a different data rate. When you author the movie, you need to create several different versions (one optimized for a 28.8 modem, a 56.6 modem, an ISDN line, a T1 line, etc.). You can use Apple's free MakeRefMovie tool (http://www.apple.com/quicktime/developers/tools.html) to associate a movie with a specific data rate. Then, all you need to do is to add a single link to the movies.

You can also create a poster movie as a placeholder. A poster movie is actually a QuickTime movie with only one frame. You can extract a frame from your clip or draw a totally different image and turn it into a single-frame QuickTime movie. However, you need to save the image in a file format that QuickTime Player Pro can import. Here are the remaining steps to create a poster movie:

1. Open QuickTime Player Pro and import the image for the poster movie.

2. Delete any audio tracks that the movie might contain.

3. Choose File | Export and make sure that the file extension is set to .mov. You also need to select the option Movie to QuickTime Movie. This action creates a fully cross-platform-compatible movie file.

4. Make sure that both the poster movie and your "real" movie are in the same directory (import both into your FrontPage Web.) If they aren't in the same directory, your main QuickTime movie opens in a new browser window.

5. Change the HTML code to show the poster movie. If I created a poster movie called "fwposter.mov" to act as a placeholder for the movie referenced in Figure 14-4, this is what the HTML should look like (with new changes in boldface):

```
<EMBED  SRC="fwposter.mov" WIDTH="320" HEIGHT="256"
CONTROLLER="false" HREF="fw5.mov" BORDER="0" TARGET="myself"
autostart="false"PLUGINSPAGE="http://www.apple.com/quicktime/download/">
```

Design Thoughts

Before adding sound or video to your page, ask yourself some important questions:

- Will your site be enhanced by this media or just bogged down? If you are a member of a rock band, adding at least a link to your music would be wise, but embedding a song so it plays over and over again could be at best tiresome—at worst, criminal. The first time a user encounters a sound linked to an event (such as a mouseover), it could seem funny. But, after the site visitor has heard the sound 30 times, it is likely to lose its humorous edge.

- Is the site visitor likely to have the needed plug-in? If not, you need to decide if you will lose your audience by forcing them to get it. Perhaps you want to create an alternate version of the site, or else try to arrange the site so that it degrades well enough to still be useful.

- Is the media small enough to download quickly? If not, you need to have some idea as to the most common modem speeds being used by your audience. You need to make long downloading items an option rather than a requirement. You also need to be sure that you've compressed the item as well as you can and used the most efficient codec for it. If you are using QuickTime, you can also create multiple versions of the movie at a variety of data rates. The plug-in will download the correct version (as set in the user's plug-in preferences).

Professional Skills Summary

You've learned how to create pages with video and audio clips so that they will play only in Internet Explorer. You've learned about the <bkgsound> and <dynsrc> tags that FrontPage uses when it places audio from the Page Properties dialog box or video using the Insert | Picture | Video. You've learned how to create Web pages that can be used on either Netscape Navigator or Internet Explorer using the Insert | Advanced | Plug-In command. You've also learned about the <embed> tag that FrontPage writes and how to extend its range by hand-coding the loop, controller, or autostart parameters into the HTML. You've also learned how to create reference and poster movies.

You've learned a bit about the various media architectures such as Windows Media Technology, Real, QuickTime, and MPEG, and where you can look on the Web for additional information. You've also learned about codecs and data compression, and the importance of making your media files as small as possible.

In Chapter 15 you'll learn about the FrontPage components and how they can help add function and energy to your site.

FrontPage Components

In this chapter, you:

- Learn how to create banner ads
- Learn how to create hover buttons
- Learn how to create a moving marquee
- Learn how to add a hit counter to your site
- Learn how to create, use, validate, and process forms
- Learn how to set up a discussion group
- Learn how to use the Include Page, Scheduled Include Page, and Scheduled Picture components

This chapter talks about components. A *component* is a FrontPage-specific feature that you can apply to your Web page. Most of the components (with the exception of the hover button) require that FrontPage extensions be installed on your server. FrontPage gives you a lot of additional value by making it easier to create things like discussion groups and forms and banner ads.

Banner Ads

A *banner ad* is a "billboard" that can display a rotating sequence of images, and provide transitions between images as well as a hyperlink for the banner. The Banner Ad Manager component helps you to create this quickly and easily. Because the banner ad uses a Java applet, this component will work correctly in a variety of level 3 browsers and above. To insert a banner ad, follow these steps:

1. In Page view, place the insertion point where you want the ad. Choose Insert | Component | Banner Ad Manager. The Banner Ad Manager Properties dialog box, shown in Figure 15-1, appears.

2. In the boxes at the top, enter the width and height of the banner ad. It's best to plan the ad beforehand so that all of the images are the same size, and use that size for the banner ad.

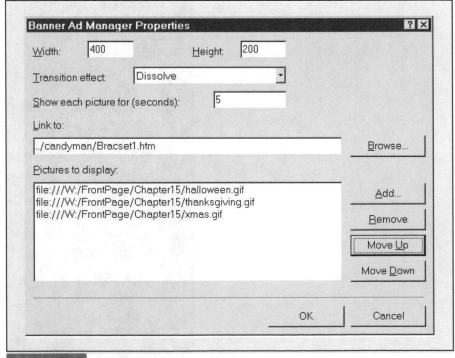

FIGURE 15-1 The Create Banner Ad dialog box

3. Choose a transition effect from the list (click on the down-pointing arrow to display the full list). Try each of these effects to see which one you like best.

4. In the "Show each picture..." box, enter the number of seconds to display each picture.

5. In the "Link to" box, enter the URL for a page that the banner will link to, if desired. Note that there is only one URL for the banner as a whole, not one for each separate image.

6. Use the Add button to add a picture to the "Pictures to display" box. Clicking the Add button opens a file selection box where you can choose the first image to display. Repeat the Add action until all of the pictures you want to use in the ad are selected. You can remove an image from the list by highlighting it and clicking the Remove button. You can also change the order of images by highlighting one and clicking the Move Up or Move Down button.

7. When you're done with the setup, click on the OK button. If you want to quit without placing the banner on the page, click the Cancel button.

Once you've placed a banner ad on your page, you can edit it at any time by opening the page, right-clicking on the banner ad, and selecting Banner Ad Manager Properties from the pop-up menu. You can delete the banner ad entirely by clicking on it to highlight it and then pressing the DELETE key.

Hover Buttons

A *hover button* is a normal button on steroids. Like any other button, it represents a link to another page or location, or to some action. A hover button, however, can also glow, display another picture, or play a sound when the cursor moves over it. The hover button is a Java applet and so works on all level 3 and higher browsers.

The hover button is usually generated by FrontPage as a rectangle of whatever size you specify in the color that you select in the dialog box. When you use the generated rectangle as your button, you can apply a variety of effects to it such as glows, bevels, and color fills. If you choose, instead, to use a picture as the hover state, the picture is your "effect" and any other effects that you enter in the dialog box are ignored. To add a hover button to your page, follow these steps:

1. Place the insertion point where you want the button to go. On the menu bar, click on Insert | Component | Hover Button. The Hover Button Properties menu appears, as shown in Figure 15-2.

2. In the "Button text" box, enter the text that should appear on the button. If you use an image for your button, the text will appear over the image. You can set the typeface, text color, font size, and font style by clicking on the Font button to open the Font dialog box.

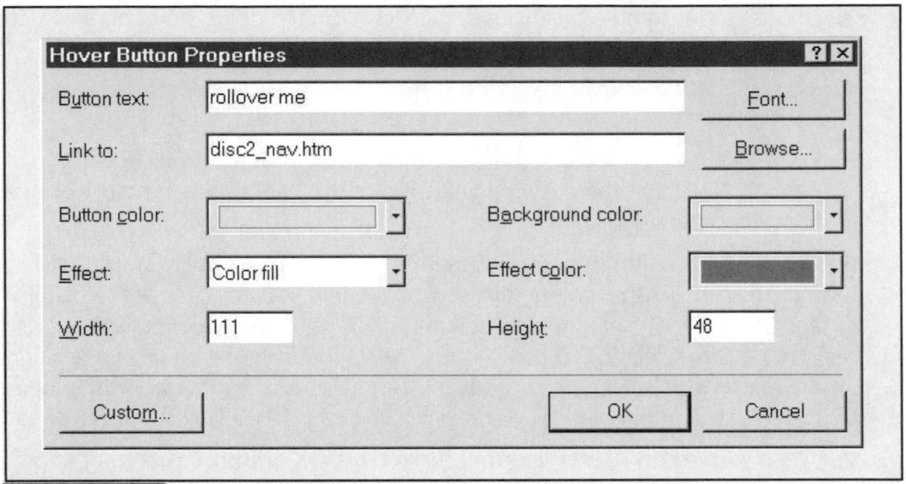

FIGURE 15-2   The Hover Button Properties dialog box

3. In the "Link to" box, enter the URL for the site the button will take the user to when clicked.

4. In the section below the "Link to" box, you can select the button and background colors, and the type and color of the effect to apply to the button when the cursor is over it. You can also set the width and height of the button. If you're planning on using images for the button, the button size should be set to the same size as the image that you want to use.

5. If you want to use pictures (rather than the other button effects), or play sounds when the cursor moves on or off the button, click the Custom button (shown in Figure 15-3). In the Custom dialog box, you can specify sounds to play when the button is clicked or when the mouse is hovering over the button. You can also specify a starting picture for the button and a different picture to display when the mouse is over the button. It's best to use two images of the same size. Remember that the text chosen in the Hover Button Properties dialog box will display over the images you choose here. When done with your selections, click on the OK button.

6. When done with all selections for the button, click on the OK button in the Hover Button Properties dialog box and your button will be placed on the page.

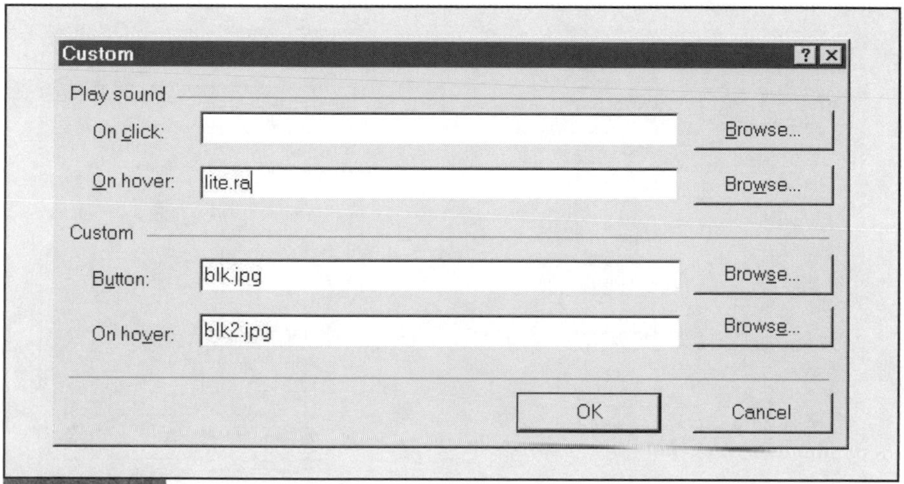

FIGURE 15-3 The Custom dialog box allows you to display pictures and attach sounds to the hover button

Marquees

A *marquee* is a component that displays a horizontally scrolling text message. The FrontPage marquee component only works for Internet Explorer pages (in fact, the selection isn't available if Netscape is selected in the Page Options Compatibility tab). To create a marquee for an Internet Explorer page, follow these steps:

1. Place the insertion point where you want the marquee to be displayed. On the menu bar, click Insert | Component | Marquee (remember that this option will be grayed out if Netscape is selected in the Page Options Compatibility tab). The Marquee Properties dialog box (shown in Figure 15-4) appears.

2. In the Text box, enter the text to be displayed in the marquee.

3. Use the Direction radio buttons to specify the direction in which the text will scroll.

4. In the Speed box, the Delay entry specifies the time in milliseconds that the text will remain stationary before each movement. The Amount entry specifies the amount, in pixels, that the text will move each time.

5. In the Behavior box, specify the way you want the text to move. If you select Scroll, the text will move in from one end of the marquee and out the other end. If you select Slide, the text will move in from one end of the marquee

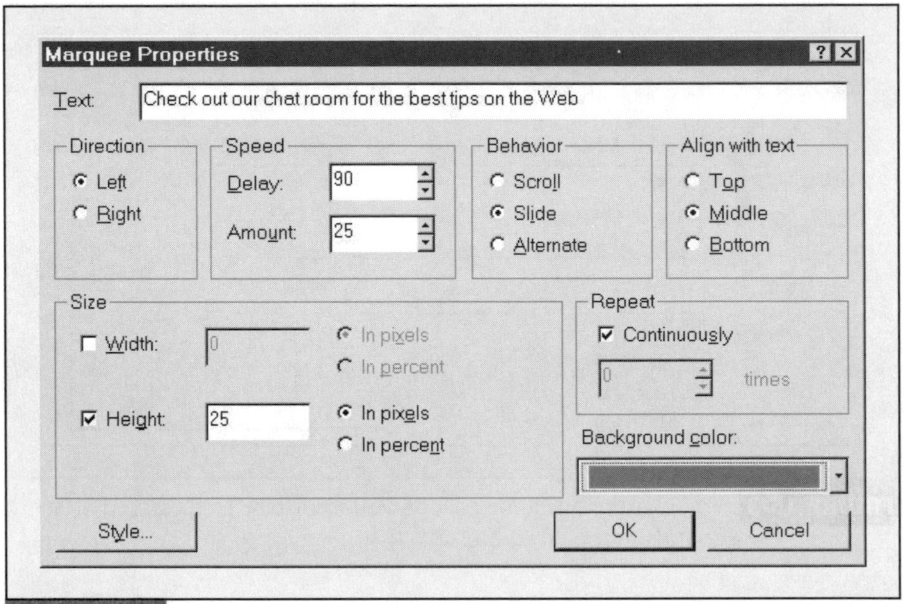

FIGURE 15-4   The Marquee Properties dialog box

and stop at the other end. If you select Alternate, the text will move in from one end of the marquee and then bounce back and forth within the marquee. Try each of these effects to see which one you like best.

6. If the marquee is on a line with other text, you can select its vertical alignment with respect to the other text on the line. Top aligns the top of the marquee with the top of the text line. Middle aligns the middle of the marquee with the middle of the text. Bottom aligns the bottom of the marquee with the bottom of the text.

7. In the Size box, specify the size of the marquee in either pixels or percent of the page width and height. It's usually best to make the marquee wide enough to fit all of the text.

8. In the Repeat box, select Continuously to make a continuously scrolling marquee, or deselect it and enter the number of times you want the scrolling to continue.

9. Use the "Background color" box to select the background color for the marquee.

10. If you want to set the text font, font size, font color, or other properties for the scrolling text, you'll need to set them by clicking on the Style button in the Marquee Properties dialog box. You need to select Style | Format | Font before you can change the color of the marquee text.

11. When you're finished making your selections, click on the OK button and your marquee appears on the page.

Hit Counter

A *hit counter* shows how many times your page has been visited. FrontPage 2000 makes it very easy to add a hit counter for your page, and to use any of several styles to display it. Hit counters are cross-browser; the only caveat for using them is that your Web server must support FrontPage 2000 Extensions. If an Internet service provider (ISP) hosts your page, you'll need to check with them to ensure that their server supports FrontPage 2000 extensions. To add a hit counter to your page, follow these steps:

1. Place the insertion point where you want the hit counter to be displayed. On the menu bar, click Insert | Component | Hit Counter. The Hit Counter Properties dialog box, shown in Figure 15-5, appears.

2. Select the style you want to use for your hit counter.

3. You can optionally specify the beginning value for the counter, and set the counter to display a fixed number of digits (leading digits will be filled with zeroes).

4. Click OK to display your counter on the page. In the Normal view, the counter is displayed as [Hit Counter]. You'll need to switch to Preview view or preview the page in a browser to see its actual appearance on the page.

Tip: There are a variety of cross-browser implementations of marquees (or "tickers") available free for public use as JavaScripts or Java applets. If you need a cross-browser marquee, use one of these rather than the standard FrontPage 2000 marquee.

Forms

Forms are used to collect information from visitors to your page. A form is just a collection of data fields into which data is entered in various ways. A form may consist of a combination of text boxes, radio buttons, checkboxes, and drop-down menus used to enter information and make selections from choices presented in the form. Forms may also include validation rules that allow them to accept only valid information. In general, a form will also contain action buttons that reset the form or send the information collected to a form handler, which might add the information to a database or perform some other processing on it.

Hit Counter Properties ✕

Counter Style

⊙ 0123456789

○ 0 1 2 3 4 5 6 7 8 9

○ 0123456789

○ 0123456789

○ 0123456789

○ Custom Picture   custom.gif

☐ Reset counter to   0

☐ Fixed number of digits   5

OK   Cancel

FIGURE 15-5 The Hit Counter Properties dialog box

To create a form, you need to lay out your page and then select the form components that you want from the Insert | Form menu. The Insert Form option on the menu

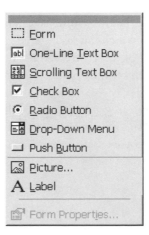

actually just adds a Submit and a Reset button to the page. That is the start of your form. You need to press the ENTER key to size the form (that pushes the Submit and Reset buttons to the bottom of the form). Once your form is created, you can add the fields that you need to it.

You can also design a form using the Form Page Wizard. When you create a new page, you can select the Form Page Wizard as your page template. You are then prompted to enter the series of questions that you want to ask your viewer. You are also given the option to specify how you want the results of the form conveyed to you and whether or not to place the form into a table. After you've entered your choices, FrontPage creates the form, which you can then modify as you want. This is a really nice feature and quite useful for the beginning designer.

Designing Forms

The following steps apply to forms in general. FrontPage 2000 also supports some specific types of forms, which we'll discuss in more detail later. The basic steps for creating a form are as follows:

- **Figure out what data you want to collect and set up your form accordingly.** The first step in creating a form that really works is to decide what information you want to collect from the user. This will be the main driver behind the form design. The other considerations are designing a logical form layout and deciding which pieces of data, if any, require some input validation. Once you've done these things, you're ready to start laying out your form on a Web page.

- **Add fields to your form.** The next step is to add fields to your form. The fields you add will be used to collect the data you want. You need to choose your fields carefully; we'll introduce you to the field types and their strengths and weaknesses below. The fields are the place where you can enter data. You add a field by selecting the field type from the Insert | Form menu. Figure 15-6 shows the Text Box Properties dialog box.

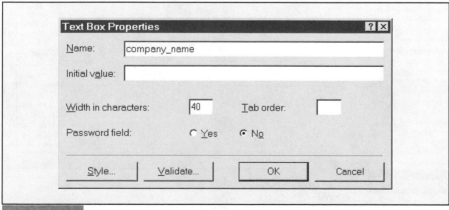

FIGURE 15-6 Creating a text field

- **Set data entry rules for your fields.** Next, decide whether and how you want individual fields validated (i.e., checked for correctness). For example, you can set a phone number field that will check for a particular area code and phone number format, or a date field that checks for a valid date (February 30 need not apply!). You can also specify a valid range of values for a field so that the user will not be allowed to enter a value outside of that range. Figure 15-7 shows the Text Box Validation dialog box. You can also limit the user's choices by your selection of the field type—a drop-down list, for example, forces the user to select from a list of values you define, and thereby prevents invalid entries.

- **Set up handlers for the form data.** You can specify what happens to the form data when the user clicks the Submit button. You can modify the default handler, if you want, and use your own script to process the form output, or you can route it to a predefined form handler. To set up a handler, you need to right-click on the form and select Form Properties. The Form Properties dialog box appears, as shown in Figure 15-8.

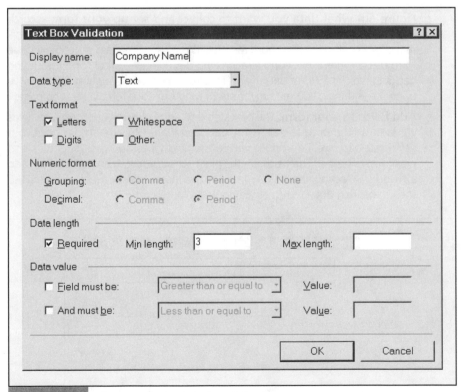

FIGURE 15-7 The Text Box Validation dialog box

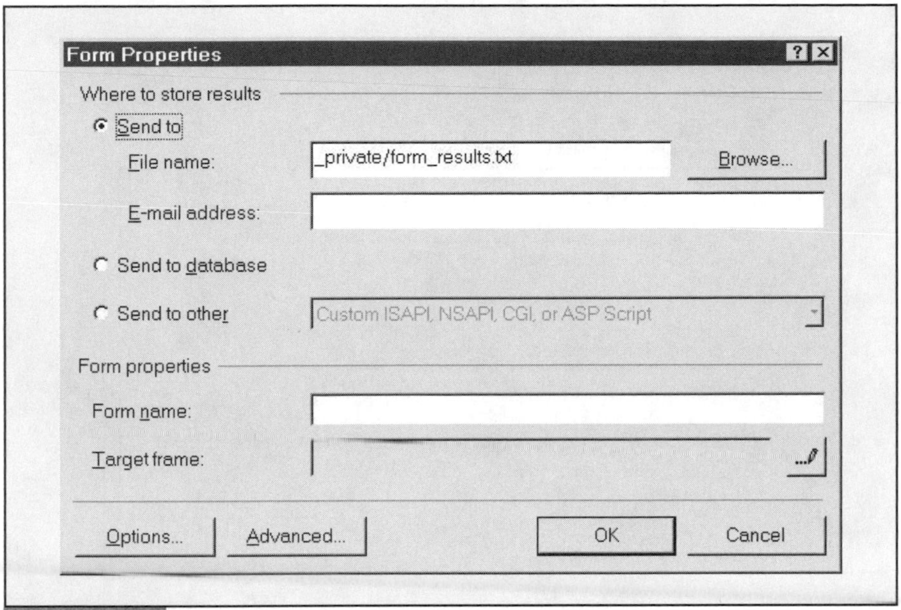

FIGURE 15-8 The Form Properties dialog box

- **Set up a confirmation page.** It's a good idea to repeat the user's inputs back to him or her and have them confirmed before processing them. FrontPage lets you set up a page to do this automatically by clicking on the Confirmation tab on the Options button in the Form Properties dialog box (phew!), as shown in Figure 15-9. Once you've completed these steps, you should be ready to use your form and handle the information it retrieves.

Choosing Form Fields

Your form can be composed of a variety of fields. The general rules for inserting fields are as follows:

- To insert any form field, open the Insert menu from the menu bar, select the Form item in the Insert menu, and then click on the type of form field you want to insert.

- After inserting a field, you can customize it by right-clicking on it and then selecting Form Field Properties from the pop-up menu. The exact options shown will depend on the type of form field selected. Typically, you can assign the field (as was shown in Figure 15-8):

  - A name (FrontPage 2000 gives each field a default name, but using a more descriptive name might help to deal with your data in the form handler and enable the user to make more sense of your confirmation page).

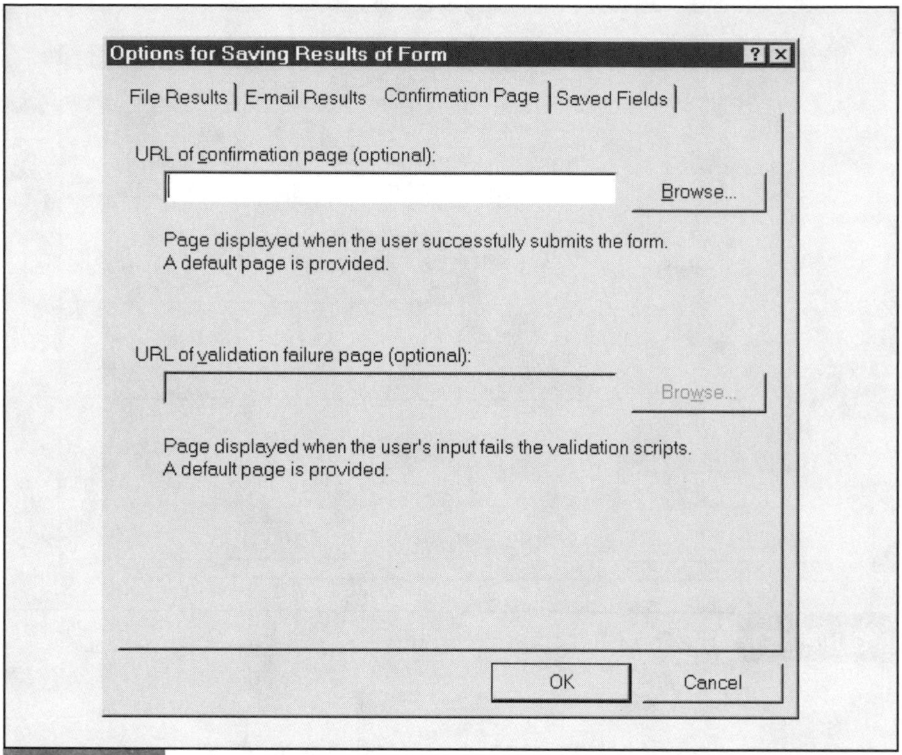

FIGURE 15-9 Setting up a confirmation page

- An initial value (the initial value that you assign becomes the default value to be used if the site visitor does not place any entry in that field).
- A field size for text fields.
- A tab order sets the order in which fields are accessed by a customer using the TAB key to move between fields. For example, you could use this to make sure that when a user enters his or her last name in the appropriate field and hits the TAB key, the insertion point will move to the First Name field to take the next entry. If you don't specify a tab order, fields are accessed in the order in which you enter them on the form.
- Whether a text field is a password field. For text fields, you can specify whether the field is a password. To prevent onlookers from viewing the user's password, password fields are filled with asterisks as the user types, rather than the actual characters typed.
- Style can be specified for certain fields. You must first specify an appropriate style in a style sheet, then use the Style button to associate that style with the field.

- Validation rules can be set for some field types. You can click the Validation button to open a Validation dialog box, where you can specify:

  - **Display name**   This is a name for the field that will be displayed if there is an error validating the field inputs (something like "Please enter a value for the *DisplayName* field.").

  - **Datatype**   This is the type of data the field will accept (text, integer, number). Use Text for mixed text and numbers, Integer to accept whole number inputs only, and Number for fields like currency.

  - **Text and numeric format**   For Text inputs, you can specify what types of characters are acceptable, and for Integer and Number fields you can specify the character used for grouping hundreds units (like a comma for the American style, 1,234 or a period for the European style, 1 234), and the character used for the decimal point.

  - **Data length**   In the Data Length section, you can specify whether the user is required to input a value in this field, and the minimum and maximum length of the input (in characters).

  - **Data value**   In the Data Value field, you can specify whether the input must be greater than or less than some value.

Next, we'll discuss each field type and show when it is appropriate for use on your forms.

Labels are used only to display descriptive information about other form fields; they do not collect data themselves, but may be used to describe the expected entries in other fields, or to provide general information concerning the form. The general procedure for inserting a label for a form field is to insert the field, type the label text where you want it relative to the field, then select the field and the text and click Insert | Form | Label. A light dotted outline appears around the label text.

Text boxes allow the user to enter text into the form. The single-line text box is appropriate for short entries (last name, first name, phone number, credit card number, etc). You insert a single-line text box by clicking Insert on the menu bar, then selecting Form | One-Line Text Box. You can also use a scrolling text box if you expect the user to enter a lengthy response. These are appropriate for such things as comments, which are essentially free-form text.

Radio buttons are used in groups where only one item in the group may be selected. For relatively small groups of items, radio buttons provide a quicker selection method than a drop-down list, although they take up more room on the form. Selecting a new item deselects all other items in the group. You insert a radio button by clicking on Insert in the menu bar, then Form | Radio Button. After inserting the button, type the associated value directly on the form. You group radio buttons by assigning them a common name in the Form Field Properties dialog box.

Checkboxes are small square boxes that can be empty or checked. Checkboxes are used when the user is allowed to make multiple selections (or no selection) from a list of options. To insert a checkbox, click on Insert in the menu bar, then Form | Check Box. After inserting the checkbox, type the associated value directly on the form. It's a good idea to then right-click on the checkbox and assign it a name in the Form Field Properties dialog box.

Tip: One strong point of radio buttons, checkboxes, and drop-down menus is that they don't allow the user to enter an invalid value (the *wrong* value, possibly, but never an invalid response). You set the acceptable values when you create the form; the user is restricted to choosing between the values you have set.

Drop-down menus allow the user to select one or more items from a long list, without using up a lot of real estate on your form. The drop-down menu can be set to allow a single selection or multiple selections. It appears on your form as a text box with a Down Arrow button next to it; clicking the Down Arrow button displays the full list in a scrolling box, if necessary.

Hidden fields are fields that are included in the form results, but are hidden from the user. For example, if you use the same custom form handler for several forms, you might want the form results to include an identifier for the form used to select the appropriate processing. To insert a hidden field, right-click on a blank area of the form and select Form Properties from the pop-up menu. Click on the Advanced button, then on the Add button in the Advanced Form Properties dialog box.

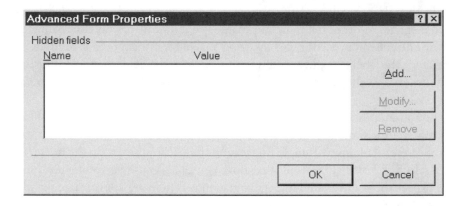

A Name/Value Pair dialog box will appear. In the Name field, enter the name of the field, and in the Value field enter its value. Then click OK, OK again, and OK again to add the field to your form.

Handling Form Content

You created a form because you wanted to collect some information from the visitors to your page. Next, you have to decide what to do with the information collected. FrontPage 2000 supplies form handlers to do the following:

- **Save the results to a text or HTML file.** If you choose this option, each time a user submits a form the results will be appended to a text or HTML file that you can view or make available to other users of your site. An example of an appropriate use of this option is a guest book page showing information about people who have signed your guest book and their comments.

- **Send the form results as e-mail.** You may also choose to have the form results mailed to you in the form of an e-mail message each time a visitor submits a form.

- **Save the results in a database.** Using this option, you can save the form results to an ODBC-compliant database whenever a user submits a form. To use this option, you must set up a connection to the database first. (You can learn more about database connections by typing **Opening a Database Connection** into the Answer Wizard of the Help Menu dialog box.)

Tip: You can only use the FrontPage 2000 form handlers if your Web server supports the FrontPage 2000 Extensions. Check with your Internet service provider if you have questions concerning this issue.

Generating Confirmation Notices

FrontPage 2000 automatically displays a confirmation page when the Submit button on a form is clicked, unless you have elected to bypass this feature with a custom form handler. The default confirmation page displays the name and value of each element of the form. This is one good argument for assigning descriptive names to the form elements.

Creating Search Forms

FrontPage 2000 makes it easy to create a page that will let your users search your site for pages containing specific words or phrases. To use this feature, the Web server hosting your Web must have the Microsoft FrontPage Server Extensions installed. The search form allows the user to input the search criteria, then searches the text index that FrontPage 2000 automatically creates for your Web.

The easiest way to create a search page is simply to create a new page using the Search Page template supplied with FrontPage 2000. You can right-click on the search form on this page and open its Properties dialog box to customize it. Figure 15-10 shows the default Search Screen page directly from the template.

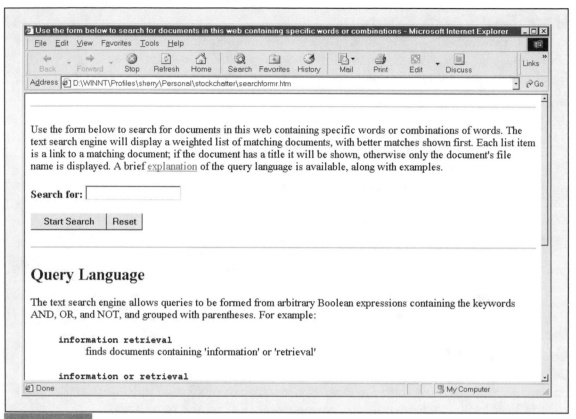

The Search Screen page generated by the Search Form template

If you want to include a search form on a page with other content, you can place the insertion point where you want the form to appear, then open the Insert menu, click on the Component item, and select Search Form. The Search Form Properties dialog box then opens. The Search Form Properties tab lets you set the label and width of the input field, and the names of the buttons on the form. The Search Results tab lets you set the word list to search, the date and time formats, and display options. The options include a score to indicate how closely the citation matches the search phrase, and whether to display the date and file size. When you click the OK button in the Search Form Properties dialog box, the search form will appear on the page at the insertion point.

Discussion Groups

You can easily set up a discussion group Web using FrontPage 2000. A discussion group is an interactive Web where users can discuss topics. The Web generally will provide a table of contents showing the topics posted, a way for users to post new topics and responses to existing topics, and a mechanism for following discussion "threads" (follow-on discussions originating from a single topic). The discussion group may also include a registration form to allow new users to become members of the discussion group, a search form to let users search for entries of interest, and a confirmation form to allow users to confirm their submissions before posting them.

Why Use a Discussion Group?

Discussion groups have a variety of uses. On an office intranet, you might set up a discussion group to allow employees to exchange ideas concerning projects, for example. Software developers often set up discussion groups to allow product testers to exchange information about bugs and desired new features. The same approach might be used on a "storefront" page to allow users to tell the organization owning the page about new products they'd like to see, problems using the page, and so forth.

A discussion Web is basically just a set of forms that allow the users to read topics and follow threads, respond to topics or other responses, search the Web, register, and so forth.

Discussion Options

The discussion group can be a separate Web (although it may be within your current Web). To create a discussion group Web, open the File menu, click on the New option, then select the Web option. In the Options section of the New dialog box, enter the location in which you want the new Web to be installed (you can click the Add to Current Web button to include the discussion group in your current Web). You can also select Secure Connection Required if you want your Web to use Secure Sockets Layer (SSL) for security—this will prevent unauthorized users from viewing the contents of your Web. Then, select Discussion Web Wizard and click on the OK button.

The Discussion Web Wizard asks you questions about the pages you want to include (the submission form is always required), the title that will appear on the discussion group pages, the folder in which you want to store the discussion topics, the fields that will appear on the submission form,

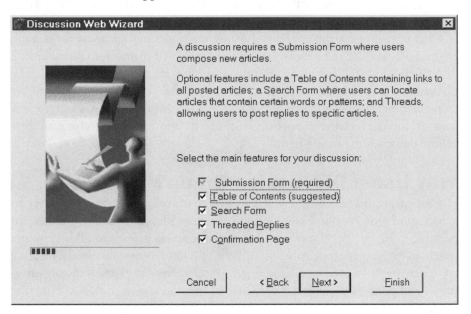

whether the Web is open to all or only registered users, how you want the table of contents sorted, whether to make the table of contents the home page for the Web, the items you want the search form to display for items found to match the search criteria,

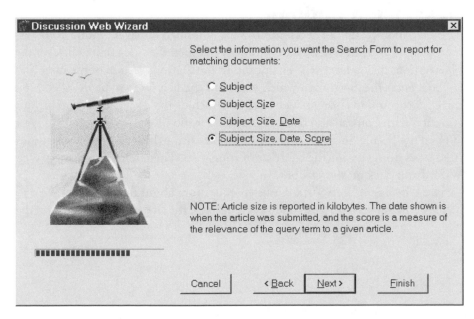

a FrontPage theme for the discussion group Web, and whether to use frames or not. Clicking Finish on the last page of the wizard creates your discussion Web for you.

Include Page Component

You can insert an Include Page component to allow you to display the contents of one page on another page in the Web. This is useful for creating reusable page sections that can be included on multiple pages in the Web. You might, for example, wish to include text and a picture on every page of your Web site (but not as a shared border). You can see here a possible top area of text and graphics to include on pages in a Web site.

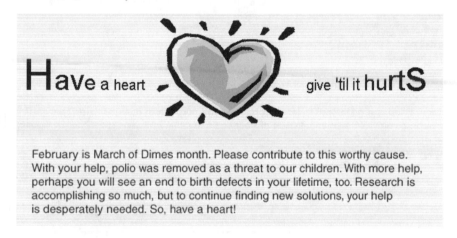

To insert an Include Page component, place the insertion point where you want the included page to appear, then open the Insert menu, then click on Component | Include Page. The Include Page Properties dialog box will then appear. Specify or browse to the path to the page that you want to include, then click on the OK button to include the page.

Figure 15-11 shows the home page of this not-really-completed site with the images and text that were in the incpage.htm document at the top of the page.

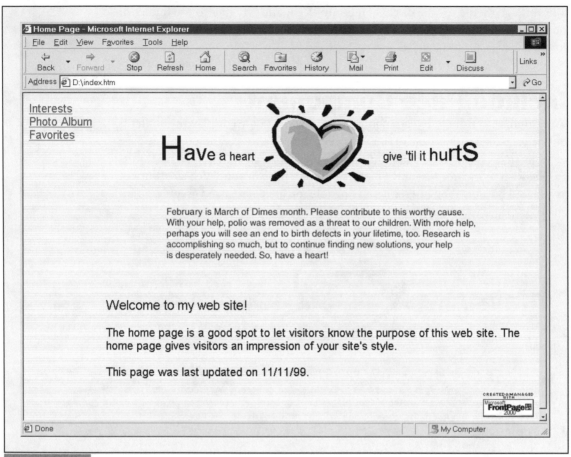

FIGURE 15-11 Including a page into another page

Scheduled Picture Component

Using the Scheduled Picture component, you can set your page to display a picture during a certain time period. For example, you might want a seasonal display that shows one picture during the Christmas season, another around New Year's Day, and so forth. The Scheduled Picture component lets you set the picture, the date and time to start showing the picture, and the date and time to stop showing the picture. It also lets you specify a picture to be used before and after the date range selected. Therefore, you may specify one picture to be displayed during the scheduled date and time range and another to be displayed at all other times. This gives you the option of displaying a particular image at all times *except* the listed time. If you didn't select a picture to display during the date range, then you would be able to black out a picture for that range.

To insert a Scheduled Picture component, place the insertion point at the point where you want the picture to be displayed, then open the Insert menu and select Component, then Scheduled Picture. In the Scheduled Picture Properties dialog box that appears, select the picture to be displayed during the scheduled time, the picture to be displayed at all other times, and the start and stop dates and times for the display period. Click OK to include the picture on your page.

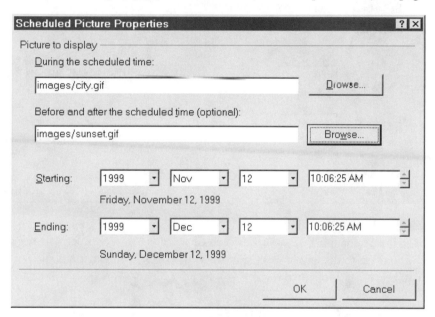

Scheduled Include Page Component

The Scheduled Include Page component is just like the Scheduled Picture component discussed above, except that it includes another HTML page rather than a picture. This is ideal for a page that changes with the seasons. It is also ideal for a storefront page where a special sale runs for a specified period of time.

To insert a Scheduled Include Page component, place the insertion point at the point where you want the picture to be displayed, then open the Insert menu and select Component, then Scheduled Include Page. In the Scheduled Include Page Properties dialog box that appears, select the page to be displayed during the scheduled time, the page to be displayed at all other times, and the start and stop dates and times for the display period. Click OK to include the page on your page.

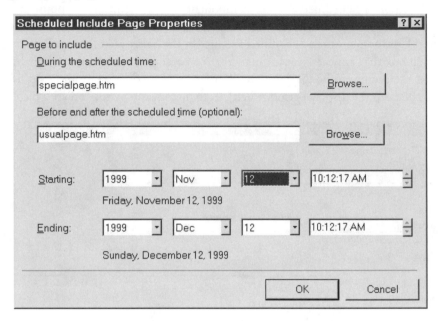

The Scheduled Include Page component is also a terrific tool for sites that need to create changing news stories. You can create a variety of lead stories and stack them up to display in a set spot on your pages. You can then specify the time to release each of the stories.

Professional Skills Summary

In this chapter, you learned how to use the large number of components that FrontPage has to offer. You learned how to create hover buttons and banner ads, hit counters and marquees. You also learned that while the hover buttons and banner ads are cross-browser, the marquee only works on Internet Explorer, and the hit counter only works if the FrontPage Extensions are installed on your ISP's server.

You also learned to create forms to process user input and to create discussion groups to facilitate online interaction between site visitors. You learned how to use the various elements of a form and how to specify rules to validate that data that is entered on a form.

In addition, you learned how to set up images and pages to be displayed at only certain times on your site using the Include page, Schedule Include Page, and Schedule Picture commands.

You've now completed the entire introduction to FrontPage. I hope that you've enjoyed the journey and I look forward to seeing your professional results online.

Index

N